# FIRST LANGUAGE LESSONS
FOR THE WELL-TRAINED MIND

LEVEL 3

This book is to be used in conjunction with the
First Language Lessons, Level 3
Student Workbook
ISBN 978-1-933339-08-5.
Available at www.peacehillpress.com
or wherever books are sold.

© 2007 Peace Hill Press

www.peacehillpress.com

Publisher's Cataloging-In-Publication Data
(Prepared by The Donohue Group, Inc.)

Wise, Jessie.
    First language lessons for the well-trained mind. Level 3 / by Jessie Wise and Sara Buffington.

        p. : ill. ; cm.

    Includes index.
    ISBN: 978-1-933339-07-8
1. English language--Grammar--Study and teaching (Primary)   2. English language--Composition and exercises--Study and teaching (Primary)   3. Language arts (Primary)   I. Buffington, Sara.   II. Title.

LB1528 .W573 2007
372.61   2007924667

FIRST LANGUAGE LESSONS
FOR THE WELL-TRAINED MIND
LEVEL 3

by Jessie Wise and Sara Buffington

Peace Hill Press
www.peacehillpress.com

Also by Jessie Wise and Sara Buffington

The Ordinary Parent's Guide to Teaching Reading
(Peace Hill Press, 2005)

First Language Lessons for the Well-Trained Mind, Level 4
(Peace Hill Press, 2008)

Also by Jessie Wise

First Language Lessons for the Well-Trained Mind, Levels 1 and 2
(Peace Hill Press, 2003)

with Susan Wise Bauer
The Well-Trained Mind: A Guide to Classical Education at Home
(W.W. Norton, Third Edition, 2009)

TABLE OF CONTENTS

Introduction...................... page 1
How to Use First Language Lessons, Level 3

Lesson 1 .... page 6
New: The Parts of This Book

Lesson 2 .... page 8
New: Nouns

Lesson 3 ....page 11
New: Forming Plurals the Usual Way
Review: Nouns

Lesson 4 ....page 14
New: Forming Plurals of Words That
     End in S, SH, CH, X, or Z
Review: Nouns
Review: Forming Plurals the Usual Way

Lesson 5 ....page 18
New: Forming Plurals of Nouns
     That End in Y
New: Irregular Plural Nouns
Review: Forming Plurals the Usual Way
Review: Forming Plurals of Words That
     End in S, SH, CH, X, or Z

Lesson 6 .... page 22
New: Common and Proper Nouns
Review: Forming Plurals

Lesson 7 .... page 26
New: Pronouns
Review: Common and Proper Nouns

Lesson 8 .... page 30
Review: Common and Proper Nouns
Review: Plurals
Review: Pronouns

Lesson 9 .... page 34
Introduction to Poem Memorization:
     "The Land of Nod"

Lesson 10 .... page 36
New: Action Verbs

Lesson 11 .... page 40
New: Definition of a Sentence
New: Sentences (Diagramming Subjects
     and Action Verbs)

Lesson 12 .... page 44
Introduction to Narration: "Bats"

Lesson 13 .... page 47
New: Adjectives
Review: Sentences

Lesson 14 ....page 51
New: Adjectives That Tell Whose
(Possessive Nouns)
Review: Adjectives

Lesson 15 .... page 56
New: Adjectives That Tell Whose
(Possessive Irregular Plural Nouns)
Review: Adjectives
Review: Forming Plurals

Lesson 16 ....page 61
New: Articles
New: Adjectives (with Diagramming)

Lesson 17 .... page 68
Review: Adjectives

Lesson 18 .... page 72
Poem Memorization: "A Tragic Story"

Lesson 19 ....page 74
New: Adverbs That Tell How
(with Diagramming)

Lesson 20 .... page 79
New: Adverbs That Tell When
(with Diagramming)

Lesson 21 .... page 84
New: Adverbs That Tell Where
(with Diagramming)

Lesson 22 .... page 88
New: Adverbs That Tell How Often
(with Diagramming)

Lesson 23 .... page 93
Review: Adjectives and Adverbs

Lesson 24 .... page 100
Review: Nouns, Pronouns, Verbs,
Adjectives, and Adverbs

Lesson 25 ....page 107
Narration: "The Mongols"

Lesson 26 ....page 110
New: Proper Nouns (with Diagramming)

Lesson 27 ....page 114
New: Helping Verbs (with Diagramming)

Lesson 28 ....page 119
Review: Proper Nouns and Helping
Verbs

Lesson 29 .... page 123
New: Direct Objects (with Diagramming)

Lesson 30 .... page 127
Review: Subjects, Verbs, Adjectives,
Adverbs, and Direct Objects

Lesson 31 ....page 132
Poem Memorization:
"I Wandered Lonely As a Cloud"

Lesson 32 .... page 134
New: Simple Versus Complete Subjects
and Predicates
Review: Subjects, Verbs, Adjectives,
Adverbs, and Direct Objects

Lesson 33 ....page 141
New: State of Being Verbs
(with Diagramming)
Review: Action and Helping Verbs

Lesson 34 ....page 147
New: Linking Verbs (with Diagramming)
New: Predicate Nominatives
(with Diagramming)
Review: Action Verbs, Helping Verbs,
and State of Being Verbs

Lesson 35 ....page 155
Review: Linking Verbs
Review: Predicate Nominatives

Lesson 36 ....page 158
Narration: "The Beaver Is a Builder"

Lesson 37 ....page 160
New: Predicate Adjectives
(with Diagramming)
Review: Linking Verbs
Review: Predicate Nominatives

Lesson 38 ....page 165
Review: Linking Verbs
Review: Predicate Adjectives
Review: Predicate Nominatives

Lesson 39 ....page 172
Review: Common and Proper Nouns
Review: Forming Plurals

Lesson 40 ....page 177
New: Four Types of Sentences

Lesson 41 ....page 180
New: You (Understood)
Subject in Command Sentences
New: Commands (with Diagramming)
Review: Statements

Lesson 42 ....page 184
Review: Statements and Commands

Lesson 43 ....page 191
Cumulative Poem Review

Lesson 44 ....page 192
New: Questions (with Diagramming)

Lesson 45 ....page 195
Review: Four Types of Sentences

Lesson 46 ....page 201
Poem Memorization: "A Time to Talk"

Lesson 47 ....page 203
Review: Four Kinds of Verbs
Review: Direct Objects, Predicate Nominatives, and Predicate Adjectives

Lesson 48 ....page 209
New: Prepositions

Lesson 49 ....page 214
New: Prepositional Phrases

Lesson 50 ....page 218
Review: Prepositional Phrases

Lesson 51 ....page 223
New: Object of the Preposition

Lesson 52 .... page 228
Review: Object of the Preposition

Lesson 53 .... page 233
Review: Prepositional Phrases

Lesson 54 .... page 237
Narration: "Isaac Newton's Laws of
　　Gravity"

Lesson 55 .... page 239
Review: Adjectives

Lesson 56 .... page 244
Review: Adverbs

Lesson 57 .... page 249
New: Adverbs That Tell to What Extent

Lesson 58 .... page 257
Poem Memorization: "The Bells"

Lesson 59 .... page 259
Review: Four Kinds of Verbs
Review: Direct Objects,
　　Predicate Nominatives, and
　　Predicate Adjectives

Lesson 60 .... page 266
Review: Simple and Complete Subjects
　　and Predicates

Lesson 61 .... page 273
New: Initials and Abbreviations for
　　Titles of Respect
New: Abbreviations for Months and
　　Days of the Week

Lesson 62 .... page 276
New: Conjunctions (with Diagramming)
New: Commas in a Series
Review: Abbreviations of Titles of
　　Respect, Days, and Months

Lesson 63 .... page 281
New: Commas in Direct Address
Review: Commas in a Series

Lesson 64 .... page 283
New: Contractions

Lesson 65 .... page 287
Cumulative Poem Review

Lesson 66 .... page 288
Narration: "Spiders"

Lesson 67 .... page 290
New: The "No" Adverbs and Contrac-
　　tions (with Diagramming)
Review: Contractions

Lesson 68 .... page 295
New: Direct Quotations
　　at the Ends of Sentences
Review: Four Types of Sentences

Lesson 69 .... page 299
New: Direct Quotations
　　at the Beginnings of Sentences
Review: Four Types of Sentences

Lesson 70 .... page 307
New: Indirect Quotations
Review: Direct Quotations

Lesson 71 .... page 312
Poem Memorization: "A Slash of Blue"

Lesson 72 .... page 314
Review: Commas in a Series and
   in Direct Address
Review: Contractions

Lesson 73 .... page 317
Review: Prepositions
Review: Conjunctions

Lesson 74 .... page 321
New: Compound Subjects
   (with Diagramming)
Review: Prepositions

Lesson 75 .... page 325
New: Compound Verbs
   (with Diagramming)
Review: Prepositional Phrases

Lesson 76 .... page 331
New: Sentences with Compound Subjects and Compound Verbs

Lesson 77 .... page 335
Narration: "Bull-Jumpers in Early Crete"

Lesson 78 .... page 337
Review: Four Kinds of Verbs
Review: Direct Objects,
   Predicate Nominatives, and
   Predicate Adjectives

Lesson 79 .... page 345
New: Comparative and
   Superlative Adjectives
Review: Adjectives

Lesson 80 .... page 350
Review: Adverbs

Lesson 81 .... page 358
Review: Four Types of Sentences

Lesson 82 .... page 364
Review: Adjectives
Review: Comparative and
   Superlative Adjectives

Lesson 83 .... page 368
New: Interjections (with Diagramming)
Review: Contractions

Lesson 84 .... page 373
Review: Nouns, Pronouns,
   Action Verbs, Sentences
Review: Simple and Complete Subjects
   and Predicates

Lesson 85 .... page 377
Review: Prepositions

Lesson 86 .... page 384
Review: Conjunctions
Review: Compound Subjects and
   Compound Verbs

Lesson 87 .... page 389
Review: Commas in a Series and
   in Direct Address
Review: Direct and Indirect Quotations

Lesson 88 .... page 394
Review: Diagramming

Lesson 89 .... page 400
Cumulative Poem Review

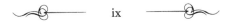

Writing Letters Lessons

Lesson 1 ....page 401
Writing Dates
Thank-You Letter Rough Draft

Lesson 2 .... page 404
Thank-You Letter Final Copy

Lesson 3 .... page 405
Addressing the Envelope

Lesson 4 .... page 407
Friendly Letter Rough Draft

Lesson 5 .... page 409
Friendly Letter Final Copy

Lesson 6 ....page 410
Addressing the Envelope

Lesson 7 ....page 411
Copying a Poem

Dictionary Skills Lessons

Lesson 1 ....page 413
Alphabetizing by First and Second Letter

Lesson 2 ....page 417
Alphabetizing by Third Letter

Lesson 3 ....page 419
Looking Up Words in the Dictionary

Lesson 4 ....page 421
Parts of the Entry

Lesson 5 .... page 424
Syllables and Phonetic Spelling

Lesson 6 .... page 428
Words with More Than One Meaning
and/or Pronunciation

Lesson 7 .... page 432
Synonyms and Antonyms

Oral Usage Lessons

Lesson 1 ....page 435
Verb Tenses: Present, Past, and Future

Lesson 2 .... page 437
Irregular Verbs

Lesson 3 .... page 439
Irregular Verbs

Lesson 4 .... page 441
Irregular Verbs: Lay Versus Lie,
Set Versus Sit

Lesson 5 .... page 444
Subject Pronouns and Object Pronouns

Lesson 6 .... page 448
Irregular Verbs: "To Be"

Lesson 7 ....page 450
Avoiding Double Negatives

Reference Materials

Definitions, Rules, and Lists ... page 455

Definitions to Be Memorized .. page 455

Glossary of Additional
    Terms to Know.............. page 456

Summary of Rules .... page 457

Lists to Be Memorized .... page 458

Sample Schedules ....page 460

Index.......................................page 463

Permissions ....page 466

INTRODUCTION
HOW TO USE FIRST LANGUAGE LESSONS, LEVEL 3

The Four-Strand Approach

This book uses four different strands to teach grammar and punctuation rules, proper usage, and writing skills.

Strand 1: Memory Work

Memorizing Poetry

Poems store beautiful language in the student's mind. Memorizing poetry gives the student confidence that he can indeed retain material. This confidence extends to his memorization of material in history, science, and literature. Also, memorization can actually train the student's attention span. He is not just passively being exposed to information; he is actively engaged in a mental exercise. There is a good memorization technique in the first poetry lesson of this book.

Memorizing Rules and Definitions

The technique for memorizing rules and definitions is practiced in the scripted lessons. A summary of the rules, definitions, and lists to be memorized is on page 457.

A note for students who have not used First Language Lessons, Levels 1 and 2: Several of the definitions and memorized lists of parts of speech were taught in the first two levels of this series. All of this material is reviewed in this book. However, you may wish to do extra review of these rules and lists. You may find it helpful to purchase the audio companion to *Levels 1 and 2* (a CD containing both chanted and sung versions of definitions and lists to be memorized) from Peace Hill Press at www.peacehillpress.com.

Strand 2: Copywork and Dictation

At this level, copywork is still the primary tool to help the student store in his mind the look and feel of properly written language. Copywork engages both the visual and motor memory of the student. It gives the student correct models while he is still struggling with the basics of written conventions: spaces between words, capital letters, punctuation, and spelling. Supervise the student carefully and correct him when he **begins** to copy incorrectly.

When you **dictate** a sentence to the student, he must write it without looking at a written model. Dictation teaches the student to picture a sentence in his mind before putting it down on paper and also trains him to hold complete sentences in his memory as he writes. Dictation should be a precursor to any original writing, since it allows the young writer to practice mechanics without also struggling to produce original content. We will discuss a good technique for giving dictation in "Dictation Exercises," later in this introduction.

Strand 3: Narration

Through copywork and dictation, a student learns to put words down on paper properly. Narration is simply the student retelling a passage that he has read or heard, putting it in his own words. Narration helps the student to listen with attention, to grasp the main point of a work, to think through a sequence of events, and to reproduce the events in his own words in proper, logical order.

Narration is also a precursor to original writing. There are no formal essays or creative writing assignments for the student to do in this book. In the primary grades, the student learns the proper structure of language through copywork and dictation. He learns basic oral composition through narration. In later grades, the student will use these skills in original writing.

Most narration beginners fall into one of two camps: they don't know where to begin **or** they don't know when to stop. If your student cannot think of anything to say, prompt him by repeating a couple of the comprehension questions, and have him answer each one in a complete sentence. If you have a very verbal student who goes on and on (and on!) when narrating, stop him and ask him to choose **only** two pieces of information and put those into sentences. For both types of students, narration is basic training in the skill of summarizing.

Strand 4: Grammar

This book teaches advanced grammar concepts to young students in a pleasant way. It is important to teach formal grammar in the early grades. Otherwise, the student may develop bad habits that he will have to unlearn later on. He will have to reorient his mind and ear to an entirely new way of constructing sentences.

This book introduces sentence diagramming. In the third grade, the student learns that a diagram is essentially a picture of a sentence. The diagram serves as a visual reinforcement of the function of each part of speech, particularly useful for visual learners.

Using the Lessons

Type Formatting in First Language Lessons
- Suggested wording for the instructor is in traditional print.
- *Suggested answers for the student are in italics.*
- **Answers to workbook exercises are in larger, darker print.**

- Notes to the instructor are in smaller, traditional print, between two lines.

Length of Lessons

This book is designed to be completed in one school year. If you do the lessons in the main part of the book but skip the end units, do about two lessons each week for the school year (36 weeks). If you decide to include the end units as well, plan on three lessons per week. See the sample schedules on page 460.

A student doing third- or fourth-grade-level work will probably need to spend thirty minutes on this subject three days per week. If the lesson time exceeds thirty minutes, stop and pick up with the remainder of the lesson the following day. If a student is struggling to understand or if he doesn't write easily, he may do some of the written exercises orally instead.

The Use of Inclusive Pronouns

A note from Jessie Wise: I studied advanced traditional grammar in the 1950s as part of my training in teaching certification. I learned that the pronouns "he" and "him" were generic pronouns, used to refer to both men and women. Although I understand why some users would prefer to see an alternate use of "he" and "she," I find this style of writing awkward; my early training shapes my usage! So I have used "he" and "him" to refer to the student throughout. If you prefer, simply change these pronouns to "she" and "her."

The Student's Workbook

All of the lesson numbers in the teacher's book match the lesson numbers in the student's workbook (ISBN 978-1-933339-08-5, Peace Hill Press, 2007). The student needs a pencil for each workbook lesson. The student should keep a bookmark in his workbook to easily find his place at the start of the lesson.

The workbook pages are perforated and three-hole punched so you can file them in a binder if you wish. If the student writes letters for the optional end-unit lessons, you may wish to photocopy them before you mail them so you can file the letters as well.

Dictation Exercises

As the student's general skills in writing and spelling improve, so will his ability to take dictation. At first, the student may struggle for a number of reasons. He may be transitioning from printing to cursive writing. He may have to stop and think about how to form a letter and lose his train of thought. He may ask you to repeat a phrase, or he may leave out a word. He may stop to correct a misspelled word that "doesn't look right." This is all very normal! Watch the student as he writes. Help him with proper spelling and punctuation as he goes. If he leaves out a word that you have dictated, let him insert it rather than making him recopy the entire sentence.

Follow this procedure when giving dictation:

1. After you read a sentence, ask the student to visualize the beginning capital letter and the end punctuation mark.
2. Repeat the sentence once more.
3. Have the student repeat what you just said.
4. Have him write what he has just said, if it is accurate. If it is not accurate, repeat steps 1 and 2.

If the student seems frustrated with dictation, have him copy the sentence first. Then dictate the same sentence for him to write from memory. If he is struggling, you may also decide to have the student write only one sentence.

We have excluded dictation exercises from lessons with extensive copywork or diagramming. And some lessons have only optional dictation sentences. Skip the optional dictation if the student is doing dictation in another subject that day.

Optional Follow-Ups

At the end of some lessons, there is an optional follow-up activity to reinforce the content of the lesson. Often these activities involve the participation of other family members. This makes learning grammar a shared family affair.

Optional End Units

The main part of this book consists of eighty-nine lessons in grammar and writing. If you wish, you may choose to complete any or all of the three optional sections at the end of the book: writing letters, dictionary skills, and oral usage. Suggested schedules for completing this book are on page 460. If you do the lessons on dictionary skills, the student will need a dictionary and thesaurus. We recommend *Merriam-Webster's Elementary Dictionary* (Merriam-Webster, 2000) and *Roget's Children's Thesaurus* (Scott-Foresman, 2000).

LESSON 1

New: **The Parts of This Book**

In this book all of the lesson numbers in the teacher's book match the lesson numbers in the student's workbook. You will use Lesson 1 (page 1) in the Student Workbook.

Instructor: In this lesson, I am going to use my book to show you the parts of a book. The title of the book is printed on the front cover. It is the full name of the book. Read the whole title to me.

Student [reading the cover]: First Language Lessons for the Well-Trained Mind, Level 3

Instructor: In **Exercise 1** of your workbook, copy the title.

Instructor: Look again at the cover of my book. Under the title, you will find the names of the authors, the people who wrote this book. Read the authors' names to me.

Student [reading the cover]: Jessie Wise and Sara Buffington

Instructor: In **Exercise 2** your workbook, copy the authors' names.

Instructor: What kind of information do you think is in this book? To find out, we need to look at my table of contents. The table of contents tells you what will be in each lesson. The titles of the lessons are written in the order they appear in the book. Turn to the table of contents on page v. Find Lesson 2. What is Lesson 2 about?

Student: *Nouns*

Instructor: Now look at the number across from Lesson 2. This is the page number on which you will find that lesson. On which page is Lesson 2 located?

Student: *Page 8*

Instructor: Now turn to that page, page 8. Does Lesson 2 start on that page?

Student: *Yes*

If this kind of exercise is new to the student, you may wish to have him look up other lessons in this book for extra practice.

Instructor: The table of contents is always printed near the beginning of a book. You can also find out more information about what is in a book by looking at the index. The index is always printed near the end of a book. The information in the index is not listed in the order in which it appears. Instead, it is listed in **ABC** (alphabetical) order.

Show the student the index at the end of this book and point out that the entries are organized alphabetically by letter. Find the index entries for *commas*, *nouns*, and *sentences*. Tell him that the numbers next to each entry show the page or pages on which these topics are found. The student should look up at least one page (in the instructor book) for each topic.

Optional Dictation Exercise

If your student is not doing dictation in another subject, dictate the sentences to him, one at a time. If he is struggling, you may also decide to have the student write only one sentence. Instruction for giving dictation are on page 4 under "Dictation Exercises."

Dictation: The title of a book is printed on the front cover.

Dictation: The author is the person who wrote the book.

Optional Follow-Up

Take a field trip to the library. Have the student look in books to find their titles, authors, tables of contents, and indexes. If the student does not yet know the difference between fiction and nonfiction, explain to him that fiction is a made-up story. The people and events in a fiction book are at least partly imaginary. Nonfiction is the opposite of fiction. The people in a nonfiction book really lived, and the events really happened. Go to the fiction and nonfiction shelves in the children's section of your local library. Flip through some of the fiction and nonfiction books and tell the student what each book is about.

LESSON 2

New: Nouns

If the student has completed *First Language Lessons, Levels 1 and 2* and already knows the content of this lesson, you may go on to Lesson 3. If you choose to do the Optional Follow-Up, you will need a blank piece of paper.

Instructor: A noun is the name of a person, place, thing, or idea. A girl is a person. The word *girl* is a noun. A grandfather is a person. The word *grandfather* is a noun. A doctor is also a person. The word *doctor* is a noun. Repeat after me: A noun is the name of a person.

Student: *A noun is the name of a person.*

Instructor: A noun is also the name of a place. A home is a place. The word *home* is a noun. A city is a place. The word *city* is a noun. A country is a place. The word *country* is a noun. Repeat after me: A noun is the name of a place.

Student: *A noun is the name of a place.*

Instructor: Now we are going to put those two parts of the definition together. Repeat after me: A noun is the name of a person, place …

Let your voice trail off to indicate that the definition is not yet complete.

Student: *A noun is the name of a person, place …*

Instructor: A noun is also the name of a thing. A pencil is a thing. The word *pencil* is a noun. A bird is a living thing. The word *bird* is a noun. A toy is a thing. The word *toy* is a noun. Repeat after me: A noun is the name of a thing.

Student: *A noun is the name of a thing.*

Instructor: Now we are going to put those three parts of the definition together. Repeat after me: A noun is the name of a person, place, thing …

Student: *A noun is the name of a person, place, thing …*

Instructor: A noun is also the name of an idea. An idea is something you think about in your mind, but cannot see or touch—like love, anger, energy, loneliness, or fear. You can name ideas, but you can't see them. Let's add *idea* to the definition of a noun.

Instructor: A noun is the name of a person, place, thing, or idea. Let's say that together three times.

Together (three times): A noun is the name of a person, place, thing, or idea.

Instructor: Answer these questions with a noun that is a person. What do you call the person who prepares food in a restaurant?

Student: *The cook [or chef]*

Instructor: *Cook* [or *chef*] is a noun. What do you call the person who checks and cleans your teeth in an office?

Student: *The dentist [or dental hygienist]*

Instructor: *Dentist* [or *dental hygienist*] is a noun. Answer these questions with a noun that is a place. What do you call the place where you can read books and check them out?

Student: *The library*

Instructor: *Library* is a noun. What do you call the place where you hang your clean clothes?

Student: *The closet*

Instructor: *Closet* is a noun. Now let's look around the room. Tell me the things that you see. Remember, a noun is the name of a thing.

Student: *[Correct answers could include book, chair, table, crayon, window, clock, counter, ruler, picture, etc., ...]*

Instructor: Nouns are also the name of ideas. Although you can name ideas, you cannot see or touch them. Love is an idea. You can think about it in your mind. In **Exercise 1** of your workbook, read aloud to me the three ideas.

Workbook: hunger

excitement

sadness

Instructor: In your workbook read aloud each sentence in **Exercise 2**. When you get to the blank, write in the correct noun from **Exercise 1** that names an idea and makes sense in the sentence.

Workbook: When I lost my favorite toy, I was filled with sadness.

I trembled with excitement as I opened my biggest birthday present.

My stomach made loud, rumbling noises because of my hunger.

Instructor: A noun is the name of a person, place, thing, or idea. Say that with me.

Together: A noun is the name of a person, place, thing, or idea.

Dictation Exercise

Dictation: A noun is the name of a person, place, thing, or idea.

Optional Follow-Up

Turn to page 3 in the Student Workbook. Have the student flip through a magazine and clip pictures of nouns to paste on the workbook page (for example, *lady, doctor, strawberry, beach, puppy,* etc..). You or the student may label the pictures with the noun words.

LESSON 3

New: **Forming Plurals the Usual Way**

Review: **Nouns**

Instructor: Let's review the definition of a noun. A noun is the name of a person, place, thing, or idea. Say that with me three times.

Together (three times): A noun is the name of a person, place, thing, or idea.

Instructor: In your workbook, look at the four columns of words in **Exercise 1**. I will read each column to you.

Person	Place	Thing	Idea
child	room	pencil	love
mother	street	toy	anger

Instructor: Look in your workbook at **Exercise 2**. I will read you a list of words, one at a time. After I say each word, I want you to tell me whether the word is a person, place, thing, or idea. Then I want you to write the word in the correct column in the blank chart.

Workbook: firefighter

store

paper

peace

car

nurse

kindness

town

(This lesson continues on the next page.)

Answer Key:

Person	Place	Thing	Idea
firefighter	store	paper	peace
nurse	town	car	kindness

Instructor: Some nouns name one, single thing. These are called singular nouns. *Car* is a singular noun, because it names one, single car. *Store* is a singular noun, because it names one, single store. Other nouns name more than one thing. These are called plural nouns. *Cars* is a plural noun. You could have two, twenty, or one hundred cars! *Stores* is a plural noun because you are naming more than one thing. There are many stores in a town.

Instructor: Usually, add **s** to a noun to form the plural. I will say this to you three times.

Instructor (three times): Usually, add **s** to a noun to form the plural.

Instructor: I will say this three more times, and I want you to say as much as you can with me.

Together (three times): Usually, add **s** to a noun to form the plural.

Instructor: Follow along in **Exercise 3** of your workbook as I read these pairs of words to you. The first word in each pair is a singular noun. The second word in each pair is a plural noun. Then I will read these words in a sentence while you follow along.

Workbook: bee

bees

The other bees in the hive feed the queen bee.

Workbook: cloud

clouds

One cloud was bigger and darker than the other clouds.

Workbook: daughter

daughters

My mother has three daughters, and I am the youngest daughter.

Instructor: Now I will read two sentences to you. Follow along in **Exercise 4** of your workbook.

Workbook: A hummingbird is a very tiny bird.

Some hummingbirds build nests the size of walnuts and lay eggs the size of peas.

Instructor: Look at each underlined word in the two sentences I just read. Circle the noun that is a singular noun. How many hummingbirds are there?

Student: *There is only one hummingbird.*

Instructor: Now put a box around the noun that is plural. How many hummingbirds are there? Is there one or more than one?

Student: *There is more than one hummingbird.*

Instructor: Usually, add **s** to a noun to form the plural. I will say this three more times, and I want you to say as much as you can with me.

Together (three times): Usually, add **s** to a noun to form the plural.

Begin by asking the student to circle the **s** at the end of each plural noun. Then have the student copy at least one of the sentences in **Exercise 5**. If the student writes easily, have him copy all four.

Workbook: 1. The evening star is brighter than the other stars.

2. The oldest boy helped the younger boys.

3. That river joins two other rivers that flow to the sea.

4. A bird in the hand is worth two birds in the bush.

Optional Follow-Up

Play the game "I Spy a Noun." Take turns choosing an object (a noun) in the room. When you have one in your mind say "I spy a noun that begins with the letter _____" (for example, **t** for "*table*").

LESSON 4

New: Forming Plurals of Words That End in S, SH, CH, X, or Z

Review: Nouns

Review: Forming Plurals the Usual Way

Instructor: We will begin this lesson by saying the definition of a noun together twice.

Together (two times): A noun is the name of a person, place, thing, or idea.

Instructor: In the last lesson we made a list of nouns in four columns: persons, places, things, and ideas. In your workbook, read aloud each column in **Exercise 1**, beginning with its title.

Person	Place	Thing	Idea
child	room	pencil	love
mother	street	toy	anger
firefighter	store	paper	peace
nurse	town	car	kindness

Instructor: Look in your workbook at **Exercise 2**. I will read you the list of words, one at a time. After I say each word, I want you to tell me whether the word is a person, place, thing, or idea. Then I want you to copy the word in the correct column in **Exercise 2**.

Workbook: button

park

honesty

playmate

Answer Key:

Person	Place	Thing	Idea
playmate	park	button	honesty

Instructor: Last lesson you learned that nouns can be either singular or plural. The word *button* is a singular noun because you have only one, single button. The word *buttons* is a plural noun because you have two or more buttons. Usually, add **s** to a singular noun to form the plural. I will say that rule to you three more times, and you will join in as much as you can.

Together (three times): Usually, add **s** to a noun to form the plural.

Instructor: In **Exercise 3** of your workbook, you will see a list of singular nouns. I want you to add an **s** to the end of each word to make it plural.

Workbook: arm

leg

painter

pond

chair

Instructor: Look again at the **singular** words in the list in **Exercise 3**. Tell me the final letter in each word as I point to it.

Student: *m, g, r, d, r*

In the following dialogue, letters and letter pairs that are printed in bold should be spelled aloud.

Instructor: None of these nouns end in **s**, **sh**, **ch**, **x**, or **z**. If a noun ends in **s**, **sh**, **ch**, **x**, or **z**, we form the plural differently. Instead of a plain **s**, we add **es**. Add **es** to nouns ending in **s**, **sh**, **ch**, **x**, or **z**. I will say this to you three times.

Point to the letters in the column in **Exercise 4** as you say them.

Workbook: s

sh

ch

x

z

Instructor (three times): Add **es** to nouns ending in **s**, **sh**, **ch**, **x**, or **z**.

Instructor: Now I will say that rule three more times, and you will join in as much as you can.

Together (three times): Add **es** to nouns ending in **s**, **sh**, **ch**, **x**, or **z**.

Instructor: Follow along in **Exercise 5** of your workbook as I read these pairs of words to you. The first word in each pair is a singular noun. The second word in each pair is a plural noun. Then I will read the words in a sentence. This first singular noun ends in **s**. You add **es** to make the word plural.

Workbook: bus

buses

The empty bus arrived before the other buses.

Instructor: In your workbook, look at the word *bus* with the line after it. Write **es** on the line to make *bus* plural. Remember, a singular noun that ends in the letter **s** becomes plural when you add **es** to the end of the word.

Instructor: This next singular noun ends in **sh**. You add **es** to make the word plural.

Workbook: dish

dishes

Do not drop a dish when you are washing the dishes.

Instructor: In your workbook, look at the word *dish* with the line after it. Write **es** on the line to make *dish* plural. Remember, a singular noun that ends in the letters **sh** becomes plural when you add **es** to the end of the word.

Instructor: This next singular noun ends in **ch**. You add **es** to make the word plural.

Workbook: inch

inches

Thirteen inches is the same as one foot plus one inch.

Instructor: In your workbook, look at the word *inch* with the line after it. Write **es** on the line to make *inch* plural. Remember, a singular noun that ends in the letters **ch** becomes plural when you add **es** to the end of the word.

Instructor: This next singular noun ends in **x**. You add **es** to make the word plural.

Workbook: box

boxes

Wait until you have opened the other boxes before you open the big box.

Instructor: In your workbook, look at the word *box* with the line after it. Write **es** on the line to make *box* plural. Remember, a singular noun that ends in the letter **x** becomes plural when you add **es** to the end of the word.

Instructor: This next singular noun ends in **z**. You add **es** to make the word plural.

Workbook: buzz

buzzes

In the game you may move one space when you hear one buzz and three spaces when you hear three buzzes.

Instructor: In your workbook, look at the word *buzz* with the line after it. Write **es** on the line to make *buzz* plural. Remember, a singular noun that ends in the letter **z** becomes plural when you add **es** to the end of the word.

Instructor: Say this with me three times: Add **es** to nouns ending in **s**, **sh**, **ch**, **x**, or **z**.

Together (three times): Add **es** to nouns ending in **s**, **sh**, **ch**, **x**, or **z**.

Instructor: Now let's add this rule to the rule you learned last lesson. Usually, add **s** to a noun to form the plural. Add **es** to nouns ending in **s**, **sh**, **ch**, **x**, or **z**. Let's say this together three times. Join in with me as soon as you can.

Together (three times): Usually, add **s** to a noun to form the plural. Add **es** to nouns ending in **s**, **sh**, **ch**, **x**, or **z**.

Begin by asking the student to circle the **es** at the end of each plural noun. Then have the student copy at least one of the sentences in **Exercise 6**. If the student writes easily, have him copy all four. If he copies the second or fourth sentence, remind him to copy the commas.

Workbook: 1. My favorite glass is part of a set of colored glasses.
2. A peach is a popular fruit in America, but peaches originally came from China.
3. Foxes have such good hearing that a red fox can hear a mouse squeak one hundred feet away.
4. Your brush probably has bristles made of nylon, but some brushes are made from the hair of pigs, camels, or squirrels.

Optional Follow-Up

Ask the student to draw a scene showing as many plural nouns as possible. After he has finished, have him point out all the plural words. Assist him as necessary to label the plural words in his picture.

LESSON 5

New:	Forming Plurals of Nouns That End in Y
New:	Irregular Plural Nouns
Review:	Forming Plurals the Usual Way
Review:	Forming Plurals of Words That End in S, SH, CH, X, or Z

If the student does not know that the vowels are **a**, **e**, **i**, **o**, **u** and that all other letters are consonants, take the time to teach it to him now.

Instructor: Let's say the definition of a noun three times together.

Together (three times): A noun is the name of a person, place, thing, or idea.

Instructor: Nouns can be either singular or plural. Usually, add **s** to a noun to form the plural. Add **es** to nouns ending in **s**, **sh**, **ch**, **x**, or **z**. Let's say those two rules together three times.

Together (three times): Usually, add **s** to a noun to form the plural. Add **es** to nouns ending in **s**, **sh**, **ch**, **x**, or **z**.

Instructor: In this lesson you will learn another way to form plural nouns. If a noun ends in **y** after a consonant, change the **y** to **i** and add **es**. I will say this to you three times.

Instructor (three times): If a noun ends in **y** after a consonant, change the **y** to **i** and add **es**.

Instructor: Now I will say the rule three more times. Say as much of it with me as you can.

Together (three times): If a noun ends in **y** after a consonant, change the **y** to **i** and add **es**.

Instructor: Look in your workbook at **Exercise 1**. Read the singular noun.

Workbook: baby

Instructor: Point to the last letter in the word *baby*. What is that letter?

Student: *It is a **y**.*

Instructor: Now circle the letter before the **y**. It is a **b**. Is **b** a vowel or a consonant?

Student: *It is a consonant.*

Instructor: *Baby* ends in **y** after a consonant. Look at the word below *baby* in your workbook. Read the plural of *baby*.

Workbook: babies

Instructor: Since the singular noun *baby* ends with the letter **y** after a consonant, you must change the **y** to **i** and add **es** to form the plural.

Instructor: In your workbook, look at the chart in **Exercise 2**. Copy the singular noun into the blank. After you have copied each noun, change the word to make it plural. Erase the **y**, change it to **i**, and add **es**.

It is okay to talk the student through the formation of each plural noun. You may use the questions in italics to prompt the student.

What is the last letter?
Is the letter before the **y** *a consonant?*
What do you change the **y** *to?*
Then what do you add after the **i**?

Answer Key:

Singular Noun	Change to a Plural Noun
penny	pennies
lady	ladies
sky	skies
fly	flies

Instructor: This rule only works for nouns that end in a consonant and then a **y**. If a noun ends in **y** after a vowel, just add **s**. I will say that to you three times.

Instructor (three times): If a noun ends in **y** after a vowel, just add **s**.

Instructor: Now I will say the rule three more times. Say as much of it with me as you can.

Together (three times): If a noun ends in **y** after a vowel, just add **s**.

Instructor: Look in your workbook at **Exercise 3**. Read the singular noun.

Workbook: day

Instructor: Point to the last letter in the word *day*. What is that letter?

Student: *It is a* **y**.

Instructor: Now circle the letter before the **y**. It is an **a**. Is **a** a vowel or a consonant?

Student: *It is a vowel.*

Instructor: Look at the word below *day.* Read the plural of *day.*

Workbook: days

Instructor: Since the singular noun *day* ends with the letter **y** after a vowel, you just add the letter **s** to form the plural.

Instructor: In your workbook, look at the chart in **Exercise 4.** Copy the singular noun into the blank. After you have copied each noun, change the word to make it plural by adding **s** after the **y.**

It is okay to talk the student through the formation of each plural noun. You may use the questions in italics to prompt the student.

What is the last letter?
*Is the letter before the **y** a vowel?*
*Then what do you add after the **y**?*

Answer Key:

Singular Noun	Change to a Plural Noun
boy	boys
key	keys
toy	toys
tray	trays

Instructor: Some words don't follow any rules to form their plurals. We call these words "irregular plurals" because they don't form their plurals the regular ways. In **Exercise 5** of your workbook, read aloud the list of singular nouns and their irregular plural forms.

Make sure the student reads across from left to right.

Singular Noun	Irregular Plural Noun
child	children
foot	feet
tooth	teeth
man	men
woman	women
mouse	mice
goose	geese
deer	deer
fish	fish
sheep	sheep

Instructor: Now I am going to use a singular noun in a sentence. Then I will start another sentence, and you will finish the sentence by telling me the plural of that singular noun. If you need help, you may look at the list you just read in **Exercise 5**.

Instructor: There was one **woman** in the front seat of the car. In the backseat there were two _____.

Student: *women*

Instructor: The **mouse** scampered off to his hole and shared his cheese with the other _____.

Student: *mice*

Instructor: Each **child** was given a chance to be "it" when playing hide-and-seek with the group of _____.

Student: *children*

Instructor: This book was written by that **man**. That book was written by those three _____.

Student: *men*

Instructor: I caught one small **fish**. You caught several huge _____.

Student: *fish*

Optional Dictation Exercise

Dictation: Each child has more than one penny.
and / or
The children spend ten pennies each.

Optional Follow-Up

Using the singular noun and irregular plural noun list from earlier in the lesson, you will say the singular noun and the student will say the irregular plural noun (without looking at the list). Try to say the list in rhythm. Pat your knees twice, and clap your hands once as you or the student say the word. For example:

[pat] [pat] [clap—Instructor says "child"]

[pat] [pat] [clap—Student says "children"]

[pat] [pat] [clap—Instructor says "foot"]

[pat] [pat] [clap—Student says "feet"]

LESSON 6

New: **Common and Proper Nouns**
Review: **Forming Plurals**

You will need index cards for the optional follow-up.

Instructor: Let's say the definition of a noun one time together.

Together: A noun is the name of a person, place, thing, or idea.

Instructor: I will say each of the rules for forming the plurals of nouns. You will repeat it after me.

Instructor: Usually, add **s** to a noun to form the plural.

Student: *Usually, add **s** to a noun to form the plural.*

Instructor: Add **es** to nouns ending in **s**, **sh**, **ch**, **x**, or **z**.

Student: *Add **es** to nouns ending in **s**, **sh**, **ch**, **x**, or **z**.*

Instructor: If a noun ends in **y** after a consonant, change the **y** to **i** and add **es**.

Student: *If a noun ends in **y** after a consonant, change the **y** to **i** and add **es**.*

Instructor: If a noun ends in **y** after a vowel, just add **s**.

Student: *If a noun ends in **y** after a vowel, just add **s**.*

Instructor: In your workbook, look at the chart in **Exercise 1**. Copy each singular noun. After you have copied each noun, I want you to make it plural. On some words you will just add **s** or **es**. On other words you will have to erase the **y** and change it to **i** before you add the **es**.

If the student forms an incorrect plural, have him say the applicable rule three times. Then make the correction. It is okay to talk the student through the formation of each plural noun.

Answer Key:

Singular Noun	Change to a Plural Noun
book	books
pan	pans
class	classes
watch	watches
city	cities
story	stories
monkey	monkeys
valley	valleys
puppy	puppies
sock	socks
turkey	turkeys
bush	bushes

As you go through the following dialogue, have the student fill in the blanks in **Exercise 2** of his workbook.

Instructor: You know that a noun is the name of a person, place, thing, or idea. The first part of that definition is "a noun is the name of a person." You are a person. Are you a boy or a girl? In **Exercise 2** write your answer in sentence **number 1**.

Student: *I am a _____.*

Instructor: *Boy* and *girl* are naming words that are common to many persons, so we call them common nouns. The words *mother, father, sister, teacher,* and *doctor* are also common nouns. What is your name?

Student: *My name is _____.*

Instructor: You are not just any boy or girl. You are _____ [use student's proper name]. At **number 2** in **Exercise 2**, write your name. This is your own special, "proper" name. Proper names are the same as proper nouns. Proper nouns all begin with capital letters. What are the names of your mother and father? If you have brothers or sisters, what are their names?

Student: *My mother's name is _____. My father's name is _____. My brother's name is …*

Instructor: A noun is also the name of a place. The words *city*, *state*, *river*, and *park* are naming words that are common to many places. These are all common nouns. What is the name of the city [or town] in which you live?

Student: *I live in _____.*

Instructor: This is not just any city [or town]. This is your own special, "proper" town.

Instructor: A noun is also the name of a thing. Some living things that are common nouns are *dog*, *cat*, *fish*, and *bird*. If you have a pet or stuffed animal, what is its name?

Student: *The name of my dog [or cat, fish, bird] is _____.*

Instructor: Your pet is not just any dog [cat, fish, bird]. This is the special, "proper" name of your pet. *[Name of pet]* is a proper noun. Complete the sentences in **number 5** of **Exercise 2**. Now I am going to read you some nouns. If the noun is a common noun, stay seated. If the noun is a proper noun, stand up.

Instructor: doctor

[the name of a pet or stuffed animal the student has]

bird

neighbor

Clifford

policeman

[name of a neighbor]

mother

teacher

Mickey Mouse

[the name of the student]

[the name of the student's doctor or dentist]

friend

Optional Dictation Exercise

Dictation: Sam Smith drives trucks and buses.

My dog Molly has three puppies.

Optional Follow-Up

Using two index cards, write "common nouns" on one and "proper nouns" on the other. Then use the lists in this lesson and the next lesson to write a noun (either common or proper) on an individual index card. (You may wish to cut the cards in half and use these "half cards" to save paper.) Then give the student the stack of cards with the mixture of common and proper nouns, and have him sort the cards. For example, if the noun is common, he will place the card in a column under the index card that says "common nouns."

LESSON 7

New: Pronouns

Review: Common and Proper Nouns

If the student completed *First Language Lessons, Levels 1 and 2*, he has already memorized the list of pronouns, and this lesson will be a review. If the student does not have the list memorized, follow this procedure when you get to the pronoun list in this lesson:

- Read the entire list to the student three times.

- Then read each line, having the student repeat the line after you.

- Next say lines one and two together and have the student repeat those.

- Read lines three and four and have the student repeat.

- Then read lines five and six together and have the student repeat.

- Say the entire list, and ask the student to say as much of it with you as he can. Do this until he is confident and can try saying it on his own.

You may break this process up over several days if the student is easily frustrated. If the student finds memorizing simple, you may do this all in a day and review as necessary.

Instructor: Say the definition of a noun with me.

Together: A noun is the name of a person, place, thing, or idea.

Instructor: In the last lesson you learned about common and proper nouns. A common noun is a name common to many persons, places, or things. *Friend, country,* and *dog* are all common nouns. A proper noun is a special, "proper" name for a person, place, or thing. *John, Mexico,* and *Rover* are all proper nouns. Proper nouns always begin with a capital letter. I am going to read you some nouns. If the noun is a common noun, stay seated. If the noun is a proper noun, stand up.

Instructor: country

The United States of America

river

state

continent

Africa

ocean

Pacific Ocean

lake

Lake Michigan

building

[name of your place of worship]

Canada

McDonald's

The Rocky Mountains

statue

Statue of Liberty

restaurant

house

church [or your place of worship]

[the name of a pet or stuffed animal the student has]

Mississippi River

[the name of your state]

city

[the name of your town/city]

The Appalachian Mountains

Instructor: A noun is the name of a person, place, thing, or idea. Today we are going to learn about a new part of speech, the pronoun. Say this with me three times: A pronoun is a word used in the place of a noun.

Together (three times): A pronoun is a word used in the place of a noun.

Pronouns

I, me, my, mine
You, your, yours
He, she, him, her, it
His, hers, its
We, us, our, ours
They, them, their, theirs

Instructor: In **Exercise 1** of your workbook, look at the list of pronouns. We are going to practice memorizing common pronouns. Let's say the first line of pronouns together three times: *I, me, my, mine.*

Together (three times): *I, me, my, mine.*

Have the student repeat the next line of pronouns to you. After he has done so, say the list of pronouns together from the beginning. Repeat this procedure with the remaining lines of pronouns. If your student has not memorized this list in previous years, follow the more thorough approach to memorizing described at the beginning of this lesson.

Instructor: A pronoun is a word that takes the place of a noun. What is your name?

Student: My name is _____.

Instructor: Instead of saying "[Student's name] went outside," you could say "I went outside." Repeat those two sentences for me.

Student: [Student's name] went outside. I went outside.

Instructor: The pronouns that stand for you are *I, me, my, mine*. We just used the pronoun *I* in a sentence. *I* is a special pronoun because it is always capitalized. Now let's use *me*. *Me* is not capitalized. Instead of saying "Please give [the student's name] a sandwich," you could say "Please give me a sandwich." Repeat those two sentences for me.

Student: Please give [student's name] a sandwich. Please give me a sandwich.

Instructor: Now we will practice using *my*. Instead of saying "These are [student name]'s shoes," you could say "These are my shoes." Repeat those two sentences to me.

Student: These are [student's name]'s shoes. These are my shoes.

Instructor: In your workbook, read each sentence in **Exercise 2**. In the blank at the end of each sentence, write the pronoun that can be used instead of the underlined noun or nouns. You may look at the list of pronouns in **Exercise 1** to help you.

If the student needs a hint, point to the line in the list in **Exercise 1** that contains the correct pronoun. Also help him with the pronunciation of the proper names.

Workbook:

1. <u>George Washington</u> was the first president of the United States. [He]

2. <u>The Roman Empire</u> was divided into two parts. [It]

3. Mother read the tale called *The Adventures of Spider* to <u>my sister and me</u>. [us]

4. The Battle of Hastings was an important event in <u>England's</u> history. [its]

5. April showers bring May flowers. The child gave <u>the flowers</u> to her friend. [them]

6. <u>Empress Theodora</u> was the wife of Justinian, who ruled the Byzantine Empire. [She]

7. That game is <u>Carla's and mine</u>. [ours]

8. <u>The Smith family's</u> car is blue. [Their]

9. One of <u>Galileo's</u> discoveries was that the moon shone by reflecting the light of the sun. [his]

10. <u>You and I</u> are able to cool ourselves by sweating and warm ourselves by exercising. [We]

11. One reason that the first Queen Elizabeth did not marry is that she wanted decisions to be solely <u>Queen Elizabeth's</u>. [hers]

12. *Pinocchio*, a book written by <u>Carlo Collodi</u>, teaches us that lying is wrong. [him]

13. <u>King Ferdinand and Queen Isabella</u> gave Columbus ships and supplies for his journey across the seas. [They]

14. My older brother read <u>my sister's and my</u> copy of *Pilgrim's Progress* to Jane. [our]

15. No two people have the same fingerprints. Mine are different from <u>my sister's and brother's</u>. [theirs]

Dictation Exercise

After the student takes the dictation, have him circle all the pronouns.

Dictation: (It) is (my) book.

(She) read (it) to June and (me).

Optional Follow-Up

The student will draw a stick figure of himself and write the personal pronouns *I, me, my,* and *mine* around the figure. Then he will draw an arrow from each of the pronouns to the picture of himself. Then, following the same procedure, he may draw a picture of the instructor (*you, your, yours*), a boy (*he, him, his*) and a girl (*she, her, hers*), and a group of people (*they, them, their, theirs*).

LESSON 8

Review: **Common and Proper Nouns**

Review: **Plurals**

Review: **Pronouns**

Instructor: Say the definition of a noun with me.

Together: A noun is the name of a person, place, thing, or idea.

Instructor: Nouns can be either common or proper. A common noun is a name common to many persons, places, or things. A proper noun is a special, "proper" name for a person, place, or thing. Proper nouns always begin with a capital letter. *Girl* is a common noun, but *Judy Fleming* is a proper noun. I am going to say a common noun to you, and I want you answer my question with a proper noun (a special, "proper" name for a common noun).

Instructor: *Man* is a common noun. What is the special, "proper" name of a man that you know?

Student: *[Acceptable answers include Daddy, Uncle _____, Mr. _____, etc.]*

Instructor: *State* is a common noun. What is the special, "proper" name of the state in which you live?

Student: *[name of state]*

Instructor: Let's review the rules for forming plurals. Repeat after me: Usually, add **s** to a noun to form the plural.

Student: *Usually, add **s** to a noun to form the plural.*

Point to the noun *fork* in the student's workbook.

Instructor: Look at **Exercise 1** in your workbook. *Fork* is singular. I have one fork. Now I want you to write the plural form of *fork* on the line. After you have written the plural, tell me how many forks you are thinking about: two, six, or one million forks?

Instructor: Repeat after me another rule: Add **es** to nouns ending in **s, sh, ch, x,** or **z.**

Student: *Add **es** to nouns ending in **s, sh, ch, x,** or **z.***

In the student's workbook, point to the five words in **Exercise 2**. Go through the following scripting with each word in the list:

Instructor: _____ is singular. I have one _____. Now I want you to write the plural form of _____ on the line below it. After you have written the plural, tell me how many _____**es** you are thinking about.

Instructor: Repeat after me this next rule: If a noun ends in **y** after a consonant, change the **y** to **i** and add **es.**

Student: *If a noun ends in **y** after a consonant, change the **y** to **i** and add **es.***

Instructor: In your workbook, look at the word *story* in **Exercise 3**. Write the plural of *story* on the line below it.

Instructor: Repeat this next rule after me: If a noun ends in **y** after a vowel, just add **s.**

Student: *If a noun ends in **y** after a vowel, just add **s.***

Instructor: In your workbook, look at the word *toy* in **Exercise 4**. Write the plural of *toy* on the line below it.

Instructor: Now let's review the definition of a pronoun: A pronoun is a word used in the place of a noun. Say that with me three times.

Together (three times): A pronoun is a word used in the place of a noun.

Instructor: Look at the list of pronouns in **Exercise 5** of your workbook. The pronouns you have learned are:

Pronouns

I, me, my, mine
You, your, yours
He, she, him, her, it
His, hers, its
We, us, our, ours
They, them, their, theirs

Instructor: Now let's say that list together.

Instructor: I am going to read you a paragraph entitled "How Animals Use Their Tails." Follow along in your workbook. I will not read the numbers out loud.

Workbook: Many animals have tails, and (1) <u>animals</u> use their tails in different ways. The squirrel uses (2) <u>the squirrel's</u> tail to help it balance in the treetops. Crocodiles use their spiked tails to help (3) <u>crocodiles</u> swim through the water. (4) <u>Crocodiles'</u> tails also help them to knock small animals into water where they can be easily captured. A mother rabbit's tiny white tail guides (5) <u>the mother rabbit's</u> babies, or kits, through bushes and tall grasses. (6) <u>The mother rabbit</u> will lead her kits back to the safety of the burrow. The male peacock uses (7) <u>the male peacock's</u> tail feathers to attract a female. (8) <u>The male peacock</u> will spread his colorful feathers and parade in front of a female peacock. The beaver has a flat tail. (9) <u>The beaver</u> uses its tail to pat down mud to make its home.

Instructor: Now I want you to read the paragraph to me. When you get to a number, I want you to replace the underlined word or group of words with a pronoun. Write the pronoun above the underlined word or words. You may use the list of pronouns to help you.

If the student needs a hint, point to the line in the list from **Exercise 5** that contains the correct pronoun.

Answer Key:

1. they
2. its
3. them
4. Their
5. her
6. She
7. his
8. He
9. It

Optional Dictation Exercise

Dictation: Two oceans border the United States of America.

They are the Atlantic Ocean and the Pacific Ocean.

Optional Follow-Up

If the student needs some active reinforcement of the pronoun list, decide together on an action that is to be done as he says each line. Here is an example:

Clap hands while saying:
I, me, my, mine

Touch toes while saying:
You, your, yours

Turn around and around while saying:
He, she, him, her, it

Crouch down low while saying:
His, hers, its

Wave hands above head while saying:
We, us, our, ours

Jump up and down while saying:
They, them, their, theirs

LESSON 9

Introduction to Poem Memorization: "The Land of Nod"

Follow this technique:

1. Read the poem to the student and discuss its meaning to make sure the student understands it.

2. Read the title, the author, and the poem aloud to the student three times in a row. Or the student may read the poem aloud three times in a row.

3. Repeat this triple reading twice more during the day. Remember to read slowly and use expression that you wish your student to copy.

4. After the first day, read the poem aloud three times in a row, once daily. (You may wish to read the poem into a tape recorder three times in a row, and then have the student replay the tape.)

5. On the second day, and everyday thereafter, ask the student to try to say specific parts of the poem along with you (or the tape recorder).

6. When he can say the entire poem with you, encourage him to repeat it to himself in a mirror and then recite it to real people. Remind him to stand up straight with his feet together and his hands still, speak clearly, and look at his audience.

Instructor: In **Lesson 9** of your workbook, you will find a poem about dreaming. Have you ever dreamed that you were in a different place? Perhaps you saw strange things in your dream or ate unusual things. The poet Robert Louis Stevenson says that dreaming is like traveling to a different place—a place he calls "The Land of Nod." Have you ever seen someone fall asleep sitting up? The person's eyes close and his head bobs up and down; he looks like he is nodding yes. That's why the expression "to nod off" means "to fall asleep." You go to "The Land of Nod" when you nod off! Now follow along in your workbook as I read the poem.

The Land of Nod

by Robert Louis Stevenson

From breakfast on through all the day
At home among my friends I stay;
But every night I go abroad
Afar into the land of Nod.

All by myself I have to go,
With none to tell me what to do—
All alone beside the streams
And up the mountainsides of dreams.

The strangest things are there for me,
Both things to eat and things to see,
And many frightening sights abroad
Till morning in the land of Nod.

Try as I like to find the way,
I never can get back by day,
Nor can remember plain and clear
The curious music that I hear.

Discuss the poem with the student. Ask him if he has any questions about the meaning of the poem. Then read the poem to the student three times in a row (or he may read it). Repeat this triple reading twice more during the day. After each reading, the student should check a box in his workbook.

Optional Dictation Exercise

Dictation: All by myself I have to go.

I never can get back by day.

Optional Follow-Up

Ask the student to draw a picture of something he has dreamed about. If he can't remember a dream, tell him to draw a picture of a place he would like to "visit" in a dream. Title the picture "The Land of Nod." He may describe his dream picture to the family.

LESSON 10

New: **Action Verbs**

You will need index cards if you do the optional follow-up.

Read "The Land of Nod" (Lesson 9) three times to the student. Then ask the student to try to say parts of the first stanza along with you (or the tape recorder).

Instructor: In this lesson you are going to learn about a part of speech called a verb. A verb can do several different things in a sentence. Let's learn the definition of a verb. Repeat after me: A verb is a word that does an action …

Student: *A verb is a word that does an action …*

Instructor: Shows a state of being …

Student: *Shows a state of being …*

Instructor: Links two words together …

Student: *Links two words together …*

Instructor: Or helps another verb.

Student: *Or helps another verb.*

Instructor: I will say the whole definition to you three times.

Instructor (three times): A verb is a word that does an action, shows a state of being, links two words together, or helps another verb.

Instructor: Now I will say that definition three more times. Say as much of it with me as you can.

Together (three times): A verb is a word that does an action, shows a state of being, links two words together, or helps another verb.

Instructor: We will look at the first part of the definition: "A verb is a word that does an action." In your workbook, read aloud the poem in **Exercise 1**.

Active Animals

Anonymous

The monkey swings.
The robin sings.

The cow moos.
The dove coos.

The cat stretches.
The dog fetches.

The camel walks.
The tiger stalks.

The mouse scurries.
The ant hurries.

The bear growls.
The wolf howls.

The lion roars.
The eagle soars.

Instructor: Now I want you to look at the poem again, and I am going to ask you some questions about it. What does the monkey do?

Student: *It swings.*

Instructor: *Swings* is an action word. It is a verb. What does the robin do?

Student: *It sings.*

Instructor: *Sings* is an action word. It is a verb. What does the cow do?

Student: *It moos.*

Instructor: *Moos* is an action word. It is a verb. Now I want you to read the poem again. There is a verb in each line of the poem. After you have read each line, circle the verb for me.

As an optional activity, the student may act out any of the verbs from the poem.

Instructor: In **Exercise 2** of your workbook, circle the action verb in each of the sentences.

If the student has trouble finding the verb, ask him, "Is there a word in the sentence that you can act out?"

Answer Key:

1. The worm (wriggles) in the dirt.
2. The parents (laugh) at the child's joke.
3. (snuggle) next to my mom.
4. My sister (sneezed.)
5. My rabbit (nibbles) his food.
6. The bird (flew) over the house.
7. The squirrel (climbs) up a tree.
8. The deer (runs) through the woods.

Instructor: Look at **Exercise 3** in your workbook. Just for fun, read aloud this poem about nouns and verbs. Be sure to read the title and the author first. The author's last name is pronounced "FAR-jun."

Verbs

by Eleanor Farjeon

Nouns are things I see and touch,

My **cake**, my **mother**, and my **ball**;

I like some nouns very much,

Though some I do not like at all.

Verbs are the things I do, and make,

And feel, in one way or another.

Thanks to verbs, I *eat* my cake,

And *throw* my ball, and *hug* my mother.

Yet verbs, which make me laugh and play,

Can also make me cry and fall,

And *tease* my mother every day,

And *spoil* my cake, and *lose* my ball!

Dictation Exercise

Once the student has written the sentences, have him circle the verbs.

Dictation: The dancer (twirls.)

The tiger (pounces.)

Optional Follow-Up

Write assorted action verbs on index cards: *sing, moo, stretch, walk, scurry, growl, howl, roar, wriggle, laugh, snuggle, nibble, climb, touch, eat,* and *hug.* Shuffle the stack, and have the student draw a card. He should act out the action written on the card.

LESSON 11

New: **Definition of a Sentence**

New: **Sentences (Diagramming Subjects and Action Verbs)**

Read "The Land of Nod" (Lesson 9) three times to the student. Then ask the student to try to say parts of the first and second stanzas along with you (or the tape recorder).

Instructor: Today we are going to learn about sentences. I will say the definition of a sentence to you three times.

Instructor (three times): A sentence is a group of words that expresses a complete thought. All sentences begin with a capital letter and end with a punctuation mark.

Instructor: Now I will say the definition three more times. Say as much of it with me as you can.

Together (three times): A sentence is a group of words that expresses a complete thought. All sentences begin with a capital letter and end with a punctuation mark.

Instructor: In your workbook, read aloud each of the three sentences in **Exercise 1**. Notice that each sentence begins with a capital letter and ends with a punctuation mark. These three sentences all end with the punctuation mark called a period.

Workbook: Emily sings.

             Bubbles float.

             Dogs bark.

Instructor: Every sentence has a verb. Every verb has a subject. To find the subject of a verb, find the verb and then ask "who" or "what." In the first sentence, what is the action verb?

Student: *Sings*

Instructor: *Sings* is the verb. Now let's find the subject. Who sings?

Student: *Emily*

Instructor: *Emily* is the subject. Now look at the second sentence. What is the verb?

Student: *Float*

Instructor: *Float* is the verb. Now let's find the subject. What floats?

Student: *Bubbles*

Instructor: *Bubbles* is the subject. Look at the third sentence. What is the verb?

Student: *Bark*

Instructor: *Bark* is the verb. Now let's find the subject. What barks?

Student: *Dogs*

Instructor: *Dogs* is the subject. Did you know you can draw pictures of how the words in a sentence work together? This is called "diagramming" the sentence. Look at **Exercise 2** in your workbook. When you diagram a sentence, you begin with a simple frame that looks like the one in your workbook:

Instructor: The verb is written to the right of the center line, and the subject is written to the left of that line. Look at the diagram of "Emily sings." *Sings* is the verb, so it is written to the right of the center line. *Emily* is the subject, so it is written to the left of that line.

Instructor: In your workbook, look at **Exercise 3**. Read aloud this sentence again.

Workbook: Bubbles float.

Instructor: You are going to diagram this sentence on the empty frame in your workbook.

Instructor: You write the verb to the right of the center line. What is the verb in the sentence "Bubbles float"?

Student: *Float*

Instructor: Write *float* on your diagram. Now find the subject. What floats?

Student: *Bubbles*

Instructor: The word *Bubbles* should be capitalized in the diagram because it is capitalized in the sentence. Write *Bubbles* to the left of the center line.

Instructor: In your workbook, I want you to diagram the three sentences in **Exercise 4**. You read the sentence and then fill in the frame. Remember to copy the words exactly as they appear in the sentences. If the word begins with a capital letter in the sentence, it should also be capitalized in the diagram. No punctuation marks go on the diagram.

Workbook: 1. Birds fly.

2. Children run.

3. He giggles.

Use the following dialogue to help the student fill in each diagram:

1. *Find the verb. Write the verb to the right of your center line.*

2. *Find the subject. Ask "who" or "what" before the verb. [Prompt the student with a specific question like "What flies?" or "Who runs?"] Write the subject to the left of the center line on your frame.*

Answer Key:

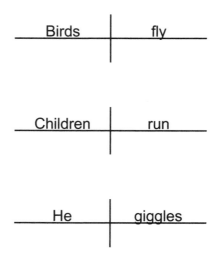

Instructor: In the sentences you just diagrammed, point to each subject. Tell me if the word is a noun or a pronoun.

Student: <u>Birds</u> *is a noun.* <u>Children</u> *is a noun.* <u>He</u> *is a pronoun.*

Instructor: Look at sentences 1 and 2. Tell me if the subjects are singular or plural nouns. Remember, *singular* means just one, single thing and *plural* means more than one.

Student: <u>Birds</u> *is a plural noun.* <u>Children</u> *is a plural noun.*

Optional Dictation Exercise

Dictation: Every sentence has a subject and a verb.

Optional Follow-Up

Tell the student that you and he will make up some sentences together. You will provide the subject, and he will think of the verb. For example, you will say "Mom" and the student may say "sings." Then you will both say "period" together to emphasize that all sentences end with a punctuation mark. Here are some subject ideas: Bubbles, Birds, Children, Dogs, Machines, [name of sibling], Dad, Doctors, Clouds, Cars, Lions, Boats.

LESSON 12

Introduction to Narration: "Bats"

Read "The Land of Nod" (Lesson 9) three times to the student. Then ask the student to try to say parts of the first, second, and third stanzas along with you (or the tape recorder).

Narration helps the student to listen with attention, to grasp the main point of a work, to think through the sequence of events, and to reproduce the events in his own words in proper, logical order. Read the following selection aloud to the student (or, the student may read it aloud himself from his workbook). After you have read the selection, follow the scripting to make sure he understands the passage and to help him practice narration. After the initial reading, the student should **not** look at the passage.

Instructor: We are going to read about bats.[1] Before we begin reading, you should know that a quadruped (pronounced KWAH-druh-ped) is an animal that has four feet.

When we have finished reading, I am going to ask you what you remember **only** about what has been read. Don't tell me information that you remember from somewhere else.

Bats

Bats are very strange little animals, having hair like mice, and wings like birds. During the day, they live in cracks of rocks, in caves, and in other dark places.

At night, they go forth in search of food; and no doubt, you have seen them flying about, catching such insects as happen to be out rather late at night.

The wings of a bat have no feathers. They are only thin pieces of skin stretched upon a framework of bones. Besides this, it may be said that while he is a quadruped, he can rise into the air and fly from place to place like a bird.

---

1. This passage is slightly adapted from *McGuffey's Second Eclectic Reader* (originally published in 1879).

Instructor: Close your eyes. Now I am going to ask you a few questions about what I just read.

The following questions are to make sure the student understands the passage. The student should answer these questions in complete sentences. If the student answers in a single word or phrase, put the phrase into a complete sentence for the student and ask him to repeat it back to you. The words in italics represent sample answers—accept other answers if they are correct and if the information was in the passage.

Instructor: What kind of animal did we read about?

Student: *We read about bats.*

Instructor: What do bats look like?

Student: *They are furry and have wings.*

Instructor: Where do bats live during the day?

Student: *They live in caves and dark areas.*

Instructor: When do they hunt for food?

Student: *They hunt at night.*

Instructor: What do they eat?

Student: *They eat bugs.*

Instructor: Do bats have feathers on their wings?

Student: *They do not have feathers on their wings.*

Instructor: Does a bat have four feet (is a bat a quadruped)?

Student: *Yes, the bat has four feet.*

(This lesson continues on the next page.)

Instructor: Now tell me two things you remember about bats. Use your own words. Speak in complete sentences.

As the student narrates in his own words, you may write his sentences down as he speaks or record them onto a tape recorder to write down when he is finished. You have three options for writing the narration:

1. Write down the student's narration for him on his workbook page.
2. Write down the student's narration for him on a separate piece of paper and have him copy some or all of the sentences onto his workbook page.
3. Write down the student's narration on a separate piece of paper and dictate it to him, as he writes it on his workbook page.

If the student repeats the author's words verbatim, use the questions about the passage to help the student form his own sentences. If the student speaks in phrases, turn his phrases into complete sentences. The student should then repeat the complete sentence back to you. The student does not need to include every aspect of the passage in his narration—he only needs to pick out two ideas. For more instructions on narration, see "Strand 3: Narration" on page 2. Here is an example of a possible narration for the passage on bats.

> Bats have wings like birds and hair like mice. They live in caves during the day, but at night they fly around and hunt insects.

Once you have written the student's narration, he should read it aloud back to you.

LESSON 13

New: Adjectives

Review: Sentences

Read "The Land of Nod" (Lesson 9) three times to the student. Then ask the student to try to say parts of the four stanzas along with you (or the tape recorder).

Instructor: In Lesson 11 you learned about sentences. A sentence is a group of words that expresses a complete thought. All sentences begin with a capital letter and end with a punctuation mark. Say that definition with me three times.

Together (three times): A sentence is a group of words that expresses a complete thought. All sentences begin with a capital letter and end with a punctuation mark.

Instructor: You also began to learn how to diagram a sentence. Remember, a sentence diagram is a picture of how the words in a sentence work together. In your workbook, read the sentence in **Exercise 1**.

Workbook: Nathan yelled.

Instructor: Diagram this sentence by filling in the empty frame.

Instructor: First you find the verb. What is the verb in the sentence "Nathan yelled"?

Student: *Yelled*

Instructor: *Yelled* is the verb. Write the verb to the right of the center line on your diagram. Now let's find the subject. Who yelled?

Student: *Nathan*

Instructor: *Nathan* is the subject. Write the subject to the left of the center line on your diagram. Your diagram is now complete.

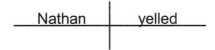

Instructor: Now I want you to diagram the sentence in **Exercise 2**. Read the sentence first. Remember to copy the words exactly as they appear in the sentence. If the word begins with a capital letter in the sentence, it should also be capitalized in the diagram.

Workbook: She looked.

Use the following dialogue to help the student fill in the diagram:

1. *Find the verb. Write the verb to the right of your center line.*

2. *Find the subject. Ask "who" or "what" before the verb. [Prompt the student with a specific question, "Who looked?"] Write the subject to the left of the center line on your frame.*

Instructor: In this lesson you will learn about the part of speech called an adjective. An adjective is a word that describes a noun or pronoun. I will say that definition to you three times.

Instructor (three times): An adjective is a word that describes a noun or pronoun.

Instructor: Now I will say the definition three more times. Say it with me.

Together (three times): An adjective is a word that describes a noun or pronoun.

Instructor: Adjectives provide you with more information about a noun or pronoun. Let's think about the noun *dog*. You don't know very much information about the dog. If you add an adjective before the noun, you can tell what kind of dog it is. In your workbook, read the list of adjectives and nouns in **Exercise 3**. Do you see how the adjectives describe each dog?

Workbook: **brown** dog

chubby dog

short dog .

friendly dog

wet dog

playful dog

Instructor: All of the adjectives you just read tell you **what kind** of dog it is. Adjectives can tell you several things about a noun. In your workbook, look with me at the list in **Exercise 4**. Adjectives tell what kind, which one, how many, and whose.

Workbook: Adjectives tell

- what kind
- which one
- how many
- whose

Instructor: Now I will say this as a chant three times. Look at the list again as I say it.

Instructor (three times): Adjectives tell what kind, which one, how many, and whose.

Instructor: Now say the chant with me three times without looking at the list.

Together (three times): Adjectives tell what kind, which one, how many, and whose.

Instructor: Friendly dog. Brown dog. Playful dog. All of these adjectives tell you what kind of dog it is. Other kinds of adjectives tell you **which** dog it is. Read aloud the list in **Exercise 5** of your workbook.

Workbook: this dog

that dog

these dogs

those dogs

Instructor: Which dog is it? It is **that** dog. The adjective *that* tells you which one. There are more adjectives that can tell you which one. Read aloud the list in **Exercise 6** of your workbook.

Workbook: first dog

second dog

next dog

last dog

Instructor: Imagine that four dogs are standing before you in a line. You point to the dog at the end of the line. Which dog is it? It is the **last** dog. The adjective *last* tells you which dog you are talking about. Adjectives can also tell you how many. Read aloud the list in **Exercise 7** of your workbook.

Workbook: one dog

two dogs

forty-three dogs

Instructor: When adjectives tell you how many, they sometimes do not tell you an exact number. In your workbook, read the list of adjectives in **Exercise 8** that tell you how many but do **not** tell you an exact number.

Workbook: **many** dogs

several dogs

all dogs

both dogs

some dogs

another dog

each dog

more dogs

most dogs

other dogs

Instructor: You know that adjectives tell what kind, which one, how many, and whose. You will learn about adjectives that tell whose in the next lesson.

Dictation Exercise

Dictation: Two people laughed.

Most snakes slither.

Optional Follow-Up

Tell the student, "I am going to say a noun with an adjective that describes it. You will draw a picture of what I say." Tell the student to draw a picture with:

- happy face
- long snake
- pretty flower
- tall house
- ugly monster
- many bugs

Then ask the student to label the items in the picture with a noun and an adjective.

LESSON 14

New: Adjectives That Tell Whose (Possessive Nouns)
Review: Adjectives

Read "The Land of Nod" (Lesson 9) three times to the student. Then ask the student to try to say the whole poem with you (or the tape recorder). The student should practice saying the whole poem to himself in a mirror.

Instructor: In the last lesson you learned the definition of an adjective. An adjective is a word that describes a noun or pronoun. Say that with me three times.

Together (three times): An adjective is a word that describes a noun or pronoun.

Instructor: Adjectives tell what kind, which one, how many, and whose. Say that with me three times.

Together (three times): Adjectives tell what kind, which one, how many, and whose.

Instructor: Adjectives tell what kind. Put your finger in your workbook at Lesson 14 and close it. Now I want you to think about a flower in your mind. Tell me words that describe this imaginary flower.

Student: [*Answers will vary.*]

If the student has trouble thinking of at least five adjectives, ask the student questions about the flower. For example, "What color is it?" or "How does it smell?" or "How would it feel to touch?" or "How big is it?"

Instructor: Now open your workbook to Lesson 14. In **Exercise 1**, read the list of adjectives that could describe a flower. Did you think of any adjectives on this list? Did you think of any adjectives that were not on this list?

Workbook: purple

yellow

sweet

stinky

soft

smooth

prickly

velvety

huge

tiny

Instructor: All of the adjectives in the list you read tell you what kind. Adjectives can also tell you which one. In your workbook, read the list in **Exercise 2**.

Workbook: **this** flower

that flower

these flowers

those flowers

Instructor: Repeat after me: *This, that, these,* and *those* are adjectives that tell which one.

Student: *This, that, these, and those are adjectives that tell which one.*

Instructor: Adjectives like *first, second, next,* and *last* can also tell you which one. In your workbook, read aloud the list in **Exercise 3**.

Workbook: **first** flower

second flower

next flower

last flower

Instructor: Adjectives can also tell you how many. Sometimes these adjectives tell you an exact number like "one cookie," and sometimes they tell you a general amount like "several cookies." In your workbook, read the sentences in **Exercise 4** and point to the adjective in bold that tells you how many.

Workbook: 1. **Three** cats mewed.

2. **Twenty** worms squirmed.

3. **All** people blink.

4. **Both** clowns juggled.

Instructor: Now, in this lesson you will learn about adjectives that tell **whose**. In your workbook, read aloud the two sentences in **Exercise 5**.

Workbook: This shirt belongs to the boy.

It is the **boy's** shirt.

Instructor: To whom does the shirt belong? It belongs to the boy. The boy possesses the shirt. Look at the word in bold print in the sentence you just read: *boy's*. Do you see the apostrophe that comes before the letter **s**? This is a tiny mark, but it is very powerful. The punctuation mark called an apostrophe changes the way a word acts in the sentence. The word *boy* (without the apostrophe and the **s**) is a noun that names a person. But when you add an apostrophe and the letter **s** to *boy*, the new word, *boy's*, tells you whose shirt it is. The apostrophe-**s** turns the noun into an adjective that tells whose! In your workbook, read aloud the list in **Exercise 6**. The adjectives are printed in bold.

Workbook: the **librarian's** desk

the **painter's** brush

the **farmer's** tractor

the **player's** trophy

the **lion's** roar

Aunt Glinda's pie

Mother's dinner

Taylor's guitar

Jennifer's ticket

Instructor: In your workbook, look at the chart in **Exercise 7**. First you will read a singular noun. Then, you will fill in the blank with that word and add an apostrophe-**s** to it. The noun will then turn into an adjective that tells whose.

Noun	Adjective That Tells Whose	Answer Key
man	the _____ head	man's
bird	the _____ nest	bird's
child	the _____ toy	child's
Juan	_____ shoes	Juan's
Uncle Abram	_____ car	Uncle Abram's

Instructor: Now you know how an apostrophe-**s** can turn a singular noun into an adjective. But how can you turn a plural noun into an adjective? Remember, plural nouns name more than one thing. In your workbook, read aloud the sentences in **Exercise 8**.

Workbook: These shirts belong to the boys.

These are the **boys'** shirts.

Instructor: To whom do the shirts belong? They belong to the boys. They all possess shirts. Look at the word in bold print in the sentence you just read: *boys'*. Do you see the apostrophe? This time the apostrophe comes at the end of the word. It is not followed by the letter **s**. That is because the plural noun *boys* already ends in an **s**! You don't need to add another one. If you did, it would sound funny: *boys's*. The *boys's* shirts. That doesn't sound right! In order to change a plural noun that already ends in **s** into an adjective that tells whose, all you need to do is add that powerful punctuation mark called an apostrophe. In your workbook, read aloud the examples in **Exercise 9**. The adjectives in bold print all tell whose.

Workbook: two **friends'** lollipops

several **kittens'** mews

many **singers'** voices

the **actors'** costumes

the **Parkers'** cars

Instructor: In your workbook, look at the chart in **Exercise 10**. First you will read a plural noun. Then you will fill in the blank with that word and add an apostrophe to it. The noun will turn into an adjective that tells whose.

Noun	Adjective That Tells Whose	Answer Key
shoppers	the _____ baskets	shoppers'
girls	the _____ dresses	girls'
Richards	the _____ children	Richards'
trees	the _____ leaves	trees'

Instructor: Continuing in **Exercise 10**, read the first sentence aloud.

Workbook: 1. The shoppers' baskets are here.

Instructor: Remember, one of the things that adjectives tell is **whose**. Whose baskets are they?

Student: *The shoppers'*

Instructor: *Shoppers'* is an adjective that tells whose baskets they are. *Shoppers'* describes *baskets*. Read the second sentence aloud.

Workbook: 2. The painter's brush dripped.

Instructor: Whose brush is it?

Student: *The painter's*

Instructor: *Painter's* is an adjective that tells whose brush it is. *Painter's* describes *brush*. On the lines in your workbook, copy the sentences in **Exercise 11**. After you have copied each sentence, circle the adjective that tells whose.

Workbook: 1. The (actors') costumes are in that room.

2. (Mother's) dinner was ham and potatoes.

3. The (trees') leaves droop.

Optional Follow-Up

Have the student find something in the house that belongs to each family member. Then have the student write, for example, "Mom's purse" on a piece of paper and tape it to the purse. If it is something that belongs to the entire family, the student may write "the family's table" or "the Morrisons' table."

LESSON 15

New: Adjectives That Tell Whose (Possessive Irregular Plural Nouns)

Review: Adjectives

Review: Forming Plurals

Read "The Land of Nod" (Lesson 9) three times to the student. Then ask the student to say the poem along with you or the tape recorder. If the student is ready, he should recite the poem to real people today. If he is not, continue practicing daily until he is ready.

Instructor: In the last lesson you reviewed the definition of an adjective. An adjective is a word that describes a noun or pronoun. Say that with me three times.

Together (three times): An adjective is a word that describes a noun or pronoun.

Instructor: Adjectives tell what kind, which one, how many, and whose. Say that with me three times.

Together (three times): Adjectives tell what kind, which one, how many, and whose.

Instructor: Adjectives tell what kind. Look at your shirt. What color is it?

Student: *[Answers will vary.]*

Instructor: *[Color of shirt]* is an adjective that tells what kind of shirt. Feel your shirt's material. How would you describe it: thin, thick, soft, scratchy, or smooth?

Student: *[Answers will vary.]*

Instructor: *[Adjective the student chose]* is an adjective that tells what kind of shirt. Adjectives can also tell which one. In your workbook, read the list in **Exercise 1**.

Workbook: **this** shirt

that shirt

these shirts

those shirts

Instructor: Repeat after me: *This, that, these,* and *those* are adjectives that tell which one.

Student: <u>*This, that, these, and those are adjectives that tell which one.*</u>

Instructor: There are other adjectives that can tell you which one. In your workbook, read aloud the list in **Exercise 2**.

Workbook: **first** flower

eighth flower

next flower

final flower

Instructor: Adjectives like *first, eighth, next,* and *final* tell you which one. Adjectives can also tell you how many. Sometimes these adjectives tell you an exact number like "one rock," and sometimes they tell you a general amount like "several rocks." Answer this question with a number. How many fingers do you have?

Student: *Ten*

Instructor: Ten fingers. *Ten* is an adjective that tells how many fingers. Could you count how many eyelashes are on your eyes? Well, maybe you could, but it would take a very long time. If I asked you how many eyelashes you have, you could just say "I have many eyelashes." *Many* is an adjective that tells how many eyelashes, even if it doesn't tell you the exact number. In **Exercise 3** of your workbook, read the list of adjectives that tell you how many but do not tell you an exact number.

Workbook: **several** cars

all cars

both cars

some cars

another car

each car

more cars

most cars

other cars

Instructor: In the last lesson you learned about adjectives that tell whose. In **Exercise 4** of your workbook, read the sentence aloud.

Workbook: It is the **boy's** shirt.

Instructor: Whose shirt is it? The boy's. *Boy's* is an adjective that tells whose. Look at the word *boy's* in the sentence. Do you see the apostrophe that comes before the letter **s**? The punctuation mark called an apostrophe changes the way a word acts in the sentence. The word *boy* (without the apostrophe and the **s**) is a noun that names a person. But when you add an apostrophe and the letter **s** to *boy*, the new word, *boy's*, tells you whose shirt it is. The apostrophe-**s** turns the noun into an adjective that tells whose!

Instructor: In your workbook, look at the chart in **Exercise 5**. First you will read a singular noun. Then, you will write that word in the blank and add an apostrophe-**s** to it. The noun will turn into an adjective that tells whose.

The student should write the possessive form of the word in the student workbook.

Noun	Adjective That Tells Whose	Answer Key
cat	the _____ fur	cat's
book	the _____ cover	book's
Lee	_____ coat	Lee's

Instructor: Now you know how an apostrophe-**s** can turn a singular noun into an adjective. Do you remember how to turn a plural noun into an adjective? Remember, plural nouns name more than one thing. In **Exercise 6** of your workbook, read the sentence aloud.

Workbook: The **girls'** dresses are all white.

Instructor: Whose dresses are they? The girls'. *Girls'* is an adjective that tells whose. Look at the word *girls'* in the sentence. Do you see the apostrophe? This time the apostrophe comes at the end of the word. It is not followed by the letter **s**. That is because the plural noun *girls* already ends in an **s**. You don't need to add another one. If you did, it would sound funny: *girls's*. The *girls's* dresses. That doesn't sound right! In order to change a plural noun that already ends in **s** into an adjective that tells whose, all you need to do is add that powerful punctuation mark called an **apostrophe**.

Instructor: Look at the chart in **Exercise 7** of your workbook. First you will read a plural noun. Then you will write that word in the blank and add an apostrophe to it. The plural noun will turn into an adjective that tells whose.

The student should write the possessive form of the word in the student workbook.

Noun	Adjective That Tells Whose	Answer Key
foxes	the _____ dens	foxes'
flowers	the _____ seeds	flowers'
Wilders	the _____ pets	Wilders'

Instructor: When a plural noun ends in **s**, as many plurals do, you add an apostrophe to turn the plural noun into an adjective that tells whose. But there are some plurals that do not end in **s**. This should sound familiar, because we learned about these plurals in Lesson 5 of this book. These nouns don't follow any rules to form their plurals. We call these "irregular plurals" because they don't form their plurals the regular ways. In **Exercise 8** of your workbook, read this list of singular nouns and their irregular plural forms to me.

Make sure the student reads across from left to right.

Singular Noun	Plural Noun
child	children
foot	feet
tooth	teeth
man	men
woman	women
mouse	mice
goose	geese
deer	deer
sheep	sheep
fish	fish

Instructor: These irregular plurals don't follow the rules when it comes to turning them into adjectives that tell whose, either. Normally, you just add an apostrophe to a plural noun to turn it into an adjective. But with irregular plurals (because they don't already end in **s**), you need to add an apostrophe **and** the letter **s**. Read **Exercise 9** to me. The adjectives in bold print all tell whose.

Workbook: two **deer's** antlers

many **fish's** scales

several **mice's** nests

Instructor: Look at the chart in **Exercise 10** of your workbook. First you will read an irregular plural noun. Then you will write the word in the blank and add an apostrophe-**s** to it. The noun will turn into an adjective that tells whose.

The student should write the possessive form of the word in the student workbook.

Noun	Adjective That Tells Whose	Answer Key
children	the _____ games	children's
men	the _____ ties	men's
sheep	the _____ pens	sheep's

Instructor: Let's finish today's lesson with a review of the regular ways to form a plural. Repeat after me: Usually, add **s** to a noun to form the plural.

Student: *Usually, add **s** to a noun to form the plural.*

Instructor: In your workbook, look at **Exercise 11**. Read the first singular and plural nouns.

Singular Noun	Plural Noun
kitten	kittens

Instructor: Repeat the second rule: Add **es** to nouns ending in **s**, **sh**, **ch**, **x**, or **z**.

Student: *Add **es** to nouns ending in **s**, **sh**, **ch**, **x**, or **z**.*

Instructor: Read the next list of singular and plural nouns in your workbook. Start with *glass* and read across.

Singular Noun	Plural Noun
glass	glasses
brush	brushes
peach	peaches
box	boxes
buzz	buzzes

Instructor: Repeat the third rule: If a noun ends in **y** after a consonant, change the **y** to **i** and add **es**.

Student: *If a noun ends in **y** after a consonant, change the **y** to **i** and add **es**.*

Instructor: Read the next singular noun and its plural form.

Singular Noun	Plural Noun
family	families

Instructor: Repeat the fourth rule: If a noun ends in **y** after a vowel, just add **s**.

Student: *If a noun ends in **y** after a vowel, just add **s**.*

Instructor: Read the last singular noun and its plural form.

Singular Noun	Plural Noun
day	days

Optional Follow-Up

There is no optional follow-up for this lesson.

LESSON 16

New: Articles
New: Adjectives (with Diagramming)

You will need a container of crayons for this lesson.

Instructor: In the last lesson you reviewed the definition of an adjective. An adjective is a word that describes a noun or pronoun. Say that with me three times.

Together (three times): An adjective is a word that describes a noun or pronoun.

Instructor: Adjectives tell what kind, which one, how many, and whose. Say that with me three times.

Together (three times): Adjectives tell what kind, which one, how many, and whose.

Instructor: Adjectives tell what kind. Put your finger in your workbook at Lesson 16 and close it. I want you to think about a cake in your mind. Now tell me words that describe this imaginary cake.

Student: *[Answers will vary.]*

If the student has trouble thinking of at least five adjectives, ask the student questions about the cake. For example, "What flavor of cake is it?" or "What color is it?" or "How does it taste?" or "How would it feel to touch?" or "How does it smell?"

Instructor: Now open your workbook to **Lesson 16**. In **Exercise 1**, read the list of adjectives that could describe a cake. Did you think of any adjectives on this list? Did you think of any adjectives that were not on this list?

Workbook: sweet

crumbly

chocolate

strawberry

white

thick

gooey

delicious

birthday

Instructor: All of the adjectives you just read tell you what kind. Adjectives can also tell you which one.

Take out a container of crayons and remove two. Put one crayon in front of the student, and put another crayon on an empty chair.

Instructor: The adjectives *this* and *that* tell you which one. Point to each of the crayons and tell me, "This crayon is on the table," and "That crayon is on the chair."

Student (pointing): This crayon is on the table. That crayon is on the chair.

Instructor: Repeat after me: *This* and *that* are adjectives that tell you which one.

Student: This *and* that *are adjectives that tell you which one.*

Take the crayon from the chair, and put it next to the crayon on the table. Set the container of crayons on the table near the two crayons.

Instructor: The adjectives *these* and *those* tell you which one. Point to the crayons and tell me, "These crayons are in the container," and "Those crayons are out of the container."

Student: These *crayons are in the container.* Those *crayons are out of the container.*

Instructor: Repeat after me: *These* and *those* are adjectives that tell you which ones.

Student: These *and* those *are adjectives that tell you which ones.*

Take out two more crayons and put the container aside. Make sure the crayons are of different colors. Set the four crayons in a straight line in front of the student.

Instructor: There are other adjectives that tell you which ones. You have a line of crayons in front of you. Point to the first crayon, and say "First crayon."

Student: First crayon

Instructor: Point to the second crayon and say "Second crayon."

Student: Second crayon

Instructor: Point to the next crayon and say "Next crayon."

Student: Next crayon

Instructor: Point to the last crayon and say "Last crayon."

Student: Last crayon

Instructor: Adjectives like *first, second, next,* and *last* tell you which one. Adjectives can also tell you how many. Sometimes these adjectives tell you an exact number like "one crayon," and sometimes they tell you a general amount like "several crayons." In **Exercise 2** of your workbook, read each sentence and circle the adjective that tells you how many.

Workbook:
1. (Two) people laughed.
2. (Sixty) geese flew.
3. (All) windows close.
4. (Both) feet itch.
5. (Some) plants froze.
6. (Another) child yells.
7. (Each) flower opens.
8. (More) rain falls.
9. (Most) birds hop.
10. (Other) birds waddle.

Instructor: Adjectives can also tell whose. You can turn a singular noun into an adjective that tells whose by adding an apostrophe-**s**. You can turn a plural noun ending in **s** into an adjective that tells whose by adding just an apostrophe. And in the last lesson you learned that you turn irregular plural nouns into adjectives in an irregular way: you add an apostrophe-**s**, even though the word is plural.

Instructor: Look at the chart in **Exercise 3** of your workbook. First you will read a noun. Then you will fill in the blank with the adjective that tells whose.

Noun	Adjective That Tells Whose	Answer Key
cricket	the _____ body	cricket's
turkeys	the _____ necks	turkeys'
women	the _____ class	women's

Instructor: There are three special, little adjectives that we have not talked about yet. These adjectives are called articles. The articles are *a, an, the.* Here is a little poem to help you learn them. Follow along in **Exercise 4** while I read the poem.

If the student already knows this poem from *First Language Lessons, Levels 1 and 2,* you need only read it once and have the student repeat it after you from memory. If this is the first time the student is learning about articles, read the poem to the student three times in a row at three different times during the day. Have the student join you when he is able. Review this poem on subsequent days if necessary.

Workbook: Articles are little words,

You need know only three.

The articles that describe nouns

are **a**, **an**, **the**.

Instructor: You use the article *a* before a word that begins with a consonant sound. A book. A pet. A car. You use the article *an* before a word that begins with a vowel sound. An apple. An egg. An icicle. An octopus. An umbrella. Continue in **Exercise 4**, and circle the article in each of the sentences. Remember, articles act like adjectives— they describe nouns.

If the student asks, the article *the* is pronounced "thuh" before a word that begins with a consonant sound. It is pronounced "thee" before a word that begins with a vowel sound or if you are trying to emphasize a word ("It is **the** car to buy.").

Workbook: (An) automobile speeds.

(The) kettle whistles.

(A) truck rattles.

(The) snake slithers.

(A) camel spits.

(An) owl hoots.

Instructor: In **Exercise 5**, I want you to diagram a sentence. It has a subject and a verb. You read the sentence. I will ask you questions as you fill in the diagram. Remember to copy the words exactly as they appear in the sentence. If the word begins with a capital letter in the sentence, it should also be capitalized in the diagram. Now read me the sentence.

Workbook: Cats purr.

Use the following dialogue to help the student fill in the diagram:

1. *Find the verb. Write the verb to the right of your center line.*

2. *Find the subject. Ask "who" or "what" before the verb. [Prompt the student with a specific question, "What purrs?"] Write the subject to the left of the center line on your frame.*

Instructor: Now you will learn how to add adjectives to a sentence diagram. In the sentence "Cats purr," the word *Cats* is the subject. It is a noun. Let's add an adjective that describes the noun *Cats*. Read the next sentence in **Exercise 5**.

Workbook: Fat cats purr.

Instructor: The subject of the sentence is still *cats*. What purrs? Cats purr. But now there is an adjective that tells us more about the *cats*. What kind of cats are they? **Fat** cats. The adjective is written on a slanted line under the word it describes. Look at this diagram. Point to the adjective.

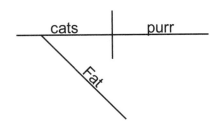

Instructor: Now in **Exercise 6** you will diagram sentences with adjectives in them. You read the sentence. I will ask you questions as you fill in the diagram. Remember to copy the words exactly as they appear in the sentence. If the word begins with a capital letter in the sentence, it should also be capitalized in the diagram.

Workbook: 1. Hot cocoa steams.

2. Three friends shop.

3. Most gold shines.

4. Children's bikes zip.

5. The alarm rang.

(This lesson continues on the next page.)

Use the following dialogue to help the student fill in the diagrams:

1. *Find the verb. Write the verb to the right of your center line.*

2. *Find the subject. Ask "who" or "what" before the verb. [Prompt the student with a specific question like "What steams?" or "Who shops?"] Write the subject to the left of the center line on your frame.*

3. *Now you have found the two most basic parts of the sentence. Go back and look again at the subject. Is there a word that describes the subject? This is an adjective that could tell what kind, which one, how many, or whose. Also look for the articles (a, an, the), because they act like adjectives. Write the adjective on the slanted line below the subject it describes.*

Answer Key:

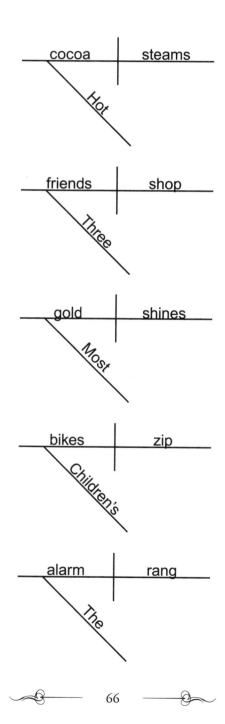

Optional Follow-Up

Remind the student that the article *a* is used before words beginning with a consonant sound and *an* is used before words beginning with a vowel sound. Tell the student to read each noun in the Optional Follow-Up, and then say it again using the correct article before the word.

Workbook:

engine	<u>an</u> engine
potato	<u>a</u> potato
insect	<u>an</u> insect
leaf	<u>a</u> leaf
umbrella	<u>an</u> umbrella
onion	<u>an</u> onion
car	<u>a</u> car

LESSON 17

Review: Adjectives

Instructor: Let's review the definition of an adjective. An adjective is a word that describes a noun or pronoun. Say that with me once.

Together: An adjective is a word that describes a noun or pronoun.

Instructor: Adjectives tell what kind, which one, how many, and whose. Say that with me once.

Together: Adjectives tell what kind, which one, how many, and whose.

Instructor: Adjectives tell what kind. In **Exercise 1** of your workbook, read the first sentence.

Workbook: Tall trees sway.

Instructor: What is the adjective in the sentence? **What kind** of trees sway?

Student: *Tall*

Instructor: Adjectives tell which one. Read the next sentence.

Workbook: That door squeaks.

Instructor: What is the adjective in the sentence? **Which one** of the doors squeaks?

Student: *That*

Instructor: Adjectives tell how many. Read the next sentence.

Workbook: Several cars race.

Instructor: What is the adjective in the sentence? **How many** cars race?

Student: *Several*

Instructor: Adjectives also tell whose. Read the next sentence.

Workbook: Mandy's horse neighs.

Instructor: What is the adjective in the sentence? **Whose** horse neighs?

Student: *Mandy's*

Instructor: Do you remember the three special, little words called articles? Articles act like adjectives—they describe nouns. What are the three articles?

Student: *A, an, the*

If the student cannot remember the articles, repeat the poem from the last lesson.

Instructor: In your workbook, read the sentences in **Exercise 2** and circle the articles.

Workbook: (An) engine roared.

(The) soup boiled.

(A) team cheered.

Instructor: In **Exercise 3** of your workbook, there is a sentence with only a subject and a verb. Read the sentence and look at the diagram.

Workbook: Cats purr.

Instructor: In the last lesson you learned how to add adjectives to a sentence diagram. Read this next sentence and look at its diagram.

Workbook: Fat cats purr.

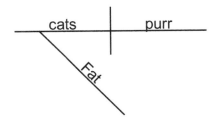

Instructor: Remember, you write an adjective on a slanted line under the word it describes. If there is more than one adjective that describes a noun, you will need more than one slanted line. Read the next sentence and look at its diagram.

Workbook: Furry, fat cats purr.

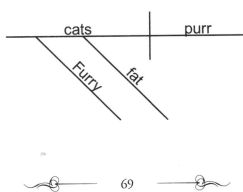

Instructor: There are two adjectives in this sentence that describe the noun *cats*. What kind of cats purr? Furry and fat cats purr. Now you will diagram sentences with **two** adjectives in them. You read the sentence out loud. I will ask you questions as you fill in the diagram. Remember to copy the words exactly as they appear in the sentence. If the word begins with a capital letter in the sentence, it should also be capitalized in the diagram.

Workbook: 1. Ten white swans swim.

2. The musicians' trumpets sound.

3. Many cheerful robins chirp.

4. Snakes' beady eyes shine.

Use the following dialogue to help the student fill in the diagrams for each of the four numbered sentences.

---

1. *Find the verb. Write the verb to the right of your center line.*

2. *Find the subject. Ask "who" or "what" before the verb. [Prompt the student with a specific question like "What swims?" or "What sounds?"] Write the subject to the left of the center line on your frame.*

3. *Now you have found the two most basic parts of the sentence. Go back and look again at the subject. Are there any words that describe the subject? These adjectives can tell what kind, which one, how many, or whose. Also look for the articles (a, an, the), because they act like adjectives. Write each adjective on a slanted line below the subject it describes.*

Answer Key:

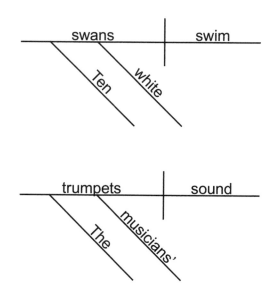

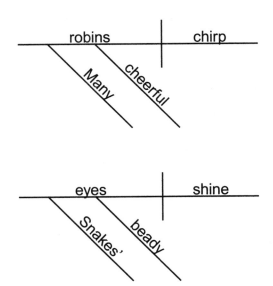

Optional Follow-Up

Tell the student, "In your workbook there is a list of nouns with adjectives that describe them. Draw a picture of each and then label the items in your picture."

- a tall, green tree
- ten tiny, blue flowers
- a fat, lazy cat
- a huge yellow house
- first dog; next dog; last dog
- some birds; more birds; many birds

LESSON 18

Poem Memorization: "A Tragic Story"

Instructor: In **Lesson 18** of your workbook, you will find a poem about a man who can't solve a problem. But before I begin reading, I want to tell you what a few words mean.

As you explain each definition, point to the word where it appears in the poem. *Sage* and *yore* appear in the first stanza. *Mused* is in the second stanza, and *stout* is in the fifth.

Instructor: A *sage* is a very wise person. *Yore* is a time long past. The sage lived long ago. *Mused* means thought over carefully. The sage thought over his problem. *Stout* means thick. The sage had a thick pigtail. Now follow along in your workbook as I read the poem.

A Tragic Story
by William Makepeace Thackeray

There lived a sage in days of yore,
And he a handsome pigtail wore;
But wondered much and sorrowed more,
Because it hung behind him.

He mused upon the curious case,
And swore he'd change the pigtail's place,
And have it hanging at his face,
Not dangling there behind him.

Says he, "The mystery I've found—
I'll turn me round"—he turned him round;
But still it hung behind him.

Then round and round, and out and in,

All day the puzzled sage did spin;

In vain—it mattered not a pin—

The pigtail hung behind him.

And right and left, and round about,

And up and down, and in and out,

He turned; but still the pigtail stout

Hung steadily behind him.

And though his efforts never slack,

And though he twist, and twirl, and tack,

Alas! still faithful to his back,

The pigtail hangs behind him.

Read the poem to the student three times in a row. Repeat this triple reading twice more during the day. Have the student check the boxes in his workbook when this is done. Doing the optional follow-up activity will help him understand the sage's dilemma (how **can** he get his pigtail to the front)?

Dictation Exercise

The student may look at the spelling of *sage* and *yore* before you dictate the first sentence.

Dictation: There lived a sage in days of yore.

All day the puzzled sage did spin.

Optional Follow-Up

Have the student act out the poem. He will need to "fashion a pigtail": Tie some yarn to the back of a baseball cap. Before he begins, he must know the line "The mystery I've found—I'll turn me round."

The instructor reads the poem as the student acts out the scenes: The sage sits, saddened that he cannot see his pigtail. He gets an idea. The student must say the line "The mystery …" when the instructor gets to it. The sage turns round and round. He spins to the right, then to the left, then up and down, then forward and backward. For a dramatic ending, the sage can collapse in exhaustion.

LESSON 19

New: **Adverbs That Tell How (with Diagramming)**

Read "A Tragic Story" (Lesson 18) three times to the student. Then ask the student to try to say parts of the first stanza along with you (or the tape recorder).

Instructor: Let's review the definition of an adjective. Say this with me two times: An adjective is a word that describes a noun or pronoun.

Together (two times): An adjective is a word that describes a noun or pronoun.

Instructor: In this lesson you will learn another part of speech that describes words: an adverb. An adverb is a word that describes a verb, an adjective, or another adverb. I will say that definition to you three times.

Instructor (three times): An adverb is a word that describes a verb, an adjective, or another adverb.

Instructor: Now I will say that definition three more times. Say it with me.

Together (three times): An adverb is a word that describes a verb, an adjective, or another adverb.

Instructor: We will talk about adverbs that describe adjectives and other adverbs later in this book. In this lesson we will focus on adverbs that describe verbs. In your workbook, put your finger on **Exercise 1**. Follow along as I read. Adverbs tell how, when, where, how often, and to what extent.

Workbook: Adverbs tell

- how
- when
- where
- how often
- to what extent

Instructor: Say that with me three times. Adverbs tell how, when, where, how often, and to what extent.

Together (three times): Adverbs tell how, when, where, how often, and to what extent.

Instructor: Adverbs tell **how. How** do you laugh? In **Exercise 2**, read each of the sentences to me. The adverb that tells how is in bold print.

Workbook: I laugh **quietly**.

I laugh **happily**.

I laugh **quickly**.

I laugh **nervously**.

I laugh **loudly**.

Instructor: We are going to practice identifying adverbs that tell how. Look at **Exercise 3**. I will ask you a "How" question and you will read the three choices. Choose your favorite adverb and say the answer to the question in a complete sentence. Then write your adverb of choice in the blank.

Instructor: How do you eat?

Workbook: quickly

quietly

slowly

Student: *I eat [adverb of choice].*

Instructor: *[Adverb of choice]* is an adverb that tells how you eat.

Instructor: How do you sing?

Workbook: loudly

sweetly

merrily

Student: *I sing [adverb of choice].*

Instructor: *[Adverb of choice]* is an adverb that tells how you sing.

Instructor: How do you write?

Workbook: carefully

clearly

neatly

Student: *I write [adverb of choice].*

Instructor: *[Adverb of choice]* is an adverb that tells how you write.

Instructor: How do you smile?

Workbook: shyly

broadly

warmly

Student: *I smile [adverb of choice].*

Instructor: *[Adverb of choice]* is an adverb that tells how you smile.

Instructor: How do you play?

You may need to help the student read the word *rambunctiously*. It means "wildly and with uncontrolled exuberance."

Workbook: joyously

busily

rambunctiously

Student: *I play [adverb of choice].*

Instructor: *[Adverb of choice]* is an adverb that tells how you play.

Instructor: In **Exercise 4**, read the first sentence and look at its diagram:

Workbook: Cats purr.

```
_____Cats____|____purr_____
               |
```

Instructor: In this lesson you will learn how to add adverbs to a sentence diagram. In the sentence "Cats purr," the word *Cats* is the subject. The verb is *purr.* Let's add an adverb that tells **how** the cats purr. Read the new sentence and look at its diagram.

Workbook: Cats purr softly.

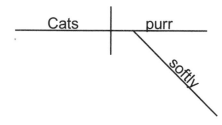

Instructor: *Softly* is an adverb that tells how the cats purr. An adverb is written on a slanted line under the verb it describes.

Instructor: Read the next simple sentence about waterfalls and look at its diagram.

Workbook: Waterfalls tumble.

Instructor: The word *Waterfalls* is the subject. The verb is *tumble*. Let's add an adverb that tells how the waterfalls tumble. Read the new sentence and look at its diagram.

Workbook: Waterfalls tumble rapidly.

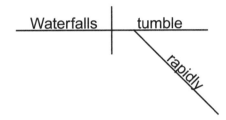

Instructor: *Rapidly* is an adverb that tells how the waterfalls tumble. You write an adverb on a slanted line under the verb it describes.

Instructor: Now in **Exercise 5** you will diagram sentences with adverbs in them. You read the sentence. I will ask you questions as you fill in the diagram. Remember to copy the words exactly as they appear in the sentence. If the word begins with a capital letter in the sentence, it should also be capitalized in the diagram.

Workbook: 1. Ants work busily.

2. Clouds float silently.

3. Bears sleep deeply.

4. Pigs snort noisily.

Use the following dialogue to help the student fill in the diagrams:

1. *Find the verb. Write the verb to the right of your center line.*

2. *Find the subject. Ask "who" or "what" before the verb. [Prompt the student with a specific question like "What works?" or "What floats?"] Write the subject to the left of the center line on your frame.*

3. *Now you have found the two most basic parts of the sentence. Go back and look again at the verb. Is there a word that describes the verb? This is an adverb that tells how. Write the adverb on the slanted line below the verb it describes.*

Answer Key:

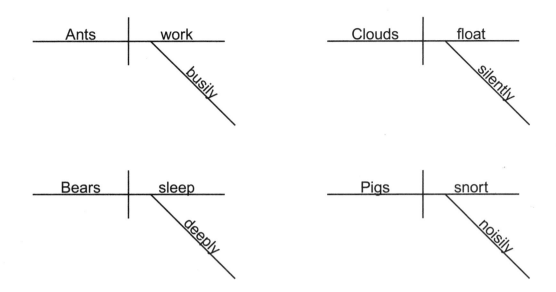

Optional Follow-Up

Have the student read the first word in each column to make a sentence (for example, "Knights battle fiercely.") Repeat this for the remaining rows. After the student has read all the "sensible sentences" by reading across, he can pick a subject and match it with any verb and adverb from the columns. He can create some very silly sentences! The student may do this orally or write down his sentences.

Subject	Verb	Adverb
Knights	battle	fiercely
Turtles	lumber	cautiously
Spies	wink	mysteriously
Dancers	leap	gracefully
Eagles	cry	shrilly
Babies	toddle	awkwardly

LESSON 20

New: Adverbs That Tell When (with Diagramming)

Read "A Tragic Story" (Lesson 18) three times to the student. Then ask the student to try to say parts of the first and second stanzas along with you (or the tape recorder).

Instructor: In the last lesson you learned a new part of speech called an adverb. An adverb is a word that describes a verb, an adjective, or another adverb. I will say that definition to you three times.

Instructor (three times): An adverb is a word that describes a verb, an adjective, or another adverb.

Instructor: Now I will say that definition three more times. Say it with me.

Together (three times): An adverb is a word that describes a verb, an adjective, or another adverb.

Instructor: In **Exercise 1** of your workbook, you will see: Adverbs tell how, when, where, how often, and to what extent. Read that with me three times.

Workbook: Adverbs tell

⊙ how

• when

• where

• how often

• to what extent

Together (three times): Adverbs tell how, when, where, how often, and to what extent.

Instructor: Adverbs tell **when. When** do you leave? In **Exercise 2**, read each of the sentences to me. The adverb that tells when is in bold print.

Workbook: I leave **tonight**.

I leave **tomorrow**.

I leave **soon**.

I leave **now**.

I leave **immediately**.

Instructor: Look at **Exercise 3**. We are going to practice identifying adverbs that tell when. I will ask you a "When" question and you will read the three choices. Choose your favorite adverb and answer the question in a complete sentence. Then write your adverb of choice in the blank.

Instructor: When do you eat?

Workbook: early

now

late

Student: *I eat [adverb of choice].*

Instructor: *[Adverb of choice]* is an adverb that tells when you eat.

Instructor: When did you sing?

Workbook: yesterday

earlier

already

Student: *I sang [adverb of choice].*

Instructor: *[Adverb of choice]* is an adverb that tells when you sang.

Instructor: When did you write?

Workbook: today

again

promptly

Student: *I wrote [adverb of choice].*

Instructor: *[Adverb of choice]* is an adverb that tells when you wrote.

Instructor: When did you smile?

Workbook: then

lately

before

Student: *I smiled [adverb of choice].*

Instructor: *[Adverb of choice]* is an adverb that tells when you smiled.

Instructor: When do you play?

Workbook: momentarily

later

tonight

Student: *I play [adverb of choice].*

Instructor: *[Adverb of choice]* is an adverb that tells when you play.

Instructor: Now find **Exercise 4** in your workbook. Read the first sentence and look at its diagram.

Workbook: Taylor whistled.

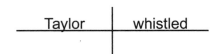

Instructor: In this sentence "Taylor whistled," the word *Taylor* is the subject. The word *whistled* is the verb. Let's add an adverb that tells **when** Taylor whistled. Read the new sentence and look at its diagram.

Workbook: Taylor whistled yesterday.

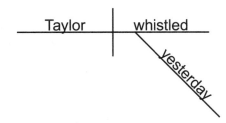

Instructor: *Yesterday* is an adverb that tells when Taylor whistled. You write an adverb on a slanted line under the verb it describes.

Instructor: Read the next simple sentence and look at its diagram.

Workbook: She arrived.

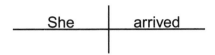

Instructor: The word *She* is the subject. The word *arrived* is the verb. Let's add an adverb that tells when she arrived. Read the new sentence and look at its diagram.

Workbook: She arrived early.

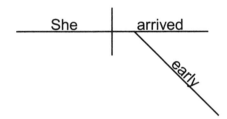

Instructor: *Early* is an adverb that tells when she arrived. You write an adverb on a slanted line under the verb it describes.

Instructor: In **Exercise 5**, **you** will diagram sentences with adverbs in them. You read the sentence. I will ask you questions as you fill in the diagram. Remember to copy the words exactly as they appear in the sentence. If the word begins with a capital letter in the sentence, it should also be capitalized in the diagram.

Workbook:
1. Lee sneezed already.
2. Mom shopped yesterday.
3. Lizards laze today.
4. I yawn now.

Use the following dialogue to help the student fill in the diagrams:

1. *Find the verb. Write the verb to the right of your center line.*

2. *Find the subject. Ask "who" or "what" before the verb. [Prompt the student with a specific question like "Who sneezed?" or "Who shopped?"] Write the subject to the left of the center line on your frame.*

3. *Now you have found the two most basic parts of the sentence. Go back and look again at the verb. Is there a word that describes the verb? This is an adverb that tells when. Write the adverb on the slanted line below the verb it describes.*

Answer Key:

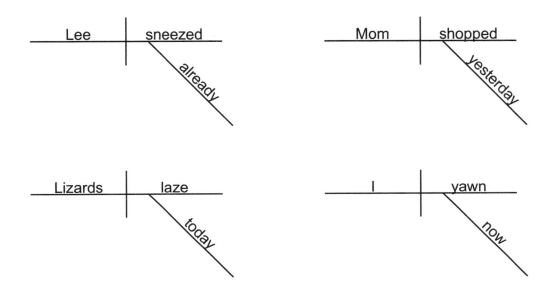

Optional Follow-Up

There is no optional follow-up for this lesson.

LESSON 21

New: Adverbs That Tell Where (with Diagramming)

Read "A Tragic Story" (Lesson 18) three times to the student. Then ask the student to try to say parts of the first through third stanzas along with you (or the tape recorder).

Instructor: An adverb is a word that describes a verb, an adjective, or another adverb. Adverbs tell how, when, where, how often, and to what extent. I will say that to you again. An adverb is a word that describes a verb, an adjective, or another adverb. Adverbs tell how, when, where, how often, and to what extent. Now I will say that three more times. Say it with me.

Together (three times): An adverb is a word that describes a verb, an adjective, or another adverb. Adverbs tell how, when, where, how often, and to what extent.

Instructor: Adverbs tell **where**. **Where** do you run? In **Exercise 1** of your workbook, read each of the sentences to me. The adverb that tells where is in bold print.

Workbook: I run **nearby**.

I run **outside**.

I run **upstairs**.

I run **away**.

I run **far**.

Instructor: We are going to practice identifying adverbs that tell where. Look at **Exercise 2**. I will ask you a "Where" question and you will read the three choices. Choose your favorite adverb and answer the question in a complete sentence. Then write your adverb of choice in the blank.

Instructor: Where do you eat?

Workbook: here

inside

downstairs

Student: *I eat [adverb of choice].*

Instructor: *[Adverb of choice]* is an adverb that tells where you eat.

Instructor: Where do you sing?

If the student asks, the following words are not used as nouns in this situation because they describe the verb *play*. They answer the question "play **where**?" The words would be nouns if they acted as a subject: "Outside is my favorite place."

Workbook: everywhere

outside

nearby

Student: *I sing [adverb of choice].*

Instructor: *[Adverb of choice]* is an adverb that tells where you sing.

Instructor: Where do you play?

Workbook: outdoors

anywhere

upstairs

Student: *I play [adverb of choice].*

Instructor: *[Adverb of choice]* is an adverb that tells where you play.

Instructor: Where do you walk?

Workbook: away

far

forward

Student: *I walk [adverb of choice].*

Instructor: *[Adverb of choice]* is an adverb that tells where you walk.

Instructor: In **Exercise 3**, read the first sentence and look at its diagram:

Workbook: Hummingbirds fly.

Hummingbirds	fly

Instructor: In the sentence "Hummingbirds fly," the word *Hummingbirds* is the subject. The word *fly* is the verb. Let's add an adverb that tells where hummingbirds fly. Read the new sentence and look at its diagram.

Workbook: Hummingbirds fly backward.

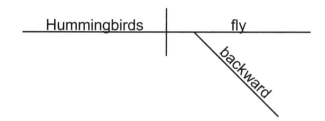

Hummingbirds can indeed fly backward! They are the only kind of bird that can.

Instructor: *Backward* is an adverb that tells where hummingbirds fly. You write an adverb on a slanted line under the verb it describes. Read the next simple sentence and look at its diagram.

Workbook: Columbus traveled.

Instructor: The word *Columbus* is the subject. The word *traveled* is the verb. Let's add an adverb that tells where Columbus traveled. Read the new sentence and look at its diagram.

Workbook: Columbus traveled far.

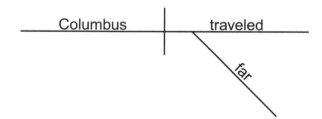

Instructor: *Far* is an adverb that tells where. You write an adverb on a slanted line under the verb it describes.

Instructor: In **Exercise 4** you will diagram sentences with adverbs in them. You read the sentence. I will ask you questions as you fill in the diagram. Remember to copy the words exactly as they appear in the sentence. If the word begins with a capital letter in the sentence, it should also be capitalized in the diagram.

Workbook: 1. Bubbles drift upward.

2. I searched everywhere.

3. Children play outside.

4. Abby came here.

Use the following dialogue to help the student fill in the diagrams:

1. *Find the verb. Write the verb to the right of your center line.*

2. *Find the subject. Ask "who" or "what" before the verb. [Prompt the student with a specific question like "What drifts?" or "Who searched?"] Write the subject to the left of the center line on your frame.*

3. *Now you have found the two most basic parts of the sentence. Go back and look again at the verb. Is there a word that describes the verb? This is an adverb that tells where. Write the adverb on the slanted line below the verb it describes.*

Answer Key:

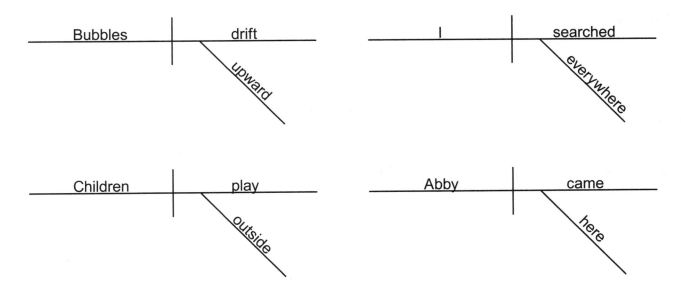

Optional Follow-Up

Have the student read each sentence and do what the sentence states. Remind the student that these adverbs tell where.

I walk **nearby**.

I walk **backward**.

I walk **upstairs**.

I walk **away**.

I walk **far**.

I walk **sideways**.

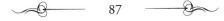

LESSON 22

New: **Adverbs That Tell How Often (with Diagramming)**

Read "A Tragic Story" (Lesson 18) three times to the student. Then ask the student to try to say parts of the first through fourth stanzas along with you (or the tape recorder).

Instructor: An adverb is a word that describes a verb, an adjective, or another adverb. Adverbs tell how, when, where, how often, and to what extent. I will say that to you again. An adverb is a word that describes a verb, an adjective, or another adverb. Adverbs tell how, when, where, how often, and to what extent. Now I will say that three more times. Say it with me.

Together (three times): An adverb is a word that describes a verb, an adjective, or another adverb. Adverbs tell how, when, where, how often, and to what extent.

Instructor: Adverbs tell **how often. How often** do you exercise? In **Exercise 1** of your workbook, read each of the sentences to me. The adverb that tells how often is in bold print.

Workbook: I exercise **daily**.

I exercise **hourly**.

I exercise **rarely**.

I exercise **usually**.

I exercise **frequently**.

Instructor: We are going to practice identifying adverbs that tell how often. Look at **Exercise 2**. I will ask you a "How often" question and you will read the three choices. Choose your favorite adverb and answer the question in a complete sentence. Then write your adverb of choice in the blank.

Instructor: How often do you read?

Workbook: sometimes

nightly

hourly

Student: *I read [adverb of choice].*

Instructor: *[Adverb of choice]* is an adverb that tells how often you read.

Instructor: How often do you nap?

Workbook: seldom

often

daily

Student: *I nap [adverb of choice].*

Instructor: *[Adverb of choice]* is an adverb that tells how often you nap.

Instructor: How often do you share?

Workbook: regularly

rarely

weekly

Student: *I share [adverb of choice].*

Instructor: *[Adverb of choice]* is an adverb that tells how often you share.

Instructor: How often did you complain last week?

Workbook: once

frequently

daily

Student: *I complained [adverb of choice].*

Instructor: *[Adverb of choice]* is an adverb that tells how often you complained.

Instructor: In **Exercise 3**, read the first sentence and look at its diagram:

Workbook: You breathe.

Instructor: In the sentence "You breathe," the word *You* is the subject. The word *breathe* is the verb. Let's add an adverb that tells how often you breathe. Read the new sentence and look at its diagram.

Workbook: You breathe constantly.

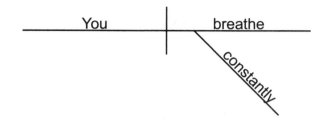

Instructor: *Constantly* is an adverb that tells how often you breathe. You write an adverb on a slanted line under the verb it describes. Read the next simple sentence and look at its diagram.

Workbook: Logan tripped.

Instructor: The word *Logan* is the subject. The word *tripped* is the verb. Let's add an adverb that tells how often Logan tripped. Read the new sentence and look at its diagram.

Workbook: Logan tripped twice.

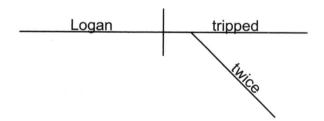

Instructor: *Twice* is an adverb that tells how often. You write an adverb on a slanted line under the verb it describes.

Instructor: In **Exercise 4** you will diagram sentences with adverbs in them. You read the sentence. I will ask you questions as you fill in the diagram. Remember to copy the words exactly as they appear in the sentence. If the word begins with a capital letter in the sentence, it should also be capitalized in the diagram.

Workbook: 1. Owls hunt nightly.

2. Musicians tune often.

3. I relax sometimes.

4. Kayla studies daily.

Use the following dialogue to help the student fill in the diagrams:

1. *Find the verb. Write the verb to the right of your center line.*

2. *Find the subject. Ask "who" or "what" before the verb. [Prompt the student with a specific question like "What hunts?" or "Who tunes?"] Write the subject to the left of the center line on your frame.*

3. *Now you have found the two most basic parts of the sentence. Go back and look again at the verb. Is there a word that describes the verb? This is an adverb that tells how often. Write the adverb on the slanted line below the verb it describes.*

Answer Key:

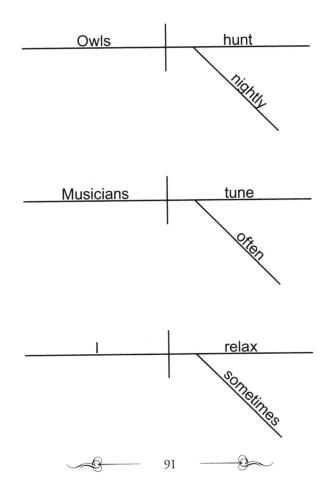

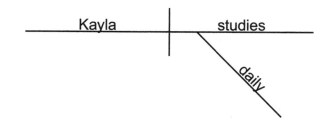

Instructor: The adverbs you have practiced so far have come **after** the verb in the sentence. Sometimes adverbs come **before** the verb, but they are diagrammed in the same way. In **Exercise 5**, read each of the sentences to me. Each sentence contains an adverb that tells how often. In these sentences, the adverbs come **before** the verbs.

Workbook: I **always** think.

She **never** quarrels.

Tom **seldom** drives.

Adverbs that tell to what extent will be covered in Lesson 57. These adverbs describe adjectives and other adverbs (not just verbs), which is why they are not covered at this time.

Optional Follow-Up

There is no optional follow-up for this lesson.

LESSON 23

Review: Adjectives and Adverbs

Read "A Tragic Story" (Lesson 18) three times to the student. Then ask the student to try to say parts of the first through fifth stanzas along with you (or the tape recorder).

Instructor: Let's review the definition of an adjective. An adjective is a word that describes a noun or pronoun. Say that with me once.

Together: An adjective is a word that describes a noun or pronoun.

Instructor: Adjectives tell what kind, which one, how many, and whose. Say that with me once.

Together: Adjectives tell what kind, which one, how many, and whose.

Instructor: Adjectives tell what kind. In **Exercise 1** of your workbook, read the first sentence.

Workbook: Fresh buds open.

Instructor: What is the adjective in the sentence? **What kind** of buds open?

Student: *Fresh*

Instructor: Adjectives tell which one. Read the next sentence.

Workbook: That insect bites.

Instructor: What is the adjective in the sentence? **Which one** of the insects bites?

Student: *That*

Instructor: Adjectives tell how many. Read the next sentence.

Workbook: Six teams travel.

Instructor: What is the adjective in the sentence? **How many** teams travel?

Student: *Six*

Instructor: Adjectives can tell whose. Read the next sentence.

Workbook: Chip's foot twitches.

Instructor: What is the adjective in this sentence? **Whose** foot twitches?

Student: *Chip's*

Instructor: Do you remember the three special, little words called articles? Articles act like adjectives—they describe nouns. What are these three articles?

Student: *A, an, the*

If the student cannot remember the articles, repeat the poem from Lesson 16.

Instructor: In your workbook, read the sentences in **Exercise 2** and circle the articles.

Workbook: (A) sword clanked.

(The) potato exploded.

(An) anteater snuffled.

Instructor: In **Exercise 3** you will diagram a sentence with one adjective in it. You read the sentence. I will ask you questions as you fill in the diagram. Remember to copy the words exactly as they appear in the sentence. If the word begins with a capital letter in the sentence, it should also be capitalized in the diagram.

Workbook: Green worms inch.

Use the following dialogue to help the student fill in the diagram:

1. *Find the verb. Write the verb to the right of your center line.*

2. *Find the subject. Ask "who" or "what" before the verb. [Prompt the student with a specific question, "What inches?"] Write the subject to the left of the center line on your frame.*

3. *Now you have found the two most basic parts of the sentence. Go back and look again at the subject. Are there any words that describe the subject? These adjectives can tell what kind, which one, how many, or whose. Also look for the articles (a, an, the), because they act like adjectives. Write each adjective on a slanted line below the subject it describes.*

Answer Key:

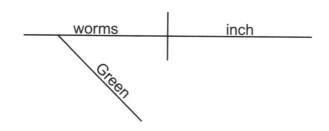

Instructor: An adverb is a word that describes a verb, an adjective, or another adverb. Adverbs tell how, when, where, how often, and to what extent. I will say that to you again. An adverb is a word that describes a verb, an adjective, or another adverb. Adverbs tell how, when, where, how often, and to what extent. Now I will say that three more times. Say it with me.

Together (three times): An adverb is a word that describes a verb, an adjective, or another adverb. Adverbs tell how, when, where, how often, and to what extent.

Instructor: Adverbs tell **how. How** do you speak? Read each sentence in **Exercise 4** to me. The adverb that tells how is in bold print.

Workbook: I speak **clearly**.

I speak **rapidly**.

I speak **quietly**.

I speak **slowly**.

I speak **plainly**.

Instructor: In **Exercise 5** in your workbook, I will ask you a "How" question and you will read the three choices. Choose your favorite adverb and answer the question in a complete sentence. Then write your adverb of choice in the blank.

Instructor: How do you sneeze?

Workbook: quickly

quietly

loudly

sweetly

Student: *I sneeze [adverb of choice].*

Instructor: *[Adverb of choice]* is an adverb that tells how you sneeze. Adverbs tell **when. When** did you speak? In **Exercise 6** read each of the sentences to me. The adverb that tells when is in bold print.

Workbook: I spoke **earlier**.

I spoke **today**.

I spoke **yesterday**.

I spoke **afterward**.

I spoke **promptly**.

Instructor: In **Exercise 7** I will ask you a "When" question and you will read the three choices. Choose your favorite adverb and answer the question in a complete sentence. Then write your adverb of choice in the blank.

Instructor: When did you hiccup?

Workbook: yesterday

earlier

today

Student: *I hiccupped [adverb of choice].*

Instructor: *[Adverb of choice]* is an adverb that tells when you hiccupped. Adverbs tell **where**. **Where** do you tiptoe? In **Exercise 8** read each of the sentences to me. The adverb that tells where is in bold print.

Workbook: I tiptoe **here**.

I tiptoe **there**.

I tiptoe **forward**.

I tiptoe **inside**.

I tiptoe **upstairs**.

Instructor: In **Exercise 9** I will ask you a "Where" question and you will read the three choices. Choose your favorite adverb and answer the question in a complete sentence. Then write your adverb of choice in the blank.

Instructor: Where do you cook?

Workbook: downstairs

outside

nearby

Student: *I cook [adverb of choice].*

Instructor: *[Adverb of choice]* is an adverb that tells where you cook. Adverbs tell **how often**. **How often** do you bathe? In **Exercise 10** read each of the sentences to me. The adverb that tells how often is in bold print.

Workbook: I bathe **daily**.

I bathe **yearly**.

I bathe **often**.

I **always** bathe.

I **never** bathe.

Instructor: In **Exercise 11**, I will ask you a "How often" question and you will read the three choices. Choose your favorite adverb and answer the question in a complete sentence. Then write your adverb of choice in the blank.

Instructor: How often do you travel?

Workbook: yearly

rarely

frequently

Student: *I travel [adverb of choice].*

Instructor: *[Adverb of choice]* is an adverb that tells how often you travel. Adverbs also tell to what extent. We will talk about these adverbs later in this book.

Instructor: Now in **Exercise 12** you will diagram a sentence with one adverb in it. You read the sentence. I will ask you questions as you fill in the diagram. Remember to copy the words exactly as they appear in the sentence. If the word begins with a capital letter in the sentence, it should also be capitalized in the diagram.

Workbook: Worms inch forward.

Use the following dialogue to help the student fill in the diagram:

1. *Find the verb. Write the verb to the right of your center line.*
2. *Find the subject. Ask "who" or "what" before the verb. [Prompt the student with a specific question like "What inches?"] Write the subject to the left of the center line on your frame.*
3. *Now you have found the two most basic parts of the sentence. Go back and look again at the verb. Is there a word that describes the verb? This is an adverb that could tell how, when, where, or how often. Write the adverb on the slanted line below the verb it describes.*

Answer Key:

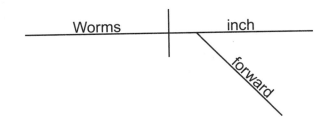

Instructor: Now in **Exercise 13** I will show you a diagram with both an adjective and an adverb in it. Read the sentence and look at its diagram.

Workbook: Green worms inch forward.

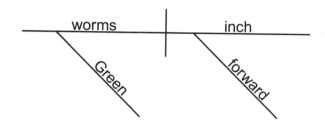

Instructor: In **Exercise 14** you will diagram four sentences with adjectives **and** adverbs in them. You read each sentence. I will ask you questions as you fill in each diagram. Remember to copy the words exactly as they appear in the sentence. If the word begins with a capital letter in the sentence, it should also be capitalized in the diagram.

Workbook: 1. Each horse gallops easily.

  2. Strong winds blew again.

  3. The alarm rang downstairs.

  4. Lazy lizards lounge often.

Use the following dialogue to help the student fill in the diagram:

1. *Find the verb. Write the verb to the right of your center line.*

2. *Find the subject. Ask "who" or "what" before the verb. [Prompt the student with a specific question like "What gallops?" or "What blew?"] Write the subject to the left of the center line on your frame.*

3. *Now you have found the two most basic parts of the sentence. Go back and look again at the subject. Are there any words that describe the subject? These adjectives can tell what kind, which one, how many, or whose. Also look for the articles (a, an, the), because they act like adjectives. Write each adjective on a slanted line below the subject it describes.*

4. *Go back and look again at the verb. Is there a word that describes the verb? This is an adverb that could tell how, when, where, or how often. Write the adverb on the slanted line below the verb it describes.*

Answer Key:

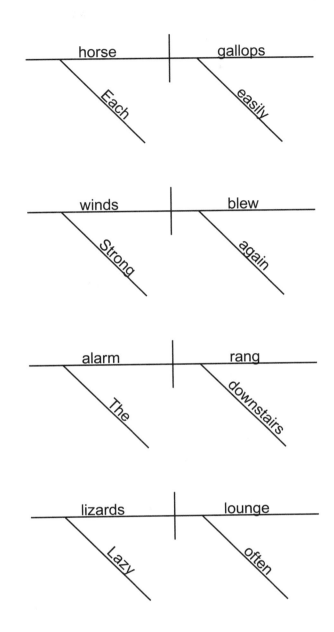

Optional Follow-Up

Give the student a magazine or newspaper and ask him to cut out pictures of people doing actions: running, talking, shaking hands, cooking, laughing, driving, etc. He should paste the pictures (about 5-10) onto pieces of paper. The instructor should write a very simple sentence at the top of each picture. For example, if you have a picture of a woman driving, you may write "The woman drives _____." Then the student fills in the blank with an adverb that could accurately describe the action. For example, "The woman drives fast."

LESSON 24

Review: Nouns, Pronouns, Verbs, Adjectives, and Adverbs

Read "A Tragic Story" (Lesson 18) three times to the student. Then ask the student to try to say parts of the six stanzas along with you (or the tape recorder).

This may look like a very long lesson, but it is mostly done orally. There is no dictation exercise.

Instructor: A noun is the name of a person, place, thing, or idea. Say that definition with me.

Together: A noun is the name of a person, place, thing, or idea.

Instructor: There are two types of nouns: common and proper. A common noun is a name common to many persons, places, or things. The words *car*, *river*, and *game* are all common nouns. A proper noun is a special, "proper" name for a person, place, or thing. *Ford*, *Amazon River*, and *Scrabble* are all proper nouns. Proper nouns always begin with a capital letter. I am going to read you some nouns. If the noun is a common noun, stay seated. If the noun is a proper noun, stand up.

Instructor: Atlantic Ocean

bird

China

city

country

doctor

Dr. Elizabeth Blackwell (the first woman physician in the United States)

Europe

inventor

lake

Nile River

ocean

restaurant

Sally Ride (the first woman astronaut)

state

statue

The Great Salt Lake

The Washington Monument

Instructor: Nouns can be either singular or plural. The word *stick* is a singular noun because you have only one, single stick. The word *sticks* is a plural noun because you have two or more sticks. Repeat after me: Usually, add **s** to a noun to form the plural.

Student: *Usually, add **s** to a noun to form the plural.*

Instructor: Look at the chart in **Exercise 1** of your workbook. Copy each singular noun in the blank. After you have copied each noun, I want you to make it plural by adding **s**.

Singular Noun	Change to a Plural Noun
kitten	kittens
street	streets

Instructor: Repeat this second rule: Add **es** to nouns ending in **s**, **sh**, **ch**, **x**, or **z**.

Student: *Add **es** to nouns ending in **s**, **sh**, **ch**, **x**, or **z**.*

Instructor: Look at the chart in **Exercise 2** of your workbook. Copy each singular noun in the blank. After you have copied each noun, I want you to make it plural by adding **es**.

Singular Noun	Change to a Plural Noun
glass	glasses
brush	brushes
peach	peaches
box	boxes
buzz	buzzes

Instructor: Repeat the third rule: If a noun ends in **y** after a consonant, change the **y** to **i** and add **es**.

Student: *If a noun ends in **y** after a consonant, change the **y** to **i** and add **es**.*

Instructor: Look at the chart in **Exercise 3** of your workbook. Copy each singular noun in the blank. After you have copied each noun, I want you to make it plural. You will have to erase the **y** and change it to **i** before you add the **es**.

Singular Noun	Change to a Plural Noun
family	families
lady	ladies

Instructor: Repeat the fourth rule: If a noun ends in **y** after a vowel, just add **s**.

Student: *If a noun ends in **y** after a vowel, just add **s**.*

Instructor: Look at the chart in **Exercise 4** of your workbook. Copy the singular noun in the blank. After you have copied each noun, I want you to make it plural by adding **s**.

Singular Noun	Change to a Plural Noun
day	days
key	keys

Instructor: Now look at **Exercise 5** in your workbook. You already know the definition of a pronoun. A pronoun is a word used in the place of a noun. Say that with me.

Together: A pronoun is a word used in the place of a noun.

Instructor: Now we are going to practice the list of common pronouns.

Pronouns

I, me, my, mine
You, your, yours
He, she, him, her, it
His, hers, its
We, us, our, ours
They, them, their, theirs

If the student already knows the list of pronouns, have him say them alone from memory once. If he needs to review, follow this procedure:

1. Have the student say the first line of pronouns with you three times. He may look at the list in his workbook.

2. Then ask him to say the first line alone from memory.

3. Together, say the second line three times, looking at the list.

4. Then, from memory, say the list of pronouns together from the beginning.

5. Repeat Steps 3 and 4 with each of the remaining four lines of pronouns.

The following oral exercise helps the student understand the relationship between a noun and the pronoun that replaces it.

Instructor: Look at **Exercise 6** in your workbook. Each sentence contains a pronoun. After you read each sentence, substitute a noun for which the underlined pronoun could stand.

Workbook: Nancy gave grape juice to <u>me</u>.

Student: *Nancy gave grape juice to [student's name].*

Workbook: I will ask <u>you</u> for permission.

Student: *I will ask [Daddy, Mommy, the teacher] for permission.*

Workbook: Return <u>it</u> to the library.

Student: *Return [the book, the video] to the library.*

Workbook: The family will take <u>her</u> to the zoo.

Student: *The family will take [any girl's name, the girl] to the zoo.*

Instructor: Now I am going to help you review verbs. A verb is a part of speech that can do several different things in a sentence. Let's practice the definition of a verb. A verb is a word that does an action, shows a state of being, links two words together, or helps another verb. Say this with me three times.

Together (three times): A verb is a word that does an action, shows a state of being, links two words together, or helps another verb.

Instructor: In **Exercise 7** read each **action** verb. After you read the verb, I want you to do the action and then use the word in a sentence. For example, if you read the action verb *jump*, you would jump up and down and say "I jump."

Workbook: sing

run

dance

skip

squat

bend

laugh

sit

Instructor: Now let's talk about adjectives. An adjective is a word that describes a noun or pronoun. Adjectives tell what kind, which one, how many, and whose. Say that with me.

Together: An adjective is a word that describes a noun or pronoun. Adjectives tell what kind, which one, how many, and whose.

Instructor: Look at **Exercise 8** in your workbook. I am going to read you some adjectives that tell **what kind**. I want you to use each adjective I say to describe any noun you wish. For example, if I say "pretty," you might say "pretty flowers."

Workbook: loud

new

tall

beautiful

silver

warm

Instructor: Look at **Exercise 9** in your workbook. I am going to read you some adjectives that tell **which one**. I want you to use each adjective I say to describe any noun you wish. For example, if I say "that," you might say "that pumpkin."

Workbook: this

these

those

first

second

next

last

Instructor: Look at **Exercise 10** in your workbook. I am going to read you some adjectives that tell **how many**. I want you to use each adjective I say to describe any noun you wish. For example, if I say "five," you might say "five pencils."

Workbook: one

ten

seventy

many

each

another

all

Instructor: Look at **Exercise 11** in your workbook. I am going to read you some adjectives that tell **whose**. I want you to use each adjective I say to describe any noun you wish. For example, if I say "Leo's," you might say "Leo's wig." Follow along with your eyes as I read. The adjective that tells whose is in bold print.

Workbook: **Jenny's**

the **man's**

the **dog's**

all the **cats'**

several **cooks'**

the **children's**

the **women's**

Instructor: Now let's talk about adverbs. An adverb is a word that describes a verb, an adjective, or another adverb. Adverbs can tell how, when, where, how often, and to what extent. Say that with me.

Together: An adverb is a word that describes a verb, an adjective, or another adverb. Adverbs can tell how, when, where, how often, and to what extent.

Instructor: Read the sentence at the beginning of **Exercise 12** in your workbook.

Workbook: I jump quickly.

Instructor: *Jump* is the action I am doing—it is the verb in the sentence. *Quickly* is an adverb that tells how I jump. Read each column of adverbs in **Exercise 12** of your workbook. Begin with each column's title.

How	When	Where	How Often
happily	tonight	around	hourly
loudly	today	down	daily
quickly	now	far	nightly
quietly	again	inside	sometimes
sadly	immediately	nearby	rarely
softly	afterward	up	often
fast	momentarily	there	regularly

Instructor: Now read the sentences below the columns. Choose two adverbs from each column to tell how, when, where, and how often I jump.

How do I jump?   Possible answers:

    I jump _____.   fast

    I jump _____.   happily

When do I jump?

    I jump _____.   now

    I jump _____.   tonight

Where do I jump?

    I jump _____.   up

    I jump _____.   around

How often do I jump?

    I jump _____.   sometimes

    I jump _____.   daily

Instructor: In **Exercise 13** there is a mixed-up list containing adverbs that tell how, when, where, or how often. Read each adverb and say whether it tells how or when or where or how often. I am going to cover up the columns in **Exercise 12**, but if you get stuck I will let you use the list to help you.

Workbook: quietly

today

rarely

nearby

happily

sometimes

again

inside

Answer Key: How: quietly, happily; When: today, again; Where: nearby, inside; How often: rarely, sometimes

Optional Follow-Up

Say a word as you throw a soft item (like a Nerf ball or balled-up socks), and the student has to say whether the word is a noun or action verb when he catches the soft item. Here are some examples:

Nouns: bird, pencil, book, boy, truck, city, river

Action verbs: sing, kick, write, skip, jump, grow, chew

LESSON 25

Narration: "The Mongols"

Read "A Tragic Story" (Lesson 18) three times to the student. Then ask the student to try to say the whole poem with you (or the tape recorder). The student should practice saying the whole poem to himself in a mirror.

Read the following selection aloud to the student (or, the student may read it aloud himself from his workbook). After the selection has been read, follow the scripting to to make sure he understands the passage. After the initial reading, the student should **not** look at the passage.

Instructor: We are going to read about a fierce tribe called the Mongols who roamed China hundreds of years ago (in the 13th century). When we have finished reading, I am going to ask you what you remember **only** about what has been read. Don't tell me information that you remember from somewhere else.

The Mongols

The Mongols came from the wild, cold mountains north of China. They lived in felt tents which they took down each morning, leaving nothing but ashes behind. They were nomads who swept over the countryside, conquering and killing. The bone-chilling cold of the north didn't stop them; they wore furs and leather and rubbed their skin with grease to keep the wind away. They never settled down and grew crops; instead they ate foxes, rabbits, and other small wild creatures. But they could go without food for days at a time. If they were in danger of starving, they would open the veins of their horses, drink some blood, and then close the vein and ride on.

This passage on the Mongols is excerpted from *The Story of the World, Volume 2: The Middle Ages* by Susan Wise Bauer (Peace Hill Press, second edition, 2007).

Instructor: Close your eyes. Now I am going to ask you a few questions about what I just read.

The following questions are to make sure the student understands the passage. The student should answer these questions in complete sentences. If the student answers in a single word or phrase, put the phrase into a complete sentence for the student and ask him to repeat it back to you. The words in italics represent sample answers—accept other answers if they are correct and if the information was in the passage.

Instructor: Who is this paragraph about?

Student: *It is about the Mongols OR nomads from China.*

Instructor: Where did the Mongols sleep at night?

Student: *They slept in tents.*

Instructor: How did the Mongols protect themselves from the cold?

Student: *They wore furs and leather and/or rubbed grease on their skin.*

Instructor: Did the Mongols grow crops for food or did they hunt for food?

Student: *They hunted.*

Instructor: Were the Mongols peaceful people?

Student: *No, they were warlike.*

Instructor: What would the Mongols drink if they were starving?

Student: *They drank their horses' blood.*

Instructor: Now tell me two things you remember about the Mongols. Use your own words. Speak in complete sentences.

As the student narrates in his own words, you may write his sentences down as he speaks or record them onto a tape recorder to write down when he is finished. You have three options for writing the narration:

1. Write down the student's narration for him on his workbook page.
2. Write down the student's narration for him on a separate piece of paper and have him copy some or all of the sentences onto his workbook page.
3. Write down the student's narration on a separate piece of paper and dictate it to him, as he writes it on his workbook page.

If the student repeats the author's words verbatim, use the questions about the passage to help the student form his own sentences. If the student speaks in phrases, turn his phrases into complete sentences. The student should then repeat the complete sentence back to you. The student does not need to include every aspect of the passage in his narration—he only needs to pick out two ideas. Here is an example of a possible narration:

> The Mongols lived in tents and moved from place to place. They killed lots of people.

Once you have written the student's narration, he should read it aloud back to you.

LESSON 26

New: **Proper Nouns (with Diagramming)**

Read "A Tragic Story" (Lesson 18) three times to the student. Then ask the student to say the poem along with you or the tape recorder. If the student is ready, he should recite the poem to real people today. If he is not, continue practicing daily until he is ready.

Instructor: Remember there are two types of nouns: common and proper. A common noun is a name common to many persons, places, or things. The noun *boy* is a common noun. A proper noun is a special, "proper" name for a person, place, or thing. *Sam Goldberg* is a proper noun. In this lesson we will practice writing many proper nouns. A proper noun always begins with a capital letter. Read the full name printed in **Exercise 1** of your workbook.

Workbook: George Washington Carver

Instructor: Many proper nouns are made up of more than one word. You just read one, single proper noun: *George Washington Carver*. Although his full name is made up of three words, he is just one person. George Washington Carver is a proper noun. Each word in the proper noun begins with a capital letter. I am going to write out the full names of two members of our family in the blanks in **Exercise 1** of your workbook. Then you will copy each name on the line below it.

Write the full names of two siblings, parents, aunts, uncles, or grandparents on the first and third blanks in **Exercise 1** (so the student can copy directly below each name).

Now dictate a short sentence about one of these relatives to the student for him to write on the blank lines at the end of **Exercise 1**. The sentence should include one of the names the student has copied. For example, "Elvin James Jefferson is my father." Help the student as needed with spelling, capitalization, and punctuation.

Instructor: In **Exercise 2** of your workbook, let's look at a diagram with a proper noun as the subject.

Workbook: George Washington Carver farmed.

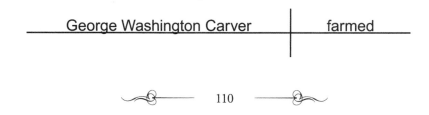

Instructor: Remember, *George Washington Carver* is one proper noun because he is one man. That is why his full name is written on the subject line. In **Exercise 3** you will diagram two sentences with proper nouns. These proper nouns are made up of more than one word. You read the sentence. I will ask you questions as you fill in the diagram. Remember to copy the words exactly as they appear in the sentence. If the words begin with a capital letter in the sentence, they should also be capitalized in the diagram. All the words that make up one proper noun are written on the subject line.

Workbook: 1. Thomas Alva Edison invented.

2. Marian Anderson sang.

Use the following dialogue to help the student fill in the diagrams for **Exercise 3**:

---

1. *Find the verb. Write the verb to the right of your center line.*

2. *Find the subject. Ask "who" or "what" before the verb. [Prompt the student with a specific question like "Who invented?" or "Who sang?"] Write the subject to the left of the center line on your frame.*

Answer Key:

Thomas Alva Edison	invented

Marian Anderson	sang

Instructor: Now look at **Exercise 4** in your workbook. The special, "proper" name of a **place** is sometimes made up of more than one word. Read the proper nouns that are places. I will tell you where these places are located after you read each one.

"Chobe" is pronounced "cho-bee."

Workbook: Yellowstone National Park   (located in Mammoth, Wyoming)

Central Park   (located in New York City)

Chobe National Park   (located in Botswana, Africa)

Empire State Building   (located in New York City)

Sistine Chapel   (located in Rome, Italy)

Instructor: Remember, even though Yellowstone National Park is made up of three words, it is still one proper noun. Yellowstone National Park is the special, "proper" name for that place. If you were diagramming it, all three words would go together on the subject line.

Instructor: In **Exercise 5** you will look at some other proper nouns. The days of the week and the months of the year are proper nouns. They each begin with a capital letter. Read the names of the months and days.

Months of the Year	Days of the Week
January	Monday
February	Tuesday
March	Wednesday
April	Thursday
May	Friday
June	Saturday
July	Sunday
August	
September	
October	
November	
December	

In **Exercise 5** of the student's workbook, you will fill in the blanks with the student's birthday month and the current day of the week, respectively. The student will then copy each complete sentence.

Workbook: My birthday is in [student's birthday month].

Today is [day of the week].

Remind the student that months of the year and days of the week are capitalized because they are proper nouns.

Instructor: Although the days of the week and the months of the year begin with capital letters, the names of the four seasons do not. They are not proper nouns. Read the list of seasons in **Exercise 6** of your workbook.

Seasons
spring
summer
fall
winter

Optional Dictation Exercise

Remind the student that the days of week and the months of the year are capitalized because they are proper nouns, but the names of the seasons are not. Assist the student in placing the commas correctly, if necessary. (Commas in a series will be covered in a later lesson.)

Dictation: I will have art lessons on Monday and Friday.

The summer months are June, July, and August.

Optional Follow-Up

Look up one of the historical figures from this lesson (George Washington Carver, Thomas Alva Edison, or Marian Anderson) in an encyclopedia or online. Read portions of the entry to the student, and ask the student to tell you back as much as he can remember. Prompt him with questions as necessary.

LESSON 27

New: **Helping Verbs (with Diagramming)**

Instructor: A verb is a part of speech that can do several different things in a sentence. Let's practice the definition of a verb. A verb is a word that does an action, shows a state of being, links two words together, or helps another verb. Say this with me three times.

Together (three times): A verb is a word that does an action, shows a state of being, links two words together, or helps another verb.

Instructor: You already know about verbs that do actions. In **Exercise 1** of your workbook there is a list of verbs. I want you to read each verb, do the action, and then use the verb in a sentence. For example, if you read the action verb *whisper*, you would whisper the sentence "I whisper."

Workbook: point

stretch

wink

smile

hop

sigh

fall

roar

crawl

Instructor: A verb is a word that does an action, shows a state of being, links two words together, or helps another verb. You already know about action verbs, and you will learn about verbs that show state of being and link two words together in a later lesson. In this lesson we are going to talk about the last part of that definition: a verb can help another verb. Listen to this sentence: The men were fixing cars. The men were doing something active. What were they doing? Answer me in a complete sentence starting with "They were …"

Student: *They were fixing cars.*

Instructor: But if I just said "They fixing cars," that wouldn't sound right! *Fixing* needs **another** verb to help it. The verb *were* is helping the verb *fixing*. Working together, the verbs make sense in the sentence. The verb *were* is called a helping verb because it helps the main verb, *fixing*. In order to recognize a helping verb, you need to know all of them. Read the list in **Exercise 2** of your workbook one time. Then we will practice chanting them together without your looking at them.

After the student has read through the list in his workbook, say the helping verbs chant and demonstrate the claps.

Instructor: Am [clap]
Is [clap]
Are, was, were. [clap]
Be [clap]
Being [clap]
Been. [clap] [clap]

Instructor: Listen as I say the rest of the helping verbs in a chant.

Have, has, had [clap]
Do, does, did [clap]
Shall, will, should, would, may, might, must [clap, clap]
Can, could!

Instructor: Now let's say the entire chant together three times. Clap along with me.

Together (three times):
Am [clap]
Is [clap]
Are, was, were. [clap]
Be [clap]
Being [clap]
Been. [clap] [clap]
Have, has, had [clap]
Do, does, did [clap]
Shall, will, should, would, may, might, must [clap, clap]
Can, could!

If the student did not memorize the list of helping verbs in *First Language Lessons, Levels 1 and 2* (or he can't remember the helping verbs), practice the chant with him daily until he learns it.

Instructor: Helping verbs can help other verbs by showing time. Read the sentences in **Exercise 3** to me, and I will show you what I mean:

Workbook: 1. Today you **play**.

2. Yesterday you **did play**.

3. Tomorrow you **will play**.

Instructor: A verb can show present time, past time, or future time. In grammar, we call the time a verb is showing its *tense*. "Tense" means "time." In the first sentence "Today you play," the verb tense, or time, is present. You play at the present moment. In the second sentence "Yesterday you did play," the verb tense, or time, is past. You played in the past. In the third sentence "Tomorrow you will play," the verb tense, or time, is future. The helping verb *will* helps the verb *play* show future time. You **will play** in the future.

Instructor: You will read the sentences in **Exercise 4**. After you have read each sentence, tell me if the verb in bold print is in the present, past, or future tense. In other words, is the time in the present moment, is it in the past, or will it be in the future?

Workbook: 1. Mr. Park **was painting** his house last year.

2. I **will bake** a cake tomorrow.

3. Yesterday, the baby **crawled** for the first time.

4. I **open** the door.

5. You **shall help** me next week.

6. He **smiles** at the joke.

Answer Key:
1. past tense
2. future tense
3. past tense
4. present tense
5. future tense
6. present tense

Tenses are covered in more detail in Oral Usage End Unit Lessons 1, 2, and 3.

Instructor: You will learn more about tenses later in your studies. Right now, you just need to know that helping verbs can help other verbs show time. In **Exercise 5** look at a diagram of a sentence with a helping verb and an action verb in it. Read the sentence and look at its diagram.

Workbook: I am singing.

Instructor: Do you see that two words are on the verb line? The helping verb *am* helps the action verb *singing* to make this sentence sound right. "I singing" sounds funny, doesn't it? You need the helping verb for the sentence to make sense. Since the two verbs work together, they are both written on the verb line.

Instructor: In **Exercise 6** you will diagram four sentences with helping verbs and action verbs. Remember, these verbs work together so they are **both** written on the verb line. You read the sentence. I will ask you questions as you fill in the diagram. Remember to copy the words exactly as they appear in the sentence. If the words begin with a capital letter in the sentence, they should also be capitalized in the diagram.

Workbook: 1. They have eaten.

2. Mice will nibble.

3. We should watch.

4. Lucy had finished.

Use the following dialogue to help the student fill in each diagram:

1. *Find the verb. There are two verbs in this sentence. What is the helping verb? Look in Exercise 2 of your workbook if you need help remembering the list of helping verbs. What is the action verb? You write both these verbs on your verb line.*

2. *Find the subject. Ask "who" or "what" before the verb. [Prompt the student with a specific question like "Who has eaten?" or "What will nibble?"] Write the subject to the left of the center line on your frame.*

Answer Key:

They	have eaten

Mice	will nibble

We	should watch

Lucy	had finished

Optional Follow-Up

Before this follow-up, make a "time gauge." Glue the time gauge template and the arrow from the Student Workbook (end of Lesson 27, page 87) onto a piece of cardstock. Cut them out. Using a brad, secure the arrow to the time gauge, so that you can use it to point to "Past," "Present," or "Future."

First say the verb alone (printed in bold in the sentence). Then read the entire sentence to the student. The student should move the arrow so it points to the correct tense of the verb. If he points the arrow correctly, he gets one point. The student wins the game when he has earned eight points. Save this "time gauge" for Oral Usage Lesson 1 (if you plan to do it).

Mr. Park **has painted** his house last year. (past tense)

I **will bake** a cake tomorrow. (future tense)

Yesterday, the baby did **crawl** for the first time. (past tense)

Victor **plays** the piano. (present tense)

I **open** the door. (present tense)

You **shall help** me next week. (future tense)

Sandra **did kick** the ball. (past tense)

He **smiles** at the joke. (present tense)

LESSON 28

Review: **Proper Nouns and Helping Verbs**

Instructor: There are two types of nouns: common and proper. A common noun is a name common to many persons, places, or things. The noun *cousin* is a common noun. Remember, the seasons are also common nouns. In **Exercise 1** of your workbook, read the list of seasons.

Seasons
spring
summer
fall
winter

Instructor: A proper noun is a special, "proper" name for a person, place, or thing. *Julia Stevens* is a proper noun. Remember, the days of the week and the months of the year are also proper nouns. They each begin with a capital letter. In **Exercise 2** read the names of the months and days.

Months of the Year	Days of the Week
January	Monday
February	Tuesday
March	Wednesday
April	Thursday
May	Friday
June	Saturday
July	Sunday
August	
September	
October	
November	
December	

Instructor: Remember, many proper nouns are made up of more than one word. Look at the full name in **Exercise 3** of your workbook. I will read it to you first, and then you will read it back to me.

Workbook: Ferdinand Magellan

Instructor: You just read one, single proper noun: *Ferdinand Magellan*. Although his full name is made up of two words, he is just one person. Each word in the proper noun begins with a capital letter. In **Exercise 4**, look at a diagram with a proper noun as the subject.

Workbook: Ferdinand Magellan sailed.

Ferdinand Magellan	sailed

Instructor: Remember, *Ferdinand Magellan* is one proper noun because he is one man. That is why his full name is written on the subject line. Now in **Exercise 5 you** will diagram a sentence with a proper noun. *Louisa May Alcott* is a proper noun made up of more than one word. You read the sentence. I will ask you questions as you fill in the diagram. Remember to copy the words exactly as they appear in the sentence. If the words begin with a capital letter in the sentence, they should also be capitalized in the diagram.

Workbook: Louisa May Alcott wrote.

Use the following dialogue to help the student fill in the diagram:

1. *Find the verb. Write the verb to the right of the center line.*

2. *Find the subject. Ask "who" or "what" before the verb. [Prompt the student with a specific question, "Who wrote?"] Write the subject to the left of the center line on your frame.*

Answer Key:

Louisa May Alcott	wrote

Instructor: Let's practice the definition of a verb. A verb is a word that does an action, shows a state of being, links two words together, or helps another verb. Say this with me two times.

Together (two times): A verb is a word that does an action, shows a state of being, links two words together, or helps another verb.

Instructor: The last part of that definition tells you that a verb "helps another verb." Let's review your list of helping verbs. I will break it up into two parts.

Instructor: Am [clap]
Is [clap]
Are, was, were. [clap]
Be [clap]
Being [clap]
Been. [clap] [clap]

Instructor: Listen as I say the rest of the helping verbs in a chant.

Have, has, had [clap]
Do, does, did [clap]
Shall, will, should, would, may, might, must [clap, clap]
Can, could!

Instructor: Now let's say the entire chant together three times.

Together (three times): [say chant above]

Instructor: In **Exercise 6** of your workbook read the sentence and look at its diagram. This sentence has a helping verb and an action verb in it.

Workbook: We are chanting.

```
                          |
        We                |        are chanting
_____|_____
                          |
                          |
```

Instructor: Do you see that two words are on the verb line? The helping verb *are* helps the action verb *chanting* to make this sentence sound right. "We chanting" sounds funny, doesn't it? You don't know when the people were chanting. Are they chanting in the present? Were they chanting in the past? Will they be chanting in the future? You need a helping verb to show time in order to make the other verb in the sentence make sense. "We are chanting." Since the two verbs work together, they are both written on the verb line of a diagram. Now in **Exercise 7** you will diagram four sentences with helping verbs and action verbs. Remember, these verbs work together so they are **both** written on the verb line. These sentences also have proper nouns for subjects. The proper nouns are made up of more than one word. After you read each sentence, I will ask you questions as you fill in the diagram. Remember to copy the words exactly as they appear in the sentence. If the words begin with a capital letter in the sentence, they should also be capitalized in the diagram.

Workbook: 1. Bill Gates has donated.

2. Pope Benedict XVI is praying.

3. George Washington was fighting.

4. Winston Churchill was speaking.

Use the following dialogue to help the student fill in each diagram:

1. *Find the verb. There are two verbs in this sentence. What is the helping verb? What is the action verb? You write both these verbs on your verb line.*

2. *Find the subject. Ask "who" or "what" before the verb. [Prompt the student with a specific question like "Who has donated?" or "Who is praying?"] Write the subject to the left of the center line on your frame. [In the second sentence, if the student is not familiar with the pope, explain that the Roman numerals XVI are considered a part of the pope's name. XVI means "the sixteenth."]*

Answer Key:

Bill Gates	has donated

Pope Benedict XVI	is praying

George Washington	was fighting

Winston Churchill	was speaking

Optional Follow-Up

At a family meal, have the student use sentences with helping verbs to describe past and present activities. The student should say what each person was doing before the meal. For example, "Mom was cooking. Ben and Judy were playing. Dad was working." Then the student will say what each person is doing now at the table. For example, "The baby is laughing. Mom is chewing. Dad is waiting. Ben is eating."

LESSON 29

New: Direct Objects (with Diagramming)

Review "The Land of Nod" (Lesson 9) today. If the student has trouble remembering the poem, have him practice it daily until he is confident.

Instructor: Let's begin this lesson by saying the definition of a sentence. A sentence is a group of words that expresses a complete thought. All sentences begin with a capital letter and end with a punctuation mark. Say that with me three times.

Together (three times): A sentence is a group of words that expresses a complete thought. All sentences begin with a capital letter and end with a punctuation mark.

Instructor: Read the sentence in **Exercise 1** of your workbook.

Workbook: Leroy kicks.

Instructor: Every sentence has a verb and a subject. What is the action verb in the sentence?

Student: *Kicks*

Instructor: Kicks is the verb. Now let's find the subject. Who kicks?

Student: *Leroy*

Instructor: Leroy kicks. Remember, *kicks* is the action verb. Sometimes there is a word that follows the verb that receives the action of the verb. I will show you what I mean. Read the sentence in **Exercise 2** of your workbook.

Workbook: Leroy kicks rocks.

Instructor: *Leroy* is the subject. *Kicks* is the verb. What does Leroy kick? Rocks. *Rocks* receives the action of the verb. The noun *rocks* is called the direct object. To find the direct object, ask "whom" or "what" after the verb. Now you will try to find the direct object in a sentence. Direct objects receive the action of the verb. You will read each sentence in **Exercise 3**, and I will ask you a question that will help you find the direct object.

Workbook: Ted cracked peanuts.

Instructor: Cracked **what**?

Student: *Peanuts*

Instructor: *Peanuts* is the direct object. It receives the action of the verb *cracked*. Read the next sentence.

Workbook: Mary kissed Mother.

Instructor: Kissed **whom**?

Student: *Mother*

Instructor: *Mother* is the direct object. It receives the action of the verb *kissed*. Read the next sentence.

Workbook: Bethany scrubbed dishes.

Instructor: Scrubbed **what**?

Student: *Dishes*

Instructor: *Dishes* is the direct object. It receives the action of the verb *scrubbed*. Read the next sentence.

Workbook: We invited guests.

Instructor: Invited **whom**?

Student: *Guests*

Instructor: *Guests* is the direct object. It receives the action of the verb *invited*. In **Exercise 4**, read this sentence one more time and look at its diagram:

Workbook: Leroy kicks rocks.

| Leroy | kicks | rocks |

Instructor: The direct object is written next to the verb. It is divided from the verb by a short line that does not go through the main horizontal line. Now **you** will diagram four sentences with direct objects in **Exercise 5** of your workbook. You read the sentence. I will ask you questions as you fill in the diagram. Remember to copy the words exactly as they appear in the sentence. If the words begin with a capital letter in the sentence, they should also be capitalized in the diagram.

Workbook: 1. Ted cracked peanuts.

2. Mary kissed Mother.

3. Bethany scrubbed dishes.

4. We invited guests.

Use the following dialogue to help the student fill in each diagram:

1. *Find the verb. Write the verb to the right of your center line.*

2. *Find the subject. Ask "who" or "what" before the verb. [Prompt the student with a specific question like "Who cracked?" or "Who kissed?"] Write the subject to the left of the center line on your frame.*

3. *Is there a direct object that receives the action of the verb? I will ask you a question that will help you find the direct object.*

   Sentence 1: Cracked what?

   Sentence 2: Kissed whom?

   Sentence 3: Scrubbed what?

   Sentence 4: Invited whom?

4. *Write the direct object to the right of the verb on your diagram. The direct object is separated from the verb by a short, straight line.*

Answer Key:

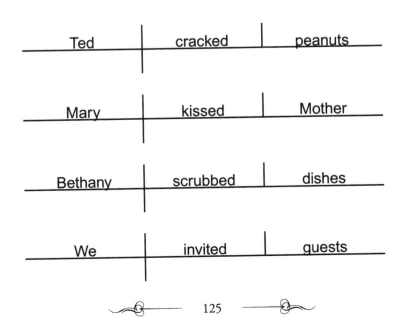

Optional Dictation Exercise

Before beginning dictation, have the student follow along in his workbook as you read the paragraph to him.

> Jane Addams started a program in 1889 to help people who had come to live in America from other countries. Newcomers came to live at a mansion called Hull House where they could study, learn crafts and skills, and live in a safe, healthy place. Although Jane Addams helped all kinds of people, she particularly cared for children and women.

In the paragraph, point out the proper nouns *Jane Addams* and *Hull House* to the student. Explain that although these nouns each have two words, each is still one proper noun. Dictate the two sentences about Jane Addams that follow.

Dictation: Jane Addams started Hull House.

              She helped children.

After the student has correctly written each of the sentences, help him find the direct object by asking the following questions:

Sentence 1: Started what? (Hull House is the direct object.)

Sentence 2: Helped whom? (Children is the direct object.)

Have the student write "d.o." over the direct object in each sentence.

Optional Follow-Up

The student should go around the house doing things that receive action. For example, *write name, clap hands, throw ball, open door, touch wall, play piano, pat dog, shake hands,* or *eat apple.* As the student does each activity he should say, for example, "Hit wall. *Hit,* verb. *Wall,* direct object." The student should not use articles (*a, an, the*) for this exercise.

LESSON 30

Review: **Subjects, Verbs, Adjectives, Adverbs, and Direct Objects**

In the exercises in this lesson, point to parts of each diagram as you explain them. **Exercises 2** *through* **4** *in the workbook show more and more of the solution as the student works through the exercise. Place a blank sheet of paper over the part of the exercise the student hasn't yet reached, to keep him from seeing the answers prematurely.*

Instructor: In the last lesson you learned about direct objects. A direct object follows the verb and receives the action of the verb. Read the first sentence in **Exercise 1** of your workbook.

Workbook: John stirs soup.

Instructor: Find the verb. *Stirs* is the verb. Now find the subject. Who stirs? John stirs. Stirs what? Soup. *Soup* receives the action of the verb *stirs*. The noun *soup* is the direct object. Look at the diagram of this sentence.

| John | stirs | soup |

Instructor: The direct object is written to the right of the verb. The direct object is separated from the verb by a short, straight line. Let's add to this sentence an adjective that describes John. Read the new sentence and look at its diagram.

Workbook: Helpful John stirs soup.

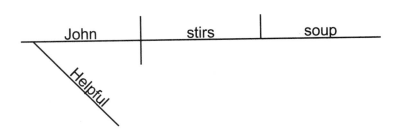

Instructor: The adjective *Helpful* is written on a slanted line beneath the subject *John* because *Helpful* describes *John*. Adjectives describe nouns. There is another noun besides *John* in this sentence: *soup*. Let's add an adjective that describes the noun *soup*. This adjective will tell what kind of soup it is. Read the next sentence and look at its diagram.

Workbook: Helpful John stirs hot soup.

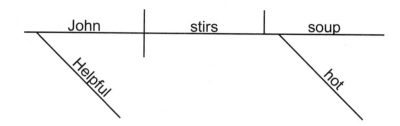

Instructor: The adjective *hot* is written on a slanted line beneath the word it describes, *soup*. Let's add one final word to the sentence: an adverb. Remember, adverbs can describe verbs. This adverb follows the verb, but it does not come directly after the verb. The adverb is at the end of the sentence. Read the last sentence in **Exercise 1** and look at its diagram.

Workbook: Helpful John stirs hot soup slowly.

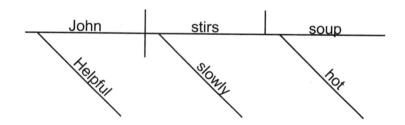

Instructor: How does John stir? Slowly. The adverb *slowly* is written on a slanted line below the verb because it describes the verb *stirs*.

Instructor: Now in **Exercises 2**, **3**, and **4** of your workbook, you will diagram three new groups of sentences: one about spiders, one about eating squid, and one about mothers. You read each sentence. As you work through each group of sentences, the parts of the diagram that you have filled in will be already printed on the next diagram. You will only have to add new words as you answer my questions. I will cover the diagrams below where you are working so you don't see the answers.

Group 1 (Exercise 2 in the Student Workbook)

Spiders spin webs.	(Ask questions 1, 2, and 3)
Most spiders spin webs.	(Ask question 4)
Most spiders spin sticky webs.	(Ask question 5)
Most spiders spin sticky webs beautifully.	(Ask question 6)

Group 2 (Exercise 3 in the Student Workbook)

Trish eats squid.	(Ask questions 1, 2, and 3)
Bold Trish eats squid.	(Ask question 4)
Bold Trish eats fried squid.	(Ask question 5)
Bold Trish eats fried squid downstairs.	(Ask question 6)

Group 3 (Exercise 4 in the Student Workbook)

Mothers rock babies.	(Ask questions 1, 2, and 3)
Many mothers rock babies.	(Ask question 4)
Many mothers rock tiny babies.	(Ask question 5)
Many mothers rock tiny babies daily.	(Ask question 6)

Use the following dialogue in italics to help the student fill in each diagram. After the student reads a sentence in each sentence group (about spiders or Trish or mothers), you will prompt him with the question(s) in italics listed across from that sentence (for example, "Ask questions 1, 2, and 3").

---

1. *Find the verb. Write the verb to the right of the center line on your frame.*

2. *Find the subject. Ask "who" or "what" before the verb. [Prompt the student with a specific question like "What spins?" or "Who eats?"] Write the subject to the left of the center line on your frame.*

3. *Is there a direct object that receives the action of the verb? I will ask you a question that will help you find the direct object.*

   Sentence Group 1: Spin what?

   Sentence Group 2: Eats what?

   Sentence Group 3: Rocks whom?

   Write the direct object to the right of the verb on your diagram. The direct object is separated from the verb by a short, straight line.

4. *Go back and look again at the subject. Are there any words that describe the subject? These adjectives can tell what kind, which one, how many, or whose. Also look for the articles (a, an, the), because they act like adjectives. Write each adjective on a slanted line below the subject it describes.*

5. *Look again at the direct object. Are there any words that describe the direct object? These adjectives can tell what kind, which one, how many, or whose. Also look for the articles (a, an, the), because they act like adjectives. Write each adjective on a slanted line below the direct object it describes.*

6. *Look at the verb. Is there a word that describes the verb? This is an adverb that could tell how, when, where, or how often. This adverb does not directly follow the verb in the sentence; it comes a little bit later. Write the adverb on the slanted line below the verb it describes.*

Answer Key:

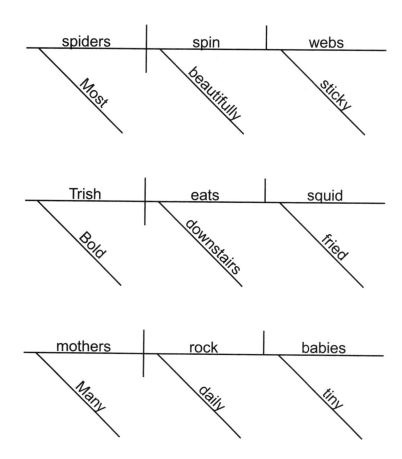

Optional Follow-Up

If the student enjoyed diagramming the sentences by adding descriptive elements (or he needs extra practice), he can diagram the next two sentences as well. Use the dialogue printed in this lesson.

Group 1

Ostriches lay eggs.	(Ask questions 1, 2, and 3)
Tall ostriches lay eggs.	(Ask question 4)
Tall ostriches lay enormous eggs.	(Ask question 5)
Tall ostriches lay enormous eggs here.	(Ask question 6)

Group 2

Lions chase ostriches.	(Ask questions 1, 2, and 3)
Fearsome lions chase ostriches.	(Ask question 4)
Fearsome lions chase speedy ostriches.	(Ask question 5)
Fearsome lions chase speedy ostriches sometimes.	(Ask question 6)

Answer Key:

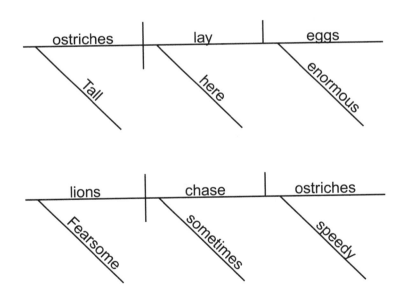

LESSON 31

Poem Memorization: "I Wandered Lonely As a Cloud"

Instructor: In **Lesson 31** of your workbook, you will find a poem about a field of daffodils. Follow along as I read the poem to you. Before I begin reading, you should know that a *vale* is a valley.

I Wandered Lonely As a Cloud
by William Wordsworth

I Wandered Lonely As a Cloud
That floats on high o'er vales and hills,
When all at once I saw a crowd,
A host, of golden daffodils;

Beside the lake, beneath the trees,
Fluttering and dancing in the breeze.
Continuous as the stars that shine
And twinkle on the milky way,

They stretched in never-ending line
Along the margin of the bay;
Ten thousand saw I at a glance,
Tossing their heads in sprightly dance.

Discuss the poem with the student. Can he picture the scene the poet is describing? Ask:

Instructor: Was the person by himself?

Student: *Yes, he was alone.*

Instructor: What did he see?

Student: *He saw lots of daffodils.*

Instructor: To what did he compare the daffodils?

Student: *He compared them to the stars.*

Instructor: Were the daffodils moving?

Student: *Yes, they looked like they were dancing.*

Read the poem to the student three times in a row. Repeat this triple reading twice more during the day. Have the student check the boxes in his workbook when this is done.

Optional Dictation Exercise

Dictation: I Wandered Lonely As a Cloud.

Ten thousand saw I at a glance.

Optional Follow-Up

The last two stanzas of this poem have been omitted because of length and complexity. Find the rest of the poem online or in a volume of Wordsworth's poetry and read the entire poem with your student.

LESSON 32

New: Simple Versus Complete Subjects and Predicates

Review: Subjects, Verbs, Adjectives, Adverbs, and Direct Objects

---

Read "I Wandered Lonely As a Cloud" (Lesson 31) three times to the student. Then ask the student to try to say parts of the first stanza along with you (or the tape recorder). As with Lesson 30, exercises in the workbook show more and more of the solution as the student works through each exercise. Place a blank sheet of paper over the part of the exercise the student hasn't yet reached, to keep him from seeing the answers prematurely.

Instructor: Two lessons ago you diagrammed some long sentences with subjects, verbs, direct objects, adjectives, and adverbs. For review, read the sentence in **Exercise 1** of your workbook and look at its diagram.

Workbook: Hot chocolate warms cold children quickly.

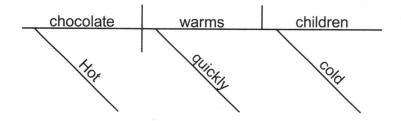

Instructor: Every sentence has a subject and a verb. On a diagram, the subject and the verb are separated by a straight line that runs down the center of the frame.

Point to the line that divides *chocolate* and *warms* on the diagram.

Instructor: To the left of this center line, you will find all the words that tell you more about the subject, *chocolate*. The subject of the sentence is simply the word *chocolate*, so it is called the **simple subject**. But when you add other words that tell you more about *chocolate* you get a longer, more complete description of the subject. *Hot* tells us more about *chocolate*. *Hot chocolate* is the **complete subject**. The simple subject is always written on the subject line (*chocolate*).

On the diagram in the workbook, point to the horizontal subject line and the simple subject, *chocolate*.

Instructor: The complete subject is the simple subject and all the words that hang off the simple subject (*Hot chocolate*). The complete subject includes all the words to the left of the straight line that runs down the center of the frame.

On the diagram in the workbook, point to the different words in the complete subject. Show the student that all these words are printed to the left of the straight, center line.

Instructor: We are going to use a sentence from Lesson 30 to learn more about subjects and predicates. Now read the sentence in **Exercise 2** of your workbook. Then look at its diagram.

Workbook: Most spiders spin sticky webs beautifully.

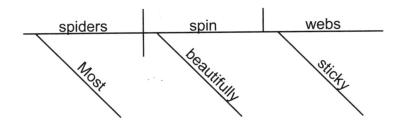

Instructor: On a diagram, the subject and the verb are separated by a straight line that runs down the center of the frame. Look at the word to the left of the center line. What is the simple subject of the sentence? The simple subject is always written on the subject line.

Student: Spiders

Instructor: But when you add other words that tell you more about the subject, *spiders*, you get a longer, more complete description of the subject. On a diagram, the **complete subject** includes all the words to the left of the straight line that runs down the center of the frame. What is the complete subject of the sentence?

Student: Most spiders

Instructor: Look again at the diagram of the sentence about spiders. The words to the right of the center, straight line are the verb and other words that tell us what is said about the subject. The verb in this sentence is simply the word *spin*. But more is said about the spiders than just "spiders spin." We know that they "spin sticky webs beautifully." All these words tell us what is said about the subject, *spiders*. These words together are called the **complete predicate**.

Since the "simple predicate" of a sentence is the verb, we are not requiring the student to learn two terms for the same word at this time.

Instructor: Let's look closely at the words in the complete predicate.

- *Spin* is the verb. The verb is always written on the **verb line.**

- *Beautifully* tells us more about the verb *spin*. It is an adverb that tells us how the spider spins.

- *Webs* is the direct object. It tells us what the spider spins.

- *Sticky* is an adjective that also belongs in the complete predicate, because it tells us what kind of webs the spiders spin.

The complete predicate is the verb and all the words attached to the verb line (*spin sticky webs beautifully*). The complete predicate includes **all the words to the right of the straight line that runs down the center of the frame.**

Instructor: Read again the sentence in **Exercise 1** and look at its diagram.

Workbook: Hot chocolate warms cold children quickly.

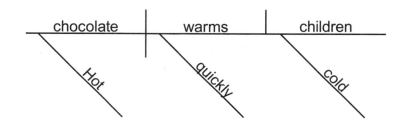

Instructor: What is the verb in the sentence?

Student: *Warms*

Instructor: The complete predicate is the verb and all the words attached to the verb line. It includes all the words to the right of the straight line that runs down the center of the frame. What is the complete predicate of the sentence?

Student: *Warms cold children quickly [It is okay if the student says the words in a different order.]*

Instructor: Now in **Exercises 3**, **4**, and **5**, I will help you diagram three groups of sentences: one about tornadoes, one about hail, and one about rain. You will read each sentence. As you work through each group of sentences, the parts of the diagram that you have filled in will be already printed on the next diagram. You will only have to add new words as you answer my questions. Remember to copy the words exactly as they appear in the sentence. I will cover the filled-in diagrams that are below where you are working so you don't see the answers.

Group 1 (Exercise 3 in the Student Workbook)

Tornadoes uproot trees.	(Ask questions 1, 2, and 3)
Twisty tornadoes uproot trees.	(Ask question 4)
Twisty tornadoes uproot giant trees.	(Ask question 5)
Twisty tornadoes uproot giant trees easily.	(Ask question 6)

Group 2 (Exercise 4 in the Student Workbook)

Hail pounds crops.	(Ask questions 1, 2, and 3)
Icy hail pounds crops.	(Ask question 4)
Icy hail pounds valuable crops.	(Ask question 5)
Icy hail pounds valuable crops yearly.	(Ask question 6)

Group 3 (Exercise 5 in the Student Workbook)

Rains flooded rivers.	(Ask questions 1, 2, and 3)
Heavy rains flooded rivers.	(Ask question 4)
Heavy rains flooded several rivers.	(Ask question 5)
Heavy rains flooded several rivers nearby.	(Ask question 6)

Use the following dialogue in italics to help the student fill in each diagram. After the student reads **each** sentence in the sentence group (about tornadoes or hail or rain), you will prompt him with the question(s) in italics listed across from that sentence (for example, *Ask questions 1, 2, and 3*).

---

1. *Find the verb. Write the verb to the right of the center line on your frame.*

2. *Find the subject. Ask "who" or "what" before the verb. [Prompt the student with a specific question like "What uproots?" or "What pounds?"] Write the subject to the left of the center line on your frame.*

3. *Is there a direct object that receives the action of the verb? I will ask you a question that will help you find the direct object.*

   Sentence Group 1: Uproot what?

   Sentence Group 2: Pounds what?

   Sentence Group 3: Flooded what?

   Write the direct object to the right of the verb on your diagram. The direct object is separated from the verb by a short, straight line.

4. *Go back and look again at the subject. Are there any words that describe the subject? These adjectives can tell what kind, which one, how many, or whose. Also look for the articles (a, an, the), because they act like adjectives. Write each adjective on the slanted line below the subject it describes.*

5. *Look again at the direct object. Are there any words that describe the direct object? These adjectives can tell what kind, which one, how many, or whose. Also look for the articles (a, an, the), because they act like adjectives. Write each adjective on the slanted line below the direct object it describes.*

6. *Is there a word that describes the verb? This is an adverb that could tell how, when, where, or how often. This adverb does not directly follow the verb in the sentence; it comes a little bit later. Write the adverb on the slanted line below the verb it describes.*

Answer Key:

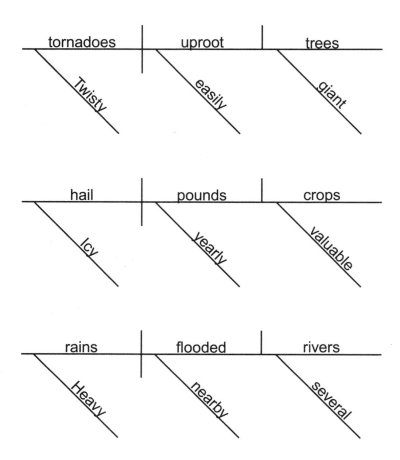

Use the following dialogue to help the student practice identifying the simple subject, complete subject, verb, and complete predicate in the sentences he just diagrammed. You will need to go through the entire dialogue below for each of the three sentences: first for the tornado sentence, second for the hail sentence, and third for the rain sentence.

Instructor: Look again at the last completed diagram in **Exercise** [**3**, **4**, **5**]. [*Instructor reads sentence*]. On a diagram, the subject and the verb are separated by a straight line that runs down the center of the frame. Point to the word on the subject line [*tornadoes, hail, rains*]. What is the simple subject of the sentence? The simple subject is always written on the subject line.

Student: [*tornadoes; hail; rains*]

Instructor: But when you add other words that tell you more about the subject [*Instructor says tornadoes or hail or rains*], you get a longer, more complete description of the subject. On a diagram, the complete subject includes all the words to the left of the straight line that runs down the center of the frame. What is the complete subject of the sentence?

Student: [*Twisty tornadoes; Icy hail; Heavy rains*]

Instructor: Look again at the same diagram. The words to the right of the center, straight line are in the complete predicate. What is the verb?

Student: [*uproot; pounds; flooded*]

Instructor: The verb tells us what the subject does. The verb answers the question "What does the subject do?" But there are other words that tell us more completely what is said about the subject. All of these words together are called the complete predicate. The complete predicate is written to the right of the straight line that runs down the center of the frame. What is the complete predicate of the sentence?

Student: [*uproot giant trees easily; pounds valuable crops yearly; flooded several rivers nearby*]

Optional Follow-Up

If the student enjoyed diagramming the sentences by adding descriptive elements (or he needs extra practice), he can diagram the next two sentences as well. Use the numbered questions printed in this lesson. After he has diagrammed each sentence, you may follow the italicized dialogue in this lesson to help him identify the simple subject, complete subject, verb, and complete predicate in each sentence.

Group 1

Tractors push dirt.	(Ask questions 1, 2, and 3)
Huge tractors push dirt.	(Ask question 4)
Huge tractors push heavy dirt.	(Ask question 5)
Huge tractors push heavy dirt steadily.	(Ask question 6)

Group 2

Cranes shift beams.	(Ask questions 1, 2, and 3)
Giant cranes shift beams.	(Ask question 4)
Giant cranes shift long beams.	(Ask question 5)
Giant cranes shift long beams sideways.	(Ask question 6)

Answer Key:

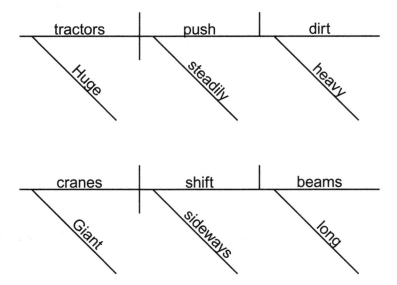

LESSON 33

New: State of Being Verbs (with Diagramming)

Review: Action and Helping Verbs

Read "I Wandered Lonely As a Cloud" (Lesson 31) three times to the student. Then ask the student to try to say parts of the first and second stanzas along with you (or the tape recorder).

Instructor: You already know the definition of a verb. A verb is a word that does an action, shows a state of being, links two words together, or helps another verb. Say that with me three times.

Together (three times): A verb is a word that does an action, shows a state of being, links two words together, or helps another verb.

Instructor: You have been reading and diagramming sentences that contain action verbs. In your workbook, read the sentences in **Exercise 1** and circle the action verb in each sentence:

Workbook: 1. The boat (floats).

2. She (drank) lemonade.

3. The eagle (soared) above.

Instructor: You have also learned about helping verbs. These verbs help other verbs. In order to recognize a helping verb, you need to know all of them. I will say a chant of the helping verbs to you. I will break it up into two parts.

Instructor: Am [clap]

Is [clap]

Are, was, were. [clap]

Be [clap]

Being [clap]

Been. [clap] [clap]

Instructor: Listen as I say the rest of the helping verbs in a chant.

Have, has, had [clap]
Do, does, did [clap]
Shall, will, should, would, may, might, must [clap, clap]
Can, could!

Instructor: Now let's say the entire chant together two times.

Together (two times): [say chant above]

Instructor: Read the sentence in **Exercise 2** and look at its diagram. This sentence has a helping verb and an action verb in it.

Workbook: Squirrels are leaping.

Squirrels	are leaping

Instructor: Do you see that two words are on the verb line? The helping verb *are* helps the action verb *leaping* to make this sentence sound right. "Squirrels leaping" sounds funny, doesn't it? You don't know when the squirrels were leaping. Are they leaping in the present? Were they leaping in the past? Will they be leaping in the future? You need a helping verb to show time in order to make the other verb in the sentence sound right. "Squirrels **are** leaping." Since the two verbs work together, they are both written on the verb line of a diagram.

Instructor: In this lesson you are going to learn about another kind of verb: a state of being verb. Some verbs are words that you can do, like the action verbs *climb, push, bounce,* and *munch.* Some verbs help other verbs make sentences sounds right. But the verbs in some sentences show that you just are! You can **do** an action verb, but a state of being verb just shows that you exist. Here are the state of being verbs: *am, is, are, was, were, be, being, been.* I am going to say this list of state of being verbs three times.

Instructor (three times):
Am [clap]
Is [clap]
Are, was, were. [clap]
Be [clap]
Being [clap]
Been. [clap] [clap]

Instructor: Now say the state of being verbs with me three more times.

Together (three times):
>   Am [clap]
>   Is [clap]
>   Are, was, were. [clap]
>   Be [clap]
>   Being [clap]
>   Been. [clap] [clap]

Instructor: Does this chant sound familiar? It should. The verbs that show state of being are from the first part of the helping verb chant. The verbs in this list can either help another verb **or** they can stand alone in a sentence, to show that someone or something exists. When these verbs come before another verb in the sentence, they are helping verbs. When they are all alone, they are state of being verbs. Look at **Exercise 3** in your workbook. I am going to read you a question and you will read the answer. Each answer you read contains a state of being verb printed in bold.

Workbook: Are you in the car?

I **am**.

Is your brother in the car with you?

He **is**.

Is your mother in the car with you?

She **is**.

Is your book on the seat?

It **is**.

Who is in the car?

We **are**.

Who is beside you?

You **are**.

Who is outside the car?

They **are**.

Who was at the library yesterday?

You **were**.

Who else was at the library?

She **was**.

Instructor: You just read some really short sentences with the state of being verbs *am, is, are, was,* and *were. Am, is, are, was,* and *were* are state of being verbs that can just be by themselves in sentence. But the state of being verbs *be, being,* and *been* almost always need another verb to help them. Often, they don't make sense if they stand alone. You would never say "I be." But if you add the helping verb *will,* you get a sentence that makes sense: "I will be." In **Exercise 4**, follow along while I read each question. Then you read each answer. In each answer, the state of being verb is in bold print, but the helping verb is not.

Workbook: Will you be at the campsite?

I will **be**.

Will Tim be at the campsite, too?

He might **be**.

Who has been there before?

They have **been**.

Instructor: Now go back and read each answer again. Underline the state of being verb in bold print, and then circle the helping verb that helps it.

Instructor: Let's say the state of being verbs together one more time.

Together: Am [clap]
Is [clap]
Are, was, were. [clap]
Be [clap]
Being [clap]
Been. [clap] [clap]

Instructor: In **Exercise 5** you will diagram some sentences with state of being verbs. These sentences are not long and complicated like the sentences you have been diagramming in the past few lessons. They are simple and short, so you can clearly see how a sentence with a state of being verb is diagrammed. You read the sentence. I will ask you questions as you fill in the diagram. Remember to copy the words exactly as they appear in the sentence. If the words begin with a capital letter in the sentence, they should also be capitalized in the diagram.

Workbook: 1. It is.

2. They are.

3. You were.

Use the following italicized dialogue to help the student fill in the diagrams for the sentences in **Exercise 5** of the student's workbook.

1. *What is the state of being verb? This verb tells us that something just exists. Write the verb to the right of your center line.*

2. *Find the subject. Ask "who" or "what" before the verb. [Prompt the student with a specific question like "What is?" or "Who are?"] Write the subject to the left of the center line on your frame.*

Answer Key:

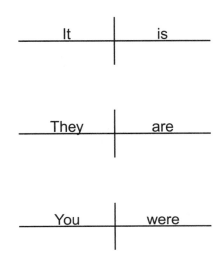

It | is

They | are

You | were

Dictation Exercise

After the student has written the sentences, have him underline the state of being verbs.

Dictation: I <u>am</u> at the bakery.

The baker <u>is</u> behind the counter.

Optional Follow-Up

Before you begin this activity, say the state of being verbs together with the student (they are printed in this lesson, "am, is, are ..."). Then very slowly read the sentences below (starting with "You are in the car") to the student. The student should not look at what you are reading; this is a listening exercise. Every time the student hears a state of being verb, he should say something silly like "Whoopee!" He may choose his own alert word.

You **are** in the car.

I **am** in the car.

Your brother **is** in the car.

Your book **is** in the car.

Other people **are** in the car.

You **were** at the library.

She **was** at the library.

LESSON 34

New:	Linking Verbs (with Diagramming)
New:	Predicate Nominatives (with Diagramming)
Review:	Action Verbs, Helping Verbs, and State of Being Verbs

Read "I Wandered Lonely As a Cloud" (Lesson 31) three times to the student. Then ask the student to try to say the whole poem with you (or the tape recorder). The student should practice saying the whole poem to himself in a mirror.

Instructor: A verb is a word that does an action, shows a state of being, links two words together, or helps another verb. Say that definition with me two times.

Together (two times): A verb is a word that does an action, shows a state of being, links two words together, or helps another verb.

Instructor: Action verbs show action. In your workbook, read the sentences in **Exercise 1** and circle the action verb in each sentence:

Workbook: 1. An artist (paints) pictures.

2. Engineers (design) skyscrapers.

3. Composers (write) music.

Instructor: Verbs that help other verbs are called helping verbs. Let's say the first part of the helping verb chant together.

Instructor: Am [clap]
Is [clap]
Are, was, were. [clap]
Be [clap]
Being [clap]
Been. [clap] [clap]

Instructor: Now let's say the second part together.

> Have, has, had [clap]
> Do, does, did [clap]
> Shall, will, should, would, may, might, must [clap, clap]
> Can, could!

Instructor: Now let's say the chant together one more time without stopping in the middle.

Together: [say chant]

Instructor: In **Exercise 2** read the sentence. This sentence has a helping verb and an action verb in it. Write "h.v." over the helping verb and "a.v." over the action verb in the sentence.

>   h.v.   a.v.
>
> **Workbook:** The chicken may squawk.

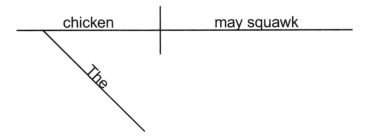

Instructor: Now look at the diagram. Do you see that two words are on the verb line? The helping verb *may* helps the action verb *squawk* to make this sentence sound right. "The chicken squawk" sounds funny, doesn't it? You need the helping verb for the sentence to make sense. Since the two verbs work together, they are both written together on the verb line in the diagram.

Instructor: In the last lesson you learned about state of being verbs. Let's say the chant of state of being verbs together three times.

Together (three times):
> Am [clap]
> Is [clap]
> Are, was, were. [clap]
> Be [clap]
> Being [clap]
> Been. [clap] [clap]

Instructor: State of being verbs just show that you exist. In the last lesson we read some questions and answers together. Let's do that again. Breakfast is ready and a mother is asking her child some questions. The child just wants to stay in bed! Look at **Exercise 3** in your workbook and follow along as I read each question. Then you will read the answer. Each answer contains a state of being verb printed in bold.

Workbook: Are you still in bed?

I **am**.

Is your sister still in the room, too?

She **is**.

Was she in bed?

She **was**.

Is your breakfast on the table?

It **is**.

Who is at the bottom of the stairs?

You **are**.

Who is upstairs?

We **are**.

Is your father in the kitchen?

He **is**.

Are the twins at the table already?

They **are**.

Who was just in the kitchen with the rest of the family?

You **were**.

Is French toast on the breakfast table?

It **is**.

Are you still in bed?

Now I **am** not!

Instructor: I just used the state of being verbs *am*, *is*, *are*, *was*, and *were*. These verbs can stand alone in a sentence, but the state of being verbs *be*, *being*, and *been* almost always need another verb to help them. In **Exercise 4**, follow along while I read each question. Then you read each answer. The state of being verb in each answer is in bold print, but the helping verb is not.

Workbook: Will you be in the yard?

I (will) **be**.

Should Tim be in the yard, too?

He (should) **be**.

Who has been in the yard this morning?

She (has) **been**.

Instructor: Now go back and read each answer again. Underline the state of being verb in bold print, and then circle the helping verb that helps it.

Instructor: There is one type of verb that we haven't talked about yet: a verb that links two words together. These verbs are easy to recognize because they are the same verbs as the state of being verbs: *am*, *is*, *are*, *was*, *were*, *be*, *being*, *been*. These verbs can do one of several different things in a sentence. Read **Exercise 5** to me.

Workbook: The verbs *am*, *is*, *are*, *was, were*, *be*, *being*, *been* can

- help another verb
- show a state of being
- link two words together

Instructor: Verbs that link two words together are called linking verbs. Do you know how to link hands with someone else? Let's link hands. We are joining hands. Now we are connected together. Do you know what we call the parts of a chain that are joined together? We call the parts of a chain "links." A link is something that connects or joins things. Linking verbs can link or connect words together in a sentence. In **Exercise 6**, read the sentence with a linking verb in it. The linking verb is followed by a noun.

Workbook: Honeybees **are** insects.

Instructor: *Are* is the linking verb in the sentence. The linking verb *are* links the subject *Honeybees* with a noun that **renames** the subject (*renames* means "gives the subject another name"). What are honeybees? Honeybees are insects. In **Exercise 7**, read the sentence to me.

Workbook: I **am** Sara.

Instructor: What is the linking verb in this sentence? *Am* is the linking verb. It connects the subject *I* with a proper noun, *Sara*, that renames the subject. *Sara* tells who the subject is. In this sentence, **who** is *I*? *Sara*. In **Exercise 8**, read the sentence to me.

Workbook: They **were** firefighters.

Instructor: What is the linking verb in this sentence? *Were* is the linking verb. It connects the subject *They* with a noun, *firefighters*, that renames the subject. Who were they? They were firefighters. *Firefighters* is in the complete predicate of the sentence. Remember, the complete predicate includes all the words that tell us what is said about the subject. *Firefighters* is a noun. A noun or pronoun in the complete predicate that renames the subject is called a **predicate nominative**. The word *nominative* is probably new to you, but you know a similar word. Have you ever heard the word *nominate*? If you nominate a person for President, you name the person you would like to be President. *Nominate* means "name." So a **predicate nominative** is a noun or pronoun in the complete predicate that *renames* the subject. Remember, *renames* means "gives the subject another name." In **Exercise 9**, look at a diagram of the sentence "They were firefighters."

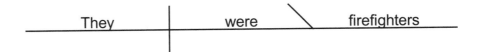

Instructor: *Firefighters* renames the subject *They*. It is written to the right of the verb on the diagram because it follows the verb in the sentence. Because the noun *firefighters* is in the complete predicate of the sentence, it is a **predicate nominative**. I will say that again: predicate nominative. *Predicate* tells you where the word is in the sentence. *Nominative* tells you that it *renames* the subject.

In order to keep the student's eyes focused on what you are explaining, physically point out the words and lines on the student's diagram as they appear in the Instructor's script.

Instructor: Look again at the diagram of "They were firefighters." Do you see the slanted line that separates the linking verb *were* from the predicate nominative? That slanted line points back toward the subject to remind you that *firefighters* is a predicate nominative that renames the subject *They*. Imagine that the slanted line is an arrow that points back to the subject. Look at the diagram with the arrow.

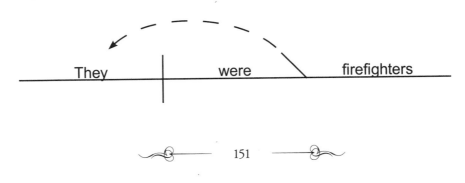

Instructor: The arrow isn't really printed on a normal diagram; you will just see the slanted line. But it is helpful to imagine that an arrow is there. Look at the diagrams in **Exercise 10**. Earlier in the lesson, you read these sentences. In the first diagram, put your pencil on the slanted line next to the predicate nominative *insects*. Start drawing an arrow that points back to the subject, *Honeybees*. This reminds you that *insects* is a predicate nominative that renames the subject *Honeybees*.

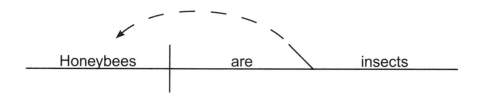

Instructor: Now look at the next diagram. Draw an arrow from the predicate nominative *Sara* back to the subject *I*. This reminds you that *Sara* is a predicate nominative that renames the subject *I*.

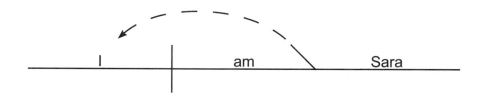

Instructor: In **Exercise 11**, we will look at another sentence with a linking verb and a predicate nominative. Read the sentence about juncos to me.

Workbook: Juncos are snowbirds.

Instructor: What is the linking verb in the sentence?

Student: *Are*

Instructor: What is the subject of the sentence?

Student: *Juncos*

Instructor: This sentence contains a predicate nominative. This noun is in the complete predicate of the sentence, and it renames the subject. What is the predicate nominative?

Student: *Snowbirds*

Instructor: *Snowbirds* is the predicate nominative. A snowbird is a bird that you see mostly in the winter. Look at the diagram of the sentence "Juncos are snowbirds."

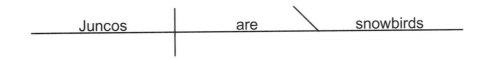

Instructor: The word *snowbirds* is a noun that renames the subject *Juncos*. It is the predicate nominative. The predicate nominative *snowbirds* is separated from the linking verb by a slanted line. That slanted line points back toward the subject to remind you that a predicate nominative renames the subject.

Instructor: In this lesson you have been reading sentences with nouns that follow linking verbs. These nouns rename the subject; they are called predicate nominatives. But, remember, a noun can follow an **action** verb, too. These nouns are direct objects, and you practiced them in Lessons 29, 30, and 32. Direct objects can **only** follow action verbs—they cannot follow linking verbs. Let's review that. Read the first sentence in **Exercise 12** to me. This sentence does not contain a linking verb. It contains an action verb and a direct object.

Workbook: Kim baked a cookie.

Instructor: The action verb *baked* is followed by the direct object *cookie*. *Cookie* receives the action of the verb *baked*. What did Kim bake? A cookie. Now we will compare the direct object sentence with a sentence that has a linking verb in it. The linking verb is also followed by a noun. Read the next sentence about Kim.

Workbook: Kim is a girl.

Instructor: There is no action in the sentence. Kim is not doing anything. What is the linking verb? *Is* is the linking verb. It links the subject *Kim* with a noun in the complete predicate that **renames** the subject. What is Kim? Kim is a girl. *Girl* is the predicate nominative because it renames the subject. Predicate nominatives can **only** follow linking verbs—they cannot follow action verbs.

Instructor: Remember, direct objects can only follow **action** verbs. They can't follow linking verbs! And predicate nominatives can't follow action verbs. They can **only** follow linking verbs! Read aloud the sentences in **Exercise 12** again.

Instructor: Is *baked* an action verb or a linking verb?

Student: *Action verb*

Instructor: Is *cookie* a direct object or a predicate nominative? Remember, predicate nominatives can't follow action verbs!

Student: *Direct object*

Instructor: *Cookie* is a direct object because *baked* is an action verb. *Girl* is a predicate nominative because *is* is a linking verb. Now read the first sentence in **Exercise 13**, and write the predicate nominative *girl* in the blank. This is where the direct object *cookie* used to be. What does the new sentence say?

Student: *Kim baked a girl.*

Instructor: That doesn't make sense, does it? Put a large "X" over the word *girl* to show that it is wrong. Now read the second sentence in **Exercise 13**, and write the direct object *cookie* in the blank. This is where the predicate nominative *girl* used to be. What does the new sentence say?

Student: *Kim is a cookie.*

Instructor: Put a large "X" over the word *cookie* to show that it is wrong. So you see, a direct object can't follow a linking verb—and a predicate nominative can't follow an action verb!

Dictation Exercise

After the student has written each sentence, have him circle the linking verb.

Dictation: Crocodiles (are) reptiles

A hammer (is) a tool.

Optional Follow-Up

The student will fill in the blank with the relative's proper name (the first name is fine). Explain to the student that the proper noun tells who the subject is. It is a predicate nominative: a noun or pronoun in the complete predicate of the sentence that renames the subject.

Workbook: I am _____.

My mother is _____.

My father is _____.

My sister is _____.

My cousin is _____.

My grandfather is _____.

LESSON 35

Review: Linking Verbs

Review: Predicate Nominatives

Read "I Wandered Lonely As a Cloud" (Lesson 31) three times to the student. Then ask the student to say the poem along with you or the tape recorder. If the student is ready, he should recite the poem to real people today. If he is not, continue practicing daily until he is ready.

Instructor: Let's begin by saying the definition of a verb. A verb is a word that does an action, shows a state of being, links two words together, or helps another verb. Say that with me two times.

Together (two times): A verb is a word that does an action, shows a state of being, links two words together, or helps another verb.

Instructor: Verbs that link two words together are called linking verbs. Linking verbs can link or connect words together in a sentence. Let's say the chant of the linking verbs. I will do the chant first, and you will join me the second time through.

Instructor, then together:
Am [clap]
Is [clap]
Are, was, were. [clap]
Be [clap]
Being [clap]
Been. [clap] [clap]

Instructor: Linking verbs can link the subject with a noun or pronoun in the complete predicate that renames the subject. In **Exercise 1** of your workbook, read the sentence to me. The linking verb is in bold print.

Workbook: Boy Scouts **are** volunteers.

Instructor: Look at a diagram of the sentence you just read.

Boy Scouts | are \ volunteers

Instructor: The noun *volunteers* is written to the right of the slanted line on the diagram. Remember, the slanted line points back to the subject that is renamed. *Volunteers* renames who the *Boy Scouts* are. *Volunteers* is in the complete predicate. Remember, the complete predicate includes the verb and all the words that follow the verb in the sentence. The complete predicate tells us what is said about the subject. So, a noun or pronoun in the complete predicate of the sentence that renames the subject is called a **predicate nominative**. The word *nominative* is similar to the word *nominate*. Do you remember that the word *nominate* means "name"? If you nominate a person for President, you name the person you would like to be President. So a predicate nominative is a noun or pronoun in the complete predicate that **renames the subject**.

Instructor: In **Exercise 2** I will help you diagram four sentences with linking verbs that link the subject to a predicate nominative. You read each sentence. I will ask you questions as you fill in the diagram. Remember to copy the words exactly as they appear in the sentence. If the words begin with a capital letter in the sentence, they should also be capitalized in the diagram.

Workbook: 1. She is Carrie.

2. Yesterday was Tuesday.

3. Indians were hunters.

4. Settlers were farmers.

Use the following dialogue to help the student fill in each of the four diagrams in **Exercise 2:**

---

1. *What is the linking verb? This verb links the subject to a word in the complete predicate. Write the verb to the right of your center line.*

2. *Find the subject. Ask "who" or "what" before the verb. [Prompt the student with a specific question like "Who is?" or "What was?"] Write the subject to the left of the center line on your frame.*

3. *This sentence contains a predicate nominative. This noun is in the complete predicate of the sentence, but it **renames the subject**. What is the predicate nominative in this sentence? Because the predicate nominative follows the verb in the sentence, it is written to the right of the verb on the diagram. Write the predicate nominative to the right of the slanted line on your diagram. That slanted line points back toward the subject to remind you that a predicate nominative renames the subject.*

Answer Key:

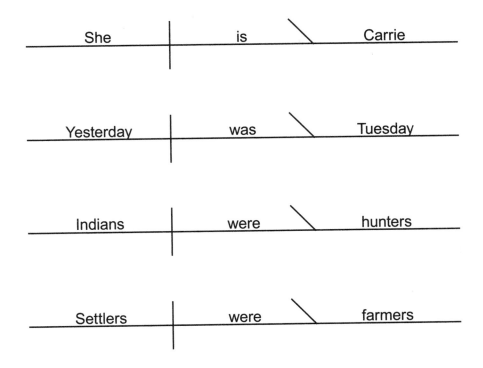

Optional Follow-Up

Tell the student, "I will show you some fill-in-the-blank sentences. I want you to circle the predicate nominative that renames the subject and makes the sentence true." You will probably need to consult an encyclopedia or the internet when doing this exercise.

Workbook: 1. Wombats are _____.

        a. marsupials

        b. amphibians

        c. birds

Workbook: 2. Pangolins are _____.

        a. lizards

        b. plants

        c. anteaters

Workbook: 3. The duck-billed platypus is a _____.

        a. bird

        b. mammal

        c. creature from outer space

Answer Key: 1. a; 2. c; 3. b

LESSON 36

Narration: "The Beaver Is a Builder"

Read the following selection aloud to the student (or, the student may read it aloud himself from his workbook). After the selection has been read, follow the scripting to make sure he understands the passage. After the initial reading, the student should **not** look at the passage.

Instructor: We are going to read about beavers. When we have finished reading, I am going to ask you what you remember **only** about what has been read. Don't tell me information that you remember from somewhere else. This passage may sound a little bit odd to you in some places, because it was written over a hundred years ago.

The Beaver Is a Builder

Beavers build themselves most curious huts to live in, and quite frequently a great number of these huts are placed close together, like the buildings in a town. They always build their huts on the banks of rivers or lakes, for they swim much more easily than they walk, and prefer moving about in the water.

When they build on the bank of a running stream, they make a dam across the stream for the purpose of keeping the water at the height they want. These dams are chiefly of mud and stones, and the branches of trees. They are sometimes six or seven hundred feet in length.

Their huts are made of the same materials as the dams, and are round in shape. The walls are very thick, and the roofs are finished off with a thick layer of mud. They commence building their houses in the summer, but do not get them finished before the early frosts. The freezing makes them tighter and stronger.

"The Beaver Is a Builder" is slightly adapted from *McGuffey's Second Eclectic Reader* (originally published in 1879).

Instructor: Close your eyes. Now I am going to ask you a few questions about what I just read.

The following questions are to make sure the student understands the passage. The student should answer these questions in complete sentences. If the student answers in a single word or phrase, put the phrase into a complete sentence for the student and ask him to repeat it back to you. The words in italics represent sample answers—accept other answers if they are correct and if the information was in the passage.

Instructor: What kind of animal did we read about?

Student: *We read about beavers.*

Instructor: Where do beavers live?

Student: *They live in huts OR next to rivers or lakes.*

Instructor: How do beavers make a running stream deep enough to swim in?

Student: *They build a dam across the stream.*

Instructor: What materials do beavers use to make their dams and huts?

Student: *They use mud, stones, and branches.*

Instructor: What does freezing do to the beavers' houses?

Student: *It makes them tighter and stronger.*

Instructor: Now tell me two things you remember about beavers. Use your own words. Speak in complete sentences.

As the student narrates in his own words, you may write his sentences down as he speaks or record them onto a tape recorder to write down when he is finished. You have three options for writing the narration:

1. Write down the student's narration for him on his workbook page.
2. Write down the student's narration for him on a separate piece of paper and have him copy some or all of the sentences onto his workbook page.
3. Write down the student's narration on a separate piece of paper and dictate it to him, as he writes it on his workbook page.

If the student repeats the author's words verbatim, use the questions about the passage to help the student form his own sentences. If the student speaks in phrases, turn his phrases into complete sentences. The student should then repeat the complete sentence back to you. The student does not need to include every aspect of the passage in his narration—he only needs to pick out two ideas. Here is an example of a possible narration.

> Beavers build huts out of mud and tree branches. They live next to lakes or rivers.

Once you have written the student's narration, he should read it aloud back to you.

LESSON 37

New: Predicate Adjectives (with Diagramming)
Review: Linking Verbs
Review: Predicate Nominatives

Review "The Land of Nod" (Lesson 9) today. If the student has trouble remembering the poem, have him practice it daily until he is confident.

Instructor: Let's begin by saying the definition of a verb. A verb is a word that does an action, shows a state of being, links two words together, or helps another verb. Say that with me two times.

Together (two times): A verb is a word that does an action, shows a state of being, links two words together, or helps another verb.

Instructor: Verbs that link two words together are called linking verbs. Linking verbs can link or connect words together in a sentence. Let's say the chant of the linking verbs. I will do the chant first, and you will join me the second time through.

Instructor, then together:
   Am [clap]
   Is [clap]
   Are, was, were. [clap]
   Be [clap]
   Being [clap]
   Been. [clap] [clap]

Instructor: Linking verbs can link the subject with a noun or pronoun in the complete predicate that renames the subject. Imagine that a mother comes into the kitchen to find the table already set and her two daughters sitting quietly at the table. The mother asks, "Who was the person who set this table so beautifully?" One of the daughters points to her sister and answers her mother with a sentence that contains a linking verb. In **Exercise 1**, read the daughter's answer to me and look at its diagram.

Workbook: It was she.

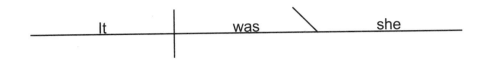

Instructor: *Was* is a linking verb. It connects the subject *It* with a **pronoun** that renames the subject. *She* renames the subject. Who was it who set the table? *She. She* is in the complete predicate of the sentence. Remember, the complete predicate includes the verb and all the words that follow it in the sentence. The complete predicate tells us what is said about the subject. A noun or pronoun in the complete predicate that renames the subject is called a **predicate nominative.** *She* renames the subject *It* and is written to the right of the verb on the diagram because it follows the verb in the sentence.

In order to keep the student's eyes focused on what you are explaining, physically point out the words and lines on the student's diagram as you mention them in the explanation below.

Instructor: Look again at the diagram. Do you see the slanted line that separates the linking verb *was* from the predicate nominative? That slanted line points back toward the subject to remind you that *she* is a predicate nominative that renames the subject *It*. Now I will help you diagram a sentence with a predicate nominative in **Exercise 2.**

Workbook: Snakes are reptiles.

Use the following dialogue to help the student fill in the diagram in **Exercise 2:**

1. *What is the linking verb? This verb links the subject to a word in the complete predicate. Write the verb to the right of your center line.*

2. *Find the subject. Ask "who" or "what" before the verb. [Prompt the student with a specific question, "What are?"] Write the subject to the left of the center line on your frame.*

3. *This sentence contains a predicate nominative. This noun is in the complete predicate of the sentence, but it **renames the subject.** What is the predicate nominative in this sentence? Because the predicate nominative follows the verb in the sentence, it is written to the right of the verb on the diagram. Write the predicate nominative to the right of the slanted line on your diagram. That slanted line points back toward the subject to remind you that a predicate nominative renames the subject.*

Answer Key:

$$\underline{\text{Snakes}} \quad \bigg| \quad \underline{\text{are}} \quad \backslash \quad \underline{\text{reptiles}}$$

Instructor: You have learned that linking verbs can link the subject with a noun or pronoun that **renames the subject**. But linking verbs can also link the subject with an **adjective** in the complete predicate. Look at **Exercise 3**. I will read you a noun and a linking verb and let you complete the sentence by writing in an **adjective** that describes the subject. The linking verb in bold print will link, or connect, the subject noun with the adjective you choose. Follow along as I read and point to the parts of the sentences in **Exercise 3**.

Workbook: The sky **is** _____.

Instructor: Can you tell me what color the sky is?

Student: *The sky is blue [or gray, or orange].*

Instructor: The linking verb *is* connects *sky* with its color! Can you tell me something about pencils that describe the way they look?

Workbook: Pencils **are** _____.

Student: *Pencils are [yellow, long, sharp].*

Instructor: The linking verb *are* connects or links the word *pencils* with the word *[the word the student chose]*. Now finish this sentence:

Workbook: The fried chicken **was** _____.

Student: *The fried chicken was [delicious, crispy, hot].*

Instructor: The linking verb *was* connects or links the word *chicken* with the word that describes the chicken: *[the word the student chose]*.

Instructor: In **Exercise 4**, read the sentence about mountains. This sentence contains a linking verb.

Workbook: Mountains are enormous.

Instructor: The linking verb *are* links the subject of the sentence, *Mountains*, with the adjective *enormous*. The adjective *enormous* describes the subject *Mountains*. Because *enormous* follows the linking verb *are*, it is located in the complete predicate. Remember, the complete predicate includes all the words that tell us what is said about the subject. Adjectives that describe the subject but are found in the complete predicate are called **predicate** adjectives. Look at the diagram of the sentence.

Instructor: *Enormous* is an adjective that describes the subject *Mountains*. It is written to the right of the verb on the diagram because it follows the verb in the sentence. Because the adjective is in the complete predicate of the sentence, it is a **predicate** adjective.

In order to keep the student's eyes focused on what you are explaining, physically point out the words and lines on the student's diagram as you mention them in the explanation below.

Instructor: Do you see the slanted line that separates the linking verb *are* from the predicate adjective? That slanted line points back toward the subject to remind you that *enormous* is an adjective that describes the subject *Mountains*. As you can see, predicate adjectives are diagrammed the same way that predicate nominatives are diagrammed, because they both refer back to the subject.

Instructor: In **Exercise 5**, I will help you diagram some sentences with linking verbs that link the subject to a predicate adjective. You read the sentence. I will ask you questions as you fill in the diagram. Remember to copy the words exactly as they appear in the sentence. If the words begin with a capital letter in the sentence, they should also be capitalized in the diagram.

Workbook: 1. Kittens are cute.

2. I am kind.

3. John is tall.

4. They were clean.

Use the following dialogue to help the student fill in each of the four diagrams:

1. What is the linking verb? This verb links the subject to a word in the complete predicate. Write the verb to the right of your center line.

2. Find the subject. Ask "who" or "what" before the verb. [Prompt the student with a specific question like "What are?" or "Who is?"] Write the subject to the left of the center line on your frame.

3. *This sentence contains a predicate adjective. This adjective is in the complete predicate of the sentence, but it describes the subject. A predicate adjective can tell what kind, which one, how many, or whose. Can you find an adjective in the complete predicate that describes the subject? Because the predicate adjective follows the verb in the sentence, it is written to the right of the verb on the diagram. Write the predicate adjective to the right of the slanted line on your diagram. That slanted line points back toward the subject to remind you that a predicate adjective describes the subject.*

Answer Key:

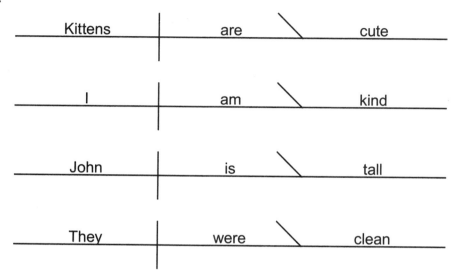

Optional Follow-Up

You need four people to do this activity. One person will be the **director** (preferably the student doing this book). The other three people are the players: the **subject** player, the **linking verb** player, and the **predicate adjective** player.

The subject player will need the following nine words (or phrases) each written on separate pieces of paper: *Suitcases, Snakes, Oranges, The gorilla, Clowns, The candy bar, Grandpa, The soup, I.*

The linking verb player will need these five words each written on separate pieces of paper: *am, is, are, was, were.*

The predicate adjective player will need these nine words each written on separate pieces of paper: *heavy, quick, juicy, immense, ridiculous, sticky, wise, thin, obedient.*

The director chooses a subject for the subject player to tape to her front. Then the director chooses a predicate adjective for the predicate adjective player to tape to his front. Then the director must choose the linking verb that will link the two words together (he may need help with this). For example, if the director chooses *Clowns* and *ridiculous*, he must select either the linking verb *are* or *were* to complete the sentence. Once every player has his word taped to his front, the players link hands in proper sentence order, facing the director. Then each player reads his word, saying the (possibly very silly) sentence. Mix and match the words to create new sentences—and feel free to giggle!

LESSON 38

Review: Linking Verbs

Review: Predicate Adjectives

Review: Predicate Nominatives

Review "A Tragic Story" (Lesson 18) today. If the student has trouble remembering the poem, have him practice it daily until he is confident.

Instructor: Let's begin by saying the definition of a verb. A verb is a word that does an action, shows a state of being, links two words together, or helps another verb. Say that with me two times.

Together (two times): A verb is a word that does an action, shows a state of being, links two words together, or helps another verb.

Instructor: Verbs that link two words together are called linking verbs. Linking verbs can link or connect words together in a sentence. Let's say the chant of the linking verbs. I will do the chant first, and you will join me the second time through.

Instructor, then together:
Am [clap]
Is [clap]
Are, was, were. [clap]
Be [clap]
Being [clap]
Been. [clap] [clap]

Instructor: In **Exercise 1** of your workbook, you will practice using some linking verbs in sentences. I will read you a noun and a linking verb and let you complete the sentence by choosing a predicate adjective that describes the subject. You will write the predicate adjective in your workbook. The linking verb in bold print will link, or connect, the subject noun with the predicate adjective you choose. Follow along in your workbook as I read and point to the parts of the sentences. Can you tell me what grass looks like? Finish this sentence and write your answer in the blank.

Workbook: The grass **is** _____.

Student: *The grass is green [or short, or brown].*

Instructor: The linking verb *is* connects *grass* with the adjective *[the word the student chose]*! Can you tell me something about porcupines that describe how they feel to the touch? Finish this sentence and write your answer in the blank.

Workbook: Porcupines **are** _____.

Student: *Porcupines are [prickly, sharp, painful].*

Instructor: The linking verb *are* connects the word *porcupines* with the adjective *[the word student chose]*. Now finish this sentence with an adjective that tells how a doughnut tasted. Write your answer in the blank.

Workbook: The doughnut **was** _____.

Student: *The doughnut was [sweet, sugary, delicious].*

Instructor: In **Exercise 2** of your workbook, read the sentence and look at its diagram. It contains a linking verb.

Workbook: The tractors **were** dusty.

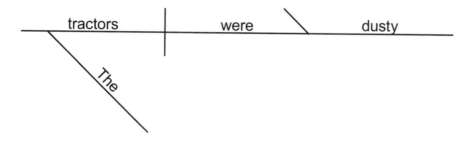

In order to keep the student's eyes focused on what you are explaining, physically point out the words and lines on the student's diagram as they appear in the following three paragraphs of the instructor's script.

Instructor: The linking verb *were* connects the subject of the sentence, *tractors*, with the adjective *dusty*. *Dusty* describes *tractors*. Because *dusty* follows the linking verb *were*, it is part of the complete predicate. Remember, the complete predicate tells us what is said about the subject. These words are the verb and all the words attached to the verb line on a diagram. Adjectives that describe the subject but are found in the complete predicate are called **predicate** adjectives. Look again at the diagram of the sentence. *Dusty* is an adjective that describes the subject *tractors*. It is written to the right of the verb on the diagram because it follows the verb in the sentence. It is a predicate adjective because it is in the complete predicate of the sentence.

Instructor: Do you see the slanted line that separates the linking verb *were* from the predicate adjective? That slanted line points back toward the subject to remind you that *dusty* is an adjective that describes *tractors*.

Instructor: There is another word besides *tractors* in the complete subject of the sentence. The article *The* describes *tractors*, so it is written on the slanted line below the simple subject, *tractors*.

Instructor: In **Exercise 3**, I will help you diagram three sentences with linking verbs that link the subjects to predicate adjectives. You read each sentence. I will ask you questions as you fill in the diagram. Remember to copy the words exactly as they appear in the sentence. If the words begin with a capital letter in the sentence, they should also be capitalized in the diagram.

Workbook: 1. Tall gates are heavy.

2. Ten pigs were lazy.

3. The Sahara Desert is dry.

Before the student diagrams the third sentence, tell him that *Sahara Desert* is the proper name of a desert in Africa. Even though *Sahara Desert* is two words, it is one proper noun (Lesson 26). *Sahara Desert* is written on the subject line of the diagram (*The* is an article that describes the proper noun).

Use the following dialogue to help the student fill in each diagram.

---

1. *What is the linking verb? This verb links the subject to a word in the complete predicate. Write the verb to the right of your center line.*

2. *Find the subject. Ask "who" or "what" before the verb. [Prompt the student with a specific question like "What are?" or "What were?"] Write the subject to the left of the center line on your frame.*

3. *This sentence contains a predicate adjective. This adjective is in the complete predicate of the sentence, but it describes the subject. A predicate adjective can tell what kind, which one, how many, or whose. Can you find an adjective in the complete predicate that describes the subject? Because the predicate adjective follows the verb in the sentence, it is written to the right of the verb on the diagram. Write the predicate adjective to the right of the slanted line on your diagram. That slanted line points back toward the subject to remind you that a predicate adjective describes the subject.*

4. *Go back and look again at the subject. Are there any words that describe the subject that come before the verb in the sentence? This adjective is in the complete subject. An adjective can tell what kind, which one, how many, or whose. Also look for an article (a, an, the), because it acts like an adjective. Write the adjective on a slanted line below the subject it describes.*

Answer Key:

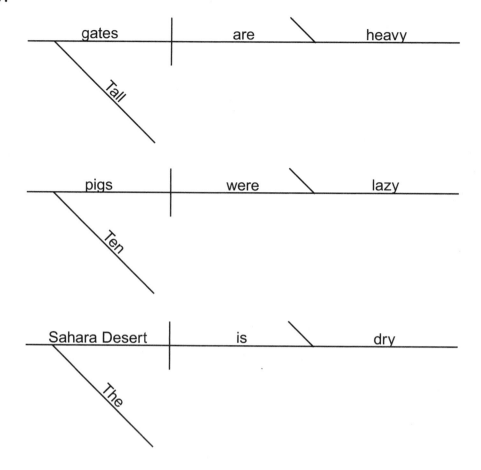

Instructor: Now we will review predicate nominatives. Remember, linking verbs can also link the subject with a **noun** or **pronoun** in the predicate that renames the subject. Read the sentences in **Exercise 4** to me. The linking verbs are in bold print.

If more review of predicate nominatives is needed, refer back to Lessons 34, 35, and 37.

Workbook: I **am** Levi.

The queen **is** a ruler.

Pythons **are** snakes.

The man **was** a leader.

Instructor: In **Exercise 5**, look at a diagram of the first sentence you just read.

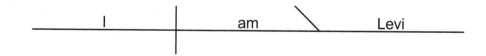

Instructor: The proper noun *Levi* is written to the right of the slanted line on the diagram. *Levi* renames the subject. Who is *I*? *Levi*. A noun or pronoun in the complete predicate of the sentence that renames the subject is called a predicate nominative. The word *nominative* is similar to the word *nominate*. Do you remember that the word *nominate* means "name"? If you nominate a person for President, you name the person you would like to be President. So a predicate nominative is a noun or pronoun in the complete predicate that renames the subject. Read the first sentence in **Exercise 6** to me.

Workbook: Pythons are snakes.

Instructor: What is the linking verb in the sentence?

Student: Are

Instructor: What is the subject of the sentence? What **are**?

Student: Pythons

Instructor: This sentence contains a predicate nominative. This noun is in the complete predicate of the sentence, but it renames the subject. What is the predicate nominative?

Student: Snakes

Instructor: Look at the diagram of the sentence "Pythons are snakes."

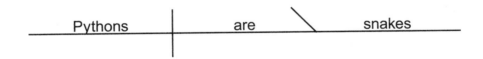

Instructor: The predicate nominative *snakes* is separated from the linking verb by a slanted line. That slanted line points back toward the subject to remind you that a predicate nominative renames the subject. Read the next sentence in **Exercise 6** to me.

Workbook: The queen is a ruler.

Instructor: What is the linking verb in the sentence?

Student: Is

Instructor: What is the subject of the sentence? Who **is**?

Student: Queen

Instructor: This sentence contains a predicate nominative. This noun is in the complete predicate of the sentence, but it renames the subject. What is the predicate nominative?

Student: *Ruler*

Instructor: Look at the diagram of the sentence "The queen is a ruler."

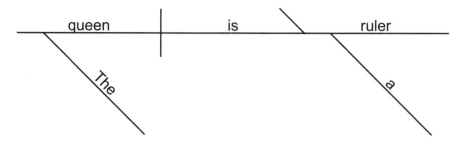

Instructor: The word *ruler* is a noun that renames the subject *queen*. It is the predicate nominative. The predicate nominative *ruler* is separated from the linking verb by a slanted line. That slanted line points back toward the subject to remind you that a predicate nominative renames the subject. Look again at the predicate nominative. It has an adjective of its own. The article *a* describes *ruler*, so it is written on the slanted line below the predicate nominative *ruler*.

Instructor: In **Exercise 7**, I will help you diagram three sentences with linking verbs that link the subject to a predicate nominative. You read each sentence. I will ask you questions as you fill in the diagram for that sentence. Remember to copy the words exactly as they appear in the sentence. If the words begin with a capital letter in the sentence, they should also be capitalized in the diagram.

Workbook: 1. A platypus is an unusual mammal.

2. Hermit crabs are amusing small pets.

3. The Lincoln Memorial is a famous monument.

Before the student diagrams the third sentence, tell him that *Lincoln Memorial* is the proper name of a monument in Washington, D.C. Even though *Lincoln Memorial* is two words, it is one proper noun. *Lincoln Memorial* is written on the subject line of the diagram (*The* is an article that describes the proper noun).

Use the following dialogue to help the student fill in each diagram:

---

1. What is the linking verb? This verb links the subject to a word in the complete predicate. Write the verb to the right of your center line.

2. Find the subject. Ask "who" or "what" before the verb. [Prompt the student with a specific question like "What is?" or "What are?"] Write the subject to the left of the center line on your frame.

3. This sentence contains a predicate nominative. This noun is in the complete predicate of the sentence, but it renames the subject. What is the predicate nominative in this sentence? Because the predicate nominative follows the verb in the sentence, it is written to the right of the verb on the diagram. Write the predicate nominative to the right of the slanted line on your diagram. That slanted line points back toward the subject to remind you that a predicate nominative renames the subject.

4. *Look at the predicate nominative again. Are there any words that describe this noun? These adjectives can tell what kind, which one, how many, or whose. Also look for articles (a, an, the), because they act like an adjective. Write each adjective on a slanted line below the predicate nominative it describes.*

5. *Go back and look again at the subject. Are there any words that describe the subject that come before the verb in the sentence? This adjective is in the complete subject. An adjective can tell what kind, which one, how many, or whose. Also look for an article (a, an, the), because it acts like an adjective. Write each adjective on a slanted line below the subject it describes.*

Answer Key:

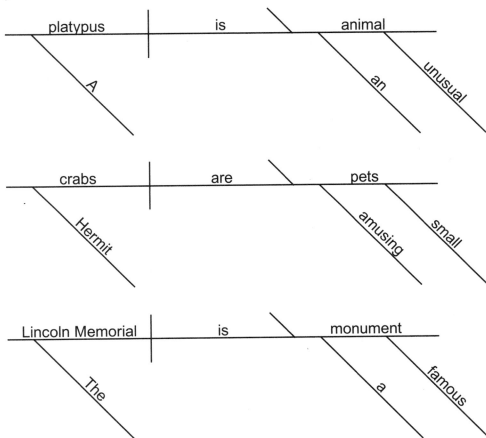

Optional Follow-Up

In an encyclopedia or on the internet, look up one of the subjects from today's lesson (the platypus, the hermit crab, the Lincoln Memorial, the python, or the Sahara Desert). Read and talk about interesting facts with your student.

LESSON 39

Review: **Common and Proper Nouns**

Review: **Forming Plurals**

Instructor: Say the definition of a noun with me.

Together: A noun is the name of a person, place, thing, or idea.

Instructor: Nouns can be either common or proper. A common noun is a name common to many persons, places, or things. A proper noun is a special, "proper" name for a person, place, or thing. Proper nouns always begin with a capital letter. The word *girl* is a common noun, but *Audrey* is a proper noun. I am going to say a common noun to you, and I want you answer my question with a proper noun (a special, "proper" name for a common noun).

Instructor: *Man* is a common noun. What is the special, "proper" name of a man that you know?

Student: *[Acceptable answers include Daddy, Uncle _____, Mr. _____]*

Instructor: *State* is a common noun. What is the special, "proper" name of the state in which you live?

Student: *[name of state]*

Instructor: Now I am going to read you some nouns. If the noun is a common noun, stay seated. If the noun is a proper noun, stand up.

Instructor: pond
cat
Salt Lake City
astronaut
Atlantic Ocean
sister
island
Dennis
shopping center
town
[name of the student's dentist]
Hawaii

Mexico
mountain
Colorado River
Mount Whitney
ocean
soldier
India
New York

Instructor: The seasons are all common nouns. They do not begin with a capital letter. Read the list of seasons in **Exercise 1** of your workbook. Circle the first letter of each word.

Seasons
spring
summer
fall
winter

Instructor: The days of the week and the months of the year are proper nouns. They each begin with a capital letter. In **Exercise 2**, read aloud the names of the months and days to me.

Months of the Year	Days of the Week
January	Monday
February	Tuesday
March	Wednesday
April	Thursday
May	Friday
June	Saturday
July	Sunday
August	
September	
October	
November	
December	

Instructor: Many proper nouns are made up of more than one word. Look at **Exercise 3**. I am going to read you the full name of the man who first ran a mile in less than four minutes.

Workbook: Roger Bannister

Instructor: We just read one, single proper noun: *Roger Bannister*. Although his full name is made up of two words, he is just one person. Each word in the proper noun begins with a capital letter. In your workbook, let's look at the diagram with a proper noun as the subject.

Workbook: Roger Bannister ran.

Roger Bannister	ran

Instructor: Remember, *Roger Bannister* is one proper noun because he is one man. That is why his full name is written on the subject line. In **Exercise 4**, I will help you diagram two sentences, each with a proper noun and a predicate adjective. You read the sentence. I will ask you questions as you fill in the diagram. Remember to copy the words exactly as they appear in the sentence. If the words begin with a capital letter in the sentence, they should also be capitalized in the diagram. Read the two sentences in **Exercise 4**.

Tell the student that Saint Peter's Basilica is one proper name for a church building in Rome and that Mount Rushmore is one proper name for a huge carving on a cliff in South Dakota.

Workbook: 1. Mount Rushmore is spectacular.

2. Saint Peter's Basilica is gigantic.

Use the following dialogue to help the student fill in the two diagrams:

1. What is the linking verb? This verb links the subject to a word in the complete predicate. Write the verb to the right of your center line.

2. Find the subject. Ask "who" or "what" before the verb. [Prompt the student with a specific question, "What is?"] This subject is a proper noun made up of more than one word. Write the subject to the left of the center line on your frame.

3. This sentence contains a predicate adjective. This adjective is in the complete predicate of the sentence, but it describes the subject. A predicate adjective can tell what kind, which one, how many, or whose. Can you find an adjective in the complete predicate that describes the subject? Because the predicate adjective follows the verb in the sentence, it is written to the right of the verb on the diagram. Write the predicate adjective to the right of the slanted line on your diagram. That slanted line points back toward the subject to remind you that a predicate adjective describes the subject.

Answer Key:

Mount Rushmore	is \ spectacular

Saint Peter's Basilica	is \ gigantic

Instructor: Now in **Exercise 5** of your workbook, we will review singular and plural nouns. A singular noun names one, single thing. Plural nouns name more than one thing. Let's review the rules of forming plurals. Repeat after me: Usually, add **s** to a noun to form the plural.

Student: *Usually, add* **s** *to a noun to form the plural.*

Instructor: Look at the singular noun *desk*. Then write the plural form of the word beneath it (*desks*).

Instructor: Repeat after me: Add **es** to nouns ending in **s**, **sh**, **ch**, **x**, or **z**.

Student: *Add* **es** *to nouns ending in* **s**, **sh**, **ch**, **x**, *or* **z**.

Instructor: Look at the next five singular nouns that follow this rule (*kiss, wish, peach, fox, buzz*). Write the plural form beneath each singular noun (*kisses, wishes, peaches, foxes, buzzes*).

Instructor: Now we will review the next plural rule. Repeat after me: If a noun ends in **y** after a consonant, change the **y** to **i** and add **es**.

Student: *If a noun ends in* **y** *after a consonant, change the* **y** *to* **i** *and add* **es**.

Instructor: Look at the singular noun *sky*. Then write the plural form of the word beneath it (*skies*).

Instructor: And for the last plural rule, repeat after me: If a noun ends in **y** after a vowel, just add **s**.

Student: *If a noun ends in* **y** *after a vowel, just add* **s**.

Instructor: Look at the singular noun *holiday*. Then write the plural form of the word beneath it (*holidays*).

Instructor: In **Exercise 6**, look at the singular and plural list. Some words don't follow any rules to form their plurals. We call these words "irregular plurals" because they don't form their plurals the regular ways. Read this list of singular nouns and their irregular plural forms to me. Read across from left to right.

Singular Noun	Plural Noun
child	children
foot	feet
tooth	teeth
man	men
woman	women
mouse	mice
goose	geese
deer	deer
fish	fish

Instructor: Now I am going to use a singular noun in a sentence. Then I will start another sentence and you will finish that sentence with the irregular plural noun. If you need help, you may look at the list you just read.

Instructor: I can balance on one **foot**. But I most often stand on two _____.

Student: *feet*

Instructor: I lost another **tooth** yesterday. It was one of my bottom _____.

Student: *teeth*

Instructor: Each **child** will take a turn hitting the piñata for the other _____.

Student: *children*

Instructor: My father is this **man**. My uncles are those three _____.

Student: *men*

Instructor: I saw one **goose** chase away several smaller _____.

Student: *geese*

Optional Follow-Up

Test the student's memory of the irregular plurals. The student will write the plural forms of the singular nouns under the column "Plural Nouns" in the chart on page 131 of the Student Workbook. He may refer back to Exercise 6 (page 130) if he needs help.

LESSON 40

New: Four Types of Sentences

Review "I Wandered Lonely As a Cloud" (Lesson 31) today. If the student has trouble remembering the poem, have him practice it daily until he is confident.

Instructor: Near the beginning of this book (Lesson 11), you learned the definition of a sentence. A sentence is a group of words that expresses a complete thought. All sentences begin with a capital letter and end with a punctuation mark.

Instructor: Now I will say the definition three times. Say as much of it with me as you can.

Together (three times): A sentence is a group of words that expresses a complete thought. All sentences begin with a capital letter and end with a punctuation mark.

Instructor: There are four different types of sentences: statements, commands, questions, and exclamations. A statement gives information. Answer this question. How old are you?

Student: *I am [eight] years old.*

Instructor: "I am [eight] years old" is a statement. It gives information; it tells me how old you are. Statements always end with a period. Read the four statements in **Exercise 1** of your workbook.

Workbook: I am a person.

You are my friend.

I like to run.

Trucks make noise.

Instructor: The second type of sentence is a command. A command gives an order or makes a request. In your workbook, read each of the command sentences in **Exercise 2**, and then do what the sentence requests.

Workbook: Stand up.

Stretch your hands into the air.

Make a silly face!

Hop up and down on one foot!

Instructor: Now look again at the command sentences. A command sentence ends with either a period or an exclamation point. Show me the punctuation mark at the end of each command sentence you just read, and tell me what it is.

Instructor: The third type of sentence is a question. A question asks something. A question always ends with a question mark. Let's pretend we are on a long car trip together. In **Exercise 3**, read the questions that we might ask the driver.

Workbook: Are we there yet?

How far do we have to go?

When do we eat?

May we turn up the radio?

Instructor: The fourth type of sentence is an exclamation. An exclamation shows sudden or strong feeling. An exclamation always ends with an exclamation point. Read the sentences in **Exercise 4**. Remember to read exclamation sentences with lots of expression because they show strong feeling!

Workbook: Our new puppy has stolen my shoe!

He is chewing it up!

That puppy is too sneaky!

I will definitely not leave my shoes out anymore!

Instructor: In **Exercise 5**, read the sentences and write either "S" for statement, "C" for command, "Q" for question, or "E" for exclamation after each sentence.

Workbook: 1. Water covers almost three-quarters of the earth's surface. <u>S</u>

2. Find the five oceans on your map. <u>C</u>

3. What are the names of these oceans? <u>Q</u>

4. You are right! <u>E</u>

5. The names of the oceans are the Pacific, Atlantic, Indian, Southern, and Arctic. <u>S</u>

6. Water expands as it freezes. <u>S</u>

7. Don't put a full bottle of water in the freezer. <u>C</u>

8. Why not? <u>Q</u>

9. It might break the bottle! <u>E</u>

10. The word "hippopotamus" means "river horse." <u>S</u>

11. Picture that large animal in your mind. <u>C</u>

12. Do you think the hippopotamus is a kind of horse? <u>Q</u>

13. It is actually a type of pig! <u>E</u>

14. Listen to this fact. <u>C</u>

15. How much does an ostrich egg weigh? <u>Q</u>

16. It weighs three pounds. <u>S</u>

17. That is a really heavy egg! <u>E</u>

Optional Dictation Exercise

Dictate the following four sentences. After the student has written each sentence, have him tell you if the sentence is a statement, command, question, or exclamation.

Dictation: 1. Sit still.   (command)

2. May I eat a cupcake?   (question)

3. This dog is filthy!   (exclamation)

4. I have ten fingers.   (statement)

Optional Follow-Up

Tell the student that he is going to play a game where **he'll** tell **you** what to do. He will **command** you. Copy the command sentences below on eight index cards, one command per card. Or you can have the student copy the sentences from his workbook. If he wishes, he may come up with his own (reasonable) commands instead of copying the ones provided.

1. Hop on one foot.

2. Bark like a dog!

3. Walk backward.

4. Turn around three times.

5. Clap your hands behind your back.

6. Take three giant steps.

7. Sing a silly song!

8. Pretend you are a kangaroo.

Once he has all the command cards, he may show you a card, read aloud his sentence, and then you must do what the card says. You can play this game with other members of the family as well.

LESSON 41

New: **You (Understood) Subject in Command Sentences**

New: **Commands (with Diagramming)**

Review: **Statements**

Instructor: In your workbook, look at **Exercise 1**. Read the two short statement sentences to me.

If the word *kernels* is not familiar to the student, explain that they are the corn seeds. Corn kernels, when heated, burst into fluffy, white popcorn.

Workbook: Hannah runs.

Kernels pop.

Instructor: In Lesson 11, you learned that every sentence has a subject and a verb. In the first sentence, what is the verb?

Student: *Runs*

Instructor: *Runs* is the verb in the sentence. Now find the subject. Who runs?

Student: *Hannah*

Instructor: *Hannah* is the subject of the sentence. Now look at the second sentence. What is the verb?

Student: *Pop*

Instructor: *Pop* is the verb in the sentence. Now find the subject. What pops?

Student: *Kernels*

Instructor: *Kernels* is the subject of the sentence. It is easy to find the subject and the verb in these statement sentences because they are only two words long. One word is the subject; the other word is the verb. It is easy to diagram these sentences. They are just like the sentences you have been diagramming so far in this book. You have been diagramming statements, but some command sentences contain only one word. What do you do if a sentence has only one word in it? Read the sentence in **Exercise 2**. This is what Hannah's mother commands her to do when they need to hurry.

Workbook: Run.

Instructor: This command is a complete sentence, although it only consists of one word. It has a subject, but the subject is not written because it is understood to be the word *you*. Hannah's mother is telling her to run. She does not command her by saying "You run"; she simply says "Run." Look at the diagram of the short command sentence "Run."

Remind the student that he is not to put punctuation on the diagram.

          (you) | Run

Instructor: Notice that the word *you* is written inside parentheses. This shows us that although the word *you* is not actually written in the sentence, it is still understood to be the subject. Read the command sentences in **Exercise 3**. Although these sentences do not have a subject that is written, the subject is understood to be *you*.

Workbook: Look!

Walk quickly!

Instructor: Now we will diagram the first sentence "Look!" onto the empty frame in **Exercise 4** of your workbook.

Instructor: What is the verb in the sentence?

Student: *Look*

Instructor: *Look* is the verb in the sentence. Write the word *Look* on the verb line. Remember to capitalize *Look* because it is capitalized in the sentence. Now find the subject. What one word tells us who is commanded to look? Remember, this word is not written in the command sentence, but it is understood to be the subject.

Student: *You*

Instructor: *You* is the subject. Write the word *you* on the subject line. Because the subject *you* is not written in the sentence but is just understood, you should put *you* in parentheses. Now your diagram is complete.

          (you) | Look

Instructor: Now we will diagram the sentence "Walk quickly!" onto the empty frame in **Exercise 5** of your workbook.

Instructor: What is the verb in the sentence?

Student: *Walk*

Instructor: *Walk* is the verb in the sentence. Write the word *Walk* on the verb line. Remember to capitalize *Walk* because it is capitalized in the sentence. Now find the subject. What one word tells us who is commanded to walk? Remember, this word is not written in the command sentence, but it is understood to be the subject.

Student: *You*

Instructor: *You* is the subject. Write the word *you* on the subject line. Because the subject *you* is not written in the sentence but is just understood, you should put *you* in parentheses.

Instructor: Look again at the verb *Walk*. Is there a word that describes the verb? This is an adverb that could tell how, when, where, or how often you should walk.

Student: *Quickly*

Instructor: *Quickly* is an adverb that tells how you are commanded to walk. Write *quickly* on the slanted line beneath the word *Walk*. Now you have finished diagramming the sentence.

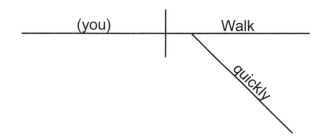

Instructor: So now you know the key to diagramming command sentences. In a command sentence, remember that the subject is not written down; it is simply understood to be *you*.

Dictation Exercise

Dictate each of the following sentences to the student. After he has written each sentence, ask him to write the subject of that sentence in the blank provided. If the student cannot remember the subject of these command sentences, remind him that *you* is always the subject of a command sentence.

Dictation: Pick up your pencil.

Write your name.

Practice your poem.

Optional Follow-Up

This activity emphasizes that *you* is understood to be the subject of command sentences. The student will point to the instructor (or someone else in the family) and give the following commands. Before he reads each command, he must point and say the word "you."

Workbook: Sit down.

Stand up.

Walk across the room.

Pick up a book.

Tiptoe around the room.

Cluck like a chicken.

Clap your hands behind your back.

Hop on one foot.

Wiggle only two fingers.

LESSON 42

Review: **Statements and Commands**

Instructor: In your workbook, read the short statement sentence in **Exercise 1** to me.

Workbook: John jumped.

Instructor: Every sentence has a subject and a verb. What is the verb in this sentence?

Student: *Jumped*

Instructor: *Jumped* is the verb in the sentence. Now find the subject. Who jumped?

Student: *John*

Instructor: *John* is the subject of the sentence. It is easy to find the subject and the verb in the statement sentence "John jumped," because it is only two words long. One word is the verb; the other word is the subject. Look at the diagram of this sentence in **Exercise 1**.

John	jumped

Instructor: But what do you do if a sentence has only one word in it, like certain command sentences? You learned how to diagram command sentences in the last lesson. Read the sentence in **Exercise 2**. This is what John's brother commanded him to do

Workbook: Jump.

Instructor: This command is a complete sentence, although it only consists of one word. It has a subject, but the subject is not written because it is understood to be the word *you*. John's brother is commanding him to jump. The brother does not command John by saying "You jump"; he simply says "Jump." In your workbook, look at the diagram of the short command sentence "Jump."

Instructor: Notice that the word *you* is written inside parentheses. This shows us that although the word *you* is not actually written in the sentence, it is still understood to be the subject. Read the command sentences in **Exercise 3**. Although these sentences do not have a subject that is written, the subject is understood to be *you*.

Workbook: Study ancient history.

Wash the dishes!

Instructor: Now we will diagram the first sentence "Study ancient history," on the first empty frame in your workbook.

Instructor: What is the verb in the sentence?

Student: *Study*

Instructor: *Study* is the verb. Write the word *Study* on the verb line. Remember to capitalize *Study* because it is capitalized in the sentence.

Instructor: Now we will find the subject. Who should study? Remember, this word is not written in the command sentence, but it is understood to be the subject.

Student: *You*

Instructor: *You* is the subject. Write the word *you* on the subject line. Because the subject *you* is not written in the sentence but is just understood, you should put *you* in parentheses.

Instructor: Again, *study* is the action verb in this sentence. Is there a direct object that receives the action of the verb? I will ask you a question that will help you find the direct object. Answer me with **one** word. Study what?

Student: *History*

If the student says "ancient history," tell him that he needs to give you only **one** word: *history* (it doesn't make sense to say you studied "ancient"!).

Instructor: Write the direct object *history* to the right of the verb on your diagram. The direct object is separated from the verb by a short, straight line. Are there any words that describe the direct object *history*? This adjective can tell what kind, which one, how many, or whose.

Student: *Ancient*

Instructor: *Ancient* is an adjective that tells what kind of history it is. Write the word *ancient* on the slanted line beneath *history*. Now your diagram is complete.

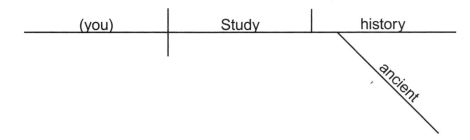

Instructor: Let's diagram the second sentence "Wash the dishes!" onto the next empty frame.

Instructor: What is the verb in the sentence?

Student: *Wash*

Instructor: *Wash* is the verb. Write the word *Wash* on the verb line. Remember to capitalize *Wash* because it is capitalized in the sentence. Now find the subject. Who should wash? Remember, this word is not written in the command sentence, but it is understood to be the subject.

Student: *You*

Instructor: *You* is the subject. Write the word *you* on the subject line. Because the subject *you* is not written in the sentence but is just understood, you should put *you* in parentheses.

Instructor: Again, *wash* is the action verb in this sentence. Is there a direct object that receives the action of the verb? I will ask you a question that will help you find the direct object. Answer me with **one** word. Wash what?

Student: *Dishes*

Instructor: Write the direct object *dishes* to the right of the verb on your diagram. The direct object is separated from the verb by a short, straight line. Are there any words that describe the direct object *dishes*? This word is an article (*a, an, the*).

Student: *The*

Instructor: *The* is an article. It is also an adjective that describes *dishes*. Write the word *the* on the slanted line beneath *dishes*. Now your diagram is complete.

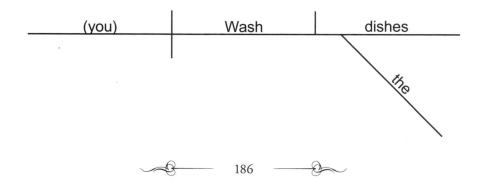

Instructor: Read the sentences in **Exercise 4** and look at their diagrams. The first sentence is a statement; the second sentence is a command.

Workbook: 1. Fred walked briskly.

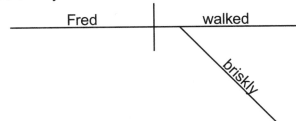

Workbook: 2. Walk briskly.

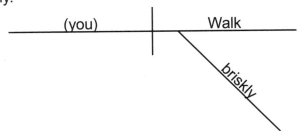

Instructor: In the statement sentence "Fred walked briskly," the subject *Fred* is written in the sentence. You would just copy his name onto the subject line of the diagram. In the command sentence "Walk briskly," the subject is not in the sentence, but it is understood to be the word *you*. That is why you put the word *you* in parentheses on the diagram. Now in **Exercises 5** through **8** you will diagram some pairs of statement sentences and command sentences. Remember, the subject of a command sentences is **always** the word *you*. You read each sentence. I will ask you questions as you fill in the diagram. Remember to copy the words exactly as they appear in the sentence. If the words begin with a capital letter in the sentence, they should also be capitalized in the diagram.

Workbook: Exercise 5

Peg runs fast.   (Ask questions 1a, 2a, and 7)
Run fast.   (Ask questions 1a, 2b, and 7)

Workbook: Exercise 6

Ray eats juicy pears.   (Ask questions 1a, 2a, 4, and 6)
Eat juicy pears.   (Ask questions 1a, 2b, 4, and 6)

Workbook: Exercise 7

Jane is polite.   (Ask questions 1b, 2a, and 3)
Be polite.   (Ask questions 1b, 2b, and 3)

Workbook: Exercise 8

Brad breaks the ice.   (Ask questions 1a, 2a, 4, and 6)
Break the ice.   (Ask questions 1a, 2b, 4, and 6)

Use the following dialogue in italics to help the student fill in each diagram in **Exercises 5** through **8**. After the student reads a sentence, you will prompt him with the questions in italics listed across from that sentence (for example, *Ask questions 1a, 2a, and 7*).

1a. *What is the verb? Write the verb to the right of your center line.*

1b. *What is the linking verb? This verb links the subject to a word in the complete predicate. Write the verb to the right of your center line.*

2a. *Find the subject. Ask "who" or "what" before the verb. [Prompt the student with a specific question like "Who runs?" or "Who eats?"] Write the subject to the left of the center line on your frame.*

2b. *Find the subject. Ask "who" or "what" before the verb. [Prompt the student with a specific question like "Who should run?" or "Who should eat?" or "Who should be?"] In a command sentence, the subject is understood to be the word <u>you</u>. Write the subject to the left of the center line on your frame. Remember to put <u>you</u> in parentheses.*

3. *This sentence contains a predicate adjective. This adjective is in the complete predicate of the sentence, but it describes the subject. A predicate adjective can tell what kind, which one, how many, or whose. Can you find an adjective in the complete predicate that describes the subject? Because the predicate adjective follows the verb in the sentence, it is written to the right of the verb on the diagram. Write the predicate adjective to the right of the slanted line on your diagram. That slanted line points back toward the subject to remind you that a predicate adjective describes the subject.*

4. *Is there a direct object that receives the action of the verb? I will ask you a question that will help you find the direct object.*

   Exercise 6: *Eats what?*

   Exercise 8: *Breaks what?*

   Write the direct object to the right of the verb on your diagram. The direct object is separated from the verb by a short, straight line.

5. *Go back and look again at the simple subject. Are there any words in the complete subject that describe the simple subject? These adjectives can tell what kind, which one, how many, or whose. Also look for the articles (<u>a</u>, <u>an</u>, <u>the</u>), because they act like adjectives. Write each adjective on a slanted line below the subject it describes.*

6. *Look again at the direct object. Are there any words that describe the direct object? These adjectives can tell what kind, which one, how many, or whose. Also look for the articles (<u>a</u>, <u>an</u>, <u>the</u>), because they act like adjectives. Write each adjective on a slanted line below the direct object it describes.*

7. *Look again at the verb. Is there a word that describes the verb? This is an adverb that could tell how, when, where, or how often. Write the adverb on the slanted line below the verb it describes.*

Answer Key:

Exercise 5

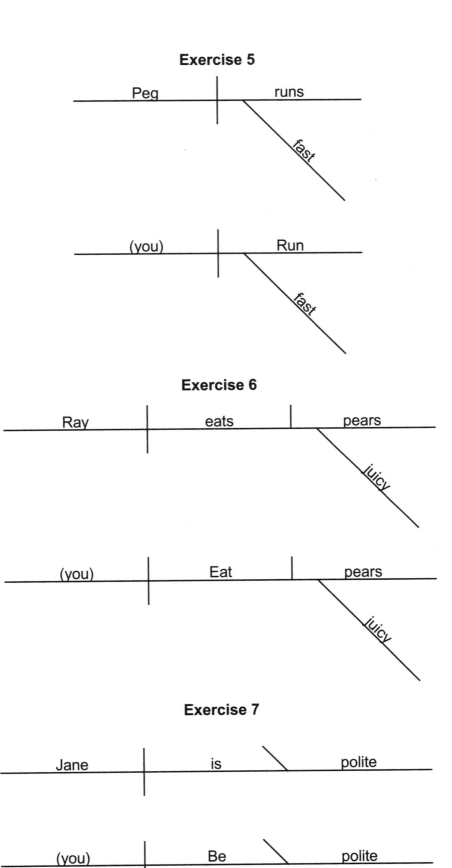

Exercise 6

Exercise 7

Exercise 8

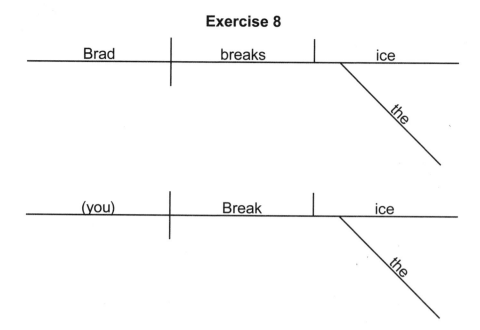

Optional Follow-Up

The student may diagram more complicated statements. Just as you did in the lesson, ask the questions beside each sentence.

Workbook: 1. Giant plows pushed heavy snowdrifts aside.

(Ask questions 1a, 2a, 4, 5, 6, and 7)

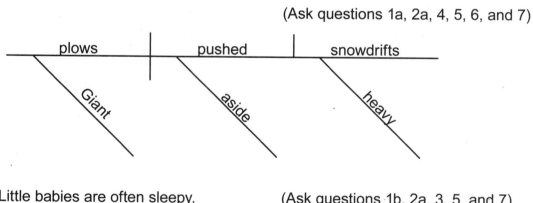

Workbook: 2. Little babies are often sleepy. (Ask questions 1b, 2a, 3, 5, and 7)

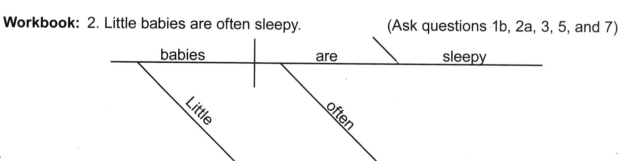

LESSON 43

Cumulative Poem Review

Instructor: Today you are going to review the poems you have memorized so far. When you recite a poem, you begin with the title and author. I will give you the title and author for each poem. Say the title and the author back to me, and then recite the poem. Remember to stand up straight! Don't fidget while you're reciting! And speak in a nice, loud, slow voice.

You may prompt the student as necessary. If the student repeats the poem accurately, he may check the box in his workbook and move on to the next poem. If he stumbles, ask him to repeat the line he cannot remember three times.

Lesson	Poem	Author
9	"The Land of Nod"	Robert Louis Stevenson
18	"A Tragic Story"	William Makepeace Thackeray
31	"I Wandered Lonely As a Cloud"	William Wordsworth

LESSON 44

New: **Questions (with Diagramming)**

Instructor: You already know that every sentence has two parts: a subject and a verb. Today you will learn that in some sentences, the subject is not at the beginning of the sentence; it is in the middle! Read the question sentence in **Exercise 1** of your workbook.

Workbook: Are they sitting?

Instructor: In order to find the subject of a question sentence, it is helpful to rearrange the words in the question so that it becomes a statement. In **Exercise 2**, read the question sentence again, and then read the statement sentence beneath it.

Workbook: Are they sitting?

They are sitting.

Instructor: Each of these sentences has a helping verb and an action verb. What are the two verbs that work together in these sentences?

Student: *Are sitting*

Instructor: *Are sitting* are the two verbs in both the question and the statement sentences. Now find the subject. Who are sitting?

Student: *They*

Instructor: *They* is the subject of both the question and the statement sentences. In **Exercise 3**, read another question sentence.

Workbook: Can snakes swim?

Instructor: Let's rearrange the words in the question sentence so that we have a statement sentence. In **Exercise 4**, read the question sentence again, and then read the statement sentence beneath it.

Workbook: Can snakes swim?

Snakes can swim.

Instructor: Each of these sentences has a helping verb and an action verb. What are the two verbs that work together in these sentences?

Student: *Can swim*

Instructor: *Can swim* are the two verbs in both the question and the statement sentences. Now find the subject. What can swim?

Student: *Snakes*

Instructor: *Snakes* is the subject of both the question and the statement sentences. In **Exercise 5**, we will practice rearranging more question sentences so that they become statement sentences. Read each question, and then say it as a statement. I will help you if you need it.

Answer Key:

1. Will Colin run?	(Colin will run.)
2. May I play?	(I may play.)
3. Could they clean?	(They could clean.)
4. Do whales sing?	(Whales do sing.)
5. Does ice float?	(Ice does float.)

Instructor: To diagram a question sentence, you must first turn it into a statement. In **Exercise 6** you will fill in the diagram for each question. Remember to copy the words exactly as they appear in the sentence. If the words begin with a capital letter in the sentence, they should also be capitalized in the diagram. Remember, punctuation marks are not put on diagrams.

	Question	**Statement (for Instructor's use)**
Workbook:	1. Will Colin run?	(Colin will run.)
	2. May I play?	(I may play.)
	3. Could they clean?	(They could clean.)
	4. Do whales sing?	(Whales do sing.)
	5. Does ice float?	(Ice does float.)

Use the following dialogue to help the student fill in the diagrams:

---

1. *Before you diagram a question sentence, you need to rearrange the words to make a statement sentence. What is the statement? [The student may need to write down the statement on the long line after each question in his workbook.]*

2. *Find the verb. There are two verbs in this sentence. What is the helping verb? What is the action verb? You write both these verbs on your verb line.*

3. *Now find the subject. Ask "who" or "what" before the verb. [Prompt the student with a specific question like "Who will run?" or "Who may play?"] Write the subject to the left of the center line on your frame.*

Answer Key:

Colin	Will run
I	May play
they	Could clean
whales	Do sing
ice	Does float

Optional Follow-Up

Play the "May I?" game to practice commands, questions, and statements. The instructor stands at one end of the room, opposite the student and at least one other person. The instructor tells one person to do something (for example, "Touch your toes."). The person must ask, "May I touch my toes?" Then the instructor replies, "Yes, you may." Then the student must repeat the question as a statement, "I may touch my toes." Once he has touched his toes, he may take a step toward the instructor. If the student does not ask "May I touch my toes?" before he does the action, he doesn't get to do the action or take a step forward. Each student takes a turn. The first person to get to the instructor wins (and he may be the instructor for the next game).

Here is a sample script:

Instructor: Wave at me.

Student: *May I wave at you?*

Instructor: Yes, you may.

Student: *I may wave at you. [student waves]*
[student takes a step forward]

Some other commands include: cover your ears, close one eye, do two jumping jacks, wiggle your tongue, smack your lips.

LESSON 45

Review: Four Types of Sentences

Instructor: In this lesson you are going to diagram the four types of sentences. Let's begin by saying the definition of a sentence. A sentence is a group of words that expresses a complete thought. All sentences begin with a capital letter and end with a punctuation mark. Say that with me.

Together: A sentence is a group of words that expresses a complete thought. All sentences begin with a capital letter and end with a punctuation mark.

Instructor: There are four different types of sentences: statements, commands, questions, and exclamations. A statement gives information. In **Exercise 1** of your workbook, read the statement sentence.

Workbook: I ate spinach earlier.

Instructor: This is a statement: "I ate spinach earlier." It gives information. Statements always end with a period. Let's diagram the sentence onto the empty frame in **Exercise 1** of your workbook. I will help you by asking questions and giving commands!

Instructor: What is the verb?

Student: *Ate*

Instructor: *Ate* is your verb. Write the verb on the verb line. Now find the subject. Who ate?

Student: *I*

Instructor: *I* is the subject. Write the subject to the left of the center line on your frame.

Instructor: Look again at the verb *ate*. Is there a direct object that receives the action of the verb? I will ask you a question that will help you find the direct object. Ate what?

Student: *Spinach*

Instructor: *Spinach* is the direct object. Write the direct object to the right of the verb on your diagram. The direct object is separated from the verb by a short, straight line.

Instructor: Look at the verb one more time. Is there a word that describes the verb? This is an adverb that tells **when** you ate.

Student: *Earlier*

Instructor: Write the adverb *earlier* on the slanted line below the verb it describes. Now your diagram is complete.

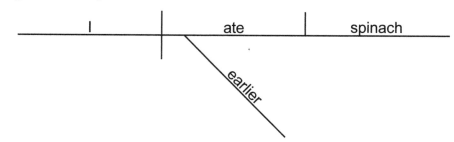

Instructor: The second type of sentence is a command. A command gives an order or makes a request. It ends with either a period or an exclamation point. In **Exercise 2**, read the command sentence.

Workbook: Pass the cheese sauce.

Instructor: Now I will help you diagram this sentence onto the empty frame in **Exercise 2** of your workbook. What is the verb?

Student: *Pass*

Instructor: *Pass* is the verb. Write the word *Pass* on the verb line. Remember to capitalize *Pass* because it is capitalized in the sentence. Now find the subject. Remember, command sentences do have a subject, but the subject is not written in the sentence. It is understood to be the word *you*. Someone is telling you to pass the cheese sauce. She does not command you by saying "You pass the cheese sauce;" she simply says "Pass the cheese sauce." So, again, what is the subject of this command sentence? Who should pass the cheese sauce?

Student: *You*

Instructor: *You* is the subject. Write the word *you* on the subject line. Because the subject *you* is not written in the sentence but is just understood, put *you* in parentheses.

Instructor: Look again at the verb *pass*. Is there a direct object that receives the action of the verb? I will ask you a question that will help you find the direct object. Answer me with one word. Pass what?

Student: *Sauce*

If the student answers "cheese," ask him to read the command sentence again. Say "Now are you asking someone to pass blocks of cheese? Or are you asking someone to pass a sauce? *Sauce* is the direct object."

Instructor: Write the direct object *sauce* to the right of the verb on your diagram. The direct object is separated from the verb by a short, straight line. Are there any words that describe the direct object *sauce*? There are two in this sentence. First, find the article (*a, an, the*).

Student: *The*

Instructor: *The* is an article that acts like an adjective that describes *sauce*. Write the word *the* on the first slanted line beneath *sauce*.

Instructor: Look again at the direct object *sauce*. Are there any other words besides the article *the* that describe the direct object? This adjective tells what kind of sauce it is.

Student: *Cheese*

Instructor: Write the adjective *cheese* on the second slanted line below the direct object *sauce*. *The* is written on the first adjective line and *cheese* is written on the second adjective line because that is the order in which they appear in the sentence. Your diagram is complete.

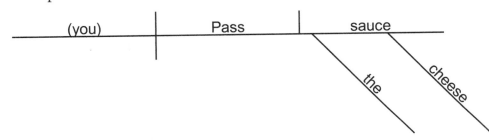

Instructor: The third type of sentence is a question. A question asks something. A question always ends with a question mark. In **Exercise 3**, read the question.

Workbook: Do you cook broccoli?

Instructor: Now I will help you diagram this sentence.

Instructor: In order to find the subject of a question sentence, it is helpful to rearrange the words in the question so that it becomes a statement. Read the question in **Exercise 3** again, and then read the statement beneath it.

Workbook: Do you cook broccoli?

  You do cook broccoli.

Instructor: Now diagram this sentence on the empty frame in **Exercise 3** of your workbook. There are two verbs in this sentence: a helping verb and an action verb. What are those verbs?

Student: *Do cook*

Instructor: Write both of these verbs on your verb line. Remember to capitalize *Do* on the diagram because it is capitalized in the sentence. What is the subject of the question "Do you cook broccoli?" Think of the statement "You do cook broccoli." Who cooks broccoli?

Student: *You.*

Instructor: Look again at *do cook*. Is there a direct object that receives the action of the verb? I will ask you a question that will help you find the direct object. Do cook **what**?

Student: *Broccoli*

Instructor: Write the direct object *broccoli* to the right of the verb on your diagram. The direct object is separated from the verb by a short, straight line. Now your diagram is complete.

Remind the student that he is not to put punctuation on the diagram.

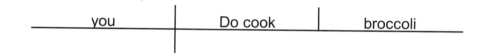

Instructor: The fourth type of sentence is an exclamation. An exclamation shows sudden or strong feeling. An exclamation always ends with an exclamation point. In **Exercise 4**, read the exclamation sentence. Read it with lots of expression because exclamations show strong feeling!

Workbook: Grandpa's chili is hot!

Instructor: Diagramming an exclamation sentence is just like diagramming a statement. I will help you diagram the sentence "Grandpa's chili is hot!" onto the empty frame in **Exercise 4**.

Instructor: What is the linking verb in this sentence?

Student: *Is*

Instructor: The verb *is* links the subject to a word in the complete predicate. Write the verb to the right of your center line. Now find the subject. Answer me with one word. **What** is?

Student: *Chili*

Instructor: Write the word *chili* on the subject line.

Instructor: This sentence contains a predicate adjective. This adjective is in the complete predicate of the sentence, but it describes the subject. What kind of chili is it?

Student: *Hot*

Instructor: Because the predicate adjective *hot* follows the verb in the sentence, it is written to the right of the verb on the diagram. Write the predicate adjective to the right of the slanted line on your diagram. That slanted line points back toward the subject to remind you that a predicate adjective describes the subject.

Instructor: Go back and look again at the subject. Are there any words in the complete subject that describe the simple subject? This adjective tells whose chili it is.

Student: *Grandpa's*

Instructor: Write the adjective *Grandpa's* on a slanted line below the subject it describes. Now your diagram is complete.

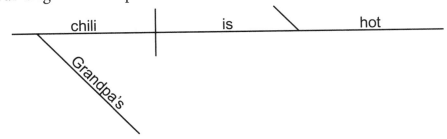

Optional Follow-Up

The student will need a large sheet of paper and colored pencils (green, blue, red, and purple) for this activity. Read the following directions to the student.

1. Draw a large square and divide it into four parts (four squares of equal size).

2. Write the word "Statement" in green at the top of the upper left-hand square.

3. Write the word "Command" in blue at the top of the upper right-hand square.

4. Write the word "Question" in red at the top of the bottom left-hand square.

5. Write the word "Exclamation" in purple at the top of the bottom right-hand square.

6. In the square labeled "Statement," draw the punctuation mark that always follows a statement sentence (*a period*). Use the green pencil.

7. In the square labeled "Command," draw the two marks of punctuation that may follow a command sentence (*a period and an exclamation point*). Use the blue pencil.

(This Optional Follow-Up continues on the next page.)

Optional Follow-Up (continued)

8. In the square labeled "Question," draw the punctuation mark that always follows a question sentence (*a question mark*). Use the red pencil.

9. In the square labeled "Exclamation," draw the punctuation mark that always follows an exclamation sentence (*an exclamation point*). Use the purple pencil.

10. Listen to this sentence: "Who are you?" Write this sentence inside the box that tells what type of sentence it is (*the Question box*). You may use a regular or colored pencil.

11. Listen to this sentence: "I stubbed my toe!" Write this sentence inside the box that tells what type of sentence it is (*the Exclamation box*).

12. Listen to this sentence: "I like to play." Write this sentence inside the box that tells what type of sentence it is (*the Statement box*).

13. Listen to this sentence: "Stop that now!" Write this sentence inside the box that tells what type of sentence it is (*the Command box*).

LESSON 46

Poem Memorization: "A Time to Talk"

Instructor: In Lesson 46 of your workbook, you will find a poem about a man who decides to stop his farm work to talk with his friend. Follow along as I read the poem to you. Before I begin reading, you should know when the friend slows his horse to a **meaning** walk, he is slowing down his horse on purpose. You should also know that when you plod, you walk slowly.

A Time to Talk

by Robert Frost

When a friend calls to me from the road

And slows his horse to a meaning walk,

I don't stand still and look around

On all the hills I haven't hoed,

And shout from where I am, What is it?

No, not as there is a time to talk.

I thrust my hoe in the mellow ground,

Blade-end up and five feet tall,

And plod: I go up to the stone wall

For a friendly visit.

Discuss the poem with the student. Can he picture the scene the poet is describing? Ask:

Instructor: What does the friend do?

Student: *The friend slows his horse.*

Instructor: What is the other person in the poem doing?

Student: *He is hoeing the ground.*

Instructor: Since there is time to talk, what does the person hoeing decide to do?

Student: *He stops to visit.*

Read the poem to the student three times in a row. Repeat this triple reading twice more during the day. Have the student check the boxes in his workbook when this is done.

Dictation Exercise

Dictation: I thrust my hoe in the mellow ground.

I go up to the stone wall for a friendly visit.

Optional Follow-Up

Have the student draw a picture to illustrate the poem. He should be sure to include the farmer with his hoe, the stone wall, and his friend on horseback. (The blade of the hoe is in the air; the handle is thrust in the mellow ground.)

LESSON 47

Review: Four Kinds of Verbs

Review: Direct Objects, Predicate Nominatives, and Predicate Adjectives

---

Read "A Time to Talk" (Lesson 46) three times to the student. Then ask the student to try to say parts of the poem along with you (or the tape recorder).

Instructor: Let's begin by saying the definition of a verb. A verb is a word that does an action, shows a state of being, links two words together, or helps another verb. Say that with me two times.

Together (two times): A verb is a word that does an action, shows a state of being, links two words together, or helps another verb.

Instructor: Action verbs show action. *Hit, run,* and *sing* are all action verbs. Action verbs are sometimes followed by a direct object that receives the action of the verb. Now you will find the direct objects in a few sentences. Look at **Exercise 1** in your workbook. After you read each sentence, I will help you find the direct object by asking you "what" or "whom" after the verb.

Workbook: Barb shook the blanket.

Instructor: Shook **what?**

Student: *Blanket*

Instructor: *Blanket* is the direct object. It receives the action of the verb *shook.* Write "d.o." for direct object over the word *blanket.* Read the next sentence.

Workbook: Cory forgave Greta.

Instructor: Forgave **whom?**

Student: *Greta*

Instructor: *Greta* is the direct object. It receives the action of the verb *forgave.* Write "d.o." for direct object over the word *Greta.* Read the third sentence.

Workbook: Pedro licked a lollipop.

Instructor: Licked **what?**

Student: *Lollipop*

Instructor: *Lollipop* is the direct object. It receives the action of the verb *licked*. Write "d.o." for direct object over the word *lollipop*. Look at the diagram of the sentence you just read, "Pedro licked a lollipop."

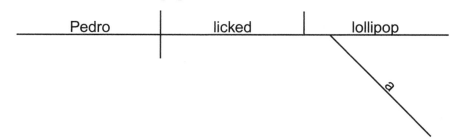

Instructor: The direct object *lollipop* is written next to the verb *licked*. It is divided from the verb by a short line.

Instructor: Helping verbs are another kind of verb. They help other verbs. Chant the first part of the list of helping verbs with me.

Together: Am [clap]
Is [clap]
Are, was, were. [clap]
Be [clap]
Being [clap]
Been. [clap] [clap]

Instructor: Now let's chant the rest of the helping verbs together.

Together: Have, has, had [clap]
Do, does, did [clap]
Shall, will, should, would, may, might, must [clap, clap]
Can, could!

Instructor: Read the sentences in **Exercise 2**. The helping verbs are in bold print. Each helping verb helps the action verb in the sentence make sense by showing time.

Workbook: Birds **will** chirp.

A flower **has** bloomed.

Bees **have** built a hive.

Instructor: Another type of verb, a state of being verb, just shows that you exist. Let's chant the state of being verbs together. This is same chant as the first part of the helping verb chant.

Together: Am [clap]
Is [clap]
Are, was, were. [clap]
Be [clap]
Being [clap]
Been. [clap] [clap]

Instructor: In **Exercise 3**, read the sentences with state of being verbs. The state of being verb is printed in bold.

Workbook: I **am**.

He **was** here.

Our parents **were** in the kitchen, too.

Instructor: State of being verbs don't show action or help other verbs—they just show that someone or something exists. There is one more type of verb: linking verbs. Linking verbs link, or join, two words together. These verbs are easy to recognize because they are the same verbs as the state of being verbs: *am, is, are, was, were, be, being, been*. These verbs can do three of the four things in your verb definition! Read aloud in **Exercise 4** of your workbook.

Workbook: The verbs *am*, *is*, *are*, *was, were*, *be*, *being*, *been* can either

- help another verb
- show a state of being
- link two words together

Instructor: So if you see the verb *am* in a sentence, you have to read the whole sentence to tell what kind of verb it is. Read aloud the first sentence in **Exercise 5**.

Workbook: I am singing.

Instructor: *Am* is a helping verb in that sentence. *Am* helps the verb *singing*. Read the next sentence.

Workbook: I am.

Instructor: The verb *am* just shows that someone exists. *Am* is a state of being verb in that sentence. Read the next sentence.

Workbook: I am happy.

Instructor: *Am* is a linking verb in that sentence. It links the subject *I* with the predicate adjective *happy*. Let's use some linking verbs in sentences. I will read you a noun and a linking verb and let you complete the sentence by choosing a predicate adjective that describes the subject. Write the word in the blank in your workbook. The linking verb in bold print will link, or connect, the subject noun with the adjective you choose. Follow along as I read and point to the parts of the sentences in **Exercise 6**. The first sentence is about fleece. You may have a jacket or a blanket made out of this fabric. Can you tell me what a fleece blanket or jacket feels like? Tell me your answer and write it in the blank.

Workbook: Fleece **is** _____.

Student: *Fleece is soft [or fuzzy, or warm].*

Instructor: The linking verb *is* connects the subject *Fleece* with the adjective *[the word the student chose]*! Can you tell me something about gorillas that describe the way they look? Tell me your answer and write it in the blank.

Workbook: Gorillas **are** _____.

Student: *Gorillas are [black, furry, huge].*

Instructor: The linking verb *are* connects the subject *Gorillas* with the adjective *[the word student chose]*. How did the macaroni taste? Tell me your answer and write it in the blank.

Workbook: The macaroni **was** _____.

Student: *The macaroni was [good, cheesy, creamy, hot].*

Instructor: The linking verb *was* connects the subject *macaroni* with the adjective *[the word student chose]*. Let's say the chant of the linking verbs. I will do the chant first, and you will join me the second time through.

Instructor, then together:
Am [clap]
Is [clap]
Are, was, were. [clap]
Be [clap]
Being [clap]
Been. [clap] [clap]

Instructor: Read the sentence in **Exercise 7** and look its diagram. This sentence contains a linking verb. I will point out words on the diagram as I explain.

Workbook: Dancers are graceful.

| Dancers | are \ graceful |

In order to keep the student's eyes focused on what you are explaining, physically point out the words and lines on the student's diagram as they appear in the following two paragraphs of the instructor's script.

Instructor: The linking verb *are* connects the subject of the sentence, *Dancers*, with the adjective *graceful*. *Graceful* is an adjective that describes the subject *Dancers*. It is written to the right of the verb on the diagram because it follows the verb in the sentence. Because the adjective is in the complete predicate of the sentence, it is a **predicate** adjective. On the diagram, draw an arrow from the predicate adjective *graceful* that points back to the subject *Dancers*.

Instructor: Remember, the complete predicate is the verb and all the words attached to the verb line on a diagram. These words tell us what is said about the subject. Do you see the slanted line on the diagram that separates the linking verb *are* from the predicate adjective? That slanted line points back toward the subject to remind you that *graceful* is an adjective that describes *Dancers*.

Instructor: Linking verbs can also link the subject with a noun or pronoun in the complete predicate that renames the subject. In **Exercise 8**, circle the sentence that correctly answers this question: Are you a boy or a girl?

Student: *I am a boy. OR I am a girl.*

Instructor: The linking verb *am* connects the subject *I* with a noun that renames the subject. *[Boy or Girl]* tells what the subject is. What are you? A *[boy or girl]*. *[Boy or Girl]* is in the complete predicate of the sentence. A noun or pronoun in the complete predicate that renames the subject is called a predicate nominative. Circle the predicate nominative in the sentence. Read the sentence in **Exercise 9** to me and look at its diagram.

Workbook: Orlando is a city.

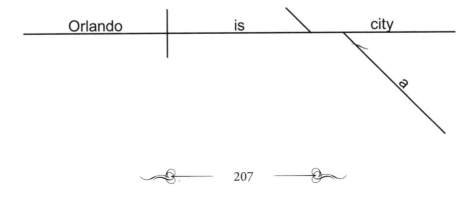

Instructor: *Is* is a linking verb. It connects the subject *Orlando* with a noun that renames the subject. *City* tells what the subject is. What is Orlando? A city. *City* is in the complete predicate of the sentence. A noun or pronoun in the complete predicate that renames the subject is called a **predicate nominative**. Even though *city* renames the subject *Orlando*, it is written to the right of the verb on the diagram because it follows the verb in the sentence. On the diagram, draw an arrow from the predicate nominative *city* that points back to the subject *Orlando*.

Instructor: Look again at the diagram. Do you see the slanted line that separates the linking verb *is* from the predicate nominative *city*? That slanted line points back toward the subject to remind you that *city* is a predicate nominative that renames the subject *Orlando*.

Dictation Exercise

After the student has written each sentence, have him circle the linking verb.

Dictation: The beetle (was) shiny.

The milkshake (is) frothy.

Optional Follow-Up

Instructor: I will read the following Mother Goose rhyme to you. Each line contains the linking verb *is* and has three predicate adjectives.

Explain to the student that a *bower* is a shelter in a garden made of trees or vines.

Spring is showery, flowery, bowery;

Summer is hoppy, croppy, poppy;

Autumn is wheezy, sneezy, freezy;

Winter is slippy, drippy, nippy.

Instructor: Look at the first line. What adjectives describe the noun *Spring*?

Student: *showery, flowery, bowery*

Instructor: Because *showery*, *flowery*, and *bowery* are located in the complete predicate of the sentence, we call these words **predicate** adjectives. The linking verb *is* links the subject, *Spring*, with the predicate adjectives, *showery*, *flowery*, and *bowery*.

Have the student find the subject noun, linking verb, and predicate adjectives in each line of the rest of the poem.

LESSON 48

New: **Prepositions**

You will need a pillow and a blanket for this lesson. Do this lesson in a room with a sofa. If you do not have a sofa, substitute the word *bed* for the word *sofa* in the explanation. In a classroom situation, have one child lie on the floor in the front of the classroom while the other students observe.

Read "A Time to Talk" (Lesson 46) three times to the student. Then ask the student to try to say parts of the poem along with you (or the tape recorder).

This lesson assumes that the student memorized the list of prepositions in *First Language Lessons, Levels 1 and 2*. If the student did not use that book, he will now start memorizing a long list of prepositions. The student will find a memorized list of prepositions invaluable when he analyzes sentences, because the object of a preposition is never the subject, direct object, or indirect object. The student will learn the definition of a preposition as well, but learning the definition is not enough. He should also memorize the list, since not all prepositions follow the definition exactly.

Instructor: This lesson is about the part of speech called a preposition. I will say the entire definition to you: A preposition is a word that shows the relationship of a noun or pronoun to another word in the sentence. Now repeat after me: A preposition is a word that shows the relationship …

Student: *A preposition is a word that shows the relationship …*

Instructor: … of a noun or pronoun to another word in the sentence.

Student: *… of a noun or pronoun to another word in the sentence.*

Instructor: Let's say the entire definition together three times.

Together (three times): A preposition is a word that shows the relationship of a noun or pronoun to another word in the sentence.

Instructor: You have worked so hard on the definition that I think you need to take a break. Toss a pillow on the sofa (or bed). Now lie down on the sofa, and rest your head on the pillow. The pillow on the sofa is soft. I will say that again: The pillow on the sofa is soft. *On* is a preposition. It shows the relationship between *pillow* and *sofa*. Which pillow is soft? It is the one **on** the sofa. Now I will put a blanket over you so you will be comfy. The blanket over you is warm.

Instructor: I will say that again: *The blanket over you is warm. Over* is a preposition and it shows the relationship between *blanket* and *you*. Which blanket is warm? It is the one **over** you. Now sit next to me, and I will tell you the definition of a preposition one more time. A preposition is a word that shows the relationship of a noun or pronoun to another word in the sentence. In **Exercise 1** of your workbook, there is a list of common prepositions that you will begin to memorize. Let's read them together.

Prepositions

Aboard, about, above, across.
After, against, along, among, around, at.

Before, behind, below, beneath.
Beside, between, beyond, by.

Down, during, except, for, from.
In, inside, into, like.

Near, of, off, on, over.
Past, since, through, throughout.

To, toward, under, underneath.
Until, up, upon.
With, within, without.

Once you have read through the list together, the student may check the box in his workbook. The student should practice the list every day until he has memorized the entire list. Focus on memorizing the first section today (*aboard* through *at*).[1] Once the student can say the first section from memory, he may check it off in his workbook.

Instructor: In **Exercise 2**, read the first sentence to me.

Workbook: 1. The captain aboard the ship whistles.

As you read the following instructions, point to the words in the example sentence ("The captain …") to make the explanation clearer to the student. These words are italicized in the instructor's script. Do this for all of the example sentences in **Exercise 2**.

---

1. The audio companion CD to *First Language Lessons, Levels 1 and 2* is an excellent practice aid, because it contains a chanted version of the list as well as a preposition song. This CD is available from Peace Hill Press (peacehillpress.com).

Instructor: *Aboard* is a preposition. Circle it. It shows the relationship between the noun *captain* and the noun *ship*. Is the captain beside the ship, on the ship, below the ship, inside the ship, or over the ship? No, the captain is **aboard** the ship. Which captain whistles? The one aboard the ship. Read the second sentence to me, and then tell me the preposition. You may look at the list of prepositions.

Workbook: 2. We read a story about bears.

Student: *About*

Instructor: *About* is a preposition. Circle it. It shows the relationship between the noun *story* and the noun *bears*. Which story is it? Answer me beginning with "It is the story …"

Student: *It is the story about bears.*

Instructor: Read the third sentence to me, and then say the preposition as you circle it.

Workbook: 3. The shelf above the desk holds books.

Student: *Above*

Instructor: *Above* is a preposition. It shows the relationship between the noun *shelf* and the noun *desk*. Which shelf is it? Answer me beginning with "It is the shelf …"

Student: *It is the shelf above the desk.*

Instructor: Read the fourth sentence to me, and then say the preposition as you circle it.

Workbook: 4. The house across the street is white.

Student: *Across*

Instructor: *Across* is a preposition. It shows the relationship between the noun *house* and the noun *street*. Which house is it? Answer me beginning with "It is the house …"

Student: *It is the house across the street.*

Instructor: Read the fifth sentence to me, and then say the preposition as you circle it.

Workbook: 5. The day after tomorrow is my birthday.

Student: *After*

Instructor: *After* is a preposition. It shows the relationship between the noun *day* and the noun *tomorrow*. Which day is it? Answer me beginning with "It is the day …"

Student: *It is the day after tomorrow.*

Instructor: Read the sixth sentence to me, and then say the preposition as you circle it.

Workbook: 6. The rose against the fence is blooming.

Student: *Against*

Instructor: *Against* is a preposition. It shows the relationship between the noun *rose* and the noun *fence*. Which rose is it? Answer me beginning with "It is the rose …"

Student: *It is the rose against the fence.*

Instructor: Read the seventh sentence to me, and then say the preposition as you circle it.

Workbook: 7. The flowers along the road are yellow.

Student: *Along*

Instructor: *Along* is a preposition. It shows the relationship between the noun *flowers* and the noun *road*. Which flowers are they? Answer me beginning with "They are the flowers …"

Student: *They are the flowers along the road.*

Instructor: Read the eighth sentence to me, and then say the preposition as you circle it.

Workbook: 8. The clowns among the crowd made people laugh.

Student: *Among*

Instructor: *Among* is a preposition. It shows the relationship between the noun *clowns* and the noun *crowd*. Which clowns are they? Answer me beginning with "They are the clowns …"

Student: *They are the clowns among the crowd.*

Instructor: Read the ninth sentence to me, and then say the preposition as you circle it.

Workbook: 9. The store around the corner is huge.

Student: *Around*

Instructor: *Around* is a preposition. It shows the relationship between the noun *store* and the noun *corner*. Which store is it? Answer me beginning with "It is the store …"

Student: *It is the store around the corner.*

Instructor: Read the tenth sentence to me, and then say the preposition as you circle it.

Workbook: 10. The man at the door delivered a package.

Student: *At*

Instructor: *At* is a preposition. It shows the relationship between the noun *man* and the noun *door*. Which man is he? Answer me beginning with "He is the man …"

Student: *He is the man at the door.*

Instructor: We are going to learn more about prepositions in the next several lessons. There are a lot of prepositions to learn, and I want to make sure you really know them. Many, many sentences have prepositions in them. You use sentences with them everyday, and you probably don't even think about it: "I am **in** my room!" "The book is **on** the table." "May I play **after** my lesson?" "Can I go **with** you **to** the store?" All of these sentences have prepositions in them. So you see why it is important that we study prepositions. You can't ignore them—they're everywhere!

Dictation Exercise

After the student has written the sentences, have him circle the prepositions.

Dictation: We watched a movie about penguins.

The store across town sells sweets.

Optional Follow-Up

To aid the student in memorizing the list of prepositions, decide together on an action that is to be done as he says each group of lines. Here is an example:

Clap hands while saying:

Aboard, about, above, across.

After, against, along, among, around, at.

Touch toes while saying:

Before, behind, below, beneath.

Beside, between, beyond, by.

Turn around and around while saying:

Down, during, except, for, from.

In, inside, into, like.

Wave hands above head while saying:

Near, of, off, on, over.

Past, since, through, throughout.

Jump up and down while saying:

To, toward, under, underneath.

Until, up, upon.

With, within, without.

LESSON 49

New: **Prepositional Phrases**

Read "A Time to Talk" (Lesson 46) three times to the student. Then ask the student to try to say the whole poem with you (or the tape recorder). The student should practice saying the whole poem to himself in a mirror.

Several of the words in the preposition list can also be adverbs. For example, "She lagged **behind**," "The treasure lies **below**," or "I went **inside**." These same words function as prepositions when they are included in a prepositional phrase: "She lagged <u>behind the other runners</u>," "The treasure lies <u>below this chamber</u>," or "I went <u>inside the house</u>." This lesson focuses on the prepositional use of these words. Do not discuss the adverb use of these words with the student at this time.

Instructor: You learned about prepositions in the last lesson. A preposition is a word that shows the relationship of a noun or pronoun to another word in the sentence. Let's say that definition together three times.

Together (three times): A preposition is a word that shows the relationship of a noun or pronoun to another word in the sentence.

If the student knows the list of prepositions in **Exercise 1**, have him review it by saying it once. If he does not yet have the whole list memorized, focus on the second section today (*before* through *by*), and review the first section. The student may check off his accomplishments in the workbook.

Prepositions

Aboard, about, above, across.
After, against, along, among, around, at.

Before, behind, below, beneath.
Beside, between, beyond, by.

Down, during, except, for, from.
In, inside, into, like.

Near, of, off, on, over.
Past, since, through, throughout.

To, toward, under, underneath.
Until, up, upon.
With, within, without.

Instructor: Read the first sentence in **Exercise 2** to me.

Workbook: 1. The presents (before) her were wrapped beautifully.

Instructor: What is the preposition in the sentence?

Student: *Before*

Instructor: Circle *before*. The presents before whom? Before **her.** "Before her" is called a **prepositional phrase**. A prepositional phrase begins with a preposition and ends with a noun or pronoun. To find the prepositional phrase, ask *whom* or *what* after the preposition. Now read the second sentence to me.

Workbook: 2. The person (behind) me is last.

Instructor: What is the preposition in the sentence?

Student: *Behind*

Instructor: Circle *behind*. To find the prepositional phrase, ask *whom* or *what* after the preposition. Behind whom? Behind me. "Behind me" is the prepositional phrase. It begins with the preposition *behind* and ends with the pronoun *me*. Read the third sentence.

Workbook: 3. The magma (below) the surface is boiling hot.

Instructor: What is the preposition in the sentence?

Student: *Below*

Instructor: Circle *below*. To find the prepositional phrase, ask *whom* or *what* after the preposition. Below what? Below the surface. "Below the surface" is the prepositional phrase. It begins with the preposition *below* and ends with the noun *surface*. Now you try. Read the fourth sentence to me.

Workbook: 4. The fish (beneath) the water swim upstream.

Instructor: Circle *beneath*. To find the prepositional phrase, ask *whom* or *what* after the preposition. Beneath what? Answer me beginning with "Beneath …"

Student: *Beneath the water*

Instructor: "Beneath the water" is a prepositional phrase. It begins with the preposition *beneath* and ends with the noun *water*.

Instructor: I will ask you to read each of the sentences, numbers 5 through 8, and circle the preposition in each sentence. Then I will ask you to underline the prepositional phrase.

Prompt the student to identify the prepositional phrase by asking him *whom* or *what* after the preposition, just as you did in the examples above.

Workbook: 5. I answered the phone (beside) the bed.

6. We hiked the mountain (between) the rivers.

7. The Pacific Ocean is the ocean (beyond) California.

8. Jacob will pick up those shoes (by) the door.

Dictation Exercise

After he has written the sentences, have him circle the prepositions.

Dictation: I lay beside the stream.

Put the bookmark between the pages.

Answer Key:

I lay (beside) the stream.

Put the bookmark (between) the pages.

Optional Follow-Up

Fold a piece of paper in half. Then fold it in half again. Then fold it in half one more time. When the paper is unfolded, you should have eight squares. Write a prepositional phrase across the top of each square. You may choose:

- under the tree
- aboard a ship
- against the fence
- on the road
- above the clouds
- below the sea
- beside a skyscraper
- near a dinosaur

Then the student will read the phrase and draw a picture of a stick person in each of the settings. For example, in the box labeled "under the tree," the student draws a picture of a person standing under a tree.

LESSON 50

Review: **Prepositional Phrases**

Read "A Time to Talk" (Lesson 46) three times to the student. Then ask the student to say the poem along with you or the tape recorder. If the student is ready, he should recite the poem to real people today. If he is not, continue practicing daily until he is ready.

Instructor: A preposition is a word that shows the relationship of a noun or pronoun to another word in the sentence. Let's say that definition together three times.

Together (three times): A preposition is a word that shows the relationship of a noun or pronoun to another word in the sentence.

If the student knows the list of prepositions in **Exercise 1**, have him review it by saying it once. If he does not yet have the whole list memorized, focus on the third section today (*down* through *like*), and review the first and second sections. The student may check off his accomplishments in the workbook.

Prepositions

Aboard, about, above, across.
After, against, along, among, around, at.

Before, behind, below, beneath.
Beside, between, beyond, by.

Down, during, except, for, from.
In, inside, into, like.

Near, of, off, on, over.
Past, since, through, throughout.

To, toward, under, underneath.
Until, up, upon.
With, within, without.

Instructor: In **Exercise 2** of your workbook, read the first sentence to me:

Workbook: 1. The cabin down the stream had no heat.

Instructor: What is the preposition in the sentence?

Student: *Down*

Instructor: Circle *down*. The cabin down what? Down the stream. Underline "down the stream." "Down the stream" is called a **prepositional phrase**. A prepositional phrase begins with a preposition and ends with a noun or pronoun. To find the prepositional phrase, ask *whom or what* after the preposition. Now read the second sentence to me.

Workbook: 2. The blackout during the storm lasted three hours.

Instructor: What is the preposition?

Student: *During*

Instructor: Circle *during*. To find the prepositional phrase, ask *whom* or *what* after the preposition *during*. During what? Answer me beginning with "During …"

Student: *During the storm*

Instructor: "During the storm" is a prepositional phrase. Underline it. It begins with the preposition *during* and ends with the noun *storm*. Do you remember the definition of a preposition? A preposition is a word that shows the relationship of a noun or pronoun to another word in the sentence. The blackout during the storm lasted three hours. Which blackout is it? It is the blackout during the storm. The preposition *during* shows the relationship between the noun in the prepositional phrase, *storm*, and the word *blackout*. Read the third sentence aloud.

Workbook: 3. The whole family except the baby rode the rollercoaster.

Instructor: What is the preposition?

Student: *Except*

Instructor: Circle *except*. Now find the prepositional phrase. Ask *whom* or *what* after the preposition *except*. Except whom? Answer me beginning with "Except …"

Student: *Except the baby*

Instructor: "Except the baby" is the prepositional phrase. Underline it. Which family is it? Answer me beginning with "It is the whole family …"

Student: *It is the whole family except the baby.*

Instructor: Read the fourth sentence aloud.

Workbook: 4. My gift for you is a surprise.

Instructor: What is the preposition?

Student: *For*

Instructor: Circle *for*. Now find the prepositional phrase. Ask *whom* or *what* after the preposition *for*. For whom? Answer me beginning with "For ..."

Student: *For you*

Instructor: "For you" is the prepositional phrase. Underline it. Which gift is it? Answer me beginning with "It is my gift ..."

Student: *It is my gift for you.*

Instructor: I will ask you to read each of the sentences, 5 through 9, in your workbook, and circle the preposition in the sentence. Then I will ask you to underline the prepositional phrase.

Have the student read each numbered sentence. Then ask him the questions below each sentence. The student's correct response is written in italics.

Workbook: 5. The man ⬭from⬭ Idaho sells potatoes.

Instructor: What is the preposition?

Student: *From*

Instructor: What is the prepositional phrase?

Student: *From Idaho*

Workbook: 6. The woman ⬭in⬭ the black dress sang a solo.

Instructor: What is the preposition?

Student: *In*

Instructor: What is the prepositional phrase?

Student: *In the black dress*

Workbook: 7. The dishes ⬭inside⬭ the cabinet are fragile.

Instructor: What is the preposition?

Student: *Inside*

Instructor: What is the prepositional phrase?

Student: *Inside the cabinet*

Workbook: 8. The path into the woods was shady.

Instructor: What is the preposition?

Student: *Into*

Instructor: What is the prepositional phrase?

Student: *Into the woods*

Workbook: 9. A subject like arithmetic takes practice.

Instructor: What is the preposition?

Student: *Like*

Instructor: What is the prepositional phrase?

Student: *Like arithmetic*

Dictation Exercise

After he has written the sentences, have him circle the prepositions and then underline the prepositional phrases. You may choose to dictate only one sentence to the student.

Dictation: The road into the valley was narrow.

An instrument like the violin plays high notes.

Optional Follow-Up

Using ten index cards, write each of the prepositional phrases below (not the words in parentheses) on a card. The student tapes a prepositional phrase to an object (suggested objects are in the parentheses below) and places the object where the prepositional phrase indicates. For example, the student will tape "in a drawer" to a spoon, and then put the spoon in a drawer.

(spoon) in a drawer

(stuffed animal) under a pillow

(a picture or drawing) over the sofa

(napkin) beside the plate

(toys) inside a box

(pencil) on the table

(bookmark) between book pages

(piece of fruit or a canned good) near the refrigerator

(hat or cap) upon my head

LESSON 51

New: Object of the Preposition

Instructor: A preposition is a word that shows the relationship of a noun or pronoun to another word in the sentence. Let's say that definition together three times.

Together (three times): A preposition is a word that shows the relationship of a noun or pronoun to another word in the sentence.

If the student knows the list of prepositions in **Exercise 1**, have him review it by saying it once. If he does not yet have the whole list memorized, focus on the fourth section today (*near* through *throughout*), and review the first, second, and third sections. The student may check off his accomplishments in the workbook.

Prepositions

Aboard, about, above, across.
After, against, along, among, around, at.

Before, behind, below, beneath.
Beside, between, beyond, by.

Down, during, except, for, from.
In, inside, into, like.

Near, of, off, on, over.
Past, since, through, throughout.

To, toward, under, underneath.
Until, up, upon.
With, within, without.

Instructor: In **Exercise 2**, read the first sentence to me.

Workbook: 1. The lamp near the sofa is blue.

Instructor: What is the preposition in the sentence?

Student: *Near*

Instructor: Circle *near*. The lamp near what? Near the sofa. Underline *near the sofa*. "Near the sofa" is called a prepositional phrase. A prepositional phrase begins with a preposition and ends with a noun or pronoun. That noun or pronoun is called the **object of the preposition**. In the prepositional phrase "near the sofa," the object of the preposition is the noun *sofa*. Read the second sentence to me.

Workbook: 2. The capital (of)Virginia is Richmond.

Instructor: What is the preposition in the sentence?

Student: *Of*

Instructor: Circle *of*. Now find the prepositional phrase. Of what?

Student: *Of Virginia*

Instructor: Underline it. The prepositional phrase "of Virginia" begins with the preposition *of* and ends with the noun *Virginia*. The noun or pronoun that follows a preposition is called the object of the preposition. What is the object of the preposition in the prepositional phrase "of Virginia"?

Student: *Virginia*

Instructor: Read the third sentence to me.

Workbook: 3. The island (off)the coast is rocky.

Instructor: What is the preposition in the sentence?

Student: *Off*

Instructor: Circle *off*. Now find the prepositional phrase. Off what?

Student: *Off the coast*

Instructor: Underline it. The prepositional phrase "off the coast" begins with the preposition *off* and ends with the noun *coast*. The noun or pronoun that follows a preposition is called the object of the preposition. What is the object of the preposition in the prepositional phrase "off the coast"?

Student: *Coast*

Instructor: The object of the preposition is just a single word—a noun or pronoun. A prepositional **phrase** contains the preposition, the object of the preposition, and any words that describe it. Read the fourth sentence to me.

Workbook: 4. The pancake (on)the griddle burned.

Instructor: What is the preposition in the sentence?

Student: *On*

Instructor: Circle *on*. Now find the prepositional phrase. On what?

Student: *On the griddle*

Instructor: Underline it. The prepositional phrase "on the griddle" begins with the preposition *on* and ends with the noun *griddle*. The noun or pronoun that follows a preposition is called the object of the preposition. What is the object of the preposition in the prepositional phrase "on the griddle"?

Student: *Griddle*

Instructor: I will ask you to read each of the sentences, numbers 5 through 8, in your workbook. Then I will ask you to underline the prepositional phrase and circle the object of the preposition in that phrase.

Have the student read each numbered sentence. Then ask him the questions below each sentence. The student's correct response is written in italics.

Workbook: 5. The black clouds (over) the city were frightening.

Instructor: What is the preposition?

Student: *Over*

Instructor: What is the prepositional phrase?

Student: *Over the city*

Instructor: What is the object of the preposition?

Student: *City*

Workbook: 6. The town (past) Williamsburg is Yorktown.

Instructor: What is the preposition?

Student: *Past*

Instructor: What is the prepositional phrase?

Student: *Past Williamsburg*

Instructor: What is the object of the preposition?

Student: *Williamsburg*

In this book, we are only using prepositional phrases that act like adjectives. A prepositional phrase beginning with *since* can only function as an adverb phrase, as in "I have been napping since lunchtime." In order to find the object of the preposition, you need to ask "Since when?" The student will learn about these in later grades.

Workbook: 7. The breeze (through) the window was cool.

Instructor: What is the preposition?

Student: Through

Instructor: What is the prepositional phrase?

Student: Through the window

Instructor: What is the object of the preposition?

Student: Window

Workbook: 8. The paintings (throughout) the museum were expensive.

Instructor: What is the preposition?

Student: Throughout

Instructor: What is the prepositional phrase?

Student: Throughout the museum

Instructor: What is the object of the preposition?

Student: Museum

Dictation Exercise

After he has written the sentences, have him circle the prepositions and then underline the prepositional phrases.

Dictation: The cabin (near) the lake is perfect.

The lights (on) the tree twinkled.

Optional Follow-Up

Play "I Spy." Take turns guessing. Try to use these prepositional phrases:

I spy something …

>across the room
>
>against the wall
>
>behind you
>
>inside this room
>
>under the table
>
>between you and me
>
>underneath your foot
>
>with red on it

LESSON 52

Review: Object of the Preposition

Instructor: A preposition is a word that shows the relationship of a noun or pronoun to another word in the sentence. Let's say that definition together three times.

Together (three times): A preposition is a word that shows the relationship of a noun or pronoun to another word in the sentence.

If the student knows the list of prepositions in **Exercise 1**, have him review it by saying it once. If he does not yet have the whole list memorized, focus on the last section today (*to* through *without*), and review the previous sections. The student may check off his accomplishments in the workbook.

Prepositions

Aboard, about, above, across.
After, against, along, among, around, at.

Before, behind, below, beneath.
Beside, between, beyond, by.

Down, during, except, for, from.
In, inside, into, like.

Near, of, off, on, over.
Past, since, through, throughout.

To, toward, under, underneath.
Until, up, upon.
With, within, without.

Instructor: Read the first sentence in **Exercise 2** to me:

Workbook: 1. He lost the key to his car.

Instructor: What is the preposition in the sentence?

Student: *To*

Instructor: The key to what? To his car. Underline *to his car*, and circle the word "to." "To his car" is the prepositional phrase. A prepositional phrase begins with a preposition and ends with a noun or pronoun. That noun or pronoun is called the **object of the preposition**. In the prepositional phrase "to his car," the object of the preposition is the noun *car.*

Instructor: Now you have worked with prepositions so much, I think you are ready to find the preposition, object of the preposition, and prepositional phrase for yourself. I will ask you to read each of the sentences, numbers two through eight, in your workbook. You will circle the preposition, write "o.p." over the object of the preposition, and underline the whole prepositional phrase.

Workbook: 2. His attitude (toward) his sister was helpful.

Instructor: What is the preposition?

Student: Toward

Instructor: What is the object of the preposition?

Student: Sister

Instructor: What is the prepositional phrase?

Student: Toward his sister

Workbook: 3. The kitten (under) the house was scared.

Instructor: What is the preposition?

Student: Under

Instructor: What is the object of the preposition?

Student: House

Instructor: What is the prepositional phrase?

Student: Under the house

Workbook: 4. The suitcase underneath my bed is dusty.

Instructor: What is the preposition?

Student: Underneath

Instructor: What is the object of the preposition?

Student: Bed

Instructor: What is the prepositional phrase?

Student: Underneath my bed

In this book, we are only using prepositional phrases that act as adjectives. A prepositional phrase beginning with *until* can only function as an adverb phrase, as in "The snow will continue until Friday." In order to find the object of the preposition, you need to ask "Until when?" The student will learn about these in later grades.

---

o.p.

Workbook: 5. The community pool up the street is open.

Instructor: What is the preposition?

Student: Up

Instructor: What is the object of the preposition?

Student: Street

Instructor: What is the prepositional phrase?

Student: Up the street

o.p.

Workbook: 6. The frog upon the log croaked.

Instructor: What is the preposition?

Student: Upon

Instructor: What is the object of the preposition?

Student: Log

Instructor: What is the prepositional phrase?

Student: Upon the log

o.p.

Workbook: 7. The lizard (with) the slender tail was green.

Instructor: What is the preposition?

Student: With

Instructor: What is the object of the preposition?

Student: Tail

Instructor: What is the prepositional phrase?

Student: With the slender tail

o.p.

Workbook: 8. The hamster will nibble the food (within) the cage.

Instructor: What is the preposition?

Student: Within

Instructor: What is the object of the preposition?

Student: Cage

Instructor: What is the prepositional phrase?

Student: Within the cage

o.p.

Workbook: 9. I would like ice cream (without) chocolate sauce.

Instructor: What is the preposition?

Student: Without

Instructor: What is the object of the preposition?

Student: Sauce

Instructor: What is the prepositional phrase?

Student: Without chocolate sauce

Dictation Exercise

After he has written the sentences, have him circle the prepositions and then underline the prepositional phrases.

Dictation: The bugs underneath the rock are small and dark.

The man with the mask stole the gold.

Optional Follow-Up

Play "I Spy." Take turns guessing. Try to use these prepositional phrases:

I spy something …

above my head

beneath a piece of furniture

upon the table

beyond the door

beside me

among the books

along the wall

LESSON 53

Review: Prepositional Phrases

Begin this lesson by having the student recite the list of prepositions. Here it is for your reference:

Prepositions

Aboard, about, above, across.
After, against, along, among, around, at.

Before, behind, below, beneath.
Beside, between, beyond, by.

Down, during, except, for, from.
In, inside, into, like.

Near, of, off, on, over.
Past, since, through, throughout.

To, toward, under, underneath.
Until, up, upon.
With, within, without.

Instructor: You now know the list of prepositions, and how to find a prepositional phrase in a sentence. So what's next? You might think that you are going to diagram prepositional phrases in this lesson, because, after all, you have learned how to diagram every other part of speech. But you're not! You will learn how to diagram prepositional phrases eventually, but not in this book. Prepositions can describe almost anything in a sentence: They can describe a subject, a verb, a direct object, a predicate nominative … even the object of the preposition in another prepositional phrase! So you see, diagramming prepositional phrases can be tricky. But you **can** diagram all the other parts of a sentence. Today we are going to practice reading a sentence, finding the prepositional phrase, and getting rid of it so that you can diagram the rest of the sentence. Read the sentence in **Exercise 1**.

Workbook: I drive the car with the dent.

Instructor: Now find the preposition in the sentence (you may have to recite the list). Circle it.

Workbook: I drive the car with the dent.

Instructor: Now find the prepositional phrase. Remember, a prepositional phrase begins with a preposition and ends with a noun or pronoun (the object of the preposition). In order to find the prepositional phrase, ask *whom* or *what* after the preposition. I drive the car with the dent. With what? With the dent. "With the dent" is the prepositional phrase. Put a box around "with the dent."

Workbook: I drive the car ⟨with⟩ the dent.

Instructor: Now read the sentence aloud, but do **not** read the prepositional phrase in the box.

Student: *I drive the car.*

Instructor: "I drive the car" is an easy sentence to diagram. It has a subject, action verb, and a direct object. Look at the diagram of this sentence in **Exercise 1.**

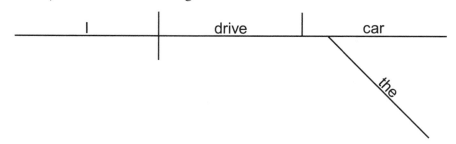

Instructor: Now you are going to diagram some sentences that, at first glance, look pretty complicated. But once you find the prepositional phrase and get rid of it, the rest of the sentence is easy to diagram.

Before the student diagrams each sentence in **Exercise 2**, he will circle each preposition and draw a box around the prepositional phrase to separate it from the rest of the sentence. Then, have the student read the sentence aloud **without reading the prepositional phrase**. That is the sentence he will diagram. Once he has done this, use the dialogue in italics to help the student fill in each diagram. Prompt him with the questions in italics listed across from that sentence (for example, *Ask questions 1a, 2, 4, and 6*).

Workbook:
1. We read a story ⟨about⟩ bears.   (Ask questions 1a, 2, 4, and 6)
2. Shady paths ⟨in⟩ the woods are cool.   (Ask questions 1b, 2, 3, and 5)
3. The lamp ⟨near⟩ the sofa is blue.   (Ask questions 1b, 2, 3, and 5)
4. Those pancake ⟨on⟩ the griddle burned.   (Ask questions 1a, 2, and 5)
5. He lost the key ⟨to⟩ his car.   (Ask questions 1a, 2, 4, and 6)

1a. *What is the verb? Write the verb to the right of your center line.*

1b. *What is the linking verb? This verb links the subject to a word in the complete predicate. Write the verb to the right of your center line.*

2. *Find the subject. Ask "who" or "what" before the verb. [Prompt the student with a specific question like "Who reads?" or "What are?"] Write the subject to the left of the center line on your frame. Remember to put <u>you</u> in parentheses.*

3. *This sentence contains a predicate adjective. This adjective is in the complete predicate of the sentence, but it describes the subject. A predicate adjective can tell what kind, which one, how many, or whose. Can you find an adjective that follows the verb that still describes the subject? Because the predicate adjective follows the verb in the sentence, it is written to the right of the verb on the diagram. Write the predicate adjective to the right of the slanted line on your diagram. That slanted line points back toward the subject to remind you that a predicate adjective describes the subject.*

4. *Is there a direct object that receives the action of the verb? I will ask you a question that will help you find the direct object.*

Sentence 1: Read what?

Sentence 5: Lost what?

Write the direct object to the right of the verb on your diagram. The direct object is separated from the verb by a short, straight line.

5. *Go back and look again at the simple subject. Are there any words that describe the subject that come before the verb? These adjectives can tell what kind, which one, how many, or whose. Also look for the articles (<u>a</u>, <u>an</u>, <u>the</u>), because they act like adjectives. Write each adjective on a slanted line below the subject it describes.*

6. *Look again at the direct object. Are there any words that describe the direct object? These adjectives can tell what kind, which one, how many, or whose. Also look for the articles (<u>a</u>, <u>an</u>, <u>the</u>), because they act like adjectives. Write each adjective on a slanted line below the direct object it describes.*

Answer Key:

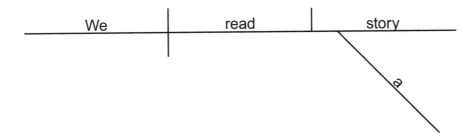

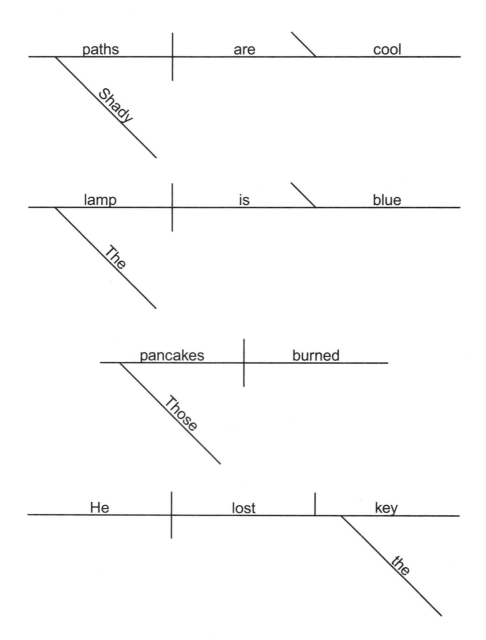

Instructor: Some sentences look **really** long and complicated, but they are just padded with a lot of prepositional phrases. Can you find and cross out all the prepositional phrases in the sentence in **Exercise 3**? You will find that a very simple sentence is left.

Workbook: In a treasure chest on the large, wooden ship across the harbor near the town, you will find a necklace with sparkling diamonds on it for the most beautiful queen in the whole world.

~~In a treasure chest~~ ~~on the large, wooden ship~~ ~~across the harbor~~ ~~near the town,~~ **you will find a necklace** ~~with sparkling diamonds~~ ~~on it~~ ~~for the most beautiful~~ ~~queen~~ ~~in the whole world~~.

Optional Follow-Up

There is no optional follow-up for this lesson.

LESSON 54

Narration: "Isaac Newton's Laws of Gravity"

Review "Land of Nod" (Lesson 9) and "I Wandered Lonely As a Cloud" (Lesson 31) today. If the student has trouble remembering the poems, have him practice them until he is confident.

Read the following selection aloud to the student (or, the student may read it aloud himself from his workbook). After the selection has been read, follow the scripting to make sure he understands the passage. After the initial reading, the student should **not** look at the passage.

Instructor: **We** are going to read about a famous scientist named Isaac Newton. When we have finished reading, I am going to ask you what you remember **only** about what has been read. Don't tell me information that you remember from somewhere else.

Isaac Newton's Laws of Gravity

One day, Isaac Newton was sitting beside a window, thinking and staring out into the family apple orchards, when he saw an apple fall to the ground. He thought, "Why does it always fall down? Why doesn't the apple ever fall sideways, or up? Some sort of force must be pulling on the apple to make it always fall in exactly the same way!"

Newton went on observing, doing experiments, and thinking until he was able to describe the force that pulls on the apple. He called it *gravity*, from the Latin word *grave*, which means "heavy." This "heavy" force means that large bodies, such as the earth, have a force that pulls objects toward them. Isaac Newton learned that he could predict, using mathematics, how strong the force would be, anywhere in the universe. The next time an apple fell, Newton could tell you exactly how fast it would fall and when it would hit the earth.

Newton's new rules, which we now call the laws of gravity, showed that every motion or action in the universe had a law that governed it. The universe wasn't a huge, mysterious, magical riddle. Instead, people could figure it out—and even predict ahead of time—what would happen.

"Isaac Newton's Laws of Gravity" is excerpted from *The Story of the World, Volume 3: Early Modern Times* by Susan Wise Bauer (Peace Hill Press, 2004).

Instructor: Close your eyes. Now I am going to ask you a few questions about what I just read.

The following questions are to make sure the student understands the passage. The student should answer these questions in complete sentences. If the student answers in a single word or phrase, put the phrase into a complete sentence for the student and ask him to repeat it back to you. The words in italics represent sample answers—accept other answers if they are correct and if the information was in the passage.

Instructor: What is the name of the scientist we just read about?

Student: **His name is** *Isaac Newton.*

Instructor: What did Isaac Newton see that gave him an idea?

Student: *He saw an apple fall.*

Instructor: Why did Newton think that apples always fell down, rather than falling up or sideways?

Student: *There was a force pulling them down.*

Instructor: What did Newton call this force that pulls objects down toward the earth?

Student: *Newton called this force gravity.*

Instructor: If people used Newton's laws and mathematics, what could they do?

Student: *They could figure out and predict what would happen.*

Instructor: Now tell me two things you remember about Isaac Newton and gravity. Use your own words. Speak in complete sentences.

As the student narrates in his own words, you may write his sentences down as he speaks or record them onto a tape recorder to write down when he is finished. You have three options for writing the narration:

1. Write down the student's narration for him on his workbook page.
2. Write down the student's narration for him on a separate piece of paper and have him copy some or all of the sentences onto his workbook page.
3. Write down the student's narration on a separate piece of paper and dictate it to him, as he writes it on his workbook page.

If the student repeats the author's words verbatim, use the questions about the passage to help the student form his own sentences. If the student speaks in phrases, turn his phrases into complete sentences. The student should then repeat the complete sentence back to you. The student does not need to include every aspect of the passage in his narration—he only needs to pick out two ideas. Here is an example of a possible narration.

Isaac Newton watched apples fall. He named this force gravity.

Once you have written the student's narration, he should read it aloud back to you.

LESSON 55

Review: **Adjectives**

Review "A Time to Talk" (Lesson 46) today. If the student has trouble remembering the poem, have him practice it until he is confident.

Instructor: Let's review the definition of an adjective. An adjective is a word that describes a noun or pronoun. Say that definition with me.

Together: An adjective is a word that describes a noun or pronoun.

Instructor: Adjectives tell what kind, which one, how many, and whose. Say that with me two times.

Together (two times): Adjectives tell what kind, which one, how many, and whose.

Instructor: In **Exercise 1** of your workbook, follow along as I read you some adjectives that tell what kind. I want you to use each adjective I say to describe any noun you wish. For example, if I say "yellow," you might say "yellow pencil."

Workbook: green

sharp

spicy

enormous

sparkly

tasty

bumpy

ferocious

Instructor: In **Exercise 2**, follow along as I read you some adjectives that tell which one. I want you to use each adjective I say to describe any noun you wish. For example, if I say "this," you might say "this book."

Workbook: this

that

these

those

first

third

next

final

Instructor: In **Exercise 3**, follow along as I read you some adjectives that tell how many. I want you to use each adjective I say to describe any noun you wish. For example, if I say "six," you might say "six jellybeans."

Workbook: seventeen

four

fifty

most

several

another

all

Instructor: In **Exercise 4**, follow along as I read you some adjectives that tell whose. I want you to use each adjective I say to describe any noun you wish. For example, if I say "girl's," you might say "girl's barrettes." Look carefully at the end of each word so you will know if the word is singular or plural.

Workbook: baby's   (singular)

artist's   (singular)

cat's   (singular)

Dad's   (singular)

Denise's   (singular)

caterpillars'   (plural)

pirates'   (plural)

knights'   (plural)

Instructor: Do you remember the three special, little words called articles? Articles act like adjectives—they describe nouns. We memorized a poem about articles. Say as much of it with me as you can. Read it in **Exercise 5** if you have forgotten parts of it.

Workbook: Articles are little words,

You need know only three.

The articles that describe nouns

are **a**, **an**, **the**.

Instructor: Again, what are the three articles?

Student: *A, an, the*

Instructor: Read the sentences in **Exercise 6** and circle the articles. Each sentence contains two articles.

Workbook: (An) octopus propels through (the) water.

(An) armadillo is (a) mammal.

(The) Egyptian pharaoh Hatshepsut was really (a) woman!

Instructor: In **Exercise 7** there is a sentence with only a subject and a verb. Read the sentence and look at the diagram.

Workbook: Monkeys chatter.

Instructor: You have already learned how to add adjectives to a sentence diagram. You diagram adjectives by writing them on a slanted line under the word they describe. Read the next sentence and look at its diagram.

Workbook: The lively monkeys chatter.

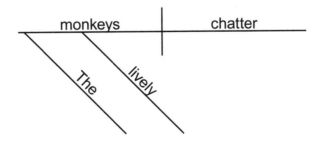

Instructor: I will point out words on the diagram as I explain. There are two adjectives in this sentence that describe the noun *monkeys*. There is an article that acts like an adjective: *The*. The monkeys. There is also an adjective that tells what kind. What kind of monkeys chatter? Lively monkeys. *The* is written before *lively* on the diagram because *The* comes before *lively* in the sentence. Now in **Exercise 8**, you will diagram sentences with **three** adjectives in them. First read the sentence. I will ask you questions as you fill in the diagram. Remember to copy the words exactly as they appear in the sentence. If the word begins with a capital letter in the sentence, it should also be capitalized in the diagram.

1. Trees' last brown leaves drop.

2. The third gigantic bubble burst.

3. All soft, golden daffodils sway.

4. Harold's two rusty cars rattle.

5. Students' heavy blue backpacks drooped.

Use the following dialogue to help the student fill in the diagrams:

1. *What is the verb? Write the verb to the right of your center line.*

2. *Find the subject. Ask "who" or "what" before the verb. [Prompt the student with a specific question like "What drops?" or "What burst?"] Write the subject to the left of the center line on your frame.*

3. *Now you have found the two most basic parts of the sentence. Go back and look again at the simple subject. Are there any words that describe the subject that come before the verb? These adjectives can tell what kind, which one, how many, or whose. Also look for the articles (a, an, the), because they act like adjectives. Write each adjective on a slanted line below the subject it describes.*

Answer Key:

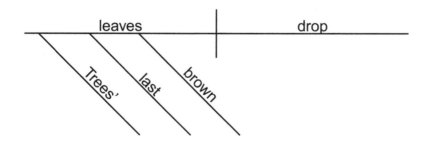

242

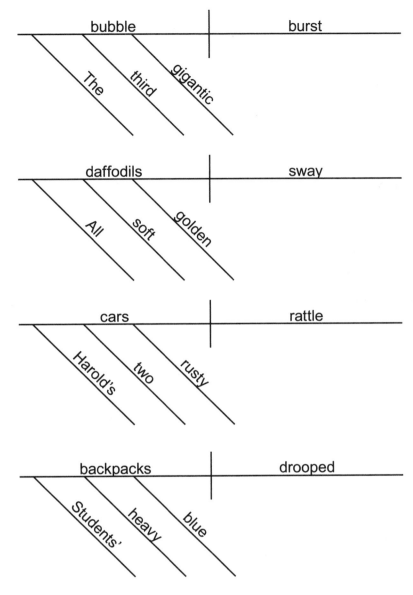

Optional Follow-Up

The student will make "picture sentences" with subjects and predicate adjectives. He will draw a picture of the underlined words with a linking verb (or helping verb and linking verb) written between them. For example, in the first sentence, the student will draw a simple picture of flowers, write the word *are*, and then color a circle red or draw the same flowers in red. You may help the student come up with ways to draw the predicate adjectives. Jessie's grandson Daniel drew *wild* (for sentence 3) as stick-figure boys jumping all over the verbs in the sentence.

1. <u>Flowers</u> are <u>red</u>.
2. <u>People</u> were <u>happy</u>.
3. <u>Two boys</u> are being <u>wild</u>.
4. <u>My cousins</u> have been <u>angry</u>.
5. <u>All the dogs</u> should be <u>hungry</u>.

LESSON 56

Review: Adverbs

Review "A Tragic Story" (Lesson 18) today. If the student has trouble remembering the poem, have him practice it daily until he is confident.

Instructor: An adverb is a word that describes a verb, an adjective, or another adverb. Adverbs tell how, when, where, how often, and to what extent. Say that with me two times.

Together (two times): An adverb is a word that describes a verb, an adjective, or another adverb. Adverbs tell how, when, where, how often, and to what extent.

If the student writes easily, have him write the answers in his workbook. Or you may choose to do the exercises orally.

Instructor: In this lesson, we will focus on adverbs that describe verbs. We will talk about adverbs that describe adjectives and other adverbs in the next lesson.

Instructor: Adverbs tell **how. How** do you sing? Read aloud each of the sentences in **Exercise 1**. The adverb that tells how is in bold print.

Workbook: I sing **quietly**.

I sing **happily**.

I sing **beautifully**.

I sing **clearly**.

I sing **loudly**.

These adverbs

Instructor: I will ask you a "How" question and you will read the four choices in **Exercise 2**. Choose your favorite adverb and answer the question in a complete sentence.

Instructor: How do you walk?

Workbook: quickly

quietly

slowly

loudly

Student: *I walk [adverb of choice].*

Instructor: *[Adverb of choice]* is an adverb that tells how you walk. Adverbs tell **when. When** do you sing? Read each of the sentences in **Exercise 3** to me. The adverb that tells when is in bold print.

Workbook: I sing **today**.

I sing **tonight**.

I sing **late**.

I sing **early**.

I sing **now**.

Instructor: I will ask you a "When" question and you will read the choices in **Exercise 4**. Choose your favorite adverb and answer the question in a complete sentence.

Instructor: When do you sleep?

Workbook: today

tonight

late

now

Student: *I sleep [adverb of choice].*

Instructor: *[Adverb of choice]* is an adverb that tells when you sleep. Adverbs tell **where. Where** do you read? Read each of the sentences in **Exercise 5** to me. The adverb that tells where is in bold print.

Workbook: I read **nearby**.

I read **outside**.

I read **upstairs**.

I read **here**.

I read **everywhere**.

Instructor: I will ask you a "Where" question and you will read the choices in **Exercise 6**. Choose your favorite adverb and answer the question in a complete sentence.

Instructor: Where do you swim?

Workbook: outdoors

nearby

here

Student: *I swim [adverb of choice].*

Instructor: *[Adverb of choice]* is an adverb that tells where you swim. Adverbs tell **how often**. **How often** do you wash your hands? Read each of the sentences in **Exercise 7** to me. The adverb that tells how often is in bold print.

Workbook: I wash **daily**.

I wash **rarely**.

I wash **seldom**.

I wash **frequently**.

I wash **often**.

Instructor: I will ask you a "How often" question and you will read the choices in **Exercise 8**. Choose your favorite adverb and answer the question in a complete sentence.

Instructor: How often do you camp?

Workbook: yearly

frequently

rarely

Student: *I camp [adverb of choice].*

Instructor: *[Adverb of choice]* is an adverb that tells how often you camp.

Instructor: In **Exercise 9** you will diagram sentences that contain adverbs. On a diagram, adverbs are written on a slanted line below the verb they describe. You read the sentence. I will ask you questions as you fill in the diagram. Remember to copy the words exactly as they appear in the sentence. If the word begins with a capital letter in the sentence, it should also be capitalized in the diagram.

Workbook: 1. Leopards creep gingerly.

2. Dolphins swam alongside.

3. Foxes sneak slyly.

4. Dad left early.

5. Dragonflies can fly backward.

6. Thomas Alva Edison napped frequently.

Use the following dialogue to help the student fill in the diagrams:

1. *What is the verb? Write the verb to the right of your center line. [**Sentence 5** contains a helping verb and an action verb. Prompt the student as necessary to include both verbs on the verb line.]*

2. *Find the subject. Ask "who" or "what" before the verb. [Prompt the student with a specific question like "What creeps?" or "What swam?"] Write the subject to the left of the center line on your frame. [**Sentence 6** has a proper name as its subject. Prompt the student as necessary to write all three words in the name on the subject line.]*

3. *Now you have found the two most basic parts of the sentence. Go back and look again at the verb. Is there a word that describes the verb? This is an adverb that could tell how, when, where, or how often. Write the adverb on the slanted line below the verb it describes.*

Answer Key:

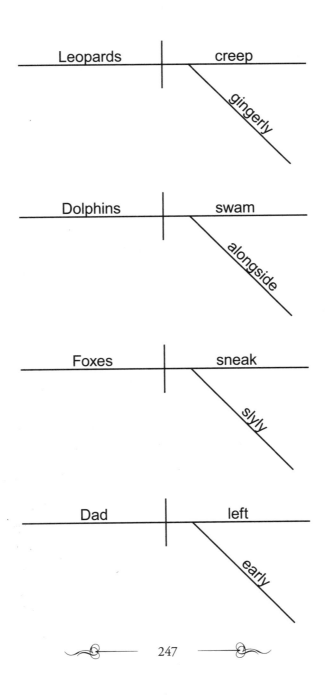

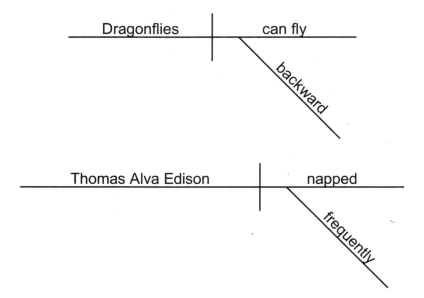

Optional Follow-Up

The student will make five "Promises for the Day." The student will select an adverb from the choices in his workbook to fill in each blank. He must do what he promises during the day. For example, in the sentence "I will make my bed _____," the student may write in "soon." If he chooses *soon*, he must fulfill his promise and go make his bed as soon as he finishes this activity. At the end of the list, the student should sign the paper, and the instructor should also sign it (as a witness).

1. I will make my bed _____ (soon, later, tomorrow).

2. I will walk across the room _____ (quickly, gracefully, sleepily).

3. I will read a book _____ (inside, nearby, there).

4. I will eat my snack _____ (slowly, greedily, later).

5. I will hug someone _____ (now, today, tenderly).

LESSON 57

New: Adverbs That Tell to What Extent

Instructor: An adverb is a word that describes a verb, an adjective, or another adverb. Say that with me two times.

Together (two times): An adverb is a word that describes a verb, an adjective, or another adverb.

Instructor: Up until this point, we have focused on adverbs that describe verbs. These adverbs tell how, when, where, and how often. In this lesson, you will see how adverbs can describe adjectives and other adverbs, too. They don't tell how, when, where, or how often. They tell you something else called "to what extent."

Instructor: Let's say this three times together: Adverbs tell how, when, where, how often, and to what extent.

Together (three times): Adverbs tell how, when, where, how often, and to what extent.

Instructor: Look at **Exercise 1**. Let's do a quick review. You read the first sentence, and I will ask you a question to help you find the adverb in that sentence.

Workbook: I will jump excitedly.

Instructor: **How** will you jump?

Student: *Excitedly*

Instructor: *Excitedly* is an adverb that tells **how** you will jump. Read the next sentence.

Workbook: I will jump immediately.

Instructor: **When** will you jump?

Student: *Immediately*

Instructor: *Immediately* is an adverb that tells **when** you will jump. Read the third sentence.

Workbook: I will jump outside.

Instructor: **Where** will you jump?

Student: *Outside*

Instructor: *Outside* is an adverb that tells **where** you will jump. Read the fourth sentence.

Workbook: I will jump daily.

Instructor: **How often** will you jump?

Student: *Daily*

Instructor: *Daily* is an adverb that tells **how often** you will jump.

Instructor: Remember, up until this lesson, we have focused on adverbs that describe verbs. These adverbs tell how, when, where, and how often. But adverbs can describe more than just verbs: they can describe adjectives and other adverbs, too. These new adverbs don't tell how, when, where, or how often. They tell you something called "to what extent." Although there are many adverbs like these, we are going to focus on five **very** common adverbs. In fact, I just used one of those adverbs: *very*! Read aloud the list of adverbs in **Exercise 2**.

Workbook: too

very

really

quite

slightly

Instructor: These adverbs can describe adjectives, like the adjective *gentle*. Read the list in **Exercise 3** to see what I mean:

Workbook: **too** gentle

very gentle

really gentle

quite gentle

slightly gentle

Instructor: All these adverbs tell "to what extent" a person is gentle. She is gentle. To what extent is she gentle? She is **very** gentle. Or she is **too** gentle, or **really** gentle, **quite** gentle, or only **slightly** gentle. Read the sentence in **Exercise 4**.

Workbook: Donkeys are too stubborn!

Instructor: What is the linking verb?

Student: *Are*

Instructor: What is the subject? What are?

Student: *Donkeys*

Instructor: This sentence has a predicate adjective that describes the subject *Donkeys*. What is the predicate adjective? **What kind** of donkeys?

Student: *Stubborn*

Instructor: What is the **adverb** that describes the predicate adjective *stubborn*? **To what extent** are the donkeys stubborn?

Student: *Too*

Instructor: Look at the diagram of the sentence "Donkeys are too stubborn!"

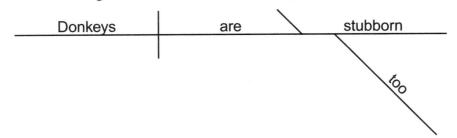

Instructor: I will point out words on the diagram as I explain. *Donkeys* is the subject. *Are* is the linking verb that links the subject with the predicate adjective *stubborn*. What kind of donkeys? Stubborn donkeys. The adjective *stubborn* is in the complete predicate of the sentence, but it describes the subject. Because the predicate adjective follows the verb in the sentence, it is written to the right of the verb on the diagram. The slanted line points back toward the subject to remind you that a predicate adjective describes the subject. There is a word in this sentence that describes the adjective *stubborn*. The adverb *too* tells us **to what extent** the donkeys are stubborn. Because *too* describes *stubborn*, it is written on the slanted line beneath the predicate adjective.

Instructor: In **Exercise 5**, I will help you diagram four sentences like this with adverbs that describe predicate adjectives.

Workbook: 1. Firemen are very courageous.

2. George was really curious.

3. Insects are quite fascinating.

4. They were slightly nervous.

1. *What is the linking verb? This verb links the subject to a word in the complete predicate. Write the verb to the right of your center line.*

2. *Find the subject. Ask "who" or "what" before the verb. [Prompt the student with a specific question like "Who is?" or "Who was?"] Write the subject to the left of the center line on your frame.*

3. *This sentence contains a predicate adjective. This adjective is in the complete predicate of the sentence, but it describes the subject. A predicate adjective can tell what kind, which one, how many, or whose. Can you find an adjective that follows the verb that still describes the subject? Because the predicate adjective follows the verb in the sentence, it is written to the right of the verb on the diagram. Write the predicate adjective to the right of the slanted line on your diagram. That slanted line points back toward the subject to remind you that a predicate adjective describes the subject.*

4. *Look again at the predicate adjective. Is there an adverb such as <u>too</u>, <u>very</u>, <u>really</u>, <u>quite</u>, or <u>slightly</u>? These adverbs tell to what extent. Write the adverb on the slanted line beneath the predicate adjective it describes.*

Answer Key:

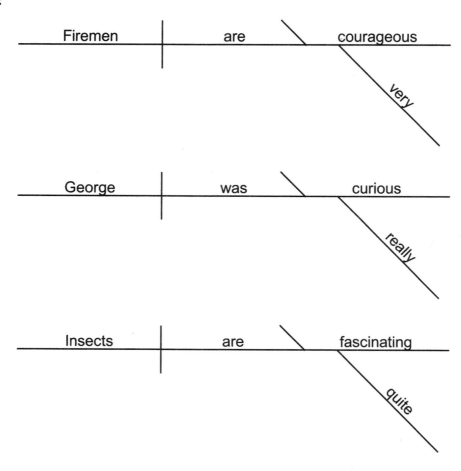

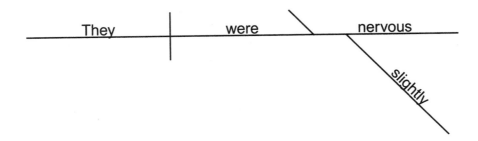

Instructor: In **Exercise 6** read the list of adverbs again.

Workbook: too

       very

       really

       quite

       slightly

Instructor: You have seen that these adverbs can describe adjectives. They can also describe other adverbs, like the adverb *early*. Read the list in **Exercise 7** to see what I mean:

Workbook: **too** early

       very early

       really early

       quite early

       slightly early

Instructor: All these adverbs tell to what extent. He is early. **To what extent** is he early? He is **too** early. Or he could be **very** early, or **really** early, **quite** early, or **slightly** early. Now read the sentence in **Exercise 8**. This sentence has **two** adverbs. One adverb describes a verb; the other adverb describes another adverb.

Workbook: Rain came very suddenly.

Instructor: What is the verb?

Student: *Came*

Instructor: Find the subject. What came?

Student: *Rain*

Instructor: There is an adverb that tells **when**. When did the rain come?

Student: *Suddenly*

Instructor: Now there is **another** adverb that describes the adverb *suddenly*. To what extent did the rain come suddenly?

Student: *Very*

Instructor: Look at the diagram of the sentence "Rain came very suddenly."

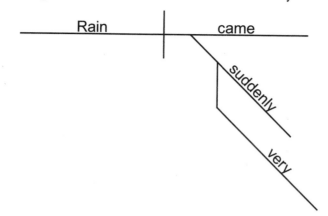

Instructor: I will point out words on the diagram as I explain. *Rain* is the subject. *Came* is the verb. When did the rain come? Suddenly. *Suddenly* is an adverb that tells when the rain came, so it is written on a slanted line beneath the verb. There is a word in this sentence that describes the adverb *suddenly*. The adverb *very* tells us **to what extent** the rain came suddenly. Because *very* describes how suddenly, *very* is written on the slanted line beneath the adverb.

Instructor: In **Exercise 9** I will help you diagram four sentences with adverbs that describe other adverbs.

Workbook: 1. Arnold slept slightly late.

2. Kris skated too fast.

3. Garcia stopped really quickly.

4. Ravens caw quite loudly.

Use this dialogue to help the student fill in the diagrams.

1. *What is the verb? Write the verb to the right of your center line.*

2. *Find the subject. Ask "who" or "what" before the verb. [Prompt the student with a specific question like "Who slept?" or "Who skated?"] Write the subject to the left of the center line on your frame.*

3. *Now you have found the two most basic parts of the sentence. Go back and look again at the verb. Is there a word that describes the verb? This is an adverb that could tell how, when, where, or how often. Write the adverb on the slanted line below the verb it describes.*

4. *Look again at the adverb. Is there another adverb in the sentence, such as <u>too</u>, <u>very</u>, <u>really</u>, <u>quite</u>, or <u>slightly</u> that describes the first adverb? <u>Too</u>, <u>very</u>, <u>really</u>, <u>quite</u>, and <u>slightly</u> are adverbs that tell to what extent. Write one of these adverbs (<u>too</u>, <u>very</u>, <u>really</u>, <u>quite</u>, or <u>slightly</u>) on the slanted line beneath the adverb it describes.*

Answer Key:

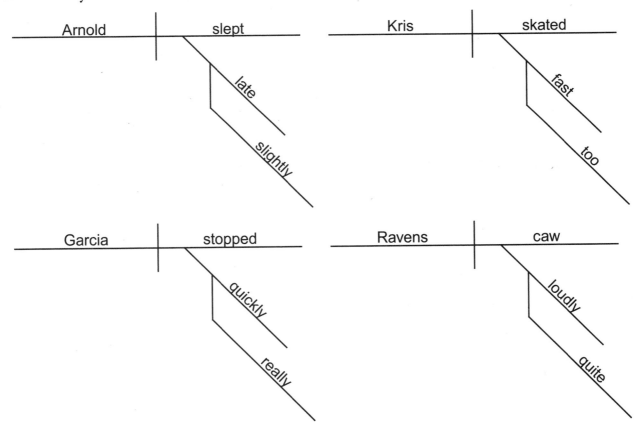

Optional Follow-Up

Instructor: Choose adverbs from the list to describe the predicate adjectives in bold print in **Sentences 1**, **2**, and **3**. Then read each completed sentence aloud.

Workbook: too

very

really

quite

slightly

Workbook: 1. The clown was _____ **silly**.

2. The hamburger was _____ **big**!

3. The baby is _____ **ticklish**.

Instructor: Choose adverbs from the list to describe the adverbs in bold print in **Sentences 4**, **5**, and **6**. Then read each completed sentence aloud.

Workbook: 4. I arrived _____ **late**.

5. I ate my ice cream _____ **quickly**.

6. The puppy was _____ **friendly**.

LESSON 58

Poem Memorization: "The Bells"

Instructor: In Lesson 58 of your workbook, you will find the first stanza of a famous poem about bells. Follow along as I read the poem to you. Before I begin reading, I want to tell you what a few words mean.

As you explain each definition, point to the words *sledges* and *tintinnabulation* in the poem.

Instructor: A *sledge* is a sleigh that horses pull in the snow. *Tintinnabulation* is a long word, but it simply means "the ringing or tinkling sound of bells." The word even sounds like what it means. Do you hear the "tin-tin" sound of bells in tin-tin-nab-u-la-tion? There is another new word in this poem: *Runic* (pronounced "ROO-nick"). After I have read the poem once, I will tell you what the word *Runic* means.

The Bells

by Edgar Allan Poe

Hear the sledges with the bells—

Silver bells!

What a world of merriment their melody foretells!

How they tinkle, tinkle, tinkle,

In the icy air of night!

While the stars that oversprinkle

All the heavens, seem to twinkle

With a crystalline delight;

Keeping time, time, time,

In a sort of Runic rhyme,

To the tintinnabulation, that so musically wells

From the bells, bells, bells, bells,

Bells, bells, bells—

From the jingling and the tinkling of the bells.

Instructor: The word *Runic* is related to the word *rune*. Runes were the written language of the Old Norse tribes who lived long ago in Northern Europe. The runes look like mysterious codes—they don't look like regular writing. You have to look at the runes carefully to find their meaning. So when Edgar Allan Poe says that the bells keep time "in a sort of Runic rhyme," he probably means that at first the sound of the bells may seem not to have any meaning. But if you listen closely, you can hear a hidden meaning in their ringing: The sleigh bells are happy and merry!

Read the poem to the student three times in a row. Repeat this triple reading twice more during the day. Have the student check the boxes in his workbook when this is done.

Dictation Exercise

You may point out the spelling of the word *sledges* before you dictate the first sentence, and point out the punctuation of the last sentence before you dictate that one.

Dictation: Hear the sledges with the bells.

How they tinkle, tinkle, tinkle in the icy air of night!

Optional Follow-Up

This poem has more stanzas. Each stanza describes a different kind of bell and the way that bell rings with emotion. Find the rest of the poem online or in a volume of Poe's works and read the entire poem with your student.

LESSON 59

Review: Four Kinds of Verbs

Review: Direct Objects, Predicate Nominatives, and Predicate Adjectives

---

Read "The Bells" (Lesson 58) three times to the student. Then ask the student to try to say parts of the poem along with you (or the tape recorder).

Instructor: Let's begin by saying the definition of a verb. A verb is a word that does an action, shows a state of being, links two words together, or helps another verb. Say that with me two times.

Together (two times): A verb is a word that does an action, shows a state of being, links two words together, or helps another verb.

Instructor: Action verbs show action. *Swim*, *play*, and *whistle* are all action verbs. Action verbs are sometimes followed by a direct object that receives the action of the verb. Now you will find the direct objects in a few sentences. To find the direct object, I will ask you "what" or "whom" after the verb. Read each sentence in **Exercise 1**.

Workbook: Max opened the door.

Instructor: Opened **what**?

Student: *Door*

Instructor: *Door* is the direct object. It receives the action of the verb *opened*. Read the next sentence.

Workbook: The waiter serves dinner.

Instructor: Serves **what**?

Student: *Dinner*

Instructor: *Dinner* is the direct object. It receives the action of the verb *serves*. Read the next sentence.

Workbook: Charles found Dave.

Instructor: Found **whom**?

Student: *Dave*

Instructor: *Dave* is the direct object. It receives the action of the verb *found*. Look at the diagram of the sentence you just read, "Charles found Dave."

Charles	found	Dave

Instructor: The direct object *Dave* is written next to the verb *found*. It is divided from the verb by a short line.

Instructor: Helping verbs are another kind of verb. They help other verbs. Chant the first part of the list of helping verbs with me.

Together: Am [clap]
Is [clap]
Are, was, were. [clap]
Be [clap]
Being [clap]
Been. [clap] [clap]

Instructor: Now let's chant the rest of the helping verbs together.

Together: Have, has, had [clap]
Do, does, did [clap]
Shall, will, should, would, may, might, must [clap, clap]
Can, could!

Instructor: Read the sentences in **Exercise 2**. The helping verbs are in bold print. Each helping verb helps the action verb in the sentence make sense by showing time.

Workbook: Carmen **shall** sleep.

The frogs **are** hiding.

We **have been** playing.

Instructor: Another type of verb, a state of being verb, just shows that you exist. Let's chant the state of being verbs together. This is the same chant as the first part of the helping verb chant.

Together: Am [clap]

             Is [clap]

             Are, was, were. [clap]

             Be [clap]

             Being [clap]

             Been. [clap] [clap]

Instructor: In **Exercise 3** read the sentences with state of being verbs. The state of being verbs are printed in bold.

Workbook: We **are** in the room.

             Anton has **been** to the city.

             The actors will **be** on stage.

Instructor: State of being verbs don't show action or help other verbs—they just show that someone or something exists. There is one more type of verb: linking verbs. Linking verbs link, or join, two words together. These verbs are easy to recognize because they are the same verbs as the state of being verbs: *am, is, are, was, were, be, being, been*. These verbs can do three of the four parts of the verb definition! Read **Exercise 4** to me.

Workbook: The verbs *am*, *is*, *are*, *was, were*, *be*, *being*, *been* can either

- help another verb
- show a state of being
- link two words together

Instructor: So if you see the verb was in a sentence, you have to read the whole sentence to tell what kind of verb it is. After you read each sentence in **Exercise 5**, I will point out to you how the verb *was* can be used as a helping verb, a state of being verb, or a linking verb.

Workbook: He was climbing.

Instructor: *Was* is a helping verb in that sentence. *Was* helps the verb *climbing* by showing it was in a past time. Read the next sentence.

Workbook: He was on a mountain.

Instructor: *Was* just shows that someone existed on a mountain. *Was* is a state of being verb in that sentence. Read the next sentence.

Workbook: He was patient.

Instructor: *Was* is a linking verb in that sentence. It links the subject *He* with the predicate adjective *patient*. Remember, adjectives tell what kind, which one, how many, whose. *Patient* describes what kind of person *He* was.

Instructor: Let's use some linking verbs in sentences. In each sentence of **Exercise 6**, I will read you a noun and a linking verb and let you complete the sentence by choosing a predicate adjective that describes the subject. The linking verb in bold print will link, or connect, the subject noun with the adjective you choose. Follow along as I read and point to the parts of the sentences in your workbook. Then write your chosen answer in the blank.

Workbook: Popcorn **is** _____.

Instructor: Can you tell me what popcorn tastes like?

Student: *Popcorn is [crunchy, salty, yummy].*

Instructor: The linking verb *is* connects the subject *Popcorn* with the adjective *[the word the student chose]*! Can you tell me something about the way marbles look?

Workbook: Marbles **are** _____.

Student: *Marbles are [round, shiny, colored].*

Instructor: The linking verb *are* connects the subject *Marbles* with the adjective *[the word student chose]*. How does clay feel?

Workbook: The clay **was** _____.

Student: *The clay was [soft, squishy, cool].*

Instructor: The linking verb *was* connects the subject *Clay* with the adjective *[the word student chose]*. Let's say the chant of the linking verbs. I will do the chant first, and you will join me the second time through.

Instructor, then together:
Am [clap]
Is [clap]
Are, was, were. [clap]
Be [clap]
Being [clap]
Been. [clap] [clap]

Instructor: In **Exercise 7** read the sentence and look its diagram. This sentence contains a linking verb.

Workbook: The costumes were fancy.

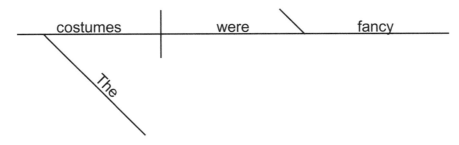

In order to keep the student's eyes focused on what you are explaining, physically point out the words and lines on the student's diagram as they appear in the next two instructor paragraphs.

Instructor: I will point out words as I explain. The linking verb *were* connects the subject of the sentence, *costumes*, with the adjective *fancy*. Even though *fancy* is an adjective that describes the subject *costumes*, it is written to the right of the verb on the diagram because it follows the verb in the sentence. Because the adjective is in the complete predicate of the sentence, it is a **predicate** adjective.

Instructor: Remember, the complete predicate is the verb and all the words attached to the verb line on a diagram. These words tell us what is said about the subject. Do you see the slanted line on the diagram above that separates the linking verb *were* from the predicate adjective? That slanted line points toward the subject to remind you that *fancy* is an adjective that describes *costumes*.

Instructor: In **Exercise 8**, the linking verbs are in bold print. Here, you will see that a linking verb can also link the subject with a noun or pronoun in the complete predicate that renames the subject. Read the three sentences to me. Now answer this question: If you had to choose one, would you like to be a veterinarian, an astronaut, or a builder when you grow up?

Student: *[veterinarian, astronaut, or builder]*

Workbook: I will be a veterinarian.

I will be an astronaut.

I will be a builder.

Instructor: The sentences in **Exercise 8** contain the helping verb *will* and the linking verb *be*. The linking verb connects the subject *I* with a noun that renames the subject. What will you be? A *[veterinarian, astronaut, or builder]*. *[Veterinarian, Astronaut, or Builder]* is in the complete predicate of the sentence. A noun or pronoun in the complete predicate that renames the subject is called a **predicate nominative**. Remember *nominate* means "to name." In **Exercise 9** read the sentence to me and look at its diagram.

Workbook: Teri is a nurse.

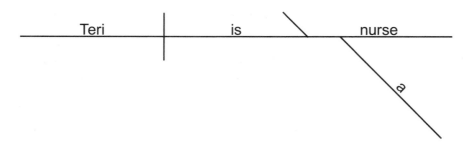

In order to keep the student's eyes focused on what you are explaining, physically point out the words and lines on the student's diagram as they appear in the next two instructor paragraphs.

Instructor: *Is* is a linking verb. It connects the subject *Teri* with a noun that renames the subject. *Nurse* tells who the subject is. Who is Teri? A *nurse*. *Nurse* is in the complete predicate of the sentence. A noun or pronoun in the complete predicate that renames the subject is called a **predicate nominative**. Even though *nurse* renames the subject *Teri*, it is written to the right of the verb on the diagram because it follows the verb in the sentence.

Instructor: Look again at the diagram. Do you see the slanted line that separates the linking verb *is* from the predicate nominative? That slanted line points back toward the subject to remind you that *nurse* is a predicate nominative that renames the subject *Teri*.

Dictation Exercise

After the student has written the sentences, have him circle the linking verbs.

Dictation: She is a zookeeper.

Ants are hardworking.

Optional Follow-Up

This activity reviews predicate adjectives. The student will choose a subject from the subject list, a linking verb (that sometimes has a helping verb with it) from the verb list, and a predicate adjective from the predicate adjective list. After he has chosen one of each, he should write the sentence he has made. He may look at the lists to help him with spelling. Remind him that the names of the seasons are common nouns: They are only capitalized here because they begin the sentences.

Subject	Verb	Predicate Adjective
Spring	will be	warm
Summer	should be	snowy
Autumn	can be	busy
Winter	was	fun
		rainy
		freezing
		sunny
		breezy

LESSON 60

Review: Simple and Complete Subjects and Predicates

Read "The Bells" (Lesson 58) three times to the student. Then ask the student to try to say parts of the poem along with you (or the tape recorder). The exercises in the workbook show more and more of the solution as the student works through the lesson. Place a blank sheet of paper over the part of the exercise the student hasn't yet reached to keep him from seeing the answers prematurely.

Instructor: In **Exercise 1** read the long sentence and look at its diagram.

Hardworking Marie plants many flowers outside.

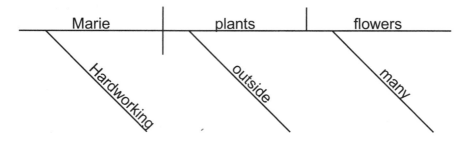

Instructor: Every sentence has a subject and a verb. On a diagram, the subject and the verb are separated by a straight line that runs down through the horizontal line.

Point to each word and line as you explain all diagrams in today's lesson.

Instructor: To the left of this straight line, you will find all the words that tell you more about the subject, *Marie*. The subject of the sentence is simply the word *Marie*, so it is called the simple subject. But when you add other words that tell you more about *Marie* you get a longer, more complete description of the subject. *Hardworking* tells us more about *Marie*. *Hardworking Marie* is the complete subject. Look at the diagram in **Exercise 1**. The simple subject is always written on the subject line (*Marie*).

Instructor: The complete subject is the simple subject (*Marie*) and all the words that hang off the simple subject (*Hardworking Marie*). The complete subject includes all the words to the left of the straight line that runs down through the horizontal line.

Instructor: In **Exercise 2** read the sentence and look at its diagram.

Workbook: Two sheepdogs herd wandering sheep efficiently.

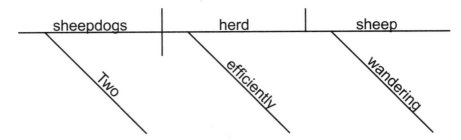

Instructor: On a diagram, the subject and the verb are separated by a straight line that runs down the center of the frame. Look at the word to the left of the center line. What is the simple subject of the sentence? The simple subject is always written on the subject line.

Student: *Sheepdogs*

Instructor: But when you add other words that tell you more about the subject, *sheepdogs,* you get a longer, more complete description of the subject. On a diagram, the **complete subject** includes **all the words to the left of the straight line that runs down the center of the frame.** What is the complete subject of the sentence?

Student: *Two sheepdogs*

Instructor: The words to the right of the center, straight line are the verb and other words that tell us what is said about the subject. All together, these words have a special name: the **complete predicate.** The verb in this sentence is simply the word *herd.* But more is said about the sheepdogs than just "sheepdogs herd." We know that they "herd wandering sheep efficiently." All these words tell us what is said about the subject, *sheepdogs.* They are the complete predicate.

On the diagram, point to each word or line that is printed in bold in the following instructor script.

Instructor: Let's look closely at the words in the complete predicate.

- *Herd* is the verb. The verb is always written on the **verb line**

- *Efficiently* tells us more about the verb *herd.* It is an adverb that tells us how the sheepdogs herd.

- *Sheep* is the direct object. It tells us what the sheepdogs herd.

- *Wandering* is an adjective that also belongs in the complete predicate, because it tells us what kind of sheep the sheepdogs herd.

Instructor: The complete predicate is the verb and all the words attached to the verb line (herd, wandering, sheep, efficiently). The complete predicate includes **all the words to the right of the straight line that runs down the center of the frame.**

Instructor: In **Exercise 3** read again the sentence and look at the diagram about hardworking Marie.

Workbook: Hardworking Marie plants many flowers outside.

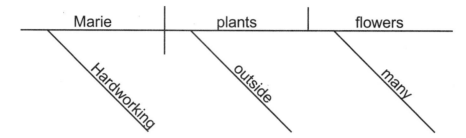

Instructor: Remember that on a diagram, the subject and the verb are separated by a straight line that runs down the center of the frame. Look at the word directly to the right of the center line. This is your verb. What is the verb in the sentence?

Student: *Plants*

Instructor: On a diagram, the complete predicate includes all the words to the right of the straight line that runs down the center of the frame. What is the complete predicate of the sentence?

Student: *Plants many flowers outside*

Instructor: Now in **Exercises 4, 5,** and **6,** you will diagram three groups of sentences: one about spacecrafts, one about clouds on the planet Mars, and one about solar flares. You read the sentences. As you work through each group of sentences, the parts of the diagram that you have filled in will be already printed on the next diagram. You will only have to add new words as you answer my questions. I will cover the diagrams that are below where you are working so you don't see the answers.

Workbook: Group 1 (Exercise 4 in the Student Workbook)

Astronauts fly spacecrafts.	(Ask questions 1, 2, and 3)
Brave astronauts fly spacecrafts.	(Ask question 4)
Brave astronauts fly sleek spacecrafts.	(Ask question 5)
Brave astronauts fly sleek spacecrafts yearly.	(Ask question 6)

Workbook: Group 2 (Exercise 5 in the Student Workbook)

Astronomers watch clouds.	(Ask questions 1, 2, and 3)
Observant astronomers watch clouds.	(Ask question 4)
Observant astronomers watch Martian clouds.	(Ask question 5)
Observant astronomers watch Martian clouds closely.	(Ask question 6)

Workbook: Group 3 (Exercise 6 in the Student Workbook)

Flares blast energy.	(Ask questions 1, 2, and 3)
Solar flares blast energy.	(Ask question 4)
Solar flares blast magnetic energy.	(Ask question 5)
Solar flares blast magnetic energy suddenly.	(Ask question 6)

Use the following italicized dialogue to help the student fill in each diagram. After the student reads a sentence in each sentence group about spacecrafts or clouds or solar flares, you will prompt him with the question(s) in italics listed across from that sentence. (For example, *Ask questions 1, 2, and 3.*)

---

1. *What is the verb? Write the verb to the right of your center line.*

2. *Find the subject. Ask "who" or "what" before the verb. [Prompt the student with a specific question like "Who flies?" or "Who watches?"] Write the subject to the left of the center line on your frame.*

3. *Is there a direct object that receives the action of the verb? I will ask you a question that will help you find the direct object.*

   Sentence Group 1: Fly what?

   Sentence Group 2: Watch what?

   Sentence Group 3: Blast what?

   Write the direct object to the right of the verb on your diagram. The direct object is separated from the verb by a short, straight line.

4. *Go back and look again at the subject. Are there any words that describe the subject? These adjectives can tell what kind, which one, how many, or whose. Also look for the articles (a, an, the), because they act like adjectives. Write each adjective on a slanted line below the subject it describes.*

5. *Look again at the direct object. Are there any words that describe the direct object? These adjectives can tell what kind, which one, how many, or whose. Also look for the articles (a, an, the), because they act like adjectives. Write each adjective on a slanted line below the direct object it describes.*

6. *Look at the verb. Is there a word that describes the verb? This is an adverb that could tell how, when, where, or how often. This adverb does not directly follow the verb in the sentence; it comes a little bit later. Write the adverb on the slanted line below the verb it describes.*

Answer Key:

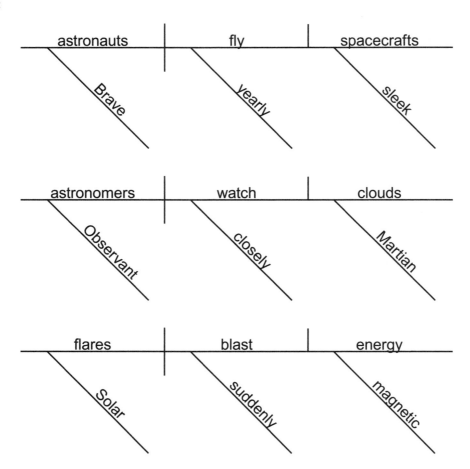

Use the following dialogue to help the student practice identifying the simple subject, complete subject, verb, and complete predicate in the sentences he just diagrammed. You will need to go through the entire dialogue below for each of the three sentences: first for the astronaut sentence, second for the astronomer sentence, and third for the solar flare sentence.

Instructor: We will look again at the last, complete diagram for **Exercises 4**, **5**, and **6** in your workbook. *[Instructor reads the appropriate sentence.]* On a diagram, the subject and the verb are separated by a straight line that runs down the center of the frame. What is the verb?

Student: *[fly; watch; blast]*

Instructor: Now look at the word to the left of the center line. What is the simple subject of the sentence? The simple subject is always written on the subject line.

Student: *[astronauts; astronomers; flares]*

Instructor: But when you add other words that tell you more about the subject, *[Instructor says astronauts or astronomers or flares]*, you get a longer, more complete description of the subject. On a diagram, the complete subject includes all the words to the left of the straight line that runs down the center of the frame. What is the complete subject of the sentence?

Student: *[Brave astronauts; Observant astronomers; Solar flares]*

Instructor: Look again at the diagram. The verb and all the words to the right of the center, straight line are in the complete predicate. The verb answers the question "What does the subject do?" But there are other words that tell us more completely what is said about the subject. They answer questions like:

[Exercise 4] "When do astronauts fly?" and "What do astronauts fly?"

[Exercise 5] "How do astronomers watch?" and "What do astronomers watch?"

[Exercise 6] "How do flares blast?" and "What do flares blast?"

Together, all of these words that tell us what is said about the subject are called the complete predicate. The complete predicate is written to the right of the straight line that runs down the center of the frame. What is the complete predicate of the sentence?

Student: *[Fly sleek spacecrafts yearly; Watch Martian clouds closely; Blast magnetic energy suddenly]*

Optional Follow-Up

If the student enjoyed diagramming the sentences by adding descriptive elements (or he needs extra practice), he may diagram the next two sentences as well. Use the numbered questions printed in this lesson. After he has diagrammed each sentence, you may follow the dialogue above to help him identify the simple subject, complete subject, verb, and complete predicate in each sentence.

Workbook: Group 1

Currents carved canyons.	(Ask questions 1, 2, and 3)
Undersea currents carved canyons.	(Ask question 4)
Undersea currents carved submarine canyons.	(Ask question 5)
Undersea currents carved submarine canyons gradually.	(Ask question 6)

Workbook: Group 2

Volcanoes ooze lava.	(Ask questions 1, 2, and 3)
Submarine volcanoes ooze lava.	(Ask question 4)
Submarine volcanoes ooze hot lava.	(Ask question 5)
Submarine volcanoes ooze hot lava underwater.	(Ask question 6)

Answer Key:

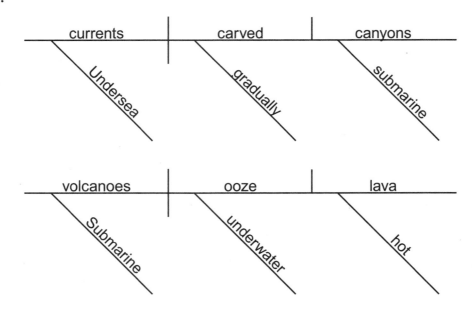

LESSON 61

New: Initials and Abbreviations for Titles of Respect
New: Abbreviations for Months and Days of the Week

Read "The Bells" (Lesson 58) three times to the student. Then ask the student to try to say parts of the poem along with you (or the tape recorder).

Instructor: Listen as I say a word: *abbreviation*. Listen to that word again slowly: *abbreviation*. Do you hear the word *brief* in the middle of *abbreviation*? *Brief* means "short." An abbreviation is the shortened form of a word. You will practice some abbreviations in this lesson.

Make sure to check the student's work as he writes the exercises in today's lesson. If he misspells an abbreviation or leaves off a period, have him rewrite it.

Instructor: In **Exercise 1** write your full name on line 1. Your full name is your first, middle, and last names. Remember, proper names all begin with capital letters.

(Student writes full name, e.g., David Patrick Stevenson)

Instructor: On line 2 in your workbook, I want you to write your initials. Your initials will be the first letter of each of your names. The word *initial* means "first" or "beginning." When you write initials, each initial is capitalized and followed by a period.

(Student writes initials, e.g., D. P. S.)

Instructor: Sometimes initials are used for only the first or middle names, but the last name is written in full. On lines 3, 5, and 7, **I** will write the full names of three family members. On lines 4, 6, and 8, I want **you** to write only the initials for the first and middle names of each person, but write out the person's last name in full. Remember, initials begin with capital letters and end with periods.

Instructor: Have you noticed that some people's names start with Mister or Mrs. [pronounced "Missus"] or Doctor or Miss? These are called "titles of respect." They show that we respect the position of that person. When these titles are written, they are often abbreviated. In **Exercise 2** of your workbook, I am going to show you the abbreviated (short) way to write some common titles of respect.

Title of Respect	Abbreviation	Used For
Mister	Mr.	This is the title for a man.
Mistress	Mrs.	This is a title for a married woman.
Doctor	Dr.	This is the title for a physician or for someone with a special degree from a university.
Miss	—	This is not an abbreviation, but a title of courtesy for an unmarried girl or woman.
Mistress or Miss	Ms.	Ms. is an abbreviation for either Mistress or Miss. You should use Ms. when you do not know whether a woman would prefer to be called Mrs. or Miss.

Instructor: In **Exercise 3** of your workbook, I want you to write two sentences I am going to read aloud to you.

Say the mother's and father's names with their preferred title of respect (for example, "Mrs. Sandra Smith" or "Mr. Christopher Green").

Dictation: 1. *[Mother's name]* is my mother.

2. [*Father's name*] is my father.

Instructor: There are also abbreviations for the days of the week and months of the year. In **Exercise 4**, read the list of the days of the week, and copy the abbreviations on the lines provided in your workbook.

Monday	Mon.
Tuesday	Tue.
Wednesday	Wed.
Thursday	Thu.
Friday	Fri.
Saturday	Sat.
Sunday	Sun.

Instructor: I am going to cover up the abbreviations in the list in **Exercise 4** in your workbook. In **Exercise 5** look at each day of the week, and write the abbreviation for it. Remember that each abbreviation begins with a capital letter and ends with a period.

Instructor: In **Exercise 6** read the list of the months of the year, and copy the abbreviations on the lines provided. May, June, and July are seldom abbreviated, so copy their full names in the blanks.

January	Jan.
February	Feb.
March	Mar.
April	Apr.
May	May
June	June
July	July
August	Aug.
September	Sept.
October	Oct.
November	Nov.
December	Dec.

Make sure to check the student's work as he writes the following exercise. If he misspells an abbreviation or leaves off a period, have him rewrite it.

Instructor: Now I am going to do as I did before: I will cover up the abbreviations in **Exercise 6**. In **Exercise 7** look at each month of the year, and write the abbreviation for it. If it is seldom abbreviated, then simply write the name of the month. Remember that each abbreviation begins with a capital letter and ends with a period.

Optional Dictation Exercise

Call out the names of the months and the days whose abbreviations the student had trouble writing. The student will write the abbreviations again. Remind him that these abbreviations begin with a capital letter and end with a period.

Optional Follow-Up

Have the student copy a calendar for one month. He will put in the abbreviations for the days of the week.

LESSON 62

New:	**Conjunctions (with Diagramming)**
New:	**Commas in a Series**
Review:	**Abbreviations of Titles of Respect, Days, and Months**

Read "The Bells" (Lesson 58) three times to the student. Then ask the student to try to say parts of the poem along with you (or the tape recorder).

Instructor: Sometimes when you are on the highway, you might see a sign that says "Junction." A "junction" sign means that two roads are joining together. *Junction* means "joining." In this lesson you will learn about a new part of speech called a conjunction. A conjunction is a word that *joins* words or groups of words together. I will say the definition of a conjunction again. Then join with me as we say it three times more: A conjunction is a word that joins words or groups of words together.

Together (three times): A conjunction is a word that joins words or groups of words together.

Instructor: In **Exercise 1** read the list of the three most common conjunctions.

Workbook: and

but

or

Instructor: In **Exercise 2** read the sentences that use the conjunction *and*. *And* is written in bold print, and the two words that it joins are underlined.

Workbook: Rabbits **and** hamsters eat lettuce.

Fish **and** tadpoles swim.

I can run **and** jump.

Dogs can bark **and** bite.

Instructor: In **Exercise 3** read the sentences that use the conjunction *or*. *Or* is written in bold print, and the two words that it joins are underlined.

Workbook: You may play **or** read.

You may eat eggs **or** cheese.

Jim **or** Leslie should stay.

Cyclists **or** joggers may use this lane.

Instructor: In **Exercise 4** read the sentences that use the conjunction *but*. *But* is written in bold print, and the words or groups of words that it joins are underlined.

Workbook: I am <u>tired</u> **but** <u>happy</u>.

<u>I want to go outside</u>, **but** <u>I cannot find my coat</u>.

<u>I would eat my spinach</u>, **but** <u>I am not hungry</u>.

Instructor: In **Exercise 5** read aloud the first sentence. Find the conjunction and circle it. Then find the two subjects that the conjunction joins and underline them once.

Workbook: My <u>dog</u> (and) <u>cat</u> are friends.

Instructor: Read aloud the second sentence. Find the conjunction and circle it. Then find the two verbs the conjunction joins and underline them twice.

The children will work or play.

Workbook: The children will <u>work</u> (or) <u>play</u>.

Instructor: In **Exercise 6** read the two short sentences.

Workbook: Jan runs.

Mel skips.

Instructor: Then read the sentence that is made up of these two smaller sentences you just read. The two small sentences are joined by a comma and then a conjunction. Find the conjunction, and circle it.

Answer Key:

Jan runs, (but) Mel skips.

Instructor: Conjunctions, such as *and, but, or*, join words or groups of words together. If you were to give me a cookie, you could also give me milk to go with it. In **Exercise 7** read the first sentence to me.

Workbook: 1. I will give you the cookie **and** the milk.

Instructor: The conjunction *and* in the sentence joins *cookie* and *milk*. But if you gave me an apple and a napkin in addition to the cookie and the milk, the sentence would be very long if you used the conjunction *and* to join the words. Read the second sentence to me.

Workbook: 2. I will give you the cookie **and** the milk **and** the apple **and** the napkin.

Instructor: There is a better way to express this idea in a sentence. Instead of placing the conjunction *and* between each one of the items, you can just put a comma between them. I will put a comma after every item you give me—except the last one in the series. (*Series* is another word for "list.") Read the third, new-and-improved sentence to me.

Workbook: I will give you the cookie, the milk, the apple, and the napkin.

Instructor: Whenever you separate items in a series by putting a comma after each item, you should keep the very last *and*. In **Exercise 8**, read the three sentences to me. Pause as you get to each comma.

Workbook: 1. I am going to play baseball. I need a ball, a bat, a glove, and a helmet.

2. I am making cookies. I mix flour, sugar, butter, vanilla, and eggs.

3. I went to the zoo. I saw tigers, elephants, lions, monkeys, and snakes.

Instructor: In **Exercise 9** copy the three sentences on the lines provided. Pay special attention to the commas.

Workbook: 1. Plants need water, sunshine, and fertilizer.

2. People need food, water, and sleep.

3. You can see the moon, stars, planets, and comets in the night sky.

Instructor: Read the sentence in **Exercise 10**. It contains a conjunction.

Workbook: I mix flour and sugar.

Instructor: What is the verb in this sentence?

Student: *Mix*

Instructor: Now find the subject. Who mixes?

Student: *I*

Instructor: Is there a direct object that receives the action of the verb? Yes, there is. In fact, there is **more than one** direct object. I will ask you a question that will help you find the direct objects. Mix what?

Student: *Flour and sugar*

Instructor: *Flour* and *sugar* receive the action of the verb *mix*. They are **both** direct objects. There is a conjunction that joins these two direct objects: *flour, sugar*. What is the conjunction?

Student: *And*

Instructor: Look at the diagram of the sentence "I mix flour and sugar."

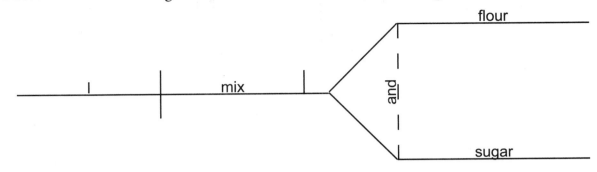

Instructor: In your workbook, I will point to what I am explaining. The subject is written on the subject line. The verb is written on the verb line. There is a short, straight line that separates the verb from the direct objects. Look at the direct objects. The first one, *flour*, is written at the top of the fork in the diagram. The second direct object, *sugar*, is written at the bottom of the fork. They are joined by a vertical, dotted line. You will see the conjunction *and* written on that dotted line.

Instructor: In **Exercise 11** of your workbook, I will help you will diagram a longer version of that same sentence. Instead of having two direct objects, this sentence has five! You read the sentence.

Workbook: 1. I mix flour, sugar, butter, vanilla, and eggs.

Remember, there are no punctuation marks on a diagram. Use the following dialogue to help the student fill in the diagram:

---

1. *What is the verb? Write the verb to the right of your center line.*

2. *Find the subject. Ask "who" or "what" before the verb. [Prompt the student with a specific question, "Who mixes?"] Write the subject to the left of the center line on your frame.*

3. *Is there a direct object that receives the action of the verb? There are five! I will ask you a question that will help you find the direct objects. Mix what?*

   Optional Sentence 2: Invited whom?

   Optional Sentence 3: Owns what?

   Write the direct object to the right of the verb on your diagram. The direct object is separated from the verb by a short, straight line.

If the student enjoyed diagramming the first sentence (or if you think he needs more practice), he may diagram Sentences 2 and 3. Sentence 3 has six direct objects!

Workbook: 2. He invited Burt, Max, Bob, Tom, and Jed.

3. She owns cats, dogs, fish, birds, lizards, and frogs.

Answer Key:

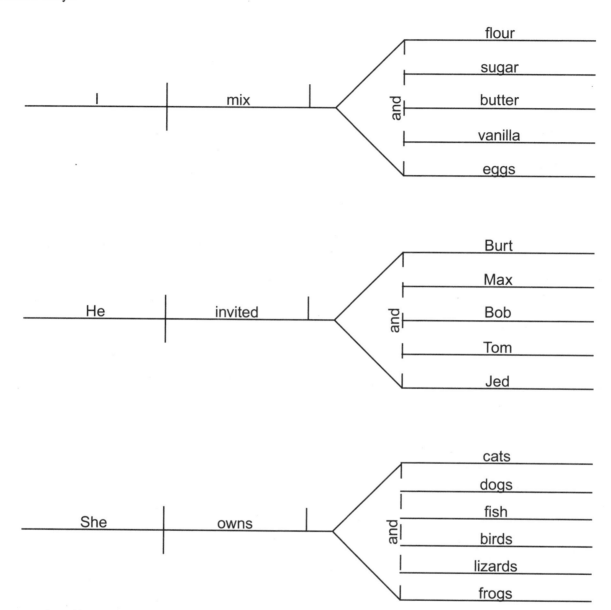

Optional Follow-Up

Draw a large comma on each of four cards, and write the word *and* on a fifth card. The student collects five objects and sets them on the table in a line. The student puts a comma between each of the first four objects, and he puts the *and* before the final object. Then he says a sentence describing what he has laid out. For example, "You can eat bread, grapes, nuts, celery, and peanut butter." OR "I see a book, a pencil, a crayon, a ruler, and paper."

LESSON 63

New: **Commas in Direct Address**

Review: **Commas in a Series**

Read "The Bells" (Lesson 58) three times to the student. Then ask the student to try to say the poem along with you (or the tape recorder). The student should practice saying the whole poem to himself in a mirror.

Instructor: In **Exercise 1** of your workbook, read the first sentence.

Workbook: I will give my brother a book **and** a stuffed animal **and** a toy car **and** Legos.

Instructor: There is a better way to express this idea in a sentence. Instead of placing the conjunction *and* between each one of the items, you can just put a comma between each one. Look at **Sentence 2**. Read this new and improved sentence to me.

Workbook: I will give my brother a book, a stuffed animal, a toy car, and Legos.

Instructor: Whenever you separate items in a series by putting a comma after each item, you should keep the very last *and*. In **Exercise 2** read the four sentences to me. Pause as you get to each comma.

Workbook: Alan, Carrie, Lucy, and I are playing together this afternoon.

Mother will make snacks for Alan, Carrie, Lucy, and me.

Jimmy, Joseph, and he went to the game with me.

I went to the game with Jimmy, Joseph, and him.

Instructor: Have the student copy two to four of the above sentences (depending on his writing ability) on the lines provided in **Exercise 2** of his workbook. Remind him to pay extra attention to the commas.

Instructor: Let's learn another way to use commas. Sometimes when you are talking to someone, you say her name to get her attention. In **Exercise 3** read the each sentence to me and then copy it onto the line just below that sentence in your workbook. Pay special attention to the comma.

Workbook: Kathy, please get me a dishcloth.

Hazel, are you ready to start to work?

Instructor: When you are talking directly to someone, you are addressing her. If you say her name at the beginning of a sentence, you are using a **direct address**. When you write a sentence that includes a direct address, you use a comma after the name or names of the people to whom you are speaking. Read both sentences aloud that you just copied. Be sure to pause when you get to each comma. That is the correct way to read a sentence that includes direct address.

Optional Follow-Up

The student will give people directions. He should begin each command with direct address. He will say loudly the name of the person he is directly addressing, whisper the word "comma," and then say the rest of the sentence in a normal voice. For example, the student might say "**Kathy** *comma* please get me a dishcloth." Five directions should be sufficient.

LESSON 64

New: **Contractions**

You will need a rubber band for this lesson. Read "The Bells" (Lesson 58) three times to the student. Then ask the student to try to say the poem along with you (or the tape recorder). If the student is ready, he should recite the poem to real people today. If he is not, continue practicing daily until he is ready.

Instructor: In this lesson you are going to learn about contractions. The word *contract* means "to draw together or shorten."

Pick up the rubber band.

Instructor: I am stretching out this rubber band. Watch as I now let it contract—it is drawing together, or shortening. So a contraction occurs when two words are drawn together and shortened by dropping some letters. Every contraction has an apostrophe in it. The apostrophe tells us where the letters were dropped to form the contraction.

Point out each element of the exercise as you explain **Exercise 1**.

Instructor: Look at **Exercise 1** in your workbook. In each group of words you will first see two words in regular black print. Next to those two words you will see the same two words, but one or more of the letters will be in different print. Those are the letters that will be left out when the contraction is formed. An apostrophe will take the place of those missing letters. We will alternate reading these groups of words. You will point to each word as you or I read. That will help you keep your place. This is the way we will read these groups of words:

1. Read aloud the two words that are first in each group.

2. Point to the letters that will be left out when the contraction is made.

3. Read aloud the contraction.

CONTRACTIONS

AM

I am	→	I am	→	I'm

IS

he is	→	he is	→	he's
she is	→	she is	→	she's
it is	→	it is	→	it's

ARE

we are	→	we are	→	we're
you are	→	you are	→	you're
they are	→	they are	→	they're

HAVE

I have	→	I have	→	I've
you have	→	you have	→	you've
we have	→	we have	→	we've
they have	→	they have	→	they've

HAS

he has	→	he has	→	he's
she has	→	she has	→	she's
it has	→	it has	→	it's

HAD

I had	→	I had	→	I'd
you had	→	you had	→	you'd
he had	→	he had	→	he'd
she had	→	she had	→	she'd
it had	→	it had	→	it'd
we had	→	we had	→	we'd
they had	→	they had	→	they'd

WILL

I will	→	I will	→	I'll
you will	→	you will	→	you'll
he will	→	he will	→	he'll
she will	→	she will	→	she'll
it will	→	it will	→	it'll
we will	→	we will	→	we'll
they will	→	they will	→	they'll

WOULD

I would	→	I would	→	I'd
you would	→	you would	→	you'd
he would	→	he would	→	he'd
she would	→	she would	→	she'd
it would	→	it would	→	it'd
we would	→	we would	→	we'd
they would	→	they would	→	they'd

LET

let us	→	let us	→	let's

NEGATIVE CONTRACTIONS

_____ NOT

is not	→	is not	→	isn't
are not	→	are not	→	aren't
was not	→	was not	→	wasn't
were not	→	were not	→	weren't
have not	→	have not	→	haven't
has not	→	has not	→	hasn't
had not	→	had not	→	hadn't
do not	→	do not	→	don't
does not	→	does not	→	doesn't
did not	→	did not	→	didn't
should not	→	should not	→	shouldn't
would not	→	would not	→	wouldn't
can not	→	can not	→	can't
could not	→	could not	→	couldn't

Instructor: There is one contraction that does not follow the normal pattern. I will read it to you. Then I want you to read it to me.

Workbook: will not → won't

Instructor: When *will not* is shortened to *won't*, the **ill** changes to **o**! This is the only contraction that has this strange change.

In **Exercise 2** have the student read aloud each sentence and then copy it, substituting a contraction for the two words in bold print. The student may look at the list in **Exercise 1** if he needs help.

Workbook: 1. **We will** eat lunch soon.

2. **It is** almost noon.

3. **You are** eating with us.

4. Antonia **could not** come.

5. She **will not** be in town.

If the student struggles to understand contractions, you may wish to have him do more copywork similar to the models in **Exercise 2**.

Optional Follow-Up

Write two words that combine to form a contraction on a strip of paper. Leave a generous space between the words, and write in large letters. Then have the student fold the strip of paper to hide the letters that are omitted when the contraction is formed. Then the student should draw a large apostrophe over the fold in the paper to complete the contraction. Do this with as many contractions from this lesson as you wish (except *won't*).

LESSON 65

Cumulative Poem Review

Instructor: Today you are going to review the poems you have memorized so far. When you recite a poem, you begin with the title and author. I will give you the title and author for each poem. Say the title and the author back to me, and then recite the poem. Remember to stand up straight! Don't fidget while you're reciting! And speak in a nice, loud, slow voice.

You may prompt the student as necessary. If the student repeats the poem accurately, he may check the box in his workbook and move on to the next poem. If he stumbles, ask him to repeat the line he cannot remember three times.

Lesson	Poem	Author
9	"The Land of Nod"	Robert Louis Stevenson
18	"A Tragic Story"	William Makepeace Thackeray
31	"I Wandered Lonely As a Cloud"	William Wordsworth
46	"A Time to Talk"	Robert Frost
58	"The Bells"	Edgar Allan Poe

LESSON 66

Narration: "Spiders"

Read the following selection aloud to the student (or, the student may read it aloud himself from his workbook). After the selection has been read, follow the scripting to make sure he understands the passage. After the initial reading, the student should **not** look at the passage.

Instructor: We are going to read to you about spiders. Before I begin reading, you should know that if you feel **aversion** to spiders, you really dislike them. When we have finished reading, I am going to ask you what you remember **only** about what has been read. Don't tell me information that you remember from somewhere else.

Spiders

Spiders are one of the marvels of the animal world and do not deserve the aversion and fear some persons feel for them. They are beneficial to mankind, for they destroy vast numbers of flies, mosquitoes, and other injurious insects; and since all but two harm neither human beings nor plants, they should not be killed.

Usually spiders have eight eyes on the front part of the head, although some species have one, two, or three pairs of eyes, and those living in caves are often entirely blind. The spider has a pair of jaws that are modified antennae; with these the prey is caught and poison is injected into the body, which is later mangled and the juices sucked out.

Instructor: Close your eyes. Now I am going to ask you a few questions about what I just read.

The following questions are to make sure the student understands the passage. The student should answer these questions in complete sentences. If the student answers in a single word or phrase, put the phrase into a complete sentence for the student and ask him to repeat it back to you. The words in italics represent sample answers—accept other answers if they are correct and if the information was in the passage.

This passage is excerpted from an article in *ChildCraft; Volume 10: Nature Excursions* (originally published in 1935). The article is entitled "Spiders and Their Kin" and was written by Mary Geisler Phillips.

Instructor: What kind of creature did we read about?

Student: *We read about spiders.*

Instructor: How do spiders help people?

Student: *They eat bad insects like flies and mosquitoes.*

Instructor: Does a spider always have only two eyes?

Student: *No, they can have more than two eyes.*

Instructor: What do spiders do with their jaws?

Student: *They catch and poison insects.*

Instructor: Now tell me two things you remember about spiders. Use your own words. Speak in complete sentences.

As the student narrates in his own words, you may write his sentences down as he speaks or record them onto a tape recorder to write down when he is finished. You have three options for writing the narration:

1. Write down the student's narration for him on his workbook page.
2. Write down the student's narration for him on a separate piece of paper and have him copy some or all of the sentences onto his workbook page.
3. Write down the student's narration on a separate piece of paper and dictate it to him, as he writes it on his workbook page.

If the student repeats the author's words verbatim, use the questions about the passage to help the student form his own sentences. If the student speaks in phrases, turn his phrases into complete sentences. The student should then repeat the complete sentence back to you. The student does not need to include every aspect of the passage in his narration—he only needs to pick out two ideas. Here is an example of a possible narration.

Spiders can have lots of eyes. They suck the juices out of their prey.

Once you have written the student's narration, he should read it aloud back to you.

LESSON 67

New: The "No" Adverbs and Contractions (with Diagramming)

Review: Contractions

Instructor: An adverb is a word that describes a verb, an adjective, or another adverb. Say that definition with me.

Together: An adverb is a word that describes a verb, an adjective, or another adverb.

Instructor: Most adverbs describe verbs. Adverbs can tell how, when, where, how often, and to what extent. In **Exercise 1** read the sentence to me.

Workbook: The truck could go nowhere.

Instructor: *Nowhere* is an adverb that tells **where**. Where could the truck go? Nowhere! The truck's wheels are probably stuck in a deep, muddy hole. Look at a diagram of that sentence.

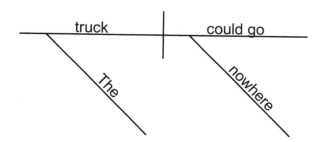

Instructor: The adverb *nowhere* is printed on a slanted line below the verb it describes.

Instructor: In **Exercise 2** read the sentence to me. It contains an adverb that comes before the verb.

Workbook: Rita never fears the dark.

Instructor: *Never* is an adverb that tells **how often**. How often does Rita fear the dark? Never! Look at a diagram of that sentence.

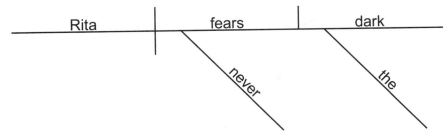

Instructor: The adverb *never* is written on a slanted line below the verb it describes.

Instructor: Now in **Exercise 3** you are going to read a sentence with a new but common adverb. You might see this sentence printed on a sign at the zoo.

Workbook: You should not feed the animals.

Instructor: What is the verb in this sentence? There are two; the helping verb *should* works together with an action verb *feed*. Both verbs—*should* and *feed*—are written together on the verb line of a diagram. There is also an adverb in this sentence, a very common little adverb: *not*. *Not* doesn't tell how, when, where, or how often. It tells "to what extent." You should not feed the animals. **To what extent** should you feed the animals? You should **not** feed them. Look at the diagram of that sentence.

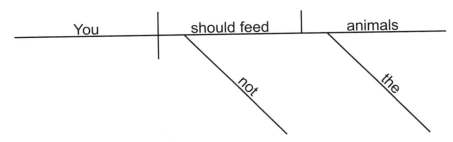

Instructor: *Not* is an adverb that describes the verbs *should feed*. It tells to what extent you should feed the animals—you should **not** feed them. Since *not* describes the verbs, it is printed on a slanted adverb line below the verbs.

Instructor: In Lesson 64 you learned about contractions. Remember, a contraction is formed when two words are drawn together and shortened by dropping some letters. In **Exercise 4** read the sentence to me.

Workbook: You shouldn't feed the animals.

Instructor: Even though the adverb *not* is shortened to *n-apostrophe-t*, we still place the shortened form *n-apostrophe-t* in the same place as the word *not* would go in the diagram. Look at the diagram of the sentence you just read.

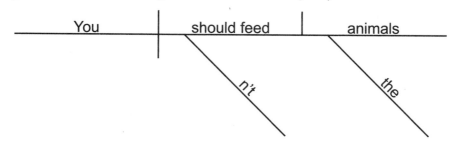

Instructor: Now in **Exercise 5**, it is your turn to diagram some sentences that contain contractions with the word *not*. You read each sentence. I will ask you questions as you fill in the diagram. Remember to copy the words exactly as they appear in the sentence. If the words begin with a capital letter in the sentence, they should also be capitalized in the diagram.

Workbook: 1. Jeremy hasn't jumped.

2. I don't swim.

Use the following dialogue in italics to help the student fill in each diagram.

1. *This sentence contains a contraction. Write out the two words that formed the contraction above the contraction itself [student writes "has not" and "do not" above the contraction in Sentences 1 and 2]. Remember to think of the contraction as two separate words.*

2. *This sentence has a helping verb and an action verb. The helping verb is part of a contraction. Write only the helping verb [has, do] and the main verb [jumped, swim], not the whole contraction, to the right of your center line.*

3. *Find the subject. Ask "who" or "what" before the verb. [Prompt the student with a specific question like "What has jumped?" or "Who does swim?"] Write the subject to the left of the center line on your frame.*

4. *This sentence contains the adverb not, although it has been shortened to n-apostrophe-t. Not tells to what extent. Write n-apostrophe-t on the slanted line below the verb it describes.*

Answer Key:

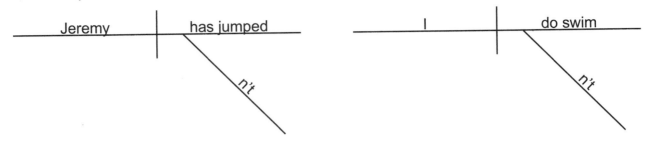

Review the list of contractions in Lesson 64. Show the student the two words that are contracted, point out the letters that are deleted to form the contraction, and then read the resulting contraction to the student. In **Exercise 6**, have the student read each sentence, and then have the student copy each sentence, substituting a contraction for the two words in bold print. The student may look at the list of contractions in Lesson 64 if he needs help.

Workbook: 1. I **will not** tease.

2. Babies **can not** walk.

3. **It is** cold today.

4. **We would** like to have dinner.

5. **You have** finished the book.

Answer Key:

1. won't

2. can't

3. It's

4. We'd

5. You've

Have the student read each sentence in **Exercise 7**. Then have him write the contraction that can be formed from the two words printed in bold. The student may look at the list of contractions in Lesson 64 if he needs help.

Workbook: 1. **She will** come with us.

2. **I am** happy.

3. **They are** my friends.

4. **Was not** she here earlier?

5. **Do not** feed the animals.

Answer Key:

1. She'll
2. I'm
3. They're
4. Wasn't
5. Don't

Optional Follow-Up

If the student enjoyed diagramming sentences with contractions (or he needs extra practice), he can diagram the next two sentences as well.

Workbook: 1. Penguins can't fly.

2. Corey doesn't type.

Answer Key:

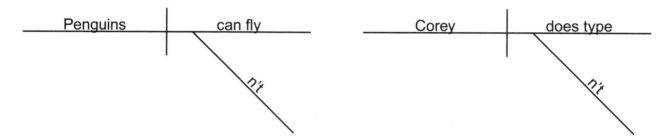

LESSON 68

New: Direct Quotations at the Ends of Sentences

Review: Four Types of Sentences

Instructor: In this lesson we are going to review the four different types of sentences: statements, commands, questions, and exclamations. A statement gives information. Statements always end with a period. In **Exercise 1** read the first statement to me.

Workbook: 1. Tuesday is a day of the week.

Instructor: The second type of sentence is a command. A command gives an order or makes a request. Read **Sentence 2** to me. A command sentence ends with either a period or an exclamation point.

Workbook: 2. Pick up all of your toys.

Instructor: The third type of sentence is a question. A question asks something. A question always ends with a question mark. Read the question aloud.

Workbook: 3. Will I need my snow boots?

Instructor: The fourth type of sentence is an exclamation. An exclamation shows sudden or strong feeling. An exclamation always ends with an exclamation point. Read **Sentence 4**. Remember to read the exclamation sentence with lots of expression because it shows strong feeling!

Workbook: 4. This box is too heavy!

Instructor: In **Exercise 2**, read the sentences and write either "S" for statement, "C" for command, "Q" for question, or "E" for exclamation after each sentence.

Workbook: 1. Put away your toy trucks. <u>C</u>

2. I need help right away! <u>E</u>

3. Is my blue coat in the closet? <u>Q</u>

4. I have one birthday each year. <u>S</u>

5. Put the lid on the jar. <u>C</u>

6. Whew, I am glad that is over! <u>E</u>

7. February is the second month of the year. <u>S</u>

8. Is our picnic lunch packed in the car? <u>Q</u>

Instructor: People use the four kinds of sentences in conversation every day. In **Exercise 3** follow along while I read the story. A family is having a conversation as they sit down to dinner.

Workbook: Mother asked, **"Did you wash your hands?"**

The children chanted together, **"We did."**

Dad said, **"Sit down."**

Carmen exclaimed, **"I am so hungry!"**

Instructor: Now we are going to read that story together. I will start each sentence, and you will read the words in bold print. These are the exact words the people said. Remember to read with expression.

In **Exercise 4** be sure to point to every punctuation mark as you explain.

Instructor: The sentences you have read are called **direct quotations**. They are the exact words that someone says. There are special punctuation marks placed before and after the exact words a person says. They are called *quotation marks*. Each of the direct quotations that you read is part of a larger sentence. When a direct quotation is at the end of a sentence, it keeps its own punctuation mark. Look at **Exercise 4** and point to the question mark at the end of the **Sentence 1**. Do you see that it is inside the quotation marks?

Workbook: 1. Mother asked, **"Did you wash your hands?"**

Instructor: "Did you wash your hands?" is a question. It ends with a **question mark**. The question mark comes **before** the last pair of **quotation marks**. Look at the sentence one more time. Notice that the direct quotation is separated from the rest of the sentence by a **comma**. And remember, when a direct quotation is at the end of a sentence, it keeps its own punctuation mark. Point to the question mark at the end of the sentence. Do you see that it is inside the quotation marks? Copy **Sentence 1** on the lines provided in your workbook.

Instructor: Read **Sentence 2**.

Workbook: 2. The children chanted together, **"We did."**

Instructor: "We did" is a statement sentence. It ends with a **period**. The period comes **before** the last pair of **quotation marks**. Look at the sentence one more time. Notice that the direct quotation is separated from the rest of the sentence by a **comma**. When a direct quotation is at the end of a sentence, it keeps its own punctuation mark. Now copy **Sentence 2** on the lines provided in your workbook.

Instructor: Read **Sentence 3**.

Workbook: 3. Dad said, "Sit down."

Instructor: "Sit down" is a command sentence. It ends with a **period**. The period comes **before** the last pair of **quotation marks**. Look at the sentence one more time. Notice that the direct quotation is separated from the rest of the sentence by a **comma**. I will say this one more time: When a direct quotation is at the end of a sentence, it keeps its own punctuation mark. Point to the period at the end of the sentence. Do you see that it is inside the quotation marks? Now copy **Sentence 3** on the lines provided in your workbook.

Instructor: Read **Sentence 4**.

Workbook: 4. Carmen exclaimed, "I am so hungry!"

Instructor: "I am so hungry!" is an exclamation sentence. It ends with an exclamation point. The exclamation point comes before the last pair of quotation marks. Look at the sentence one more time. Notice that the direct quotation is separated from the rest of the sentence by a comma. Now copy **Sentence 4** on the lines provided in your workbook.

To make sure the student is seeing and paying attention to every punctuation mark, have him read the sentences in **Exercise 5**, using the following technique: When he gets to a punctuation mark, he says the name of the punctuation mark. For example, "The children chanted together [comma] [quotation marks] We did [period] [quotation marks]."

Workbook: 1. Mother asked, "Did you wash your hands?"

2. The children chanted together, "We did."

3. Dad said, "Sit down."

4. Carmen exclaimed, "I am so hungry!"

Instructor: Now in **Exercise 6** you will copy some famous direct quotations.

Depending on the student's writing ability, choose one to three of the quotations for him to copy. As he copies, point out the rules below about a direct quotation that comes at the end of a sentence:

---

a. The exact words a person says are always enclosed by quotation marks.

b. Direct quotations begin with a capital letter.

c. The quotation is separated from the rest of the sentence by a comma.

d. The end punctuation mark always comes inside the quotation marks.

Workbook: 1. Mohandas Gandhi said, "Where there is love, there is life."

2. Patrick Henry cried, "Give me liberty or give me death!"

3. Saint Paul asked, "If God is for us, who can be against us?"

Optional Follow-Up

Tell the student that punctuation is very important because it helps you figure out the meaning of a sentence. Have the student read each pair of sentences, and discuss the different meanings.

Workbook: Jody said I ate all of the cake.

Jody said, "I ate all of the cake."

Workbook: The children cried today.

The children cried, "Today!"

Workbook: The duke declared I am now the king!

The duke declared, "I am now the king!"

Answer Key:

1. In the first sentence, Jody says that you (the person speaking) ate the cake. In the second sentence, Jody admits that she ate the cake herself.

2. In the first sentence, the children cry and sob on this day. In the second sentence, the children yell, or cry, "Today!"

3. In the first sentence, the duke declares that you (the person speaking) are the king. In the second sentence, the duke says that he himself is the new king.

LESSON 69

New: Direct Quotations at the Beginnings of Sentences
Review: Four Types of Sentences

There is a lot of writing in this lesson. If the student finds writing difficult, divide the lesson into two days (review the four types of sentences the first day and cover direct quotations the second day).

Instructor: Let's review how to diagram the four types of sentences. Let's begin by saying the definition of a sentence. A sentence is a group of words that expresses a complete thought. All sentences begin with a capital letter and end with a punctuation mark. Say that with me.

Together: A sentence is a group of words that expresses a complete thought. All sentences begin with a capital letter and end with a punctuation mark.

Instructor: There are four different types of sentences: statements, commands, questions, and exclamations. A statement gives information. In **Exercise 1** read the statement sentence.

Workbook: I play soccer weekly.

Instructor: This is a statement: "I play soccer weekly." It gives information. Statements always end with a period. Let's diagram the sentence.

Instructor: What is the verb in this sentence?

Student: *Play*

Instructor: *Play* is the verb. Write the verb on the verb line. Now find the subject. Who plays?

Student: *I*

Instructor: *I* is the subject. Write the subject to the left of the center line on your frame.

Instructor: Look again at the verb *play*. Is there a direct object that receives the action of the verb? I will ask you a question that will help you find the direct object. Play what?

Student: *Soccer*

Instructor: *Soccer* is the direct object. Write the direct object to the right of the verb on your diagram. The direct object is separated from the verb by a short, straight line.

Instructor: Look at the verb. Is there a word that describes the verb? This is an adverb that tells how often you play.

Student: *Weekly*

Instructor: Write the adverb *weekly* on the slanted line below the verb it describes. Now your diagram is complete.

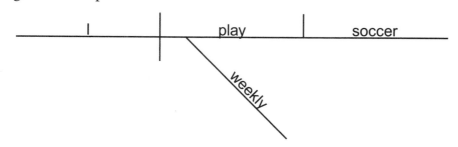

Instructor: The second type of sentence is a command. A command gives an order or makes a request. It ends with either a period or an exclamation point. In **Exercise 2** read the command sentence.

Workbook: Kick the soccer ball.

Instructor: Now you will diagram this sentence.

Instructor: What is the verb in the sentence?

Student: *Kick*

Instructor: *Kick* is the verb in the sentence. Write the word *Kick* on the verb line. Remember to capitalize *Kick* because it is capitalized in the sentence.

Instructor: Now find the subject. Remember, command sentences do have a subject, but the subject is not written in the sentence. It is understood to be the word *you*. Someone is telling you to kick the soccer ball. She does not command you by saying "**You** kick the soccer ball"; she simply says "Kick the soccer ball." So, again, what is the subject of this command sentence? Who should kick the soccer ball?

Student: *You*

Instructor: *You* is the subject. Write the word *you* on the subject line. Because the subject *you* is not written in the sentence but is just understood, you should put *you* in parentheses.

Instructor: Look again at the verb *Kick*. Is there a direct object that receives the action of the verb? I will ask you a question that will help you find the direct object. Answer me with one word. Kick what?

Student: *Ball*

Instructor: Write the direct object *ball* to the right of the verb on your diagram. The direct object is separated from the verb by a short, straight line. Are there any words that describe the direct object *ball*? There are two in this sentence. First, find the article (*a, an, the*).

Student: *The*

Instructor: *The* is an article that acts like an adjective that describes *ball*. Write the word *the* on the first slanted line beneath *ball*.

Instructor: Look again at the direct object *ball*. Are there any other words besides the article *the* that describe the direct object? This adjective tells what kind of ball it is.

Student: *Soccer*

Instructor: Write the adjective *soccer* on the second slanted line below the direct object *ball*. *The* is written on the first adjective line and *soccer* is written on the second adjective line because that is the order they appear in the sentence.

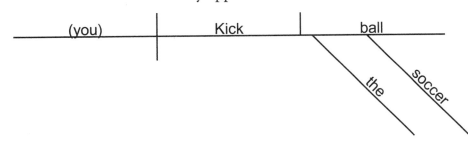

Instructor: The third type of sentence is a question. A question asks something. A question always ends with a question mark. In **Exercise 3** read the question.

Workbook: Do you play soccer?

Instructor: Diagram this question sentence.

Instructor: In order to find the subject of a question sentence, rearrange the words in the question so that it becomes a statement. Read the question again, and then read the statement beneath it.

Workbook: Do you play soccer?

You do play soccer.

Instructor: There are two verbs in this sentence: a helping and an action verb. What are those verbs?

Student: *Do play*

Instructor: Write both of these verbs on your verb line.

Instructor: What is the subject of the question "Do you play soccer?" Think of the statement "You do play soccer." Who plays soccer?

Student: *You*

Instructor: *You* is the subject of the sentence. Write the word *you* on the subject line.

Instructor: Look again at the verbs: *Do play.* Is there a direct object that receives the action of the verbs? I will ask you a question that will help you find the direct object. Do play what?

Student: *Soccer*

Instructor: Write the direct object *soccer* to the right of the verb on your diagram. The direct object is separated from the verb by a short, straight line.

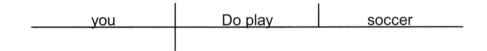

Instructor: The fourth type of sentence is an exclamation. An exclamation shows sudden or strong feeling. An exclamation always ends with an exclamation point. In **Exercise 4** read the exclamation sentence. Read it with lots of expression because exclamations show strong feeling!

Workbook: Brent's kicks were hard!

Instructor: Diagramming an exclamation sentence is just like diagramming a statement. You will diagram the sentence "Brent's kicks were hard!"

Instructor: What is the linking verb in this sentence? This verb links the subject to a word in the complete predicate.

Student: *Were*

Instructor: Write the linking verb *were* to the right of your center line.

Instructor: Now find the subject. What were hard?

Student: *Kicks*

Instructor: Write the word *kicks* on the subject line.

Instructor: This sentence contains a predicate adjective. This adjective is in the complete predicate of the sentence, but it describes the subject. What kind of kicks were they?

Student: *Hard*

Instructor: Because the predicate adjective *hard* follows the verb in the sentence, it is written to the right of the verb on the diagram. Write the predicate adjective to the right of the slanted line on your diagram. That slanted line points back toward the subject to remind you that a predicate adjective describes the subject.

Instructor: Go back and look again at the subject. Are there any words that describe the subject? This adjective tells whose kicks they were.

Student: *Brent's*

Instructor: Write the adjective *Brent's* on a slanted line below the subject it describes. Now your diagram is complete.

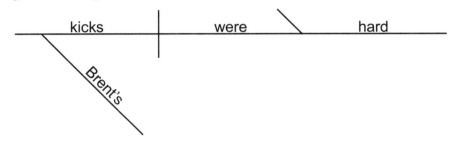

Instructor: People use the four kinds of sentences in conversation every day. Do you remember the short story we read last lesson about the family that was sitting down to dinner? In that story, each direct quotation, or exact words that a person said, came at the end of the sentence. But in some sentences, the direct quotation comes at the beginning. I am going to read the same story about the family. In **Exercise 5** follow along as I read. Notice that this time the direct quotations come at the **beginning** of the sentences.

Workbook: **"Did you wash your hands?"** Mother asked.

"We did," the children chanted together.

"Sit down," Dad said.

"I am so hungry!" Carmen exclaimed.

Instructor: Now we are going to read that story together. You will read the words in bold print. These are direct quotations—the exact words the people said. I will finish reading the words in regular print. Remember to read with expression.

As you go through the sentences in **Exercise 6**, be sure to point to every punctuation mark as you explain.

Instructor: Each of the direct quotations that you read is part of a larger sentence. Just like the direct quotations you read last lesson, these direct quotations are enclosed by quotation marks, and they each begin with a capital letter. If the direct quotation is a question or an exclamation, then the quotation itself ends with a question mark or an exclamation point. But if the direct quotation would normally end with a period, then the period is replaced by a **comma**. Let's look more closely at some of these direct quotations, and I will show you what I mean. Read the first sentence in **Exercise 6**.

Workbook: 1. **"Did you wash your hands?"** Mother asked.

Instructor: "Did you wash your hands?" is a question. It ends with a **question mark**. The question mark comes **before** the last pair of **quotation marks**. When the quotation comes at the beginning of a sentence, the end of the larger sentence needs its own mark of punctuation. Look at the larger sentence one more time. The larger sentence ends with a **period**. Now copy **Sentence 1** on the lines provided in your workbook.

Instructor: Read **Sentence 2**.

Workbook: 2. **"We did,"** the children chanted together.

Instructor: "We did" is a statement sentence. As you know, statements end with periods. But since the direct quotation statement comes at the **beginning** of a sentence, the period is replaced by a **comma**. The comma comes **before** the last pair of **quotation marks**. When the quotation comes at the beginning of a sentence, the end of the larger sentence needs its own mark of punctuation. Look at the larger sentence one more time. The sentence ends with a **period**. Now copy **Sentence 2** on the lines provided in your workbook.

Instructor: Read **Sentence 3**.

Workbook: 3. **"Sit down,"** Dad said.

Instructor: "Sit down" is a command sentence. Command sentences can end with periods. But since the direct quotation command comes at the beginning of a sentence, the period is replaced by a **comma**. The comma comes **before** the last pair of **quotation marks**. When the quotation comes at the beginning of a sentence, the end of the larger sentence needs its own mark of punctuation. Look at the larger sentence one more time. The sentence ends with a **period**. Now copy **Sentence 3** on the lines provided in your workbook.

Instructor: Read **Sentence 4**.

Workbook: 4. "I am so hungry!" Carmen exclaimed.

Instructor: "I am so hungry!" is an exclamation sentence. It ends with an **exclamation point**. The exclamation point comes **before** the last pair of **quotation marks**. When the quotation comes at the beginning of a sentence, the end of the larger sentence needs its own mark of punctuation. Look at the larger sentence one more time. The sentence ends with a **period**. Now copy **Sentence 4** on the lines provided in your workbook.

To make sure the student is seeing and paying attention to every punctuation mark, have him read the sentences in **Exercise 7** and use this technique. When he gets to a punctuation mark, he says the name of the punctuation mark. For example, "[Quotation marks] Did you wash your hands [question mark] [quotation marks] Mother asked [period]."

Workbook: 1. "Did you wash your hands?" Mother asked.

2. "We did," the children chanted together.

3. "Sit down," Dad said.

4. "I am so hungry!" Carmen exclaimed.

Instructor: In **Exercise 8**, you will copy some famous direct quotations.

Depending on the student's writing ability, choose one to three of the quotations for him to copy. As he copies, point out the following rules about a direct quotation that comes at the beginning of a sentence:

---

a. The exact words a person says are always enclosed by quotation marks.

b. Direct quotations begin with a capital letter.

c. If the direct quotation would normally end with a period, then the period is changed to a comma. This comma is always inside the quotation marks.

d. If the direct quotation ends with a question mark or exclamation point, that mark is always inside the quotation marks.

e. Since the direct quotation is only a part of the sentence, be sure to complete the sentence with its own end mark.

Workbook: 1. "No great thing is created suddenly," said Epictetus.

2. "Sing a song of seasons!" wrote Robert Louis Stevenson.

3. "Can two walk together, except they be agreed?" God asked Amos.

Optional Follow-Up

Play the game "The Silent Ruler." The student is the king or queen, and people must ask this ruler for permission to do certain things (like get a drink of water, sit down, sing a song, run around, etc.). The only problem is that the king/queen cannot speak. He/she needs to give or deny permission by giving out three notes. The student should copy the following sentences on separate pieces of paper. If the student is a boy, he should copy *king*. If the student is a girl, she should copy *queen*.

The king/queen ordered, "No, you may not!"

"Yes, you have my permission," granted the king/queen.

The king/queen asked, "Why should I allow you to do that?"

LESSON 70

New: Indirect Quotations
Review: Direct Quotations

There is a lot of writing in this lesson. If the student finds writing difficult, divide the lesson into two days (do **Exercises 1** and **2** the first day and do **Exercises 3**, **4**, and **5** the second day).

Review "The Bells" (Lesson 58) today. If the student has trouble remembering the poem, have him practice it daily until he is confident.

Instructor: In **Exercise 1** we are going to read a story together. I will start each sentence, and you will read the words in bold print. These are the exact words the people said. Remember to read with expression.

Workbook: Betty asked, **"May we make cookies?"**

Mother said, **"Get out the ingredients."**

Ralph stated, **"We will use butter, flour, and sugar."**

Betty exclaimed, **"Sugar cookies are my favorite!"**

As you go through the sentences in **Exercise 2**, be sure to point to every punctuation mark in the student's workbook as you explain.

Instructor: The sentences you have read are called **direct quotations**. They are the exact words that someone says. Quotation marks are placed before and after the exact words a person says. Each of the direct quotations that you read is part of a larger sentence. When a direct quotation is at the end of a sentence, it keeps its own punctuation mark. In **Exercise 2** read the first sentence.

Workbook: 1. Betty asked**,** "May we make cookies**?"**

Instructor: "May we make cookies?" is a question. It ends with a **question mark**. The question mark comes **before** the last pair of **quotation marks**. Look at the sentence one more time. Notice that the direct quotation is separated from the rest of the sentence by a **comma**. And remember, when a direct quotation is at the end of a sentence, it keeps its own punctuation mark. Now copy **Sentence 1** on the lines provided in your workbook.

Instructor: Read **Sentence 2**.

Workbook: 2. Mother said, **"Get out the ingredients."**

Instructor: "Get out the ingredients" is a command sentence. It ends with a **period**. When a direct quotation is at the end of a sentence, it keeps its own punctuation mark. The period comes **before** the last pair of **quotation marks**. Look at the sentence one more time. Notice that the direct quotation is separated from the rest of the sentence by a **comma**. Now copy **Sentence 2** on the lines provided in your workbook.

Instructor: Read **Sentence 3**.

Workbook: 3. Ralph stated, **"We will use butter, flour, and sugar."**

Instructor: "We will use butter, flour, and sugar" is a statement sentence. It ends with a **period**. The period comes **before** the last pair of **quotation marks**. Look at the sentence one more time. Notice that the direct quotation is separated from the rest of the sentence by a **comma**. When a direct quotation is at the end of a sentence, it keeps its own punctuation mark. Now copy **Sentence 3** on the lines provided in your workbook.

Instructor: Read **Sentence 4**.

Workbook: 4. Betty exclaimed, **"Sugar cookies are my favorite!"**

Instructor: "Sugar cookies are my favorite!" is an exclamation sentence. It ends with an **exclamation point**. The exclamation point comes **before** the last pair of **quotation marks**. Look at the sentence one more time. Notice that the direct quotation is separated from the rest of the sentence by a **comma**. When the direct quotation is at the end of a sentence, it keeps its own punctuation mark. Now copy **Sentence 4** on the lines provided in your workbook.

Instructor: In the sentences you just read, each direct quotation, or exact words that a person said, came at the end of the sentence. But in some sentences, the direct quotation comes at the beginning. In **Exercise 3** we are going to read the same story together. You will read the words in bold print. These are direct quotations—the exact words the people said. Notice that this time the direct quotations come at the beginning of the sentences. I will finish reading the words in regular print.

Workbook: **"May we make cookies?"** Betty asked.

"Get out the ingredients," Mother said.

"We will use butter, flour, and sugar," Ralph stated.

"Sugar cookies are my favorite!" Betty exclaimed.

Instructor: Each of the direct quotations that you read is part of a larger sentence. Just like the direct quotations you read earlier, these direct quotations are enclosed by quotation marks, and they each begin with a capital letter. If the direct quotation is a question or an exclamation, then the quotation itself ends with a question mark or an exclamation point. But if the direct quotation would normally end with a period, then the period is replaced by a comma. Let's look more closely at some of these direct quotations, and I will show you what I mean. In **Exercise 3** read the first sentence.

Workbook: 1. **"May we make cookies?"** Betty asked.

Instructor: "May we make cookies?" is a question. It ends with a **question mark**. The question mark comes **before** the last pair of **quotation marks**. When the quotation comes at the beginning of a sentence, the end of the larger sentence needs its own mark of punctuation. Look at the larger sentence one more time. The larger sentence ends with a **period**. Now copy **Sentence 1** of **Exercise 4** on the lines provided in your workbook.

Instructor: Read **Sentence 2** of **Exercise 4**.

Workbook: 2. **"Get out the ingredients,"** Mother said.

Instructor: "Get out the ingredients" is a command sentence. Command sentences can end with periods. But since the direct quotation command comes at the beginning of a sentence, the period turns into a **comma**. This comma comes **before** the last pair of **quotation marks**. When the quotation comes at the beginning of a sentence, the end of the larger sentence needs its own mark of punctuation. Look at the larger sentence one more time. The larger sentence ends with a **period**. Now copy **Sentence 2** on the lines provided in your workbook.

Instructor: Read **Sentence 3**.

Workbook: 3. **"We will use butter, flour, and sugar,"** Ralph stated.

Instructor: "We will use butter, flour, and sugar" is a statement sentence. As you know, statements end with periods. But since the direct quotation statement comes at the beginning of a sentence, the period turns into a **comma**. The comma comes **before** the last pair of **quotation marks**. When the quotation comes at the beginning of a sentence, the end of the larger sentence needs its own mark of punctuation. Look at the larger sentence one more time. The larger sentence ends with a **period**. Now copy **Sentence 3** on the lines provided in your workbook.

Instructor: Read **Sentence 4**.

Workbook: 4. **"Sugar cookies are my favorite!"** Betty exclaimed**.**

Instructor: "Sugar cookies are my favorite!" is an exclamation sentence. It ends with an **exclamation point**. The exclamation point comes **before** the last pair of **quotation marks**. When the quotation comes at the beginning of a sentence, the end of the larger sentence needs its own mark of punctuation. Look at the larger sentence one more time. The sentence ends with a **period**. Now copy **Sentence 4** on the lines provided in your workbook.

Instructor: All four of the sentences you have been working with contain direct quotations. You were given the **exact** words the people said. But if I change the words of a direct quotation and give the same quotation in my words, it is no longer a direct quotation. It is an **indirect** quotation. An indirect quotation tells you what a person says **without** using his or her exact words. There are no quotation marks in an indirect quotation. In **Exercise 5** read each direct quotation sentence and then read the indirect quotation beneath it.

Workbook: 1. "May we make cookies?" Betty asked.

Betty asked if Mother would let her and Ralph make cookies.

Workbook: 2. Mother said, "Get out the ingredients."

Mother told Betty to get out the ingredients.

Workbook: 3. "We will use butter, flour, and sugar," Ralph stated.

Ralph said that they would use butter, flour, and sugar to make the cookies.

Workbook: 4. Betty exclaimed, "Sugar cookies are my favorite!"

Betty exclaimed that sugar cookies were her favorite.

Optional Follow-Up

Read aloud each of the following direct quotations while the student follows along. You may need to discuss the meaning of each with him. Then he may choose three quotations and restate them in his own words as an indirect quotation (this is an oral exercise).

Workbook:
1. "The only thing we have to fear is fear itself," asserted Franklin Roosevelt.
2. Christina Rossetti stated, "There is no friend like a sister."
3. Socrates exclaimed, "How many things I can do without!"
4. "The supreme happiness in life is the conviction that we are loved," said Victor Hugo.
5. Henry David Thoreau once said, "Our life is frittered away by detail … Simplify, simplify."

Possible Answers:

1. Franklin Roosevelt said that the only thing we have to be afraid of is being afraid.
2. Christina Rossetti felt that sisters make the best of friends.
3. Socrates exclaimed that we can do without many things.
4. Victor Hugo said that being loved is one of the best things in life.
5. Henry David Thoreau said that we should simplify life.

LESSON 71

Poem Memorization: "A Slash of Blue"

Instructor: In **Lesson 71** of your workbook, you will find a poem about the colors of the sky. The author of this poem, Emily Dickinson, capitalized words in an irregular way. There are **lots** of capitalized words in this poem. Emily Dickinson also used dashes to tell the reader to pause. Follow along as I read the poem to you. Before I begin reading, you should know that a *bank* is a small hill or mound.

A Slash of Blue

by Emily Dickinson

A slash of Blue —

A sweep of Gray —

Some scarlet patches on the way,

Compose an Evening Sky —

A little purple — slipped between —

Some Ruby Trousers hurried on —

A Wave of Gold —

A Bank of Day —

This just makes out the Morning Sky.

Instructor: The author of this poem uses words to help you imagine the colors of the sky. What colors does the poet use to describe the evening sky?

Student: *Blue, gray, and scarlet*

Instructor: What colors are in the morning sky?

Student: *Purple, ruby, and gold*

Read the poem to the student three times in a row. Repeat this triple reading twice more during the day. Have the student check the boxes in his workbook when this is done.

Optional Follow-Ups

1. The student will create two pictures: one of the evening sky and one of the morning sky. Watercolors are ideal for this activity. The student should read the poem and paint the picture using the colors that Dickinson uses: gray, blue, and scarlet (red) for evening, a little purple and red, and lots of gold (yellow) for the morning sky.

2. This optional follow-up is best for an older student: Some people think that this poem is more than just a beautiful description of the sky, but that it also describes a war. Which war? The student can solve the riddle by finding the answers to these questions (look up Emily Dickinson in an encyclopedia):

   1. In what country did Emily Dickinson live? This is the country in which the war took place.

   2. When was Emily Dickinson alive? The war took place during her lifetime.

   3. What are the first two colors mentioned in the poem? These are the colors of the uniforms of the two opposing sides.

   4. Which war was fought during her lifetime (between the years of 1861 and 1865)?

Answer: The American Civil War (1861–1865). The Union soldiers wore blue; the Confederates wore gray.

LESSON 72

Review: Commas in a Series and in Direct Address

Review: Contractions

Read "A Slash of Blue" (Lesson 71) three times to the student. Then ask the student to try to say parts of the poem along with you (or the tape recorder).

Instructor: Remember, conjunctions (such as *and, but, or*) join words or groups of words together. If you lent me a baseball, you could also lend me a baseball mitt to go with it. In **Exercise 1** read the first sentence to me.

Workbook: 1. I will lend you a baseball **and** a mitt.

Instructor: The conjunction *and* in the sentence joins *baseball* and *mitt*. But if you gave me a helmet and a wooden bat in addition to the baseball and the mitt, the sentence would be very long if you used the conjunction *and* to join the words. Read the second sentence to me.

Workbook: 2. I will lend you a baseball **and** a mitt **and** a helmet **and** a bat.

Instructor: There is a better way to express this idea in a sentence. Instead of placing the conjunction *and* between each one of the items, you can just put a comma between them. I will put a comma after every item you give me—except the last one in the series. (*Series* is another word for "list.") Read the third, new-and-improved sentence to me.

Workbook: 3. I will lend you a baseball, a mitt, a helmet, and a bat.

Instructor: Whenever you separate items in a series by putting a comma after each item, you should keep the very last *and*. In **Exercise 2** read all of the sentences to me. Pause as you get to each comma.

Workbook: 1. I am going shopping. I will buy bananas, milk, eggs, and bread.

2. I set up a terrarium today. I collected beetles, ants, moths, crickets, and butter-flies.

3. I went to the park. It has a pond, a soccer field, swings, bike paths, and picnic tables.

Instructor: In **Exercise 3** copy the sentences on the lines provided. Pay special attention to the commas.

Workbook: 1. Dolphins, whales, and manatees are mammals that live in the ocean.

2. Glue can be made from animal bones, fish, milk, or vegetables.

3. We grow tomatoes, peppers, and herbs in our garden.

Instructor: You can use commas in other ways besides separating items in a series. Sometimes when you are talking to someone, you say her name to get her attention. In **Exercise 4** read both sentences to me.

Workbook: Katie, please set the table.

Margaret, did you wash your hands?

Instructor: When you are talking directly to someone, you are addressing her. If you say someone's name at the beginning of a sentence, this is called **direct address**. When you write a sentence that includes a direct address, you use a comma after the name or names of the people to whom you are speaking.

Instructor: Copy the sentences in **Exercise 4** on the lines provided. Pay extra attention to the commas.

Instructor: Now let's review contractions. Do you remember when we stretched a rubber band and then let it contract, or shorten? A contraction occurs when two words are drawn together and shortened by dropping some letters. Every contraction has an apostrophe in it. The apostrophe tells us where the letters were dropped to form the contraction. In **Exercise 5** read each pair of words. Then write the contraction that is formed when these two words are drawn together and shortened.

Answer Key:

1.	I am	I'm
2.	it is	it's
3.	she would	she'd
4.	you are	you're
5.	he will	he'll
6.	they have	they've
7.	I will	I'll
8.	it has	it's
9.	does not	doesn't
10.	will not	won't

In **Exercise 6**, have the student read each sentence and then copy it on the line provided, substituting a contraction for the two words in bold print:

Workbook: 1. **We have** eaten already.

2. **It has** been a pleasant day.

3. **Let us** leave for our camping trip now.

4. He **is not** late.

5. I **should not** bother a wasp nest.

Answer Key:

1. We've

2. It's

3. Let's

4. isn't

5. shouldn't

If the student had trouble with contractions today, go back and review Lesson 64.

Optional Follow-Up

Make "picture sentences" on a table top. Copy the following sentence starters on separate index cards for the student:

> I will eat
>
> My favorite toys are
>
> Some red items are

Then make the following punctuation cards: a large comma (make two comma cards), a "comma-*and*" card (**, and**), and a card with a period on it.

Now the student constructs a picture sentence. He places a sentence starter on one end of the table. For example, if he places "I will eat" on the table, he should put down four real food items he will eat that day. He should place a comma after each item, and place the "comma-*and*" card before the last item. He places the period card at the end of his sentence. He should then read his picture sentence, saying each punctuation mark as he gets to it ("I will eat an apple *comma* a sandwich *comma* chips *comma* and a cookie *period*"). He needs to gather four items for each sentence.

LESSON 73

Review: **Prepositions**

Review: **Conjunctions**

Read "A Slash of Blue" (Lesson 71) three times to the student. Then ask the student to try to say parts of the poem along with you (or the tape recorder).

Instructor: Let's begin this lesson reviewing prepositions. A preposition is a word that shows the relationship of a noun or pronoun to another word in the sentence. Say that definition with me three times.

Together (**three times**): A preposition is a word that shows the relationship of a noun or pronoun to another word in the sentence.

Instructor: Read the list of prepositions in **Exercise 1** one time. Then we will practice it until you can say the list from memory. You may check off your accomplishments in your workbook.

Since it has been some time since the student has practiced prepositions, use the following technique for review of the list of prepositions:

1. Have the student repeat the first section after you. If he has difficulty, chant with him until he can say it alone.

2. Have the student repeat the second section after you. If he has difficulty, chant with him until he can say it alone.

3. Then say the first *and* second sections, and have the student say both of them back to you.

4. Have the student repeat the third section after you. If he has difficulty, chant with him until he can say it alone.

5. Then say the first, second, *and* third sections, and have the student say all three back to you.

6. Continue this technique until you are finished with the list of prepositions, and the student can say the entire list by himself.

Prepositions

Aboard, about, above, across.
After, against, along, among, around, at.

Before, behind, below, beneath.
Beside, between, beyond, by.

Down, during, except, for, from.
In, inside, into, like.

Near, of, off, on, over.
Past, since, through, throughout.

To, toward, under, underneath.
Until, up, upon.
With, within, without.

If necessary, take a few minutes to review prepositions at the beginning of subsequent lessons until the student knows the list.

Instructor: When you first learned about the part of speech called a conjunction I told you this: Sometimes when you are on the highway, you might see a sign that says "Junction." A "junction" sign means that two roads are joining together. *Junction* means "joining." A conjunction is a word that **joins** words or groups of words together. I will say the definition of a conjunction again; then you join with me as we say it three times more: A conjunction is a word that joins words or groups of words together.

Together (three times): A conjunction is a word that joins words or groups of words together.

Instructor: In **Exercise 2** read the list of the three most common conjunctions.

Workbook: and

but

or

Instructor: In **Exercise 3** read sentences that use the conjunction *and* to join two words. *And* is written in bold print, and the two words that it joins are underlined.

Workbook: Pencils **and** crayons can be sharpened.

Multiplication **and** division take practice.

I study Latin **and** Spanish.

I can write **and** spell.

Instructor: In **Exercise 4** read sentences that use the conjunction *or* to join two words. *Or* is written in bold print, and the two words that it joins are underlined.

Workbook: Sherry **or** Jackie will go with us.

Skip **or** walk around the park.

You may wear a sweater **or** jacket.

We will collect shells **or** rocks.

Instructor: In **Exercise 5** read sentences that use the conjunction *but* to join words or sentences. *But* is written in bold print, and the groups of words that it joins are underlined.

Workbook: The steak was large **but** tender.

The trip was long **but** fun.

I will play the guitar, **but** I will take my violin with me.

Our house is small, **but** it is comfortable.

Instructor: In **Exercise 6** find the conjunction in the first sentence and circle it. Then find the two nouns that the conjunction joins and underline them once.

Workbook: 1. My sister (and) brother are twins.

Instructor: Find the conjunction in the second sentence and circle it. Then find the two verbs that the conjunction joins and underline them twice.

Workbook: 2. The lady hums (or) sings.

Instructor: In **Exercise 7** read the two sentences.

Workbook: Jo hides.

Keith seeks.

Instructor: Now look at the next sentence. It is made up of these two simple sentences joined by a comma and a conjunction. Find the conjunction and circle it.

Workbook: Jo hides, (but) Keith seeks.

Dictation Exercise

Before you dictate the sentences, tell the student that each dictation sentence contains a comma before a conjunction. Tell him you will pause when you get to the comma. After he has written the sentences, have him circle the conjunctions. Then you can discuss the meaning of each proverb with him.

Dictation: Ask a silly question, (and) you will get a silly answer.

A gentle answer turns anger away, (but) mean words stir up anger.

Optional Follow-Up

Put out five bowls containing bite-sized pieces of food (cereal, dried fruit, candies, bread cubes, grapes). Two people sit in front of the bowls of food. Another person (the king or queen) gives directions (the student should take a turn doing this). The king or queen grants permission to the two people to eat certain items as given in the directions below. We will use the names Meg and Bill as examples. Say a type of food when you get to a blank.

The king or queen says:

Meg **and** Bill may each eat _____.

Meg **or** Bill may eat _____. I choose Meg.

Meg may eat _____, **but** Bill may eat _____.

To continue the game, write the words *and, but,* and *or* on separate cards. Hand a card to the king or queen and have him/her make up directions using the conjunction on the card.

LESSON 74

New: Compound Subjects (with Diagramming)

Review: Prepositions

Read "A Slash of Blue" (Lesson 71) three times to the student. Then ask the student to try to say parts of the poem along with you (or the tape recorder).

Review the list of prepositions again with the student, following the technique outlined in the previous lesson.

Instructor: Let's review the definition of a sentence. A sentence is a group of words that expresses a complete thought. All sentences begin with a capital letter and end with a punctuation mark.

Instructor: Now I will say the definition three more times. Say it with me.

Together (three times): A sentence is a group of words that expresses a complete thought. All sentences begin with a capital letter and end with a punctuation mark.

Instructor: Read the first sentence in **Exercise 1**.

Workbook: Emily sings.

Instructor: Every sentence has two parts: the subject and the verb. The subject of a sentence tells who or what *does* something or who or what *is* something. In the sentence above, who sings?

Student: *Emily*

Instructor: *Emily* is the subject of the sentence. She is the only one singing. But what if someone else was also singing with Emily? Read the second sentence in **Exercise 1**.

Workbook: Emily and Ella sing.

Instructor: What is the subject of this sentence? The subject of the sentence tells who or what does something. Who sings now?

Student: *Emily and Ella*

Instructor: There are two people singing: *Emily* and *Ella*. The subject of this sentence has two parts. It is called a **compound subject**, because the word *compound* means "made up of two or more parts." The two parts of the compound subject, *Emily* and *Ella*, are joined by the conjunction *and*. Remember that a conjunction is a word that joins words or groups of words together. Look at the diagram of the sentence "Emily and Ella sing."

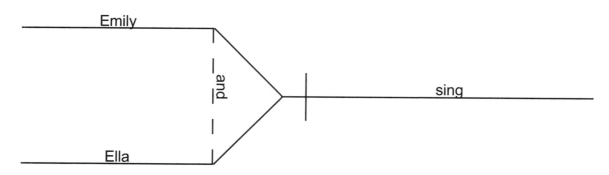

Instructor: Notice that the subject line is divided into a fork. *Emily* is written on the top line of the fork because she comes first in the sentence. *Ella* is written on the bottom line of the fork because she comes after *Emily* in the sentence. The two parts of the subject are joined by a vertical, dotted line. The conjunction *and* is printed on the dotted line because it joins the two words together.

Instructor: In **Exercise 2** of your workbook, I will ask you questions to help you diagram four sentences. Each sentence has a compound subject—it has two parts.

Workbook: 1. Fish and tadpoles swim.

2. Birds and bees fly.

3. Ted and Mark jog.

4. Balls and marbles roll.

Use the following dialogue to help the student fill in each diagram:

---

1. *What is the verb? Write the verb to the right of your center line.*

2. *Find the subject. Ask "who" or "what" before the verb. This sentence has a compound subject—it has two parts. [Prompt the student with a specific question like "What swims?" or "What flies?"] Write the first part of the subject at the top of the fork. Write the second part of the subject on the bottom of the fork.*

3. *The two parts of the compound subject are joined by a conjunction (and, but, or). What is it? Write the conjunction on the vertical, dotted line, inside the triangle formed by the fork and the dotted line.*

Answer Key:

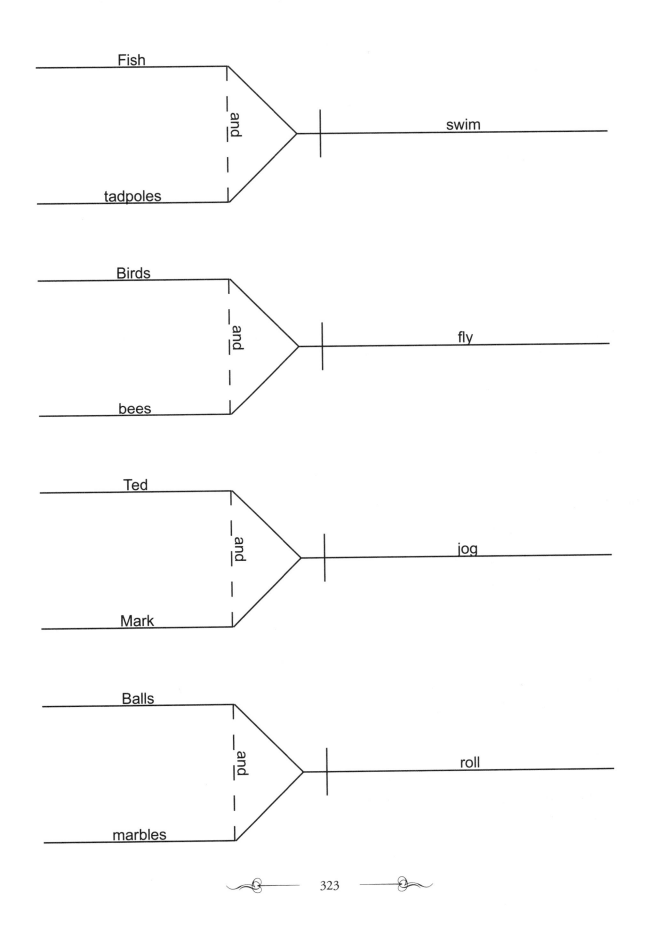

Optional Dictation Exercise

Before you dictate, show the student the compound words *firelight* and *daylight*. After he has written the sentences, have him circle the conjunction and underline the two parts of the compound subject. Cover the answers with a piece of paper so the student doesn't see the answers.

Dictation: Firelight and daylight are two kinds of light.

Wind and water break up rocks into sand.

Answer Key:

Firelight (and) daylight are two kinds of light.

Wind (and) water break up rocks into sand.

Optional Follow-Up

Give the student a direction (for example, "Ron walks to the window.").

Ron walks to the window and announces, "Now I am going to begin this sentence with a compound subject. It has two parts." It's okay to prompt the child to say this.

Ron goes back to his starting place and takes the hand of his sibling (or the instructor, or a favorite stuffed animal, or a fellow student) and they walk to the window together.

Ron says, "Ron and Mary walk to the window."

Here are some sample directions:

skip around the room

hide under a table

sit on a sofa

walk down a hall

hide behind a door

hum *The ABC Song*

LESSON 75

New: Compound Verbs (with Diagramming)

Review: Prepositional Phrases

Read "A Slash of Blue" (Lesson 71) three times to the student. Then ask the student to try to say parts of the poem along with you (or the tape recorder).

Instructor: Let's review the definition of a sentence. A sentence is a group of words that expresses a complete thought. All sentences begin with a capital letter and end with a punctuation mark.

Instructor: Now I will say the definition three more times. Say it with me.

Together (three times): A sentence is a group of words that expresses a complete thought. All sentences begin with a capital letter and end with a punctuation mark.

Instructor: Read the first sentence in **Exercise 1**.

Workbook: Emily sings.

Instructor: Every sentence has two parts: the subject and the verb. What is the verb in this sentence?

Student: *Sings*

Instructor: *Sings* is the verb. Emily sings. But what if Emily were doing something else in addition to singing? What if she were singing **and** playing the piano at the same time? Read the next sentence.

Workbook: Emily sings and plays.

Instructor: In the sentence you just read, Emily does two things. What does Emily do?

Student: *Sings and plays*

Instructor: Emily sings and Emily plays. There are two action verbs in this sentence: *sings* and *plays*. They are joined by the conjunction *and*. Remember; a conjunction is a word that joins words or groups of words together. *Sings* and *plays* joined together are called a **compound verb**. Remember, the word *compound* means "made up of two or more parts." Look at the diagram of the sentence "Emily sings and plays."

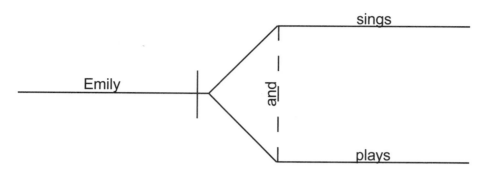

Instructor: Notice that the verb line is divided into a fork. *Sings* is written on the top line of the fork because it comes first in the sentence. *Plays* is written on the bottom line of the fork because it comes after *sings* in the sentence. The two parts of the compound verb are joined by a vertical, dotted line. The conjunction *and* is printed on the dotted line because it joins the two words together.

Instructor: In **Exercise 2** of your workbook I will help you diagram four sentences with compound verbs.

Workbook: 1. Snakes hiss and slither.

2. Wind whistles and whines.

3. Brooks tumble and swirl.

4. Soup bubbles and boils.

Use the following dialogue to help the student fill in the diagram:

1. What is the compound verb? There are two action verbs in this sentence. Write the first verb on the top of the forked verb line. Write the second verb on the bottom of the forked verb line.

2. Find the subject. Ask "who" or "what" before the verb. [Prompt the student with a specific question like "What hisses and slithers?" or "What whistles and whines?"] Write the subject to the left of the center line on your frame.

3. The two parts of the compound verb are joined by a conjunction (<u>and</u>, <u>but</u>, <u>or</u>). What is that conjunction? Write the conjunction on the vertical, dotted line, inside the triangle formed by the fork and the dotted line.

Answer Key:

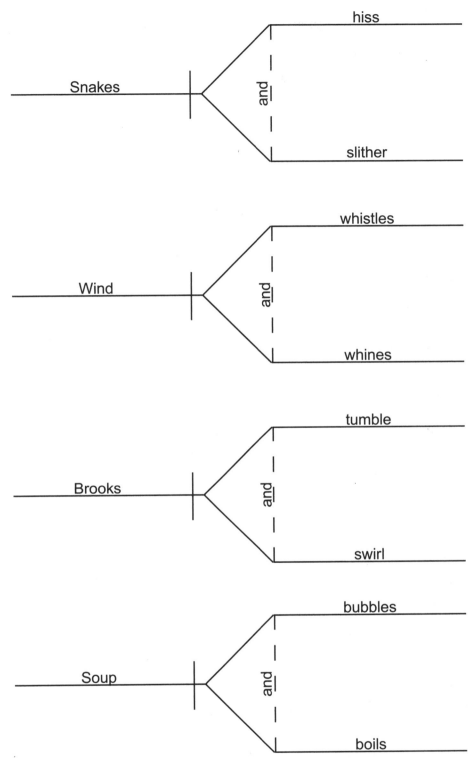

Instructor: Now let's review the definition of a preposition. A preposition is a word that shows the relationship of a noun or pronoun to another word in the sentence. Let's say that definition together three times.

Together (three times): A preposition is a word that shows the relationship of a noun or pronoun to another word in the sentence.

Student:

Prepositions

Aboard, about, above, across.
After, against, along, among, around, at.

Before, behind, below, beneath.
Beside, between, beyond, by.

Down, during, except, for, from.
In, inside, into, like.

Near, of, off, on, over.
Past, since, through, throughout.

To, toward, under, underneath.
Until, up, upon.
With, within, without.

Instructor: Read the sentence in **Exercise 3** to me:

o.p.

Workbook: Here are the keys (to) the car.

Instructor: What is the preposition in the sentence?

Student: *To*

Instructor: Circle *to*. Now find the prepositional phrase. Ask *whom* or *what* after the preposition *to*. To what? Answer me beginning with the word "To …"

Student: *To the car*

Instructor: "To the car" is the prepositional phrase. Underline it. A prepositional phrase begins with a preposition and ends with a noun or pronoun. That noun or pronoun is called the **object of the preposition**. In the prepositional phrase "to the car," the object of the preposition is the noun *car*. Write "o.p" over the object of the preposition, *car*.

Instructor: In each sentence in **Exercise 4**, you will circle the preposition, write "o.p" over the object of the preposition, and underline the prepositional phrase. You read the sentences, and I will ask you questions to help you.

Workbook: 1. His kindness ⟨toward⟩ the baby was sweet.

Instructor: What is the preposition?

Student: Toward

Instructor: What is the object of the preposition?

Student: Baby

Instructor: What is the prepositional phrase?

Student: Toward the baby

Workbook: 2. The closet ⟨under⟩ the stairs was tiny.

Instructor: What is the preposition?

Student: Under

Instructor: What is the object of the preposition?

Student: Stairs

Instructor: What is the prepositional phrase?

Student: Under the stairs

Workbook: 3. There are many bugs ⟨underneath⟩ the rock.

Instructor: What is the preposition?

Student: Underneath

Instructor: What is the object of the preposition?

Student: Rock

Instructor: What is the prepositional phrase?

Student: Underneath the rock

Workbook: 4. The kitten ⟨up⟩ the tree is scared.

Instructor: What is the preposition?

Student: *Up*

Instructor: What is the object of the preposition?

Student: *Tree*

Instructor: What is the prepositional phrase?

Student: *Up the tree*

Instructor: Some sentences look **really** long and complicated, but they are just padded with a lot of prepositional phrases. If you find and cross out all the prepositional phrases, you will see that a very simple sentence is left.

Have the student read the sentence in **Exercise 5**. Help him as needed to find and cross out all the prepositional phrases. After he has done so, he will find the sentence "A horse nibbles grass."

Workbook: In the pasture on the old farm by the banks of the James River, a horse nibbles grass near the edge of the rickety fence with chipped white paint on it.

Answer Key:

~~In the pasture~~   ~~on the old farm~~   ~~by the banks~~   ~~of the James River~~,   **a horse nibbles grass**   ~~near the edge~~   ~~of the rickety fence~~   ~~with chipped white paint~~   ~~on it~~.

Optional Follow-Up

Give the student a direction (for example, "Ron sings."). Ron sings a song.

Then give the student another direction ("Ron sits."). Ron goes to the sofa and sits down.

Then the student announces, "Now I am going to end this sentence with two verbs."

Ron says, "Ron sings and sits." He does both actions at the same time.

Here are some sample directions:

fall and roll

smile and wink

hop and bark

sigh and stretch

dance and giggle

crawl and roar

LESSON 76

New: Sentences with Compound Subjects and Compound Verbs

Read "A Slash of Blue" (Lesson 71) three times to the student. Then ask the student to try to say the poem along with you (or the tape recorder). The student should practice saying the whole poem to himself in a mirror.

Instructor: Every sentence has two parts: the subject and the verb. The subject of a sentence tells who or what **does** something or who or what **is** something. Read the sentence in **Exercise 1**.

Workbook: Sausage and bacon sizzle.

Instructor: What is the verb?

Student: *Sizzle*

Instructor: Now find the subject. What sizzles?

Student: *Sausage and bacon*

Instructor: This is a compound subject. There are two parts in this compound subject: *sausage* and *bacon*. Both meats sizzle. The two parts of the compound subject are joined by the conjunction *and*. Remember, a conjunction is a word that joins words or groups of words together. Look at the diagram of the sentence "Sausage and bacon sizzle."

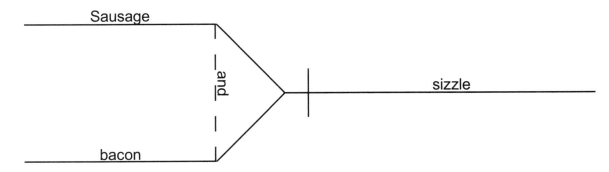

Instructor: Notice that the subject line is divided into a fork. *Sausage* is written on the top line of the fork because it comes first in the sentence. *Bacon* is written on the bottom line of the fork because it comes after *Sausage* in the sentence. The two parts of the subject are joined by a vertical, dotted line. The conjunction *and* is printed on the dotted line because it joins the two words together.

Instructor: Now read the sentence in **Exercise 2**.

Workbook: Roads twist and turn.

Instructor: In that sentence, there is a compound verb. Two action verbs are joined together by a conjunction. What do roads do?

Student: *Twist and turn*

Instructor: Roads both twist and turn. The two parts of the compound verb are joined by the conjunction *and*. Look at the diagram of the sentence "Roads twist and turn."

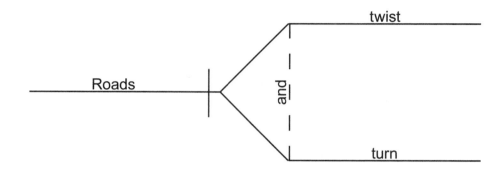

Instructor: Notice that the verb line is divided into a fork. *Twist* is written on the top line of the fork because it comes first in the sentence. *Turn* is written on the bottom line of the fork because it comes after *twist* in the sentence. The two parts of the compound verb are joined by a vertical, dotted line. The conjunction *and* is printed on the dotted line, because it joins the two words together.

Instructor: There are some sentences that have a compound subject **and** a compound verb. Read the sentence in **Exercise 3**.

Workbook: Tulips and daffodils flutter and dance.

Instructor: When we diagram sentences that have a compound subject and a compound verb, the diagram looks like this:

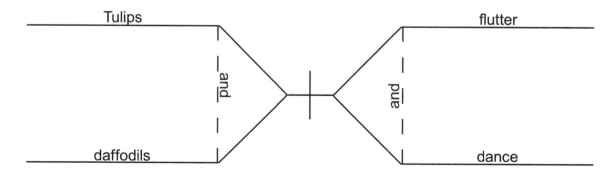

Instructor: The subject line is divided into a fork, and the verb line is divided into a fork. In **Exercise 4**, I will help you diagram three sentences that have compound subjects and compound verbs. You read each sentence and I will ask you questions.

Workbook: 1. Swallows and martins dart and swoop.

2. Walter and Brenda read and write.

3. Bees and wasps fly and sting.

Use the following dialogue to help the student fill in each diagram:

1. *What is the compound verb? There are two action verbs in this sentence. Write the first verb on the top of the forked verb line. Write the second verb on the bottom of the forked verb line.*

2. *Find the subject. Ask "who" or "what" before the verb. This sentence has a compound subject—it has two parts. [Prompt the student with a specific question like "What darts and swoops?" or "Who reads and writes?"] Write the first part of the subject at the top of the fork. Write the second part of the subject on the bottom of the fork.*

3. *The two parts of the compound verb are joined by a conjunction (and, but, or). What is that conjunction? Write the conjunction on the vertical, dotted line, inside the triangle formed by the fork and the dotted line.*

4. *The two parts of the compound subject are joined by a conjunction (and, but, or). What is it? Write the conjunction on the vertical, dotted line, inside the triangle formed by the fork and the dotted line.*

Answer Key:

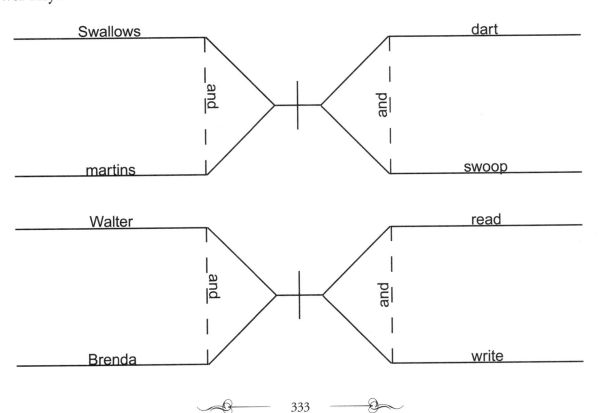

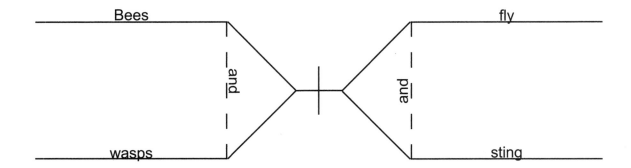

Optional Follow-Up

Gives the student a direction (for example, "Ron sings."). Ron sings a song.

Then give the student another direction ("Ron sits."). Ron goes to the sofa and sits down.

Then the instructor tells the student, "Now begin this sentence with two names and end it with two verbs."

Ron takes the hand of his sibling (or the instructor) and says, "Ron and Mary sing and sit." They do both actions at the same time.

Here are some sample directions:

sneeze and spin

wiggle and whistle

clap and waddle

blink and tiptoe

jump and wave

sleep and snore

LESSON 77

Narration: "Bull-Jumpers in Early Crete"

Read "A Slash of Blue" (Lesson 71) three times to the student. Then ask the student to try to say the poem along with you (or the tape recorder). If the student is ready, he should recite the poem to real people today. If he is not, continue practicing daily until he is ready.

Read the following selection aloud to the student (or, the student may read it aloud himself from his workbook). After the selection has been read, follow the scripting to make sure he understands the passage. After the initial reading, the student should **not** look at the passage.

Instructor: We are going to read about children who jumped over bulls.[1] When we have finished reading, I am going to ask you what you remember **only** about what has been read. Don't tell me information that you remember from somewhere else.

Bull-Jumpers in Early Crete

If you were a boy or girl in ancient Crete, you might find yourself part of a bull-jumping team! The Minoans, who lived on the island of Crete, trained athletic children to become bull-jumpers. The children learned the kind of gymnastics that children still learn today—somersaulting, balance exercises, tumbling, and vaulting. But instead of doing their vaulting over a piece of equipment, the students learned how to vault over the backs of small animals such as goats—and then finally were taught how to leap over the backs of bulls.

During bull-jumping festivals, people came from all over Crete to cheer for the bull-jumpers. Bull-jumpers were treated like royalty. They were given the best food and the nicest places to live. They were showered with presents of gold, jewelry, and beautiful clothes. But bull-jumping was a dangerous sport, because bull-jumpers were often killed by the bulls they were supposed to leap over. Few bull-jumpers lived past the age of twenty.

Instructor: Close your eyes. Now I am going to ask you a few questions about what I just read.

---

1. This passage is excerpted from *The Story of the World, Volume 1: Ancient Times* (Peace Hill Press, second edition, 2006).

The following questions are to make sure the student understands the passage. The student should answer these questions in complete sentences. If the student answers in a single word or phrase, put the phrase into a complete sentence for the student and ask him to repeat it back to you. The words in italics represent sample answers—accept other answers if they are correct and if the information was in the passage.

Instructor: What might your sport be if you were a boy or girl in ancient Crete?

Student: *Bull-jumping was a sport.*

Instructor: How did the children train to become bull-jumpers?

Student: *They learned gymnastics. OR They jumped over small animals first.*

Instructor: When did the bull-jumpers perform?

Student: *They performed during festivals*

Instructor: How were the bull-jumpers treated?

Student: *They were given gifts and treated like kings and queens.*

Instructor: What was dangerous about being a bull-jumper?

Student: *You could be killed by the bull.*

Instructor: Now tell me two things you remember about bull-jumpers. Use your own words. Speak in complete sentences.

As the student narrates in his own words, you may write his sentences down as he speaks or record them onto a tape recorder to write down when he is finished. You have three options for writing the narration:

1. Write down the student's narration for him on his workbook page.
2. Write down the student's narration for him on a separate piece of paper and have him copy some or all of the sentences onto his workbook page.
3. Write down the student's narration on a separate piece of paper and dictate it to him, as he writes it on his workbook page.

If the student repeats the author's words verbatim, use the questions about the passage to help the student form his own sentences. If the student speaks in phrases, turn his phrases into complete sentences. The student should then repeat the complete sentence back to you. The student does not need to include every aspect of the passage in his narration—he only needs to pick out two ideas. Here is an example of a possible narration.

> Bull-jumpers learned gymnastics to help them jump over the bulls. Bull-jumping was very dangerous.

Once you have written the student's narration, he should read it aloud back to you.

LESSON 78

Review: Four Kinds of Verbs

Review: Direct Objects, Predicate Nominatives, and Predicate Adjectives

Instructor: Let's begin by saying the definition of a verb. A verb is a word that does an action, shows a state of being, links two words together, or helps another verb. Say that with me two times.

Together (two times): A verb is a word that does an action, shows a state of being, links two words together, or helps another verb.

Instructor: Action verbs show action. *Fight, attack,* and *struggle* are all action verbs. Action verbs are sometimes followed by a direct object that receives the action of the verb. Now you will find the direct objects in some sentences. To find the direct object, I will ask you "what" or "whom" after the verb. Read the first sentence in **Exercise 1**. It is about a great warrior named Beowulf (pronounced "BAY-o-wolf"). There is an old, long poem about his battles and adventures.

Workbook: 1. Beowulf battled monsters.

Instructor: Battled **what**?

Student: *Monsters*

Instructor: *Monsters* is the direct object. Write "d.o." over *monsters*. It receives the action of the verb *battled*. Read the second sentence.

Workbook: 2. The monster destroys the door.

Instructor: Destroys **what**?

Student: *Door*

Instructor: *Door* is the direct object. Write "d.o." over *door*. It receives the action of the verb *destroys*. Read the third sentence.

Workbook: 3. A dragon bites Beowulf.

Instructor: Bites **whom**?

Student: *Beowulf*

Instructor: *Beowulf* is the direct object. Write "d.o." over *Beowulf*. It receives the action of the verb *bites*. Look at the diagram of the sentence you just read, "A dragon bites Beowulf."

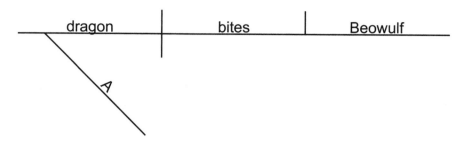

Instructor: The direct object *Beowulf* is written next to the verb *bites*. It is divided from the verb by a short line.

Instructor: Helping verbs are another kind of verb. They help other verbs. Chant the first part of the list of helping verbs with me.

Together: Am [clap]
Is [clap]
Are, was, were. [clap]
Be [clap]
Being [clap]
Been. [clap] [clap]

Instructor: Now let's chant the rest of the helping verbs together.

Together: Have, has, had [clap]
Do, does, did [clap]
Shall, will, should, would, may, might, must [clap, clap]
Can, could!

Instructor: Read the sentences in **Exercise 2**. The helping verbs are in bold print. Each helping verb helps the action verb in the sentence make sense by showing time.

Workbook: 1. The violins **should** tune.

2. The horns **will be** sounding.

3. The drums **did** beat.

Instructor: Another kind of verb, a state of being verb, just shows that you exist. Let's chant the state of being verbs together. This is same chant as the first part of the helping verb chant.

Together: Am [clap]
Is [clap]
Are, was, were. [clap]
Be [clap]
Being [clap]
Been. [clap] [clap]

Instructor: In **Exercise 3** read the sentences with state of being verbs. The state of being verbs are printed in bold.

Workbook: 1. The violins **are** in the front.

2. The horn players **were** backstage.

3. The conductor **is** on the podium.

Instructor: State of being verbs don't show action or help other verbs—they just show that someone or something exists. There is one more type of verb: linking verbs. Linking verbs link, or join, two words together. These verbs are easy to recognize because they are the same verbs as the state of being verbs: *am, is, are, was, were, be, being, been*. These verbs can do three of four parts of your verb definition! Read **Exercise 4** to me.

Workbook: The verbs *am*, *is*, *are*, *was, were*, *be*, *being*, *been* can either

- help another verb
- show a state of being
- link two words together

Instructor: So if you see the verb *is* in a sentence, you have to read the whole sentence to tell what kind of verb it is. Read the first sentence in **Exercise 5**.

               h.v.   a.v.
Workbook: 1. Daniel   is   practicing.

Instructor: *Is* is a helping verb in that sentence. *Is* helps the verb *practicing*. Write "h.v." for "helping verb" over the word *is* and write "a.v" for "action verb" over the word *practicing*. Read the second sentence.

             s.b.v.
Workbook: 2. Daniel   is   in   the   orchestra.

Instructor: *Is* just shows that someone exists among the members of the orchestra. *Is* is a state of being verb in that sentence. Write "s.b.v." for "state of being verb" over the word *is*. Read the third sentence.

Workbook:  3. Daniel is a boy.

Instructor: *Is* is a linking verb in that sentence. Write "l.v." for "linking verb" over *is*. The linking verb links the subject *Daniel* with the predicate nominative *boy*. Write "p.n." for "predicate nominative" over *boy*. Then draw an arrow from *boy* pointing back to *Daniel* to show that *boy* renames the subject *Daniel*. The verb *is* can also link the subject with an adjective in the complete predicate. Read the fourth sentence.

Workbook: 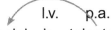 4. Daniel is talented.

Instructor: *Is* is a linking verb in this sentence, too. Write "l.v." for "linking verb" over *is*. *Is* links the subject *Daniel* with the predicate adjective *talented*. Write "p.a." for "predicate adjective" over *talented*. Then draw an arrow from *talented* pointing back to *Daniel* to show that *talented* describes the subject *Daniel*.

Instructor: In **Exercise 6**, let's look at linking verbs in sentences. I will read you a noun and a linking verb and let you complete the sentence by choosing a predicate **adjective** that describes the subject. The linking verb in bold print will link, or connect, the subject noun with the adjective you choose. Follow along as I read and point to the parts of the sentences.

Workbook: 1. Pretzels **are** _____.

Instructor: Can you tell me what pretzels tastes like?

Student: *Pretzels are [crunchy, salty, scrumptious].*

Instructor: Write your adjective in the blank. The linking verb *are* connects the subject *pretzels* with the adjective *[the word the student chose]*. Look at **Sentence 2**. Can you tell me something about the way a kaleidoscope looks?

Workbook: 2. The kaleidoscope **was** _____.

Student: *The kaleidoscope was [bright, colorful, patterned].*

Instructor: Write your adjective in the blank. The linking verb *was* connects the subject *kaleidoscope* with the adjective *[the word student chose]*. Look at **Sentence 3**. How does a hamster feel to your hand when you stroke it?

The hamster **is** _____.

Student: *The hamster is [soft, furry, warm].*

Instructor: Write your adjective in the blank. The linking verb *is* connects the subject *hamster* with the adjective *[the word student chose]*. Let's say the chant of the linking verbs. I will do the chant first, and you will join me the second time through.

Instructor, then together:

    Am [clap]

    Is [clap]

    Are, was, were. [clap]

    Be [clap]

    Being [clap]

    Been. [clap] [clap]

Instructor: In **Exercise 7** read the first sentence and look at its diagram. This sentence contains a linking verb.

Workbook: 1. The weather is gloomy.

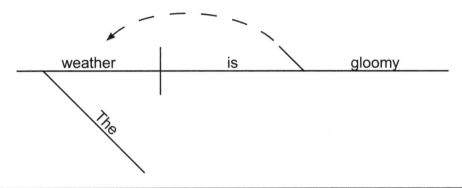

In order to keep the student's eyes focused on what you are explaining, physically point out the words and lines on the student's diagram as they appear in the next two paragraphs of the instructor's script.

Instructor: The linking verb *is* connects the subject of the sentence, *weather*, with the adjective *gloomy*. *Gloomy* is an adjective that describes the subject *weather*. It is written to the right of the verb on the diagram because it follows the verb in the sentence. Because the adjective is in the **complete predicate** of the sentence, it is a **predicate adjective**. On the diagram, draw an arrow from the predicate adjective *gloomy* that points back to the subject *weather*.

Instructor: Remember, the complete predicate is the verb and all the words attached to the verb line on a diagram. These words tell us what is said about the subject. Do you see the slanted line on the diagram that separates the linking verb *is* from the predicate adjective? That slanted line points toward the subject to remind you that *gloomy* is an adjective that describes *weather*.

Instructor: Linking verbs can also link the subject with a noun or pronoun in the complete predicate that renames the subject. This predicate noun or pronoun is called a **predicate nominative**. Read aloud **Sentence 2** and look at its diagram:

Workbook: 2. Simon was the winner.

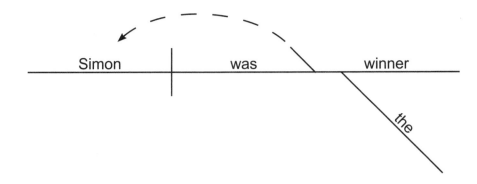

In order to keep the student's eyes focused on what you are explaining, physically point out the words and lines on the student's diagram as they appear in the next two paragraph of the instructor's script.

Instructor: *Was* is a linking verb. It connects the subject *Simon* with a noun that renames the subject. What was Simon? The *winner*. *Winner* is in the complete predicate of the sentence. A noun or pronoun in the complete predicate that renames the subject is called a **predicate nominative**. *Winner* renames the subject *Simon*. It is written to the right of the verb on the diagram because it follows the verb in the sentence. On the diagram, draw an arrow from the predicate nominative *winner* that points back to the subject *Simon* to show that *winner* renames *Simon*.

Instructor: Look again at the diagram. Do you see the slanted line that separates the linking verb *was* from the predicate nominative? That slanted line points back toward the subject to remind you that *winner* is a predicate nominative that renames the subject *Simon*.

Instructor: In **Exercise 8** of your workbook, I will help you diagram some sentences like the ones in this lesson.

1. Monsters destroyed the door.	(Ask questions 1a, 2, 3, and 7)
2. A dragon will bite Beowulf.	(Ask questions 1b, 2, 3, and 6)
3. I am.	(Ask questions 1c and 2)
4. Salty pretzels are yummy.	(Ask questions 1d, 2, 4, and 6)
5. Mother is a teacher.	(Ask questions 1d, 2, 5, and 8)

Use the following dialogue in italics to help the student fill in each diagram. After the student reads a sentence, you will prompt him with the questions in italics listed across from that sentence (for example, *Ask questions 1a, 2, 3, and 7*).

1a. What is the verb? Write the verb to the right of your center line.

1b. What is the verb? There are two verbs in this sentence. What is the helping verb? What is the action verb? You write both these verbs on your verb line.

1c. *What is the state of being verb? This verb shows that someone exists. Write the verb to the right of your center line.*

1d. *What is the linking verb? This verb links the subject to a word in the complete predicate. Write the verb to the right of your center line.*

2. *Find the subject. Ask "who" or "what" before the verb. [Prompt the student with a specific question like "What destroys?" or "What will bite?"] Write the subject to the left of the center line on your frame.*

3. *Is there a direct object that receives the action of the verb? I will ask you a question that will help you find the direct object.*

   Sentence 1: *Destroyed what?*

   Sentence 2: *Will bite whom?*

   Write the direct object to the right of the verb on your diagram. The direct object is separated from the verb by a short, straight line.

4. *This sentence contains a predicate adjective. This adjective is in the complete predicate of the sentence, but it describes the subject. A predicate adjective can tell what kind, which one, how many, or whose. Can you find an adjective that follows the verb that still describes the subject? Because the predicate adjective follows the verb in the sentence, it is written to the right of the verb on the diagram. Write the predicate adjective to the right of the slanted line on your diagram. That slanted line points back toward the subject to remind you that a predicate adjective describes the subject.*

5. *This sentence contains a predicate nominative. This noun is in the complete predicate of the sentence, but it **renames the subject**. What is the predicate nominative in this sentence? Because the predicate nominative follows the verb in the sentence, it is written to the right of the verb on the diagram. Write the predicate nominative to the right of the slanted line on your diagram. That slanted line points back toward the subject to remind you that a predicate nominative renames the subject.*

6. *Go back and look again at the subject. Are there any words that describe the subject that come before the verb? These adjectives can tell what kind, which one, how many, or whose. Also look for the articles (a, an, the), because they act like adjectives. Write each adjective on a slanted line below the subject it describes.*

7. *Look again at the direct object. Are there any words that describe the direct object? These adjectives can tell what kind, which one, how many, or whose. Also look for the articles (a, an, the), because they act like adjectives. Write each adjective on a slanted line below the direct object it describes.*

8. *Look again at the predicate nominative. Are there any words that describe the predicate nominative? These adjectives can tell what kind, which one, how many, or whose. Also look for the articles (a, an, the), because they act like adjectives. Write each adjective on a slanted line below the predicate nominative it describes.*

Answer Key:

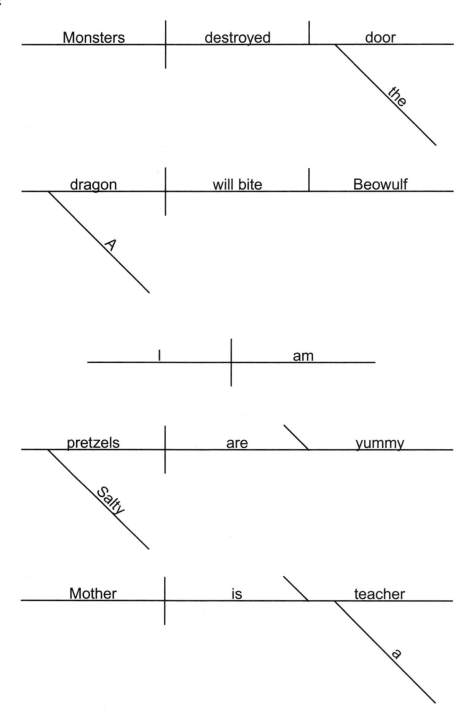

Optional Follow-Up

There is no optional follow-up for this lesson.

LESSON 79

New: Comparative and Superlative Adjectives

Review: Adjectives

Instructor: Let's review the definition of an adjective. An adjective is a word that describes a noun or pronoun. Say that definition with me.

Together: An adjective is a word that describes a noun or pronoun.

Instructor: Adjectives tell what kind, which one, how many, and whose. Say that with me two times.

Together (two times): Adjectives tell what kind, which one, how many, and whose.

Instructor: In **Exercise 1** of your workbook, I am going to read you four adjectives that tell what kind. I want you to use each adjective I say to describe any noun you wish. For example, if I say "Sleepy," you might say "Sleepy iguana."

Workbook: gentle

sugary

silly

dangerous

Instructor: In **Exercise 2** of your workbook, I am going to read you four adjectives that tell which one. I want you to use each adjective I say to describe any noun you wish. For example, if I say "That," you might say "That bicycle."

Workbook: this

those

second

last

Instructor: In **Exercise 3** of your workbook, I am going to read you four adjectives that tell how many. I want you to use each adjective I say to describe any noun you wish. For example, if I say "Five," you might say "Five pigeons."

Workbook: ten

many

several

all

Instructor: In **Exercise 4** of your workbook, I am going to read you some adjectives that tell whose. I want you to use each adjective I say to describe any noun you wish. For example, if I say "Girl's," you might say "Girl's purse." Follow along carefully with your eyes as I read each word so you will know if the word is singular or plural.

Workbook: baby's   (singular)

teacher's   (singular)

Dad's   (singular)

librarians'   (plural)

Instructor: Do you remember the three special, little words called articles? Articles act like adjectives—they describe nouns. We memorized a poem about articles. Say as much of it with me as you can. If you need help remembering, read **Exercise 5**.

Workbook: Articles are little words,

You need know only three.

The articles that describe nouns

are **a**, **an**, **the**.

Instructor: Again, what are the three articles?

Student: *A, an, the*

Instructor: Read the sentences in **Exercise 6** and circle the articles. Each sentence contains **two** articles.

Workbook: (An) eagle steals (a) fish from another bird.

(The) oil in (a) shark's liver helps it to float.

(The) actress Theodora became (an) empress.

Instructor: You already know that adjectives can tell what kind. "Young seals dive." What kind of seals? Young. But imagine you have three seals. They are all young. How can you tell them apart? Read aloud the list in **Exercise 7**.

Workbook: **young** seal

younger seal

youngest seal

Instructor: Look at the adjectives in bold print. These adjectives compare the seals. They are all young. But the second seal is younger than the first seal. And the third seal is the youngest of all. Comparative and superlative adjectives are very helpful when you have two or more of something (such as seals). You can use comparative and superlative adjectives to tell the animals or people or things apart from one another. Read aloud the four groups of sentences in **Exercise 8**. Pay special attention to the adjectives in bold print. These adjectives compare.

Workbook: There are three beds in the house.

Papa Bear's bed is **soft**.

Mama Bear's bed is **softer**.

Baby Bear's bed is the **softest**.

Pythons vary in size.

A **large** python can swallow a monkey.

A **larger** python can swallow a deer.

The **largest** python could swallow a person!

The crane fly is **small**.

The robber fly is **smaller**.

Midges are the **smallest** fly of the three.

The Arctic Ocean is **wide**.

The Atlantic Ocean is **wider**.

The Pacific Ocean is the **widest** ocean of all.

Instructor: Adjectives like "softer," "larger," and "smaller" are called *comparative*, because they *compare* two things. For example, in the story of Goldilocks, one bed is soft<u>er</u> than the other bed. Adjectives that end in "–est" are called *superlative*. The larg<u>est</u> python is the *super*-python of the whole jungle! The larg<u>est</u> python is the *super*-python of the whole jungle!

Instructor: In **Exercise 9** I will help you diagram three sentences containing comparative and superlative adjectives. You read the sentence. I will ask you questions as you fill in the diagram. Remember to copy the words exactly as they appear in the sentence. If the word begins with a capital letter in the sentence, it should also be capitalized in the diagram.

Workbook: 1. This gecko is green.   (Ask questions 1a, 2, 3, and 4)

            2. A greener gecko scurries.   (Ask questions 1b, 2, and 3)

            3. The greenest gecko hides.   (Ask questions 1b, 2, and 3)

Use the following dialogue in italics to help the student fill in each diagram. After the student reads each sentence, you will prompt him with the questions in italics listed across from that sentence.

1a. What is the linking verb? This verb links the subject to a word in the complete predicate. Write the verb to the right of the center line.

1b. What is the verb? Write the verb to the right of your center line.

2. Find the subject. Ask "who" or "what" before the verb. [Prompt the student with a specific question like "What is?" or "What scurries?"] Write the subject to the left of the center line on your frame.

3. Now you have found the two most basic parts of the sentence. Go back and look again at the subject. Are there any words that describe the subject? These adjectives can tell what kind, which one, how many, or whose. Also look for the articles (a, an, the), because they act like adjectives. Write each adjective on a slanted line below the subject it describes.

4. This sentence contains a predicate adjective. This adjective is in the complete predicate of the sentence, but it describes the subject. A predicate adjective can tell what kind, which one, how many, or whose. Can you find an adjective that follows the verb that still describes the subject? Because the predicate adjective follows the verb in the sentence, it is written to the right of the verb on the diagram. Write the predicate adjective to the right of the slanted line on your diagram. That slanted line points back toward the subject to remind you that a predicate adjective describes the subject.

Answer Key:

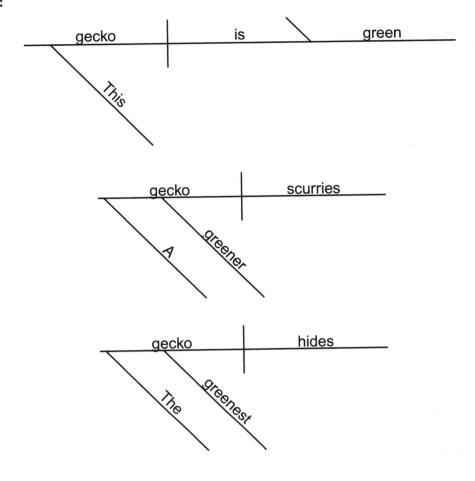

Dictation Exercise

Although it is correct to pronounce *Arctic* "AR-tik" or "ARK-tik," use the latter pronunciation when calling dictation.

Dictation: The Arctic Ocean is wide.

The Atlantic Ocean is wider.

The Pacific Ocean is the widest ocean of all.

Optional Follow-Up

The student should copy the following nine words on index cards, one word per card. He should take one set of cards and tape the cards to items in the house that can be compared.

big	long	new
bigger	longer	newer
biggest	longest	newest

LESSON 80

Review: Adverbs

Review "I Wandered Lonely As a Cloud" (Lesson 31) today. If the student has trouble remembering the poem, have him practice it daily until he is confident.

Instructor: An adverb is a word that describes a verb, an adjective, or another adverb. Adverbs tell how, when, where, how often, and to what extent. Say that with me two times.

Together (two times): An adverb is a word that describes a verb, an adjective, or another adverb. Adverbs tell how, when, where, how often, and to what extent.

Instructor: Adverbs tell **how. How** do you draw? Read each of the sentences in **Exercise 1**. The adverb that tells how is in bold print.

Workbook: I draw **quickly**.

I draw **happily**.

I draw **beautifully**.

Instructor: I will ask you a "How" question and you will read the three choices in **Exercise 2**. Choose your favorite adverb and answer the question in a complete sentence. Write the adverb in the blank provided.

Instructor: How do you sleep?

Workbook: deeply

restlessly

soundly

Student: *I sleep [adverb of choice].*

Instructor: *[Adverb of choice]* is an adverb that tells how you sleep. Adverbs tell **when. When** do you draw? Read aloud each of the sentences in **Exercise 3**. The adverb that tells when is in bold print.

Workbook: I draw **today**.

I draw **early**.

I draw **late**.

Instructor: I will ask you a "When" question and you will read the three choices in **Exercise 4**. Choose your favorite adverb and answer the question in a complete sentence. Write the adverb in the blank provided.

Instructor: When did you shop?

Workbook: earlier

yesterday

already

Student: *I shopped [adverb of choice].*

Instructor: *[Adverb of choice]* is an adverb that tells when you shopped. Adverbs tell **where**. **Where** do you draw? Read aloud each of the sentences in **Exercise 5**. The adverb that tells where is in bold print.

Workbook: I draw **outside**.

I draw **upstairs**.

I draw **everywhere**.

Instructor: I will ask you a "Where" question and you will read the three choices in **Exercise 6**. Choose your favorite adverb and answer the question in a complete sentence. Write the adverb in the blank provided.

Instructor: Where do you study?

Workbook: here

nearby

inside

Student: *I study [adverb of choice].*

Instructor: *[Adverb of choice]* is an adverb that tells where you study. Adverbs tell **how often**. **How often** do you draw? Read aloud each of the sentences in **Exercise 7**. The adverb that tells how often is in bold print.

Workbook: I draw **hourly**.

I draw **daily**.

I draw **seldom**.

Instructor: I will ask you a "How often" question and you will read the three choices in **Exercise 8**. Choose your favorite adverb and answer the question in a complete sentence.

351

Instructor: How often do you watch television?

Workbook: daily

sometimes

rarely

Student: *I watch television [adverb of choice].*

Instructor: *[Adverb of choice]* is an adverb that tells how often you watch television.

Instructor: In **Exercise 9** of your workbook, I will help you diagram four sentences with one adverb in each sentence. On a diagram, adverbs are written on a slanted line below the verb they describe. You read the sentence. I will ask you questions as you fill in the diagram. Remember to copy the words exactly as they appear in the sentence. If the word begins with a capital letter in the sentence, it should also be capitalized in the diagram.

Workbook: 1. Sloths move slowly.

2. I cooked earlier.

3. Grizzlies hibernate nearby.

4. Winston Churchill napped daily.

Use the following dialogue to help the student fill in the diagrams:

1. *What is the verb? Write the verb to the right of the center line.*

2. *Find the subject. Ask "who" or "what" before the verb. [Prompt the student with a specific question like "What moves?" or "Who cooked?"] Write the subject to the left of the center line on your frame. (Note: Sentence 4 has a proper name as its subject. Prompt the student as necessary to write both words in the name on the subject line.)*

3. *Now you have found the two most basic parts of the sentence. Go back and look again at the verb. Is there a word that describes the verb? This is an adverb that could tell how, when, where, or how often. Write the adverb on the slanted line below the verb it describes.*

Answer Key:

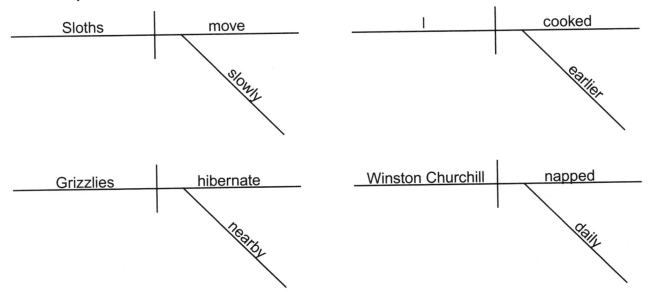

Instructor: In this review we have focused on adverbs that describe verbs. These adverbs tell how, when, where, and how often. Now let's review that adverbs can describe adjectives and other adverbs, too. Remember, these adverbs tell "to what extent." She was too tired. To what extent was she tired? **Too** tired. We are going to focus on five of these very common adverbs. Read the list of adverbs in **Exercise 10**.

Workbook: too

        very

        really

        quite

        slightly

Instructor: These adverbs can describe adjectives, like the adjective *tired*. Read the list in **Exercise 11** to see what I mean:

Workbook: **too** tired

        very tired

        really tired

        quite tired

        slightly tired

Instructor: All these adverbs tell to what extent. She was too tired. **To what extent** was she tired? **Too** tired. Or she could have been **very** tired, or **really** tired, **quite** tired, or only **slightly** tired. Now read a sentence with a predicate adjective and an adverb that describes the predicate adjective.

Workbook: Seagulls are too greedy!

Instructor: What is the predicate adjective in the sentence? **What kind** of seagulls?

Student: *Greedy*

Instructor: What is the adverb that describes the adjective *greedy*? **To what extent** are seagulls greedy?

Student: *Too*

Instructor: Look at the diagram of the sentence "Seagulls are too greedy!"

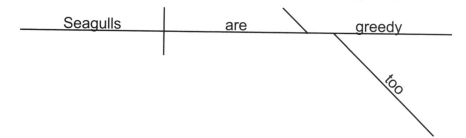

Instructor: There is a word in this sentence that describes the adjective *greedy*. The adverb *too* tells us **to what extent** the seagulls are greedy. Because *too* describes *greedy*, it is written on the slanted line beneath the predicate adjective in the diagram.

Instructor: You have seen that the adverbs *too, very, really, quite,* and *slightly* can describe adjectives. They can also describe other adverbs, like the adverb *late*. Read the list in **Exercise 12** to see what I mean:

Workbook: **too** late

very late

really late

quite late

slightly late

Instructor: All these adverbs tell to what extent. He was too late. **To what extent** was he late? **Too** late. Or he could have been **very** late, or **really** late, **quite** late, or **slightly** late. Now read a sentence with **two** adverbs. One adverb describes a verb; the other adverb describes another adverb.

Workbook: The bus stopped very quickly.

Instructor: What is the verb?

Student: *Stopped*

Instructor: What is the subject? What stopped?

Student: *Bus*

Instructor: There is an adverb that tells **how**. How did the bus stop?

Student: *quickly*

Instructor: Now there is another adverb that describes the adverb *quickly*. **To what extent** did the bus stop quickly?

Student: *Very*

Instructor: Look at the diagram of the sentence "The bus stopped very quickly." Because *very* describes to what extent the bus stopped quickly, *very* is written on the slanted line beneath the adverb.

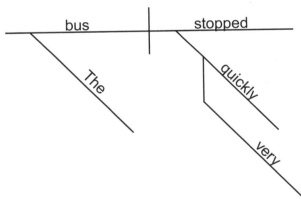

Instructor: Now I will help you diagram four sentences with adverbs that describe adjectives or other adverbs. I will ask you questions to help you fill in the diagram.

Workbook:
1. Gifts are very exciting.   (Ask questions 1a, 2, 3, and 4)
2. Grandpa was really generous.   (Ask questions 1a, 2, 3, and 4)
3. Chip wrote really carefully.   (Ask questions 1b, 2, 5, and 6)
4. They finished too early.   (Ask questions 1b, 2, 5, and 6)

Use the dialogue in italics below to help the student fill in each diagram. After the student reads a sentence, you will prompt him with the questions in italics listed across from that sentence.

1a. What is the linking verb? This verb links the subject to a word in the complete predicate. Write the verb to the right of your center line.

1b. What is the verb? Write the verb to the right of your center line.

2. Find the subject. Ask "who" or "what" before the verb. [Prompt the student with a specific question like "What are?" or "Who was?"] Write the subject to the left of the center line on your frame.

3. This sentence contains a predicate adjective. This adjective is in the complete predicate of the sentence, but it describes the subject. A predicate adjective can tell what kind, which one, how many, or whose. Can you find an adjective that follows the verb that still describes the subject? Because the predicate adjective follows the verb in the sentence, it is written to the right of the verb on the diagram. Write the predicate adjective to the right of the slanted line on your diagram. That slanted line points back toward the subject to remind you that a predicate adjective describes the subject.

4. Look again at the predicate adjective. Is there an adverb such as <u>too</u>, <u>very</u>, <u>really</u>, or <u>quite</u>? These adverbs tell how. Write the adverb on the slanted line beneath the predicate adjective it describes.

5. Now you have found the two most basic parts of the sentence. Go back and look again at the verb. Is there a word that describes the verb? This is an adverb that could tell how, when, where, or how often. Write the adverb on the slanted line below the verb it describes.

6. Look again at the adverb. Is there another adverb in the sentence, such as too, very, really, quite or slightly, that describes the first adverb? <u>Too</u>, <u>very</u>, <u>really</u>, <u>quite</u>, and <u>slightly</u> are adverbs that tell to what extent. Write one of these adverbs (<u>too</u>, <u>very</u>, <u>really</u>, <u>quite</u>, or <u>slightly</u>) on the slanted line beneath the adverb it describes.

Answer Key:

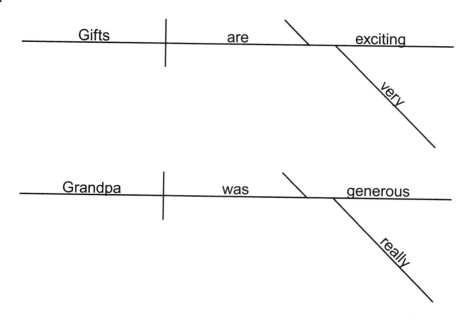

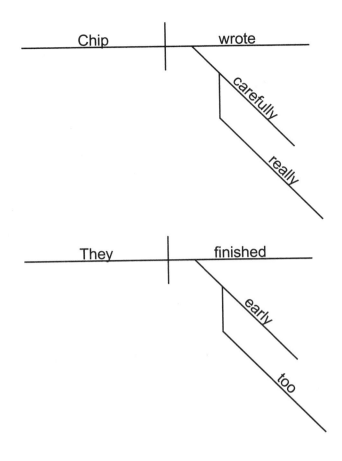

Optional Follow-Up

Play the game "The *Where* Adverb Hunt." Choose a small object (like a small teddy bear) to hide. The instructor (or another person) closes his eyes. The student hides the bear in the room in one of the following locations:

above   (hide the bear above the eye level of the person searching)

down   (somewhere on the floor)

far   (far across the room from where the person is standing)

inside   (inside something, like a box or a chest)

nearby   (near where the person is standing)

there   (when the person opens his eyes, you point generally to where the bear is hidden)

outside (outside the room)

The instructor opens his eyes and says, "Where is the bear?" The student answers, "The bear is *above* (or whatever adverb correctly describes where the bear is hidden)." When the instructor finds the bear, the game begins again. After a while the student may be the one to look for the bear.

LESSON 81

Review: Four Types of Sentences

Review "The Bells" (Lesson 58) today. If the student has trouble remembering the poem, have him practice it until he is confident.

Instructor: Let's review the four different types of sentences: statements, commands, questions, and exclamations. A statement gives information. Statements always end with a period. In **Exercise 1**, read the statement sentence to me (**Sentence 1**).

Workbook: 1. A volcanic eruption can cause a deadly mudflow.

Instructor: The second type of sentence is a command. A command gives an order or makes a request. Read the command sentence to me (**Sentence 2**). A command sentence ends with either a period or an exclamation point.

Workbook: 2. Evacuate immediately.

Instructor: The next type of sentence is a question. A question asks something. A question always ends with a question mark. Read the question to me (**Sentence 3**).

Workbook: 3. Should we cross a bridge if we see a mudflow?

Instructor: The fourth type of sentence is an exclamation. An exclamation shows sudden or strong feeling. An exclamation always ends with an exclamation point. Read the exclamation sentence with lots of expression because it shows strong feeling (**Sentence 4**)!

Workbook: 4. Mudflows can move faster than you can run!

Instructor: In **Exercise 2**, read the sentences and write either "S" for statement, "C" for command, "Q" for question, or "E" for exclamation after each sentence.

Workbook: 1. Leave the area when a volcano erupts! <u>C</u>

2. Volcanoes can be very explosive! <u>E</u>

3. How do volcanoes form? <u>Q</u>

4. Volcanic eruptions can be predicted. <u>S</u>

5. Make evacuation plans if you live near a volcano. <u>C</u>

6. Some volcanoes spew lava and rocks high into the air! <u>E</u>

7. Magma is hot, liquid rock under the earth's surface. <u>S</u>

8. Did you know that volcanic ash helps make rich soil? <u>Q</u>

Instructor: Let's review how to diagram the four types of sentences. Let's begin by saying the definition of a sentence. A sentence is a group of words that expresses a complete thought. All sentences begin with a capital letter and end with a punctuation mark. Say that with me.

Together: A sentence is a group of words that expresses a complete thought. All sentences begin with a capital letter and end with a punctuation mark.

Instructor: There are four different types of sentences: statements, commands, questions, and exclamations. A statement gives information. Read the statement sentence in **Exercise 3**.

Workbook: Volcanoes blast lava upward.

Instructor: This is a statement: "Volcanoes blast lava upward." It gives information. Statements always end with a period. I will help you diagram the sentence onto the empty frame in your workbook.

Instructor: What is the verb in this sentence?

Student: *Blast*

Instructor: *Blast* is your verb. Write the verb on the verb line.

Instructor: Now find the subject. What blast?

Student: *Volcanoes*

Instructor: *Volcanoes* is the subject. Write the subject to the left of the center line on your frame.

Instructor: Look again at the verb *blast*. Is there a direct object that receives the action of the verb? I will ask you a question that will help you find the direct object. Blast what?

Student: *Lava*

Instructor: *Lava* is the direct object. Write the direct object to the right of the verb on your diagram. The direct object is separated from the verb by a short, straight line.

Instructor: Look at the verb. Is there a word that describes the verb? This is an adverb tells where the volcanoes blast.

Student: *Upward*

Instructor: Write the adverb *upward* on the slanted line below the verb it describes. Now your diagram is complete.

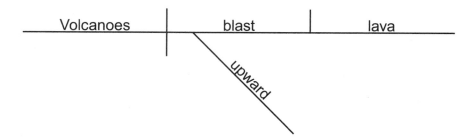

Instructor: The second type of sentence is a command. A command gives an order or makes a request. It ends with either a period or an exclamation point. Read the command sentence in **Exercise 4**.

Workbook: Leave the dangerous area!

Instructor: I will help you diagram this sentence onto the empty frame in your workbook. What is the verb?

Student: *Leave*

Instructor: *Leave* is the verb in the sentence. Write the word *Leave* on the verb line. Remember to capitalize *Leave* because it is capitalized in the sentence. Now we will find the subject. Remember, command sentences do have a subject, but the subject is not written in the sentence. It is understood to be the word *you*. Someone is telling you to leave the dangerous area. He does not command you by saying "You leave the dangerous area!" He simply orders "Leave the dangerous area!" So, again, what is the subject of this command sentence? Who should leave the dangerous area?

Student: *You*

Instructor: *You* is the subject. Write the word *you* on the subject line. Because the subject *you* is not written in the sentence but is just understood, you should put *you* in parentheses.

Instructor: Look again at the verb *Leave*. Is there a direct object that receives the action of the verb? I will ask you a question that will help you find the direct object. Answer me with one word. Leave what?

Student: *Area*

Instructor: Write the direct object *area* to the right of the verb on your diagram. The direct object is separated from the verb by a short, straight line. Are there any words that describe the direct object area? There are two in this sentence. First, find the article (*a, an, the*).

Student: *The*

Instructor: *The* is an article that acts like an adjective that describes *area*. Write the word *the* on the first slanted line beneath *area*.

Instructor: Look again at the direct object *area*. Are there any other words besides the article *the* that describe the direct object? This adjective tell what kind of area it is.

Student: *Dangerous*

Instructor: Write the adjective *dangerous* on the second slanted line below the direct object *area*. *The* is written on the first adjective line and *dangerous* is written on the second adjective line because that is the order they appear in the sentence. Now your diagram is complete.

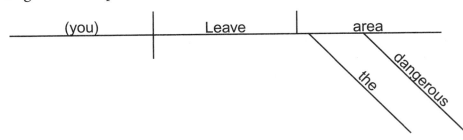

Instructor: The third type of sentence is a question. A question asks something. A question always ends with a question mark. Read the question in **Exercise 5**.

Workbook: Can we predict eruptions?

Instructor: In order to diagram a question sentence, you need to rearrange the words in the question so that it becomes a statement. Read the question again, and then read the statement beneath it.

Workbook: We can predict eruptions.

Instructor: Look at the statement sentence. What is the verb? There are two verbs in this sentence: a helping verb and an action verb. What are those verbs?

Student: *Can predict*

Instructor: Write both of these verbs on your verb line. Remember to capitalize *Can* because it is capitalized in the question sentence.

Instructor: Now find the subject. Who can predict?

Student: *We*

Instructor: *We* is the subject of the sentence. Write the word we on the subject line.

Instructor: Look again at the verbs *can predict*. Is there a direct object that receives the action of the verbs? I will ask you a question that will help you find the direct object. Can predict what?

Student: *Eruptions*

Instructor: Write the direct object *eruptions* to the right of the verb on your diagram. The direct object is separated from the verb by a short, straight line. Now your diagram is complete.

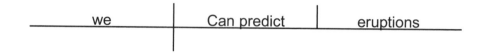

Instructor: The fourth type of sentence is an exclamation. An exclamation shows sudden or strong feeling. An exclamation always ends with an exclamation point. Read the exclamation sentence in **Exercise 6**. Read it with lots of expression because exclamations show strong feeling!

Workbook: India's mudflow was devastating!

Instructor: Diagramming an exclamation sentence is just like diagramming a statement. What is the linking verb?

Student: *Was*

Instructor: The verb *was* links the subject to a word in the complete predicate. Write the verb to the right of your center line.

Instructor: Now find the subject. Answer me with one word. What was?

Student: *Mudflow*

Instructor: Write the word *mudflow* on the subject line.

Instructor: This sentence contains a predicate adjective. This adjective is in the complete predicate of the sentence, but it describes the subject. What kind of mudflow was it?

Student: *Devastating*

Instructor: Because the predicate adjective *devastating* follows the verb in the sentence, it is written to the right of the verb on the diagram. Write the predicate adjective to the right of the slanted line on your diagram. That slanted line points back toward the subject to remind you that a predicate adjective describes the subject.

Instructor: Go back and look again at the subject. Are there any words that describe the subject? This adjective tells whose mudflow it was.

Student: *India's*

Instructor: Write the adjective *India's* on a slanted line below the subject it describes. Now your diagram is complete.

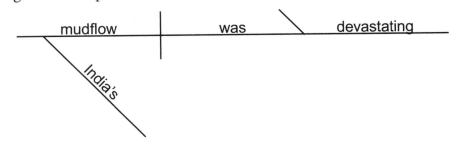

Optional Follow-Up

Make model of a volcano. Tape an empty toilet paper tube to a plate so the tube stands up. This is the "volcano." Cut red, orange, or yellow construction paper into eight long strips. Each strip should be about an inch wide. On each of the strips, copy one of the eight numbered sentences about volcanoes from earlier in this lesson. The student can curl half of each strip around a pencil. Stuff the straight end of the strip into the volcano. Once all the strips are in the volcano, the student pulls one out and reads the sentence. Then he must identify the type of sentence: statement, command, question, or exclamation. If the student correctly identifies the sentences, he can run from the erupting volcano. If he incorrectly identifies the sentence, he gets "caught in a lava flow" and must fall on the floor. He must stuff the sentence strip back into the volcano and try again later.

If you would like, the student may use Play-Doh or modeling clay to surround the tube and make it a more conical volcano shape.

LESSON 82

Review: Adjectives

Review: Comparative and Superlative Adjectives

Review "A Time to Talk" (Lesson 46) today. If the student has trouble remembering the poem, have him practice it daily until he is confident.

Instructor: Let's review the definition of an adjective. An adjective is a word that describes a noun or pronoun. Say that definition with me.

Together: An adjective is a word that describes a noun or pronoun.

Instructor: Adjectives tell what kind, which one, how many, and whose. Say that with me two times.

Together (two times): Adjectives tell what kind, which one, how many, and whose.

Instructor: In **Exercise 1** of your workbook, I am going to read some adjectives that tell what kind. I want you to use each adjective I say to describe any noun you wish. For example, if I say "Bright," you might say "Bright sun."

Workbook: dark

fuzzy

sad

active

Instructor: In **Exercise 2** of your workbook, I am going to read some adjectives that tell which one. I want you to use each adjective I say to describe any noun you wish. For example, if I say "That," you might say "That fish."

Workbook: this

these

fourth

next

Instructor: In **Exercise 3** of your workbook, I am going to read some adjectives that tell how many. I want you to use each adjective I say to describe any noun you wish. For example, if I say "Two," you might say "Two tangerines."

Workbook: twenty

most

some

Instructor: In **Exercise 4** of your workbook, I am going to read some adjectives that tell whose. I want you to use each adjective I say to describe any noun you wish. For example, if I say "Henry's," you might say "Henry's harmonica." Follow along with your eyes as I read each word so you will know if the word is singular or plural.

Workbook: bee's   (singular)

student's   (singular)

Grandpa's   (singular)

musicians'   (plural)

Instructor: Do you remember the three special, little words called articles? Articles act like adjectives—they describe nouns. In **Exercise 5** look at the poem you memorized about articles. Read it and then say as much of it with me as you can.

Workbook: Articles are little words,

You need know only three.

The articles that describe nouns

are **a, an, the**.

Instructor: Again, what are the three articles?

Student: *A, an, the*

Instructor: In **Exercise 6** read the sentences and circle the articles. Each sentence contains two articles.

Workbook: (A) jaguar is (a) large, spotted cat.

(The) space station is (an) artificial satellite of Earth.

(The) moon is (a) natural satellite.

Instructor: You already know that adjectives can tell what kind. "Old books are valuable." What kind of books? Old. But imagine you have three books. They are all old. How can you tell them apart? Read the list in **Exercise 7** to me.

Workbook: **old** book

older book

oldest book

Instructor: Look at the adjectives in bold print. These adjectives all describe the books. The books are all old. But the second book is older than the first book. And the third book is the oldest of all. "Older" is a comparative adjective. "Oldest" is a superlative adjective. Read the four groups of sentences in **Exercise 8** to me. Pay special attention to the adjectives in bold print.

Workbook: I will sip three soups.

The tomato soup is **creamy**.

The mushroom soup is **creamier**.

The potato and cheese soup is **creamiest**.

I must use up these bananas.

I will eat the **ripe** banana.

I will blend the **riper** banana in my milkshake.

I will mash up the **ripest** banana for banana bread.

Iron is **hard**.

Steel is **harder**.

Diamonds are **hardest**.

Red stars are **hot**.

White stars are **hotter**.

Blue stars are the **hottest** of all.

Instructor: In **Exercise 9** I will help you diagram three sentences that contain comparative and superlative adjectives. You read the sentence. I will ask you questions as you fill in the diagram. Remember to copy the words exactly as they appear in the sentence. If the word begins with a capital letter in the sentence, it should also be capitalized in the diagram.

Workbook: 1. That horse is dark.   (Ask questions 1a, 2, 3, and 4)

2. A darker horse whinnies.   (Ask questions 1b, 2, and 3)

3. The darkest horse gallops. (Ask questions 1b, 2, and 3)

Use the following dialogue in italics to help the student fill in each diagram. After the student reads each sentence, you will prompt him with the questions in italics listed across from that sentence.

1a. What is the linking verb? This verb links the subject to a word in the complete predicate. Write the verb to the right of the center line.

1b. What is the verb? Write the verb to the right of your center line.

2. Find the subject. Ask "who" or "what" before the verb. [Prompt the student with a specific question like "What is?" or "What whinnies?"] Write the subject to the left of the center line on your frame.

3. Now you have found the two most basic parts of the sentence. Go back and look again at the subject. Are there any words that describe the subject? These adjectives can tell what kind, which one, how many, or whose. Also look for the articles (a, an, the), because they act like adjectives. Write each adjective on a slanted line below the subject it describes.

4. This sentence contains a predicate adjective. This adjective is in the complete predicate of the sentence, but it describes the subject. A predicate adjective can tell what kind, which one, how many, or whose. Can you find an adjective that follows the verb that still describes the subject? Because the predicate adjective follows the verb in the sentence, it is written to the right of the verb on the diagram. Write the predicate adjective to the right of the slanted line on your diagram. That slanted line points back toward the subject to remind you that a predicate adjective describes the subject.

Answer Key:

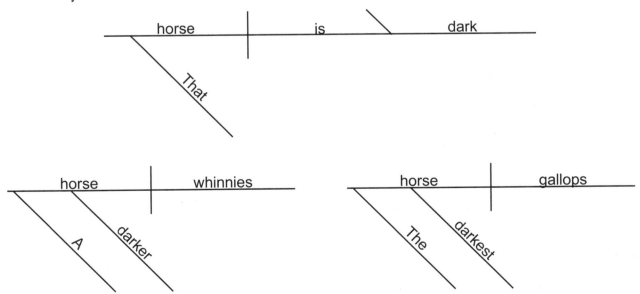

Optional Follow-Up

There is no optional follow-up for this lesson.

LESSON 83

New: Interjections (with Diagramming)

Review: Contractions

Review "A Tragic Story" (Lesson 18) today. If the student has trouble remembering the poem, have him practice it daily until he is confident.

In this lesson, the student will learn how to identify, define, and diagram an interjection. Although interjections are rarely used in formal or academic writing, the student will still encounter them in creative writing and dialogue.

Instructor: Today we are going to talk about another part of speech called an interjection. When you suddenly say just one or two words with strong feeling, we call that an interjection. Interjections might show excitement ("Yippee!") or surprise ("Wow!") or concern ("Oh no!"). An interjection is followed by a comma or an exclamation point that separates it from the main sentence. Say the definition of an interjection with me three times: An interjection is a word that expresses sudden or strong feeling.

Together (three times): An interjection is a word that expresses sudden or strong feeling.

Instructor: Read the sentences in **Exercise 1**, and read the interjection with strong feeling.

Workbook: Yikes, the bathtub is overflowing!

Wow! That is a giant watermelon!

Ouch! My sunburn is painful.

Instructor: Notice that in these sentences, each interjection is followed by a comma or an exclamation point that separates it from the main sentence. Read the list of interjections in **Exercise 2**, and then make up your own sentence using each interjection. For example, if you see the interjection "Brrr!" you might say this sentence: "Brrr, it is cold in here!"

Workbook: Quick

Eek

Great

Oops

Once the student has finished **Exercises 1** and **2**, have him copy the sentences in **Exercise 3** that have interjections. Remind him that an interjection is separated from the rest of the sentence by a comma or an exclamation point.

Workbook: 1. Quick! Come here.

2. Good! We won!

3. Oh, I spilt juice.

Instructor: Interjections are always separated from the rest of the sentence by a comma or an exclamation point. When you diagram an interjection, you need to separate it from the rest of the sentence. In **Exercise 4** look at the sentence and its diagram.

Workbook: Quick! Come here.

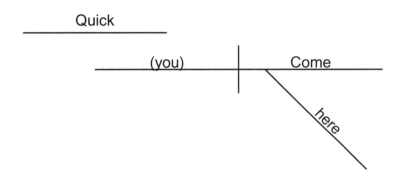

Instructor: The interjection *Quick* sits on a line that floats above the subject line in the diagram. Now in **Exercise 5** of your workbook, I will help you diagram the sentence "Good! We won!" on the empty frame in your workbook. Read the sentence again.

Workbook: Good! We won!

Instructor: Let's get the interjection out of the way. What is the interjection?

Student: *Good!*

Instructor: Write the interjection, *Good*, on the line that sits above the frame. Remember to capitalize the word *Good* because that is the way it appears in the sentence. What is the verb?

Student: *Won*

Instructor: *Won* is your verb. Write the verb on the verb line.

Instructor: Now find the subject. Who won?

Student: *We*

Instructor: *We* is the subject. Write the subject to the left of the center line on your frame. Remember to capitalize *We*, because that is the way it appears in the sentence. Now your diagram is complete.

Instructor: Now in **Exercise 6** you will diagram the sentence "Oh, I spilt juice" onto the empty frame in your workbook. Read the sentence again.

Workbook: Oh, I spilt juice.

Instructor: Let's get the interjection out of the way. What is the interjection?

Student: *Oh*

Instructor: Write the interjection, *Oh*, on the line that sits above the frame. Remember to capitalize the word *Oh* because that is the way it appears in the sentence. What is the verb?

Student: *Spilt*

Instructor: *Spilt* is your verb. Write the verb on the verb line. Now find the subject. Who spilt?

Student: *I*

Instructor: *I* is the subject. Write the subject to the left of the center line on your frame.

Instructor: Is there a direct object that receives the action of the verb? I will ask you a question that will help you find the direct object. Spilt what?

Student: *Juice*

Instructor: *Juice* is the direct object. Write the direct object to the right of the verb on your diagram. The direct object is separated from the verb by a short, straight line. Now your diagram is complete.

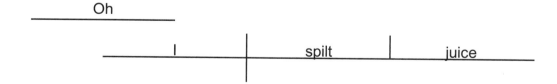

Instructor: In **Exercise 7** we will review contractions. Do you remember when we stretched a rubber band and then let it contract, or shorten? A contraction occurs when two words are drawn together and shortened by dropping some letters. Every contraction has an apostrophe in it. The apostrophe tells us where the letters were dropped to form the contraction. Read each pair of words. Then write the contraction that is formed when these two words are drawn together and shortened.

Answer Key

1.	it is	it's
2.	I would	I'd
3.	will not	won't
4.	can not	can't
5.	are not	aren't
6.	they will	they'll
7.	I have	I've
8.	I am	I'm
9.	you are	you're
10.	we have	we've

Have the student read the sentences in **Exercise 8** and then copy each sentence, substituting a contraction for the two words in bold print:

Workbook:
1. **We will** go shopping.
2. **It is** time to go now.
3. **Let us** eat lunch there.
4. There **were not** any sales at the stores.
5. We **could not** find anything we wanted.

Answer Key:
1. We'll
2. It's
3. Let's
4. weren't
5. couldn't

If the student had trouble with contractions today, go back and review Lesson 64.

Optional Follow-Up

You and the student will take turns thinking of different interjections (feel free to say some silly ones). First you will shout an interjection (because interjections show sudden or strong feeling) and then the student will shout another interjection. Try to keep in rhythm. Pat your knees twice, and clap your hands once as you or the student say the word. For example:

[pat] [pat] [clap—Instructor shouts "Yikes!"]

[pat] [pat] [clap—Student shouts "Ouch!"]

[pat] [pat] [clap—Instructor shouts "Wow!"]

[pat] [pat] [clap—Student shouts "Whew!"]

LESSON 84

Review: Nouns, Pronouns, Action Verbs, Sentences

Review: Simple and Complete Subjects and Predicates

Review "The Land of Nod" (Lesson 9) today. If the student has trouble remembering the poem, have him practice it daily until he is confident.

Instructor: Let's begin this lesson by saying the definition of a noun together. A noun is the name of a person, place, thing, or idea. Say that with me, and then say it alone.

Together, then student alone: A noun is the name of a person, place, thing, or idea.

Instructor: A common noun is a name common to many persons, places, or things. *Guest, city,* and *book* are all common nouns. A proper noun is a special, "proper" name for a person, place, or thing. *Aunt Jane, St. Louis,* and *The Hobbit* are all proper nouns. Proper nouns always begin with a capital letter. I am going to read you some nouns. If the noun is a common noun, stay seated. If the noun is a proper noun, stand up.

president

Indian Ocean

St. Jude's Children's Hospital

ocean

Abraham Lincoln

author

Washington, D.C.

book

Home Depot

Arabian Nights

park

city

Mount McKinley

E. B. White

Central Park

mountain

country

Instructor: You also know the definition of a pronoun. A pronoun is a word used in the place of a noun. Say that with me, and then say it alone.

Together, then student alone: A pronoun is a word used in the place of a noun.

Instructor: The pronouns you have learned are in **Exercise 1**. Read them to me.

Pronouns

I, me, my, mine
You, your, yours
He, she, him, her, it
His, hers, its
We, us, our, ours
They, them, their, theirs

Instructor: Let's say that list together without looking, and then you say it alone.

Instructor, then student alone:

Pronouns

I, me, my, mine
You, your, yours
He, she, him, her, it
His, hers, its
We, us, our, ours
They, them, their, theirs

Instructor: Now we will talk about verbs. A verb is a word that does an action, shows a state of being, links two words together, or helps another verb. Say that with me, and then say it alone.

Together, then student alone: A verb is a word that does an action, shows a state of being, links two words together, or helps another verb.

Instructor: We will look at the first part of the definition: "A verb is a word that does an action." Circle the action verb in each of the sentences in **Exercise 2**.

Workbook: 1. The worm wriggles in the dirt.

2. I snuggle next to my mom.

3. The doorbell rang.

4. My rabbit nibbles his food.

5. The squirrel climbs up a tree.

Instructor: Nouns and verbs can be combined to form sentences. A sentence is a group of words that expresses a complete thought. All sentences begin with a capital letter and end with a punctuation mark. Say that with me, and then say it alone.

Together, then student alone: A sentence is a group of words that expresses a complete thought. All sentences begin with a capital letter and end with a punctuation mark.

Instructor: Read the short sentence in **Exercise 3**.

Workbook: Jets race.

Instructor: Every sentence has two parts: the subject and the verb. What is the verb?

Student: *Race*

Instructor: What is the subject? What races?

Student: *Jets*

Instructor: Read the long sentence in **Exercise 3** and look at its diagram. I will point out each word and line on your diagram as I explain.

Workbook: Construction workers operate giant excavators carefully.

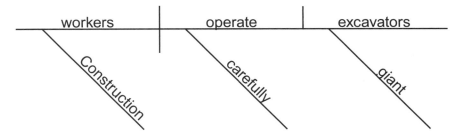

When you get to words printed in bold in the following three paragraphs of the instructor's script, point to these words or lines on the student's diagram.

Instructor: Every sentence has a subject and a verb. On a diagram, the subject and the verb are separated by **a straight line that runs down the center of the frame.** To the **left** of this center line, you will find all the words that tell you more about the subject, *workers*. The subject of the sentence is simply the word *workers*, so it is called the simple subject. But when you add other words that tell you more about the workers, you get a longer, more complete description of the subject. *Construction* tells us what kind of workers they are. *Construction workers* is the complete subject. The simple subject (*workers*) is always written on the **subject line.** The complete subject is the simple subject and all the words that hang off the simple subject (*Construction workers*). The complete subject includes **all the words to the left of the straight line that runs down the center of the frame.**

Instructor: Again, on a diagram, the subject and the verb are separated by **a straight line that runs down the center of the frame.** The words to the **right** of the center, straight line are the verb and other words that tell us what is said about the subject. All together, these words have a special name: the complete predicate. The verb in this sentence is simply the word *operate.* But more is said about the workers than just "workers operate." We know that they "operate giant excavators carefully." All these words tell us what is said about the subject, *workers.* These words together are called the complete predicate.

- *Operate* is the verb. The verb is always written on the **verb line.**

- *Carefully* tells us more about the verb *operate.* It is an adverb that tells us how the workers operate.

- *Excavators* is the direct object. It tells us what the workers operate.

- *Giant* is an adjective that also belongs in the complete predicate, because it tells us what kind of excavators the workers operate.

Instructor: The complete predicate is the verb and all the words attached to the verb line (*operate giant excavators carefully*). The complete predicate includes **all the words to the right of the straight line that runs down the center of the frame.**

Dictation Exercise

After the student has written the sentence, have him find the simple and complete subject, the verb, and the complete predicate.

Workbook: Little ladybugs eat fruit flies daily.

Answer Key:

Simple subject: ladybugs	Complete subject: Little ladybugs
Verb: eat	Complete predicate: eat fruit flies daily

Optional Follow-Up

Using a world map or a globe, have the student find one of each of the following places. (You may help him as necessary). He should copy down the proper names of each of the common names for these places in the blanks provided in his workbook.

country

ocean

river

city

lake

mountains

Review: Prepositions

Instructor: Let's review prepositions. A preposition is a word that shows the relationship of a noun or pronoun to another word in the sentence. Say that definition with me, and then say it alone.

Together, then student alone: A preposition is a word that shows the relationship of a noun or pronoun to another word in the sentence.

Have the student say the list of prepositions. If he recites them easily, he need only say them once. If he has trouble remembering the prepositions, have him read the list in **Exercise 1** and then chant it three times from memory.

Prepositions

Aboard, about, above, across.
After, against, along, among, around, at.

Before, behind, below, beneath.
Beside, between, beyond, by.

Down, during, except, for, from.
In, inside, into, like.

Near, of, off, on, over.
Past, since, through, throughout.

To, toward, under, underneath.
Until, up, upon.
With, within, without.

Instructor: Read the first sentence in **Exercise 2**.

Workbook: 1. The book before me is my grammar book.

Instructor: What is the preposition?

Student: *Before*

Instructor: Circle *before*. Before whom?

Student: *Before me*

Instructor: Underline *before me*

Instructor: "Before me" is a **prepositional phrase**. A prepositional phrase begins with a preposition and ends with a noun or pronoun. To find the prepositional phrase, ask *whom* or *what* after the preposition. Read each sentence below and circle the preposition in the sentence. Then underline the prepositional phrase.

Workbook: 2. The shoe under the bed was dusty.

Instructor: What is the preposition?

Student: *Under*

Instructor: What is the prepositional phrase? Under what?

Student: *Under the bed*

Workbook: 3. The camel in the desert drank water.

Instructor: What is the preposition?

Student: *In*

Instructor: What is the prepositional phrase? In what?

Student: *In the desert*

Instructor: A prepositional phrase begins with a preposition and ends with a noun or pronoun. That noun or pronoun is called the **object of the preposition**. In the prepositional phrase "in the desert," the object of the preposition is the noun *desert*. Read each sentence in **Exercise 3** to me. You will circle the preposition, underline the prepositional phrase, and write "o.p." over the object of the preposition.

                                       o.p.

Workbook: 1. The uniform on the conductor is fancy.

Instructor: What is the preposition?

Student: *On*

Instructor: What is the prepositional phrase? On whom?

Student: *On the conductor*

Instructor: What is the object of the preposition?

Student: *Conductor*

Workbook: 2. The sandwich without mustard is mine. [o.p.]

Instructor: What is the preposition?

Student: *Without*

Instructor: What is the prepositional phrase?

Student: *Without mustard*

Instructor: What is the object of the preposition?

Student: *Mustard*

Workbook: 3. The windows throughout the house are open. [o.p.]

Instructor: What is the preposition?

Student: *Throughout*

Instructor: What is the prepositional phrase?

Student: *Throughout the house*

Instructor: What is the object of the preposition?

Student: *House*

Workbook: 4. The player near the referee is injured. [o.p.]

Instructor: What is the preposition?

Student: *Near*

Instructor: What is the object of the preposition?

Student: *Referee*

Instructor: What is the prepositional phrase?

Student: *Near the referee*

Workbook: 5. I will wear the shirt with the purple stripes. [o.p.]

Instructor: What is the preposition?

Student: *With*

Instructor: What is the object of the preposition?

Student: *Stripes*

Instructor: What is the prepositional phrase?

Student: *With the purple stripes*

Instructor: You now know the list of prepositions, and how to find a prepositional phrase in a sentence. In **Exercise 4** we are going to practice reading a sentence, finding the prepositional phrase, and getting rid of it so that you can diagram the rest of the sentence. Read the sentence.

Workbook: I ate the muffin with raisins.

Instructor: Now find the preposition in the sentence. Circle it.

Workbook: I ate the muffin(with)raisins.

Instructor: Now find the prepositional phrase. Remember, a prepositional phrase begins with a preposition and ends with a noun or pronoun (the object of the preposition). In order to find the prepositional phrase, ask *whom* or *what* after the preposition. I ate the muffin with raisins. With what? With raisins. "With raisins" is the prepositional phrase. Put a box around the entire phrase, including the preposition.

I ate the muffin(with)raisins.

Instructor: Now read the sentence aloud, but do not read the prepositional phrase in the box.

Student: *I ate the muffin.*

Instructor: "I ate the muffin" is an easy sentence to diagram. It has a subject, action verb, and a direct object. Look at the diagram of this sentence.

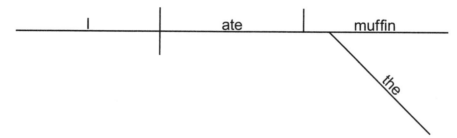

Instructor: In **Exercise 5** you are going to diagram some sentences that contain prepositional phrases. Before you begin to diagram, find the prepositional phrase and put a box around it. Then diagram the remaining sentence.

Before the student diagrams each sentence, he will **circle the preposition and put a box around the prepositional phrase.** Once he has done this, use the dialogue in italics to help the student diagram the remaining sentence. After the student reads the "preposition-free" sentence, prompt him with the questions in italics listed across from that sentence.

Workbook: 1. We saw some bugs (underneath) logs   (Ask questions 1a, 2, 4, and 6)

2. The weather (after) the storm was cooler.   (Ask questions 1b, 2, 3, and 5)

3. The cat (with) the kittens is gray.   (Ask questions 1b, 2, 3, and 5)

4. Many cars (on) the freeway sped.   (Ask questions 1a, 2, and 5)

5. Hank found two dimes (in) the grass.   (Ask questions 1a, 2, 4, and 6)

1a. What is the verb? Write the verb to the right of your center line.

1b. What is the linking verb? This verb links the subject to a word in the complete predicate. Write the verb to the right of your center line.

2. Find the subject. Ask "who" or "what" before the verb. [Prompt the student with a specific question like "Who saw?" or "What was?"] Write the subject to the left of the center line on your frame.

3. This sentence contains a predicate adjective. This adjective is in the complete predicate of the sentence, but it describes the subject. A predicate adjective can tell what kind, which one, how many, or whose. Can you find an adjective that follows the verb that still describes the subject? Because the predicate adjective follows the verb in the sentence, it is written to the right of the verb on the diagram. Write the predicate adjective to the right of the slanted line on your diagram. That slanted line points back toward the subject to remind you that a predicate adjective describes the subject.

4. Is there a direct object that receives the action of the verb? I will ask you a question that will help you find the direct object.

Sentence 1: Saw what?

Sentence 5: Found what?

Write the direct object to the right of the verb on your diagram. The direct object is separated from the verb by a short, straight line.

5. Go back and look again at the subject. Are there any words that describe the subject that come before the verb? These adjectives can tell what kind, which one, how many, or whose. Also look for the articles (a, an, the), because they act like adjectives. Write each adjective on a slanted line below the subject it describes.

6. Look again at the direct object. Are there any words that describe the direct object? These adjectives can tell what kind, which one, how many, or whose. Also look for the articles (a, an, the), because they act like adjectives. Write each adjective on a slanted line below the direct object it describes.

Answer Key:

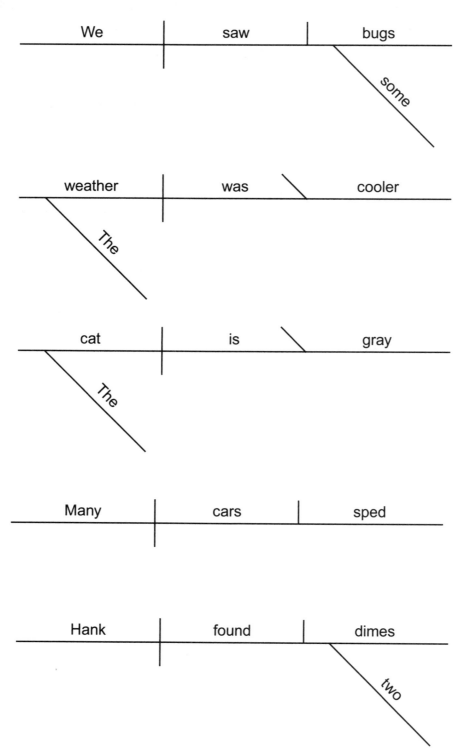

Instructor: Some sentences look **really** long and complicated, but they are just padded with a lot of prepositional phrases. Read the sentence in **Exercise 6**. Can you find and cross out all the prepositional phrases? You will find that a very simple sentence is left.

Workbook: Inside the bottom drawer of the large wooden desk in the dusty library with the tall shelves of ancient books, Jeremy uncovered a mysterious book with faded gold lettering across its tattered cover.

Answer Key:

~~Inside the bottom drawer~~ ~~of the large wooden desk~~ ~~in the dusty library~~ ~~with the tall shelves~~ ~~of ancient books,~~ **Jeremy uncovered a mysterious book** ~~with faded gold lettering~~ ~~across its tattered cover~~.

Optional Follow-Up

There is no optional follow-up for this lesson.

LESSON 86

Review: Conjunctions

Review: Compound Subjects and Compound Verbs

Review "A Slash of Blue" (Lesson 71) today. If the student has trouble remembering the poem, have him practice it until he is confident.

Instructor: A "junction" sign on the highway means that two roads are joining together. *Junction* means "joining." Remember, a conjunction is a word that joins words or groups of words together. Say that definition with me, and then say it alone.

Together, then student alone: A conjunction is a word that joins words or groups of words together.

Instructor: In **Exercise 1** read the list of the three most common conjunctions.

and

but

or

Instructor: Read the sentences in **Exercise 2** that use conjunctions. The conjunction is written in bold print, and the two words or groups of words that it joins are underlined.

Workbook: <u>Brenna</u> **and** <u>Jenna</u> make necklaces.

Nathan may play <u>football</u> **or** <u>tennis</u>.

<u>Abigail would like to stay up late</u>, **but** <u>it is time to go to bed</u>.

Instructor: Read the first sentence in **Exercise 3**. Find the conjunction and circle it. Then find the two words that the conjunction joins and underline them once.

Workbook: <u>Jane</u> ⊙r <u>Chris</u> can hide.

Instructor: Read the next sentence in **Exercise 3**. Find the conjunction and circle it. Then find the two words that the conjunction joins and underline them twice.

Workbook: The wind <u>howls</u> ⊙nd <u>moans</u>.

Instructor: Read the first two sentences in **Exercise 4**.

Workbook: Michael draws.

Vivian paints.

Instructor: Now read the next sentence. It is made up of these two simple sentences joined by a conjunction. Find the conjunction and circle it.

Workbook: Michael draws, (but) Vivian paints.

Instructor: Look at **Exercise 5**. Every sentence has two parts: the subject and the verb. The subject of a sentence tells who or what does something or who or what is something. Read the first sentence.

Workbook: 1. Frogs and bats hibernate.

Instructor: In this sentence, what hibernates?

Student: *Frogs and bats*

Instructor: This sentence has a compound subject. There are two parts to the subject: *frogs* and *bats*. Both animals hibernate. The two parts of the subject are joined by the conjunction *and*. Remember, a conjunction is a word that joins words or groups of words together. Look at the diagram of the sentence "Frogs and bats hibernate."

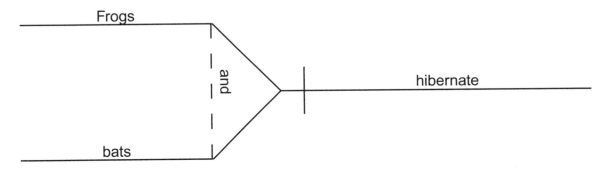

Instructor: Notice that the subject line is divided into a fork. *Frogs* is written on the top line of the fork because it comes first in the sentence. *Bats* is written on the bottom line of the fork because it comes after *Frogs* in the sentence. The two parts of the subject are joined by a vertical, dotted line. The conjunction *and* is printed on the dotted line because it joins the two words together.

Instructor: Now read the second sentence.

Workbook: 2. Branches sway and bend.

Instructor: What do branches do?

Student: *Sway and bend*

Instructor: There are two action verbs in this sentence: *sway* and *bend*. They are joined by the conjunction *and*. Remember; a conjunction is a word that joins words or groups of words together. *Sway* and *bend* joined together are called a **compound verb**. Look at the diagram of the sentence "Branches sway and bend."

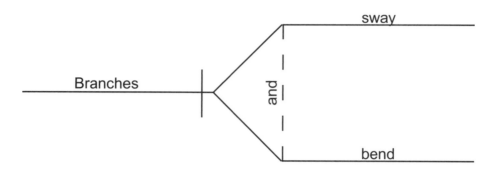

Instructor: Notice that the verb line is divided into a fork. *Sway* is written on the top line of the fork because it comes first in the sentence. *Bend* is written on the bottom line of the fork because it comes after *sway* in the sentence. The two parts of the compound verb are joined by a vertical, dotted line. The conjunction *and* is printed on the dotted line because it joins the two words together.

Instructor: There are some sentences with compound subjects **and** compound verbs. Read **Sentence 3**.

Workbook: 3. Gibbons and marmosets climb and swing.

Instructor: Look at the diagram of this sentence.

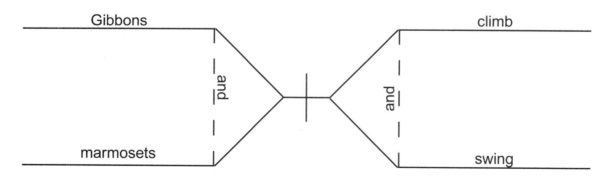

Instructor: The subject line is divided into a fork, and the verb line is divided into a fork. Now in **Exercise 6** you are going to diagram three sentences with compound subjects and compound verbs.

Workbook: 1. Dolphins and whales sing and migrate.

2. Moths and butterflies flit and flutter.

3. Gulls and pelicans swim and fly.

Use the following dialogue to help the student fill in each diagram:

1. *What is the compound verb? There are two verbs in this sentence. Write the first verb on the top of the forked verb line. Write the second verb on the bottom of the forked verb line.*

2. *Find the subject. Ask "who" or "what" before the verb. This sentence has a compound subject—it has two parts. [Prompt the student with a specific question like "What sings and migrates?" or "What flits and flutters?"] Write the first part of the subject at the top of the fork. Write the second part of the subject on the bottom of the fork.*

3. *The two parts of the compound verb are joined by a conjunction (and, but, or). What is it? Write the conjunction on the vertical, dotted line, inside the triangle formed by the fork and the dotted line.*

4. *The two parts of the compound subject are joined by a conjunction (and, but, or). What is it? Write the conjunction on the vertical, dotted line, inside the triangle formed by the fork and the dotted line.*

Answer Key:

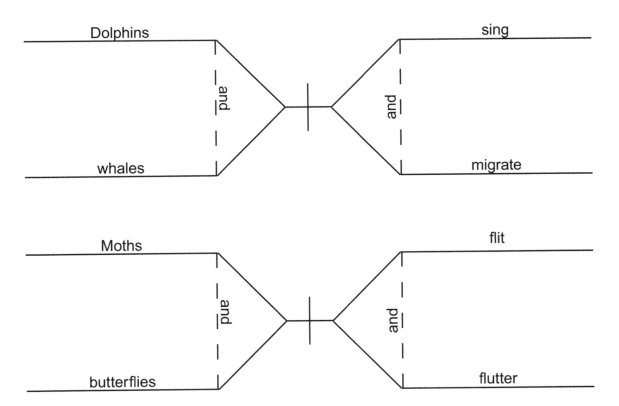

(This Answer Key continues on the next page.)

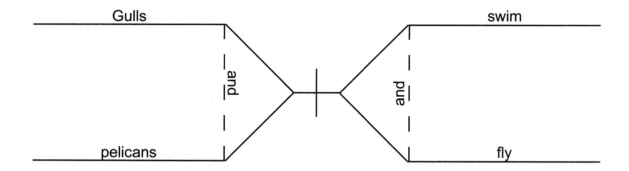

Optional Follow-Up

There is no optional follow-up for this lesson.

LESSON 87

Review: Commas in a Series and in Direct Address

Review: Direct and Indirect Quotations

Instructor: Conjunctions, such as *and, but, or,* join words or groups of words together. If I were to go on vacation, I might pack binoculars. I might also pack a swimsuit. In **Exercise 1**, read the first sentence to me.

Workbook: 1. I will pack binoculars **and** a swimsuit.

Instructor: The conjunction *and* in the sentence joins *binoculars* and *swimsuit*. But I would probably pack more in my suitcase than those two items. If I packed pajamas and a toothbrush in addition to the binoculars and swimsuit, the sentence would be very long if you used the conjunction *and* to join the words. Read the second sentence to me.

Workbook: 2. I will pack binoculars **and** a swimsuit **and** pajamas **and** a toothbrush.

Instructor: There is a better way to express this idea in a sentence. Instead of placing the conjunction *and* between each one of the items, you can just put a comma between them. I will put a comma after every item I pack—except the last one in the series. (*Series* is another word for "list.") Read this new and improved sentence to me (**Sentence 3**).

Workbook: 3. I will pack binoculars, a swimsuit, pajamas, and a toothbrush.

Instructor: Whenever you separate items in a series by putting a comma after each item, you should keep the very last *and*. In **Exercise 2**, read the sentences to me. Pause as you get to each comma.

Workbook: I am making brownies. I mix flour, sugar, oil, eggs, and chocolate.

I have many collections. I collect stickers, bugs, rocks, coins, and junk.

I went to the aquarium. I saw fish, dolphins, penguins, seals, and stingrays.

Instructor: Copy the sentences in **Exercise 3** on the lines in your workbook. Pay special attention to the commas.

Workbook: 1. Solid, liquid, and gas are the three forms of matter.

2. Cars have fenders, tires, engines, and gears.

3. Stormy weather can bring rain, sleet, snow, and wind.

Instructor: You can use commas in other ways besides separating items in a list. Sometimes when you are talking to someone, you say his name to get his attention. When you are talking directly to someone, you are addressing him. If you say his name at the beginning of a sentence, this is called **direct address**. When you write a sentence that includes a direct address, you use a comma after the name or names of the people to whom you are speaking. Read each sentence in **Exercise 4** and copy it onto the lines provided in your workbook.

Workbook: **Jordan,** stop teasing your sister.

Patricia, are you aggravating him?

Instructor: To review quotations, we are going to read the story in **Exercise 5** together. I will start each sentence, and you will read the words in bold print. These are the exact words the people said. Remember to read with expression.

Workbook: Greg asked, **"What is my job today?"**

Dad answered, **"Take out the trash."**

Brad stated, **"I'll pick up, vacuum, and dust."**

Jess exclaimed, **"We'll be through in no time!"**

As you go through the sentences in **Exercise 6**, be sure to point to every punctuation mark as you explain.

Instructor: The sentences you have read are called **direct quotations**. They are the exact words that someone says. Quotation marks are placed before and after the exact words a person says. Each of the direct quotations that you read is part of a larger sentence. When a direct quotation is at the end of a sentence, it keeps its own punctuation mark. In **Exercise 6**, read the first sentence.

Workbook: 1. Greg asked, **"What is my job today?"**

Instructor: "What is my job today?" is a question. It ends with a **question mark**. The question mark comes **before** the last pair of **quotation marks**. Look at the sentence one more time. Notice that the direct quotation is separated from the rest of the sentence by a **comma**. And remember when a direct quotation is at the end of a sentence, it keeps its own punctuation mark. Now copy **Sentence 1** on the line provided in your workbook.

Instructor: Read **Sentence 2**.

Workbook: 2. Dad answered, **"Take out the trash."**

Instructor: "Take out the trash" is a command sentence. It ends with a **period**. When a direct quotation is at the end of a sentence, it keeps its own punctuation mark. The **period** comes **before** the last pair of quotation marks. Look at the sentence one more time. Notice that the direct quotation is separated from the rest of the sentence by a **comma**. Now copy **Sentence 2** on the line provided in your workbook.

Instructor: Read **Sentence 3**.

Workbook: 3. Brad stated, **"I'll pick up, vacuum, and dust."**

Instructor: "I'll pick up, vacuum, and dust" is a statement sentence. It ends with a **period**. The period comes **before** the last pair of **quotation marks**. Look at the sentence one more time. Notice that the direct quotation is separated from the rest of the sentence by a **comma**. When a direct quotation is at the end of a sentence, it keeps its own punctuation mark. Now copy **Sentence 3** on the line provided in your workbook.

Instructor: Read **Sentence 4**.

Workbook: 4. Jess exclaimed, **"We'll be through in no time!"**

Instructor: "We'll be through in no time!" is an exclamation sentence. It ends with an **exclamation point**. The exclamation point comes **before** the last pair of **quotation marks**. Look at the sentence one more time. Notice that the direct quotation is separated from the rest of the sentence by a **comma**. When a direct quotation is at the end of a sentence, it keeps its own punctuation mark. Now copy **Sentence 4** on the line provided in your workbook.

Instructor: In the sentences you just read, each direct quotation, or exact words that a person said, came at the **end** of the sentence. But in some sentences, the direct quotation comes at the **beginning**. In **Exercise 7** we are going to read the same story together. You will read the words in bold print. These are direct quotations—the exact words the people said. Notice that this time the direct quotations come at the **beginning** of the sentences. I will finish reading the words in regular print.

Workbook: **"What is my job today?"** Greg asked.

"Take out the trash," Dad said.

"I'll pick up, vacuum, and dust," Brad stated.

"We'll be through in no time!" Jess exclaimed.

As you go through the sentences in **Exercise 8**, be sure to point to every punctuation mark as you explain.

Instructor: Each of the direct quotations that you just read is part of a larger sentence. Just like the direct quotations you read earlier, these direct quotations are enclosed by quotation marks, and they each begin with a capital letter. If the direct quotation is a question or an exclamation, then the quotation itself ends with a question mark or an exclamation point. But if the direct quotation would normally end with a period, then the period is replaced by a comma. Let's look more closely at some of these direct quotations, and I will show you what I mean. In **Exercise 8**, read **Sentence 1** aloud.

Workbook: 1. "What is my job today**?**" Greg asked.

Instructor: "What is my job today?" is a question. It ends with a **question mark**. The question mark comes **before** the last pair of **quotation marks**. When the quotation comes at the beginning of a sentence, the end of the larger sentence needs its own mark of punctuation. Look at the larger sentence one more time. The larger sentence ends with a **period**. Now copy **Sentence 1** on the line provided in your workbook.

Instructor: Read **Sentence 2**.

Workbook: 2. "Take out the trash**,**" Dad said.

Instructor: "Take out the trash" is a command sentence. Command sentences can end with periods. But since the direct quotation command comes at the beginning of a sentence, the period is replaced by a **comma**. The comma comes **before** the last pair of **quotation marks**. When the quotation comes at the beginning of a sentence, the end of the larger sentence needs its own mark of punctuation. Look at the larger sentence one more time. The sentence ends with a **period**. Now copy **Sentence 2** on the line provided in your workbook.

Instructor: Read **Sentence 3**.

Workbook: 3. "I'll pick up, vacuum, and dust**,**" Brad stated.

Instructor: "I'll pick up, vacuum, and dust" is a statement sentence. As you know, statements end with periods. But since the direct quotation statement comes at the beginning of a sentence, the period is replaced by a **comma**. The comma comes **before** the last pair of **quotation marks**. When the quotation comes at the beginning of a sentence, the end of the larger sentence needs its own mark of punctuation. Look at the larger sentence one more time. The sentence ends with a **period**. Now copy **Sentence 3** on the line provided in your workbook.

Instructor: Read **Sentence 4**.

Workbook: 4. "We'll be through in no time**!**" Jess exclaimed.

Instructor: "We'll be through in no time!" is an exclamation sentence. It ends with an **exclamation point**. The exclamation point comes **before** the last pair of **quotation marks**. When the quotation comes at the beginning of a sentence, the end of the larger sentence needs its own mark of punctuation. Look at the larger sentence one more time. The sentence ends with a **period**. Now copy **Sentence 4** on the line provided in your workbook.

Instructor: All four of the sentences you have been working with contain direct quotations. You were given the **exact** words the people said. But if I change the words of a direct quotation and give you the same information in my words, it is no longer a direct quotation. It is an **indirect quotation**. An indirect quotation tells you what a person says **without** using his or her exact words. There are no quotation marks in an indirect quotation. In **Exercise 9**, read each direct quotation sentence, and then read the indirect quotation beneath it.

Workbook: 1. "What is my job today?" Greg asked.

Greg asked his father what his job was for the day.

2. Dad said, "Take out the trash."

Dad told Greg to take out the trash.

3. "I'll pick up, vacuum, and dust," Brad stated.

Brad promised to pick up the books on the floor, vacuum the rug, and dust the table.

4. Jess exclaimed, "We'll be through in no time!"

Jess exclaimed that she thought they would be finished cleaning in no time.

Optional Follow-Up

There is no optional follow-up for this lesson.

LESSON 88

Review: **Diagramming**

Cover up the student workbook page. Move the paper down to reveal only the first sentence and the empty frame.

Instructor: Read the first simple sentence in **Exercise 1**. It contains only a subject, verb, and direct object.

Workbook: 1. Scrooge scared children.

Instructor: Scrooge is a character from Charles Dickens' book *A Christmas Carol*. You are going to diagram the sentence "Scrooge scared children."

Instructor: What is the verb? *[Student says <u>scared</u>.]* Write the verb *scared* to the right of the center line on your frame.

Instructor: Now find the subject. Who scared? *[Student says <u>Scrooge</u>.] Scrooge* is your subject. Write the subject to the left of the center line on your frame.

Instructor: Look again at the verb *scared*. Is there a direct object that receives the action of the verb? I will ask you a question that will help you find the direct object. Scared whom? *[Student says <u>children</u>.]* Write the direct object, *children*, to the right of the verb on your diagram. The direct object is separated from the verb by a short, straight line.

Instructor: I will move down the paper in your workbook so you can see the second sentence and its frame. In the second sentence, see that a word has been added.

Workbook: 2. Mean Scrooge scared children.

Instructor: Look at the subject, *Scrooge*. Are there any words that describe the subject? This adjective can tell what kind, which one, how many, or whose. *[Student says <u>Mean</u>.]* Write the adjective *Mean* on the slanted line below the subject it describes. Remember to capitalize the word because it is capitalized in the sentence.

Instructor: I will move down the paper in your workbook so you can see the third sentence and its frame. In the third sentence, see that another word has been added.

Workbook: 3. Mean Scrooge scared little children.

Instructor: Look again at the direct object, *children*. Are there any words that describe the direct object, *children*? This adjective can tell what kind, which one, how many, or whose. *[Student says little.]* Write the adjective *little* on the slanted line below the direct object it describes.

Instructor: I will move down the paper in your workbook so you can see the fourth sentence and its frame. In the fourth sentence, see that another word has been added.

Workbook: 4. Mean Scrooge scared little children often.

Instructor: Look at the verb *scared*. Is there a word that describes the verb *scared*? This is an adverb that could tell how, when, where, or how often. This adverb does not directly follow the verb in the sentence; it comes a little bit later. *[Student says often.]* Write the adverb *often* on the slanted line below the verb it describes. Now your diagram is complete.

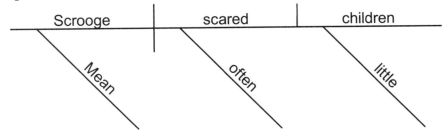

Instructor: Now in **Exercise 2**, **3**, and **4** you will diagram three new sentences about the characters in Charles Dickens' book *A Christmas Carol*. You read each sentence. As you work through each group of sentences, the parts of the diagram that you have filled in will be already printed on the next diagram. You will only have to add new words as you answer my questions. I will cover the diagrams below where you are working so you don't see the answers. Remember to copy the words exactly as they appear in the sentence. If the words begin with a capital letter in the sentence, they should also be capitalized in the diagram.

Workbook: **Group 1 (Exercise 2** in the Student Workbook)

Bob Cratchit copied numbers.	(Ask questions 1, 2, and 3)
Diligent Bob Cratchit copied numbers.	(Ask question 4)
Diligent Bob Cratchit copied Scrooge's numbers.	(Ask question 5)
Diligent Bob Cratchit copied Scrooge's numbers daily.	(Ask question 6)

Workbook: **Group 2 (Exercise 3** in the Student Workbook)

Bob Cratchit loved Tiny Tim.	(Ask questions 1, 2, and 3)
Kind Bob Cratchit loved Tiny Tim.	(Ask question 4)
Kind Bob Cratchit loved cheerful Tiny Tim.	(Ask question 5)
Kind Bob Cratchit loved cheerful Tiny Tim dearly.	(Ask question 6)

Workbook: Group 3 (Exercise 4 in the Student Workbook)

Ghosts visited Scrooge.	(Ask questions 1, 2, and 3)
Three ghosts visited Scrooge.	(Ask question 4)
Three ghosts visited stingy Scrooge.	(Ask question 5)
Three ghosts visited stingy Scrooge unexpectedly.	(Ask question 6)

Use the following italicized dialogue to help the student fill in the diagrams. After the student reads a sentence in each sentence group, you will prompt him with the question(s) in italics listed across from that sentence.

1. *What is the verb? Write the verb to the right of your center line.*

2. *Now find the subject. Ask "who" or "what" before the verb. [Prompt the student with a specific question like "Who copied?" or "Who loved?"] Write the subject to the left of the center line on your frame. [Note: The subject for Sentence Groups 1 and 2 is a proper noun. Prompt the student to write both words in the proper noun <u>Bob Cratchit</u> on the subject line.]*

3. *Is there a direct object that receives the action of the verb? I will ask you a question that will help you find the direct object.*

   Sentence Group 1: Copied what?

   Sentence Group 2: Loved whom? (<u>Tiny Tim</u> is a proper noun)

   Sentence Group 3: Visited whom?

   Write the direct object to the right of the verb on your diagram. The direct object is separated from the verb by a short, straight line.

4. *Go back and look again at the subject. Are there any words that describe the subject? This adjectives can tell what kind, which one, how many, or whose. Also look for the articles (<u>a</u>, <u>an</u>, <u>the</u>), because they act like adjectives. Write the adjective on a slanted line below the subject it describes.*

5. *Look again at the direct object. Are there any words that describe the direct object? This adjectives can tell what kind, which one, how many, or whose. Also look for the articles (<u>a</u>, <u>an</u>, <u>the</u>), because they act like adjectives. Write the adjective on a slanted line below the direct object it describes.*

6. *Look at the verb. Is there a word that describes the verb? This is an adverb that could tell how, when, where, or how often. This adverb does not directly follow the verb in the sentence; it comes a little bit later. Write the adverb on the slanted line below the verb it describes.*

Answer Key:

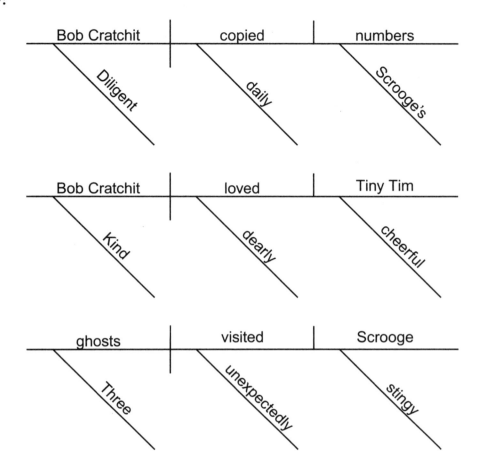

Instructor: The sentences that you just diagrammed all contained action verbs and direct objects. Now in **Exercise 5** you are going to diagram some sentences with linking verbs that link the subject to a predicate nominative or a predicate adjective.

Workbook:
1. Joseph Lister is a famous doctor.   (Ask questions 1, 2, 3, and 4)
2. Melvil Dewey was an influential librarian. (Ask questions 1, 2, 3, and 4)
3. King Solomon was very wise.   (Ask questions 1, 2, 5, and 6)
4. Lewis Carroll was quite imaginative.   (Ask questions 1, 2, 5, and 6)

For **Exercise 5**, use the following dialogue in italics to help the student fill in each diagram. After the student reads each sentence, you will prompt him with the questions in italics listed across from that sentence.

1. *What is the linking verb? This verb links the subject to a word in the complete predicate. Write the verb to the right of your center line.*

2. *Now find the subject. Ask "who" or "what" before the verb. The subject is a proper noun that consists of two words. [Prompt the student with a specific question like "Who is?" or "Who was?"] Write the subject to the left of the center line on your frame.*

3. *This sentence contains a predicate nominative. This noun is in the complete predicate of the sentence, but it **renames the subject**. What is the predicate nominative in this sentence? Because the predicate nominative follows the verb in the sentence, it is written to the right of the verb on the diagram. Write the predicate nominative to the right of the slanted line on your diagram. That slanted line points back toward the subject to remind you that a predicate nominative renames the subject.*

4. *Look again at the predicate nominative. Are there any words that describe the predicate nominative? There are two. These adjectives can tell what kind, which one, how many, or whose. Also look for the articles (<u>a</u>, <u>an</u>, <u>the</u>), because they act like adjectives. Write each adjective on a slanted line below the predicate nominative it describes.*

5. *This sentence contains a predicate adjective. This adjective is in the complete predicate of the sentence, but it describes the subject. A predicate adjective can tell what kind, which one, how many, or whose. Can you find an adjective that follows the verb that still describes the subject? Because the predicate adjective follows the verb in the sentence, it is written to the right of the verb on the diagram. Write the predicate adjective to the right of the slanted line on your diagram. That slanted line points back toward the subject to remind you that a predicate adjective describes the subject.*

6. *Look again at the predicate adjective. Is there an adverb such as <u>too</u>, <u>very</u>, <u>really</u>, <u>quite</u>, or <u>slightly</u> that describes the adjective? These adverbs tell to what extent. Write the adverb on the slanted line beneath the predicate adjective it describes.*

Answer Key:

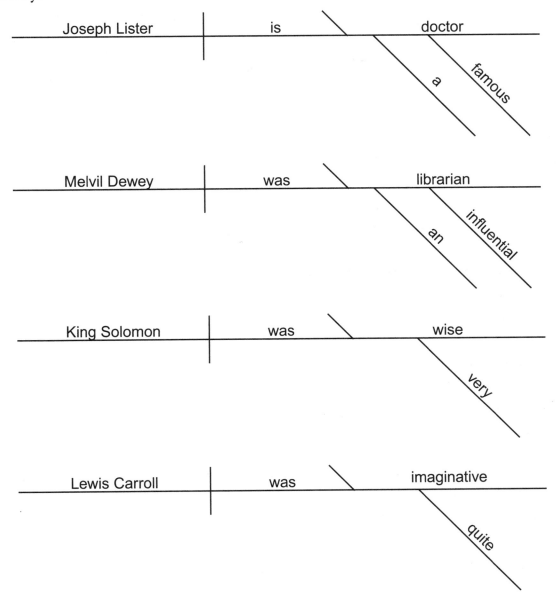

Optional Follow-Up

There is no optional follow-up for this lesson.

LESSON 89

Cumulative Poem Review

Instructor: Today you are going to review the poems you have memorized in this book. When you recite a poem, you begin with the title and author. I will give you the title and author for each poem. Say the title and the author back to me, and then recite the poem. Remember to stand up straight! Don't fidget while you're reciting! And speak in a nice, loud, slow voice.

You may prompt the student as necessary. If the student repeats the poem accurately, he may check the box in his workbook and move on to the next poem. If he stumbles, ask him to repeat the line he cannot remember three times.

Lesson	Poem	Author
9	"The Land of Nod"	Robert Louis Stevenson
18	"A Tragic Story"	William Makepeace Thackeray
31	"I Wandered Lonely As a Cloud"	William Wordsworth
46	"A Time to Talk"	Robert Frost
58	"The Bells"	Edgar Allan Poe
71	"A Slash of Blue"	Emily Dickinson

WRITING LETTERS LESSON 1

Writing Dates
Thank-You Letter Rough Draft

Instructor: Now that you are learning all of this grammar, don't forget that grammar is important because it helps us communicate well in words! You're going to use some of this grammar knowledge when you write letters.

Instructor: Every day of the year has a date. A date is made up of the month of the year, a number telling you what day of the month it is, and a number telling you what year it is. Every time you write a letter, you should include the date. Follow along in **Exercise 1** as I read a poem about the number of days in each month.

The Months

A Mother Goose Rhyme

Thirty days hath September,

April, June, and November;

All the rest have thirty-one,

Except for February alone,

Which has four and twenty-four

Till leap year gives it one day more.

If the student did not memorize the poem in first and second grade, you may have him repeat it each day until he knows it.

If you live in a country where the number of the day of the month is written **before** the name of the month, adjust the following scripting and show your student how to write a date in your country.

Instructor: To write a date, write the full name of the month, and then write the number of the day in that month. Put a comma after the number, and finish by writing the year. I will write some dates for you.

In **Exercise 2**, on the lines labeled "Instructor," write out for the student the date on which he was born and the birth dates for three other members of the family or friends.

Instructor: Do you know what this first date is? Notice that the name of the month is always capitalized. It is a proper noun.

Instructor: Now I want you to copy your birth date as well as the three other birth dates I have written for you. Copy each date on the line directly below the date I have written.

Instructor: In this lesson you are going to write a thank-you letter. You begin the letter by writing today's date. The first copy of any piece of writing is a rough draft. You will compose the letter today, and then copy it over neatly in the next lesson.

Use the following format to help the student write the rough draft of his letter in his workbook. As you see mistakes, point them out, and have the student erase and make corrections. He will make a final copy of the letter in the next lesson. If the student is a reluctant writer, he may dictate the rough draft for you to write down.

(This lesson continues on the next page.)

Date (Today's date, written on the right-
hand side of the paper)

Greeting (Dear _____,)

Explain to the student that a comma always comes after the greeting. Remind the student to include the abbreviation for the appropriate title of respect (Lesson 61). The letter may even be written to a member of the immediate family; everyone loves to get mail!

Body of the Letter

Read the following list of composition starters to the student, and have him choose one of the subjects. Ask him the prompting questions about that subject, and have him talk to you about what he would like to write. This is orally composing the body of the letter. This is an all-important step that should precede writing words down on paper.

As he writes down the body of the letter, remind the student of what he has orally composed (e.g., "What happened when you saw the penguins at the zoo?"). Aim for the student to write a paragraph of about four sentences. He should indent the paragraph about the space of two of his fingers.

This will be the message you are communicating to the receiver. In this letter, you may thank the receiver for:

- a gift
    - Why did you like it?
    - What will you use it for?
- an invitation to an occasion (accepting or declining)
    - Why are you excited about going? (Or, why will you hate to miss it?)
- having been entertained or taken somewhere
    - What was your favorite memory from the trip or visit?
- doing something special for you (a kind deed)
    - How did this help you?
    - How did the kind deed make you feel?

Closing (You may choose "Love,"
"Sincerely," or "Yours truly." A comma
always follows the closing.)

Writer's Name

WRITING LETTERS LESSON 2

Thank-You Letter Final Copy

Instructor: Today we will make a neat, final copy of the letter you wrote last lesson.

Assist the student as necessary to make a neat final version of the letter on the lined page on page 343 of his workbook (or you may choose to have him write on his own stationery). Then have him go through the Final Thank-You Letter Checklist on page 289 of his workbook. He will mail this letter.

Instructor: We will address and mail this letter in the next lesson!

WRITING LETTERS LESSON 3

Addressing the Envelope

You will need a business-size envelope and a first-class stamp.

Instructor: Can you tell me your address?

Student: *[says address, including city and state]*

Turn to **Exercise 1** of the student's workbook. Let the student watch as you write his complete address on the blank lines in the workbook. Do not include any abbreviations. Make sure you include a comma between your city and state. Include the zip code. Have the student read the address.

Instructor: Now you are going to learn how to abbreviate, or shorten, some words in addresses. In **Exercise 2** of your workbook, I will say each street name and point to its abbreviation. Notice that each abbreviation begins with a capital letter and ends with a period.

Name	Abbreviation
Avenue	Ave.
Boulevard	Blvd.
Circle	Cir.
Court	Ct.
Drive	Dr.
Highway	Hwy.
Lane	Ln.
Road	Rd.
Street	St.

Instructor: The post office also has special abbreviations for the names of states. They do not have periods like regular abbreviations. Every state abbreviation has two letters, and both letters are capitalized. The abbreviation for our state is _____. Write these two capital letters in the blank in **Exercise 3** of your workbook.

For a complete list of state postal abbreviations, go to the United States Postal Service website: www.usps.com/ncsc/lookups/abbrstate.txt

Instructor: I already wrote your complete address in **Exercise 1**. Notice that there is a comma between the name of your city [town] and your state. I want you to copy this full address in **Exercise 4**. It does not have any abbreviations.

Instructor: Now in **Exercise 5** of your workbook, I will write your full address in your workbook using abbreviations. You will copy it onto the lines in **Exercise 6**.

Have the student practice writing his address using the correct abbreviations for his street and state until he can do it from memory. (Depending on the student and the length of address, you may have to practice this over a number of days.)

Instructor: In the last lesson you wrote a thank-you note. You are going to mail it today! In order to mail a letter, you need to put it in an envelope and address it properly. The envelope has to have two names and addresses on it. The most important name and address is that of the person to whom you are sending the letter. But you also need to include your own name and address. This is called the "return address."

Write the address and the return address on the model of an envelope on page 292 of the student's workbook. The student will copy this model onto the real envelope. The addresses should include the appropriate abbreviations. If the student has completed Lesson 61 on abbreviations, he should include the abbreviation for the appropriate title of respect and an initial. Then help the student fold the letter. First, fold up the bottom third of the paper, and then fold down the top third. Put the folded letter in the stamped envelope. Seal and mail it!

WRITING LETTERS LESSON 4

Friendly Letter Rough Draft

Instructor: In this lesson you are going to write a letter to a member of your family.

The student should choose to send the letter to an adult member of the family who is not aware of what the student has been learning. Use the format on the following page to help the student write the rough draft of his letter in his workbook. As you see mistakes, point them out, and have the student erase and make corrections. If the student is a reluctant writer, he may dictate the rough draft for you to write down. The student will make a final copy of the letter in the next lesson.

If the student has completed Lesson 40 on the four types of sentences, encourage him to use each type: statement, command, question, and exclamation. Consider these options:

Would you please write back?	(Question)
Please answer soon!	(Command)
What have you been doing lately?	(Question)
Tell me something exciting you have been doing lately.	(Command)
It would be great to hear from you!	(Exclamation)

Greeting (Dear _____,)   **Date** (Today's date, written on the right-hand side of the paper)

Explain to the student that a comma always comes after the greeting. Remind the student to include the abbreviation for the appropriate title of respect (Lesson 61).

Body of the Letter

Read the following list of composition starters to the student, and have him choose one of the subjects. Ask him the prompting questions about that subject, and have him talk to you about what he would like to write. This is orally composing the body of the letter. This is an all-important step that should precede writing words down on paper. As he writes down the body of the letter, remind the student of what he has orally composed (ex., "What did you say about King Tut?"). Aim for the student to write a paragraph of about four sentences. He should indent the paragraph about the space of two of his fingers.

Instructor: This will be the message you are is communicating to the receiver. In this letter, you may tell the receiver:

- something interesting you learned this past week
  - Why did you find it interesting?
  - Have you read any books about the topic?
  - Did you learn something new?
- a special errand or outing you took recently
  - Where did you go?
  - What did you do there?
  - What special memory do you have from the trip?
- something funny that happened
  - Who were the people or animals involved?
  - What happened **before** the funny incident?
  - What did you do when you saw or heard about the funny incident?
- the weather
  - What has the weather been like—hot, cold, stormy, cloudy, etc.?
  - Has this weather been unusual?
  - Did you like this weather? If so, why? If not, why not?
- any news about you or your family
  - Who are the people you are going to tell about?
  - What special things are you going to tell about?

                                        Closing (You may choose "Love," "Sincerely," or "Yours truly." Remember that a comma always follows the closing.)

                                        Writer's Name (Student writes his own name that includes at least one initial.)

WRITING LETTERS LESSON 5

Friendly Letter Final Copy

Instructor: Today we will make a neat, final copy of the letter you wrote last lesson.

Assist the student as necessary to make a neat final version of the letter on lined page 295 in his workbook (or you may choose to have him write on his own stationery). Then have him go through the checklist on page 294. He will mail this letter.

Instructor: We will address and mail this letter in the next lesson!

Addressing the Envelope

Instructor: In the last lesson you wrote a friendly letter. You are going to mail it today! In order to mail a letter, you need to put it in an envelope and address it properly. The envelope has to have two names and addresses on it. The most important name and address is that of the person to whom you are sending the letter. But you also need to include your own name and address.

Write the address and the return address on the model of an envelope on page 297 of the student's workbook. The student will copy this model onto the real envelope. The addresses should include the appropriate abbreviations. If the student has completed Lesson 61 on abbreviations, he should include the abbreviation for the appropriate title of respect and an initial. Then help the student fold the letter. First, fold up the bottom third of the paper, and then fold down the top third. Put the folded letter in the stamped envelope. Seal and mail it!

WRITING LETTERS LESSON 7

Copying a Poem

Instructor: In your workbook, follow along with your eyes as I read the poem "Who Has Seen the Wind?"

Who Has Seen the Wind?

by Christina G. Rossetti

Who has seen the wind?

Neither I nor you;

But when the leaves hang trembling

The wind is passing through.

Who has seen the wind?

Neither you nor I;

But when the trees bow down their heads

The wind is passing by.

Instructor: In this lesson you are going to copy this poem and send it to a friend or family member. Before you do this, you need to know about the correct written form for traditional poetry.

Instructor: Point to the title of the poem I just read to you. Each word in the title of the poem is capitalized except for the word *the* (before *Wind*) because it is an article. Articles are not capitalized in titles unless the word appears first.

Instructor: Now put your finger on the author's name in the poem. This line begins with the word *by*, but this word is not capitalized. The name of the author is capitalized. Notice that the author uses her middle initial, *G.* When you write initials, each initial is capitalized and followed by a period.

Instructor: Now put your finger on the first word in the first line of the poem. This word is *Who*. It is capitalized. Run your finger down along the first words in every line of the poem. All of these words are capitalized. You always capitalize the first word of every line in traditional poetry.

Instructor: Look at the end of each line. You will see some marks of punctuation. Each poem has its own special punctuation. When you are copying a poem, make sure you punctuate it exactly as it is printed.

Instructor: The first four lines are separated from the last four lines by a space. These groups of lines are called stanzas. "Who Has Seen the Wind?" has two stanzas. When you copy a poem, leave a space between the stanzas.

Instructor: Look at the second line of the poem. I will point to the last word in that line: *you.* Now look at the fourth line of the poem. I will point to the last word in that line: *through.* The two words I pointed to are *you* and *through.* Do you hear that these two words rhyme? *You, through.* Traditional poems often contain rhyming words at the ends of lines.

The student should copy this poem onto the lined paper on page 345 of his workbook. After he has finished copying the poem, have him go through the checklist on page 298 of his workbook.

The student may wish to illustrate the poem with colored pencils, markers, or crayons. You will write an accompanying note to the friend or family member and address the envelope for the student.

Optional Follow-Up

The student will copy his favorite poem from the ones he has memorized this year. He will do this on page 347 of his workbook or on his own sheet of lined paper. When copying the poem, the student should follow this checklist.

1. Write the title of the poem on the top line of the piece of paper. Capitalize the first word. Also capitalize the rest of the words in the title, except for the following:

- Articles (*a, an, the*)

- Conjunctions (*and, but, or*)

- Prepositions that are four letters or less (such as *at, by, for, from, in, into, like, near, of, off, on, over, past, to, up, upon, with*)

2. On the second line, write the author's name beneath the title of the poem. You should write *by* before the author's name, but do not capitalize the word *by.*

3. Skip a line.

4. Copy the first stanza. Remember to capitalize the first word in each line. Copy the punctuation exactly as it is printed in the poem.

5. Skip a line.

6. Copy the next stanza, following the same rules that you did for the first stanza.

7. Repeat steps 5 and 6 until you have copied the entire poem.

DICTIONARY SKILLS LESSON 1

Alphabetizing by First and Second Letter

Before doing the dictionary skills lessons, the student needs to know the eight parts of speech or he should have completed through Lesson 83 in the book.

Instructor: In this lesson you will learn how to put words in alphabetical, or **A-B-C**, order. In your mind, you need to be able to say the alphabet in order or sing the alphabet song. If you can do that, you can put the words *carrot*, *banana*, and *apple* in alphabetical order. Read the list in **Exercise 1**. The words are in alphabetical order.

Workbook: apple

banana

carrot

Instructor: The word *apple* comes first in the list because it begins with the first letter of the alphabet, **a**. The word *banana* comes after the word *apple* because *banana* begins with the letter **b**. **A** comes before **b** in the alphabet. The word *carrot* is last in the list because it begins with the letter **c**. The letter **c** comes after the letters **a** and **b** in the alphabet. When you are alphabetizing, which means putting words in alphabetical order, just think of the alphabet in your mind, **a**, **b**, **c**, **d**, **e**, **f**, **g**, and so on. In **Exercise 2**, I will show you how to alphabetize some more words: *turtle*, *duck*, and *zebra*. The first thing you do is look at the first letter of each word.

Workbook: turtle

duck

zebra

Instructor: The word *turtle* begins with **t**, *duck* begins with **d**, and *zebra* begins with **z**. If you say the alphabet in order, which letter do you say first: **t**, **d**, or **z**? Think **a**, **b**, **c**, **d**, **e**, **f**, **g** …. The letter **d** comes first. That means that word *duck* comes before *turtle* or *zebra*. Say the alphabet again. Now, what word comes after *duck*: *turtle* or *zebra*? Does **t** or does **z** come first?

Student: **t**

Instructor: **T** comes before the letter **z**, so the word *turtle* comes next in alphabetical order. *Zebra* is last. The three words are written in alphabetical order in **Exercise 3**.

Workbook: duck

turtle

zebra

Instructor: There are five groups of words in **Exercise 4**. Rewrite each group in its own alphabetical order. Remember to think or sing the alphabet while you are doing this exercise.

Workbook: circle

fun

down

out

key

man

salt

run

under

sing

hand

bent

zoo

look

ant

Answer Key:

1. circle, down, fun

2. key, man, out

3. run, salt, under

4. bent, hand, sing

5. ant, look, zoo

Instructor: You now know how to put words that begin with different letters in alphabetical order. But what do you do if you have words that all begin with the same letter? Then you need to look at the **second** letter of each word. Again, think to yourself "**a, b, c, d, e, f, g**," and so forth. In **Exercise 5**, I will show you how to alphabetize some words that all begin with the same letter: *go, get,* and *grass.* Look at the second letter in each word.

Workbook: g<u>o</u>

g<u>e</u>t

g<u>r</u>ass

Instructor: Each word begins with the letter **g**, but the second letter in each word is different. The word *go* has **o** as the second letter, *get* has **e** as the second letter, and *grass* has **r** as the second letter. If you say the alphabet in order, which letter do you say first: **o, e,** or **r**? Think **a, b, c, d, e, f, g** …. The letter **e** comes first. That means the word *get* comes before *go* or *grass.* Say the alphabet again. Now, what word comes after *get: go* or *grass*? Does **o** or does **r** come first?

Student: **o**

Instructor: **O** comes before the letter **r**, so the word *go* comes next in alphabetical order. *Grass* is last. The three words are written in alphabetical order in **Exercise 6**.

Workbook: get

go

grass

Instructor: In **Exercise 7** rewrite the list in alphabetical order on the lines provided.

Workbook: act

away

able

after

add

Instructor: Your list should read *able, act, add, after, away,* because the alphabetical order of the words' second letters is **b, c, d, f, w**. In **Exercise 8** rewrite each of the three groups of words in its own alphabetical order.

Workbook:

List 1	List 2	List 3
get	mind	step
gold	mess	swim
grow	man	slip
glass	mold	skin
give	much	seed

Answer Key:

1. get, give, glass, gold, grow

2. man, mess, mind, mold, much

3. seed, skin, slip, step, swim

Optional Follow-Up

If the student needs extra practice, you may use these lists of words for the student to alphabetize on his own piece of paper.

List 1	List 2	List 3	List 4	List 5
ball	dive	obey	red	this
born	drop	open	race	tag
beat	date	off	ride	ten
bit	down	one	run	torn
blue	dust	old	roll	tip

Answer Key:

1. ball, beat, bit, blue, born

2. date, dive, down, drop, dust

3. obey, off, old, one, open

4. race, red, ride, roll, run

5. tag, ten, this, tip, torn

DICTIONARY SKILLS LESSON 2

Alphabetizing by Third Letter

Instructor: In the last lesson you learned how to put words in alphabetical, or **A-B-C**, order. When you have a list of words that begin with different letters, you look at the first letter and think to yourself, "**a, b, c, d, e, f, g**," and so forth. Then you rewrite the words based on where their beginning letter falls in the alphabet. The word *apple* would come before the word *banana*, because **a** comes before **b** in the alphabet. The word *turtle* would come before the word *zebra*, because **t** comes before **z** in the alphabet. You also learned how to alphabetize words that all begin with the same letter. You had to look at the **second** letter of each word. What do you do if a word begins with the same two letters, such as *off* and *often*? You need to look at the **third** letter in each word. Again, think to yourself "**a, b, c, d, e, f, g**," and so forth. In **Exercise 1** rewrite each of the four lists in alphabetical order.

Workbook:

<u>List 1</u>	<u>List 2</u>	<u>List 3</u>	<u>List 4</u>
car	fan	gas	hat
can	fat	gap	ham
cab	fast	gang	hard
cake	face	gain	hand
cage	fall	gate	have

Answer Key:

1. cab, cage, cake, can, car

2. face, fall, fan, fast, fat

3. gain, gang, gap, gas, gate

4. ham, hand, hard, hat, have

Optional Follow-Up

If the student needs extra practice with alphabetizing words, you may use these lists of words for the student to alphabetize on his own piece of paper.

Workbook:

List 1	List 2	List 3	List 4	List 5
eat	hay	fig	grab	lot
ear	hall	fin	grill	low
each	hair	fish	grow	lost
easy	hawk	five	great	love
eagle	hang	file	grudge	loud

Answer Key:

1. each, eagle, ear, easy, eat
2. hair, hall, hang, hawk, hay
3. fig, file, fin, fish, five
4. grab, great, grill, grow, grudge
5. lost, lot, loud, love, low

DICTIONARY SKILLS LESSON 3

Looking Up Words in the Dictionary

You will need a student's dictionary for this lesson. We used the hardcover version of *Merriam-Webster's Elementary Dictionary* (Merriam-Webster, 2000; ISBN 0-8779-575-4). If you use another dictionary (even the paperback version of the *Merriam-Webster's Elementary Dictionary*), you will have to adjust the page numbers and guide words.

Instructor: It is important to know how to alphabetize words so you can find them in a dictionary. A dictionary is a book of words that are written in alphabetical order. A dictionary can be very useful when you are both reading and writing. When you are reading and you encounter a word you are not familiar with, you can look it up in the dictionary to find out its pronunciation, its part of speech, and its meaning. When you are writing and you would like to use a word but you are not sure of its spelling or its meaning, you can look the word up in the dictionary so you will spell and use the word correctly. If you do not look it up, you risk making an error that will take more time to correct later.

Instructor: The first skill you need to learn is how to find words quickly in the dictionary. Words are organized in the dictionary by alphabetical, or **A-B-C**, order.
In **Exercise 1** look at these lines of the alphabet.

Demonstrate for the student that the line breaks in the alphabet occur where you pause when you sing the alphabet song (the **ABC** song).

Workbook: A B C D E F G

H I J K L M N O P

Q R S T U V W X Y Z

Instructor: If the word you are looking up begins with one of the letters in the first line (**A**, **B**, **C**, **D**, **E**, **F**, **G**), open the dictionary near the front. Then flip the pages forward or backward to find the word. There are special words written at the top of each page in the dictionary that will help speed up your search. These pairs of words are called guide words. Turn to page 273 in the dictionary. Look at the top right-hand corner of the page. The first guide word is *joyful*. Now look at the list of words on that page. *Joyful* is the first word at the top of the page in the first column. Now look at the second guide word, *junk*. *Junk* is the last word that is defined in this page's list. It is at the bottom of the page in the second column. All the words on this page come after *joyful* and before *junk* in alphabetical order. So when you are looking for a word in the dictionary, you can look at the guide words to see if the word you are looking for is on that page.

Instructor: In **Exercise 2** find these words in the dictionary. Remember to open the dictionary near the front. Use the guide words to help you quickly find the exact page.

Workbook: chill

arm

Instructor: If the word you are looking up begins with one of the letters in the middle of the alphabet (**H**, **I**, **J**, **K**, **L**, **M**, **N**, **O**, **P**), open the dictionary near the middle. Then flip the pages forward or backward to find the word. In **Exercise 3** find these words in the dictionary. Remember to open the dictionary near the middle.

Workbook: hot

loaf

Instructor: If the word you are looking up begins with one of the letters near the end of the alphabet (**Q**, **R**, **S**, **T**, **U**, **V**, **W**, **X**, **Y**, **Z**), open the dictionary near the end. Then flip the pages forward or backward to find the word. In **Exercise 4** find these words in the dictionary. Remember to open the dictionary near the end.

Workbook: shoe

under

DICTIONARY SKILLS LESSON 4

Parts of the Entry

You will need a student's dictionary for this lesson. We used the hardcover version of *Merriam-Webster's Elementary Dictionary* (Merriam-Webster, 2000; ISBN 0-8779-575-4). If you use another dictionary (even the paperback version of the *Merriam-Webster's Elementary Dictionary*), the phonetic spelling and abbreviations may be different.

Instructor: In the last lesson you learned how to find words in the dictionary. Look at the alphabet in **Exercise 1**.

Workbook: A B C D E F G

H I J K L M N O P

Q R S T U V W X Y Z

Instructor: If the word you are looking up begins with a letter in the first line, **A**, **B**, **C**, **D**, **E**, **F**, or **G**, you open the book toward the front. If the word begins with a letter in the second line, **H**, **I**, **J**, **K**, **L**, **M**, **N**, **O**, or **P**, you open the book in the middle. If the word begins with a letter in the third line, **Q**, **R**, **S**, **T**, **U**, **V**, **W**, **X**, **Y**, or **Z**, you open the book near the end. You then flip the pages forward or backward until you find the correct page. Use the guide words at the tops of the pages to help you quickly find the exact page. Find the words in **Exercise 2** in the dictionary. After you find the last word, *peanut*, keep your dictionary open to that page.

Workbook: dormouse

navigate

skeptical

peanut

Instructor: Put your finger on the word *peanut* in the dictionary. In this lesson you will begin learning some skills that will help you use your dictionary easily. The word *peanut* is called the **entry word**. It is written in bold print. Look closely at the word. You will notice a black dot in the center. This dot divides the word *peanut* into two separate parts. When you are writing a paragraph, sometimes you do not have enough space to write an entire word at the end of the line. You have two options. You can write the word on the next line like in the first sentence of **Exercise 3**. Read that sentence.

Workbook: 1. When I go to the zoo, I feed each of the enormous elephants a **peanut**. The elephants use their trunks to grab the nuts.

Instructor: Or, you can divide the word *peanut* into two parts, like in the second sentence of **Exercise 3**. Read that sentence.

Workbook: 2. When I go to the zoo, I feed each of the enormous elephants a **pea-nut**. The elephants use their trunks to grab the nuts.

Instructor: The dot in the middle of the entry word tells you where you can divide *peanut* if you need to.

Instructor: Look again at the dictionary entry for peanut. Now move your finger to the right. You will see some letters and symbols. This is called the phonetic spelling of the word, and it tells you how to pronounce the word. We will learn more about phonetic spelling in the next lesson. For now, move your finger a little more to the right. You will see an abbreviation next to the phonetic spelling of the word *peanut*. This abbreviation is written in a different kind of print called italics. The *n* is an abbreviation for a part of speech. It tells you that the word *peanut* is a noun. Point to each abbreviation in **Exercise 4** and read aloud the part of speech for which it stands.

Workbook:

adj	adjective
adv	adverb
conj	conjunction
interj	interjection
n	noun
prep	preposition
pron	pronoun
vb	verb

Instructor: There are some words that mean one thing when they are written with lowercase letters and mean another thing when they begin with a capital letter. Look up the word *east* in the dictionary. Look at the second definition. You will see the abbreviation **cap**.

Instructor: The second definition in your dictionary tells you that when *east* is capitalized, it means "regions or countries east of a certain point." It is the proper name of a region. In **Exercise 5** read a sentence that uses this definition of the word *East*.

Workbook: I live in California, but I spend holidays with my grandparents in the **East**.

Instructor: The dictionary also has abbreviations to tell you if a word is singular or plural. Look at **Exercise 6**.

Workbook: *sing*   singular

          pl   plural

These abbreviations most commonly appear to describe irregular verbs and their tenses. The definitions for these irregular verbs appear very complicated, and it is not necessary for the student to understand them at this level. But if you or the student would like to see one, look up the verbs *be* and *have*.

Instructor: Some words don't follow any rules to form their plural. We call these words irregular plurals because they don't form their plurals in any of the regular ways (Lesson 5). Dictionaries will often include the plural forms of these words. Look at **Exercise 7** in your workbook. If you were to look up the word *child* in the dictionary, this is what you would see at the beginning of the entry.

child \'chīld\ n, pl chil•dren

Instructor: Next to the entry word, you see the phonetic spelling for *child*. After the phonetic spelling, you see the letter *n*, which is the dictionary abbreviation for *noun*. Then you see the abbreviation for plural, *pl*, written before the word *children*. This tells you that *children* is the plural form of the noun *child*. Now look up the word *child* in your dictionary. Point to the abbreviation **pl**. Do you see the plural word *children* next to **pl**?

Instructor: In your dictionary, look up each singular word in **Exercise 7**. Find the abbreviation **pl** in the entry. It comes right before the plural form of the entry word. Then write the plural form of the word in the blank provided in your workbook.

Workbook: foot   *pl*, feet

           tooth   *pl*, teeth

           mouse *pl*, mice

           man   *pl*, men

All of the abbreviations we have covered are listed on page 21a of *Merriam-Webster's Elementary Dictionary*. Show that page to the student.

Optional Follow-Up

Practice "dictionary speed drills." You will need a digital watch or a watch with a second hand. Give the student a closed dictionary. Tell him to open the dictionary to a particular letter. Slowly say "Find **G**. Ready, set, go." You should alternate giving the student letters from the beginning, middle, and end of the alphabet. Can the student find a letter in less than 10 seconds?

DICTIONARY SKILLS LESSON 5

Syllables and Phonetic Spelling[1]

Instructor: In **Exercise 1** read the four words aloud.

Workbook: air

plane

base

ball

Instructor: Before we open the dictionary today, I am going to teach you about syllables. The words you just read each have one vowel sound: *air, plane, base, ball.* These are words of one **syllable**. A syllable is a part of word containing one vowel sound. If a word has two syllables, it has two vowel sounds. Follow along as I read a couple of two-syllable words in **Exercise 2**.

Workbook: airplane

baseball

Instructor: Now I will read those words again and clap on each syllable.

Read the words again, but this time clap when you say *air, plane, base,* and *ball.*

Instructor: The two-syllable words I just read are made up of two smaller words put together. *Airplane* is made up of *air* and *plane*. But not all two-syllable words are like this. In **Exercise 3** follow along with your eyes as I read some more two-syllable words.

Workbook: brother

teacher

Friday

Thursday

Tuesday

photo

---

1. Portions of this lesson have been excerpted from *The Ordinary Parent's Guide to Teaching Reading* (Peace Hill Press, 2005).

Workbook: suggest

about

among

again

divide

because

Instructor: When you say a two-syllable word, one syllable is spoken with more force than the other. This syllable is called the **accented** syllable. Follow along in **Exercise 4** while I say this list of words again. These words have been divided into syllables.

Read the list below, overemphasizing the accented syllable which is in bold print.

Workbook: **broth**-er

teach-er

Fri-day

Thurs-day

Tues-day

pho-to

sug-**gest**

a-**bout**

a-**mong**

a-**gain**

di-**vide**

be-**cause**

Instructor: Sometimes we can barely hear the vowel sound in a syllable that is not accented. Follow along and listen in **Exercise 5** while I read the words. Pay attention to the unaccented syllable. It will sound much quieter than the accented syllable. I will point to each softer, unaccented syllable when I read it.

Overemphasize the accented syllable (in bold print). Point to the unaccented syllable (in regular print) when you say it. These words all contain the *schwa* sound in the unaccented syllable. This is the same sound at the beginning and end of the word <u>A</u>meric<u>a</u>.

Workbook: **so**-fa

          so-da

          lem-on

          ex-tra

          chi-na

          ba-con

Instructor: In words of more than one syllable, often the unaccented syllable barely makes a sound. This is the same sound that you hear in the beginning and end of the word *America*. It is similar to a very quiet short-**u** vowel sound. Any of the vowels in an unaccented syllable may be pronounced with this sound, which has a strange name. It is called a *schwa*.

Instructor: Now you know that words are made up of syllables, and, when you pronounce a word, some of those syllables are accented and others are not. But how can you find out how to correctly pronounce an unfamiliar word? You can look it up in the dictionary! In the last lesson you looked up the entry for *peanut*. Find that word once more.

Instructor: Put your finger on the bolded entry word: *peanut*. Now move your finger a little to the right of the entry word in the dictionary. You will see the phonetic spelling: \\'pē-ˌnət\\.

Instructor: This is the phonetic spelling that shows you how to pronounce the word. Do you see the **e** with a line over it? This is a pronunciation symbol. This symbol represents a sound. At the bottom right-hand corner of the dictionary page there is a key that tells you the sound that each letter and symbol represents. Find this letter and symbol in the pronunciation key: \\ē\\.

Instructor: Do you see the word written next to the symbol? It is the word *easy*. The letters **ea** are written in bold print. Say the word *easy*. When you say the word *easy*, you will hear the sound the letters **ea** represent: [say the sound for the student—the sound is the name of the letter **e**]. This is the *long-vowel* sound of **e**. It is written with the symbol printed above. Look again at the phonetic spelling for the entry word *peanut*. Do you see the symbol that looks like a backward and upside-down **e**? That is the symbol for the *schwa* sound. Find this symbol in the pronunciation key: \\ə\\.

Instructor: The pronunciation key tells you that the *schwa* sound is in the word *abut* [the word *abut* means "to touch along a border" as in "America *abuts* Mexico along the river called the Rio Grande"]. The schwa sound is also in the words in the list in **Exercise 6**. Follow along as I read these words to you. Then I want you to read them back to me. The letters that stand for the *schwa* sound are in bold print. Remember, the *schwa* sound is similar to a very quiet short-**u** vowel sound. It is the sound you hear at the beginning and end of the word *America*.

Workbook: **a**mong

about

again

upon

lem**o**n

extr**a**

chin**a**

d**i**vide

Instructor: Now look at the phonetic spelling of the word *peanut* again in your dictionary: \\'pē-ˌnət\\.

Instructor: I am going to point to the tiny mark (') just before the letter **p**. It is called an accent mark. This accent mark is printed just before the first syllable to show you that this is the syllable that you should say the loudest. *PEA*-nut.

Instructor: Now I am going to point to the tiny mark (ˌ) just before the letter **n**. This is also an accent mark. This accent mark is printed just before and below the second syllable to show you that this syllable is not as loud as the first syllable. PEA-*nut*. Some syllables are not accented at all—they are said quietly.

Some dictionaries will use a bold tilted mark (´) to indicate strong stress and a plain tilted mark (´) to indicate medium stress. In that case both marks appear at the top of the word.

DICTIONARY SKILLS LESSON 6

Words with More Than One Meaning and/or Pronunciation

The student will need his dictionary for this lesson. We used *Merriam-Webster's Elementary Dictionary* (Merriam-Webster, 2000). If the student is using a different dictionary and the phonetic symbols are different, you can look up the words and copy the phonetic spelling that the dictionary uses. A different dictionary may also put the pronunciation key in a different place on the page.

Instructor: In the last lesson you learned how to pronounce words correctly by examining the phonetic spelling. The phonetic spelling of a word uses letters and symbols. A key to these letters and symbols is printed on each bottom right-hand page in the dictionary. Open your dictionary to any page with the phonetic key. Can you figure out how to pronounce each of the words in **Exercise 1**?

Workbook: 1. \'ak-shən\

2. \'skül\

3. \'näl-ij\

4. \'äp-ə-ˌrāt\

5. \'ad-vər-ˌtīz\

6. \'ak-sə-ˌdent-l\

Optional Challenge Word:

7. \kə-ˈlīd-ə-skōp\

Answer Key:
1. action
2. school
3. knowledge
4. operate
5. advertise
6. accidental
7. kaleidoscope

Instructor: Look up the word *supermarket* in the dictionary. Look at the abbreviation to the right of the phonetic spelling. What part of speech is the word *supermarket*?

Student: *noun*

Instructor: After the part of speech, you will see the definition. Read the definition of the word *supermarket* to me.

Student: *[reads definition]*

Instructor: *Supermarket* has only one definition. The word always means the same thing. But some words have more than one definition. In **Exercise 2** read these two sentences in which the word *light* has two different meanings!

Workbook: I can pick up my baby sister, because she is so **light**.

My baby sister wants **light** in her room at bedtime.

Instructor: Words that are spelled alike and pronounced alike but have different meanings are called **homonyms**. The origin of this word is from the Greek language. In Greek, *homo* means "same" and *nym* is a shortened form of the word for "name." Homonym means "same name." In these sentences, the word *light* has the **same name** but different meanings. In the first sentence, the word *light* means "not heavy." Baby sister is light; she is not heavy. In the second sentence, the word *light* means "not dark." Look up the word *light* in the dictionary.

When you read from the dictionary in the next exercise, put a folded piece of paper under the line you are reading to help the student follow along. Explain any definitions the student does not understand. The many entries for the word *light* show that the word comes from different sources or is a different part of speech. The student need not be concerned with this right now—he need only know that the word *light* has many different definitions.

Instructor: Look at all the definitions! There are six different entries for the word *light*. I will read them for you as you follow along with your eyes. Each time I get to an abbreviation, I want you to tell me what that abbreviation means. You may use the key in **Exercise 3** to help you.

Workbook: *adj*   adjective

adv   adverb

n   noun

vb   verb

Instructor: I want you to find the word *box* in your dictionary. It has many definitions. Read the first definition to me—it has has the number 1 next to the entry word.

Student: *[reads definition]*

Instructor: Now in **Exercise 4** of your workbook, I will read a sentence that uses the word *box*.

Workbook: My favorite shrub in the yard is called a **box**.

Instructor: Now read the second entry in your dictionary for the word *box*. There are three different definitions for this entry, but they are all nouns. After you read each definition, I will read you a sentence that uses that meaning of the word *box*. Follow along in **Exercise 5** as I read these sentences.

Workbook: 1. The delivery man put a **box** on our porch.

        2. Our family eats a **box** of cereal every day.

        3. The President and his wife sit in a special **box** at the theater.

Instructor: Read the third entry of the word box to me, and I will read you the sentence in **Exercise 6**. Notice that *box* is a verb.

Workbook: Will you **box** up that cake for me?

Instructor: Read the fourth definition, and read the sentence in **Exercise 7**.

Workbook: The two men plan to **box** in the ring tonight.

Instructor: There are some words that are spelled alike, but they have different meanings **and** different pronunciations. Read the two sentences in **Exercise 8**. Notice that although each word in bold print is spelled **B-O-W**, the words have different meanings **and** different pronunciations. These are called *homographs*. *Homograph* means "same writing."

Workbook: The girl in the play has a pink **bow** in her hair.

        In the play, the father and son **bow** when the girl enters the room.

Instructor: The words *bow* and *bow* are spelled alike but have different meanings and different pronunciations. In the first sentence, the word *bow* means "a loop of ribbon." In the second sentence, the word *bow* means "to bend at the waist." Often words in the dictionary will have more than one meaning and more than one phonetic spelling.

Instructor: Look up the word *wound* in the dictionary. Look at the phonetic spelling of the first entry and tell me how to pronounce the word.

Student: *wound [the* **ou** *sounds like the* **ou** *in soup]*

Instructor: Look at the abbreviation next to the phonetic spelling. What part of speech is this word?

Student: *noun*

Instructor: Read the two definitions in the first entry for *wound*. After you read the definitions, follow along in **Exercise 9** while I read you sentences that use those two different definitions.

Workbook: 1. The soldier received a **wound** in battle.

2. Her ugly words left a **wound** in my heart.

Instructor: Look at the second entry for *wound* and tell me what part of speech it is.

Student: *verb*

Instructor: Read the two definitions in the second entry for *wound*. After you read the definitions, follow along in **Exercise 10** while I read you sentences that use those two different definitions.

Workbook: 1. Stepping on glass can **wound** your foot.

2. Gossip can **wound** your reputation.

Instructor: Read the phonetic spelling for the third entry. How do you pronounce the word?

Student: *wound [the **ou** sounds like the **ou** in sound]*

Instructor: The **ou** sounds like the /ou/ in the word *sound*. This entry for *wound* is still a verb. Read the definition for the third entry.

Make sure the student reads the verb *wind* correctly—it should rhyme with *mind*.

Instructor: Follow along in **Exercise 11** as I read the sentence. Then you read it to me.

Workbook: He **wound** the kite's string when the wind grew too strong.

Optional Follow-Up

If the student needs extra practice with dictionary skills, you may use these words to follow the procedure used in this lesson.

These are words that are spelled and pronounced alike but have different meanings.

   pen

   bear

   rose

These are words that are spelled alike but have different meanings **and** different pronunciations.

   object

   present

DICTIONARY SKILLS LESSON 7

Synonyms and Antonyms

The student will need his thesaurus for this lesson. The following exercises are keyed to *Roget's Children's Thesaurus* (ISBN 0-673-65137-1) If the student is using a different children's thesaurus, be sure to read through the lesson ahead of time and make any adjustments necessary.

Instructor: Today we are going to learn about synonyms. Read the three sentences in **Exercise 1**.

Workbook: I am **afraid** of the dark.

I am **scared** of the dark.

I am **frightened** of the dark.

Instructor: The three words in bold print, *afraid, scared,* and *frightened,* all have the same meaning. They are synonyms. Synonyms are words that have the same meaning. Say that definition with me three times.

Together (three times): Synonyms are words that have the same meaning.

Instructor: You can remember that synonyms have the same meaning by thinking to yourself, "SSSSynonyms have the ssssame meaning." A thesaurus is a book that contains lists of synonyms. It can be helpful to have a thesaurus on hand when you are writing. For example, if you write the sentence "My older brother walks behind me," you could make it more descriptive by substituting a synonym for *walk*.

Help the student look up the word *walk*. Explain that you must first look up the word in the Synonym Index in the back of the thesaurus, and then turn to the page number printed next to the index entry for *walk*. Read through the page for the entry word *walk* while the student follows along.

Instructor: You are looking at the entry for the word *walk*. The entry contains a list of synonyms. Remember the sentence "My older brother walks behind me"? Now you can replace *walk* with a new, better word. "My older brother **shuffles** behind me." You shuffle when you have too little energy to lift your feet off the ground. If you use the word *shuffles* in the sentence, it make your older brother sound tired. What if you used the word *marches* instead? "My older brother **marches** behind me." When you march, you keep a steady tempo as you walk. Your older brother must be walking with a lot of energy. Or you could choose the word *strides*. "My older brother **strides** behind me." If you stride, you are taking long steps. Maybe your brother is trying to catch up with you. Using synonyms for ordinary words can make your sentences more lively and imaginative.

Instructor: Read aloud the story in **Exercise 2**. It contains the word *huge* used over and over again.

Workbook: At the National Museum of Natural History, I gazed at the skull of the Tyrannosaurus rex. It was **huge**. It was bigger than I was! Inside the jaws were **huge**, pointed teeth. I read that one tooth was thirteen inches long. That is one inch longer than my ruler. The Tyrannosaurus rex needed its **huge** teeth and powerful jaws. It could crush five hundred pounds of meat and bone in a single bite. That animal had a **huge** appetite!

Instructor: This paragraph would be much more interesting if the word *huge* was not used so much! Look up the word *huge* in the thesaurus.

Help the student look up the word *huge*. Remember to first look up the word in the Synonym Index. Turn to the page listed in the index. Read through the entire thesaurus entry for *huge* while the student follows along.

Instructor: You will see *huge* and three of its synonyms in **Exercise 3** of your workbook. Read this list to me.

Workbook: huge

enormous

immense

gigantic

Instructor: Now I am going to read the paragraph to you. This paragraph would be much better if the word *huge* were not used so many times. It's okay to have it in the paragraph once but not four times! When I get to the second time the word *huge* is used, I want you to substitute one of its synonyms from the list of words you just read in **Exercise 3**.

Instructor: *Huge, gigantic, immense,* and *enormous* are all synonyms—they have the same meaning. Look again at the thesaurus entry for the word *huge.* Look at the middle of the page. You will see the words in **Exercise 4** of your workbook.

Workbook: ANTONYM: tiny

Instructor: *Tiny* is the opposite of *huge.* These two words are antonyms. Antonyms are opposites. Say that with me three times.

Together (three times): Antonyms are opposites.

If your student has a lot of other writing to do for school today, you may do the following exercise orally instead.

Instructor: A thesaurus often includes antonyms at the bottom of the entry, after the list of synonyms. Read each of the sentences in **Exercise 5**. Look up the word in bold in the thesaurus, and find its antonym. Then rewrite the sentence with an antonym of the word in bold. The word now has the opposite meaning and could cause a few laughs!

Workbook: 1. A **tiny** insect landed on my nose.

2. My mother insists that my room always be **neat**.

3. I always bid goodbye to my guests when they **leave**.

4. I love the smell of **new** sneakers.

5. I like my bath water to be very **hot**.

6. After our Thanksgiving feast, my stomach felt so **full**.

Answer Key:

1. gigantic; 2. messy; 3. arrive; 4. old; 5. cold, cool; 6. empty

ORAL USAGE LESSON 1

Verb Tenses: Present, Past, and Future

In order to increase the effectiveness of these oral usage lessons, listen for common errors in the student's everyday speech. Quickly correct him by having him repeat the proper form after you. Students who have heard spoken errors constantly think of them as sounding correct. The more the student hears correct usage, the more likely he is to use language properly when speaking.

The student needs to have completed Lesson 30 before this lesson.

Instructor: A verb can show present time, past time, or future time. In **Exercise 1** read the sentences to me.

Workbook: 1. Today you **play**.

2. Yesterday you **played**.

3. Tomorrow you **will play**.

Instructor: In grammar, we call the time a verb is showing its *tense*. *Tense* means "time." In the first sentence "Today you play," the verb tense, or time, is present. You play at the present moment. In the second sentence "Yesterday you played," the verb tense, or time, is past. You played in the past. In the third sentence "Tomorrow you will play," the verb tense, or time, is future. You will play in the future.

Instructor: Read the sentences in **Exercise 2**. Then tell me if the verb in bold print is in the present, past, or future tense. In other words, is the time in the present moment, is it in the past, or will it be in the future?

Workbook: 1. Sally **planted** some flowers yesterday.

2. He **will collect** seashells at the beach tomorrow.

3. Last week, the baby **walked** to me.

4. I **smell** cookies baking in the oven.

5. You **shall clean** your room this afternoon.

6. She **chases** butterflies.

Answer Key:

1. past tense
2. future tense
3. past tense
4. present tense
5. future tense
6. present tense

This next exercise was also the optional follow-up for Lesson 27 (helping verbs), but it is fun to repeat with a different set of sentences, Use the time gauge you created for that lesson.

Instructor: Look at **Exercise 3**. First I will say the verb in each sentence. The verb is in bold print. Then I will read the whole sentence to you. I want you to move the arrow on your "time gauge" so it points to the correct tense of the verb. For every correct answer, you get one point.

If he points the arrow correctly, he gets one point. The student wins the game when he has earned eight points. You may need to go back through the sentences a second time.

Answer Key:

1. Manuel **floats** in the pool.   present tense
2. Bobby **winked** at his sister.   past tense
3. The kitten **will drink** milk from a saucer. future tense
4. A flock of bids **flew** across the sky. past tense
5. Many bees **buzz** around the flowers.   present tense
6. We **shall rest** after the hike.   future tense
7. I **laughed** at the joke.   past tense
8. The baker **will sell** us bread.   future tense

ORAL USAGE LESSON 2

Irregular Verbs

The student needs to have completed Lesson 30 before this lesson.

This oral usage lesson focuses on using the correct forms of the verbs "to eat," "to do," "to see," "to sing," "to go," "to drink," "to come," and "to write." Here is a chart for your reference.

Present	Past	Past with Helping Verb (like *have*, *has*, or *had*)
eat	ate	eaten
do	did	done
see	saw	seen
sing	sang	sung
go	went	gone
drink	drank	drunk
come	came	come
write	wrote	written

Instructor: Sometimes people use the wrong verb—so we want to practice saying the correct verb. Read each group of sentences in **Exercise 1** to me. The first sentence in each group has a verb that shows present time, or tense. The second sentence has the form of that same verb that shows past tense. The third sentence has a special past form of the verb that needs a helping verb to go along with it.

Workbook: I **eat** an apple today.

I **ate** an apple yesterday.

I **have eaten** an apple every day this week.

I **do** my school work today.

I **did** my school work yesterday.

I **have done** my school work every day this week.

(This lesson continues on the next page.)

I **see** the moon today.

I **saw** the moon yesterday.

I **have seen** the moon every day this week.

I **sing** a song today.

I **sang** a song yesterday.

I **have sung** a song every day this week.

I **go** to the library today.

I **went** to the library yesterday.

I **have gone** to the library every day this week.

I **drink** water today.

I **drank** water yesterday.

I **have drunk** water every day this week.

I **come** home today.

I **came** home yesterday.

I **have come** home every day this week.

I **write** spelling words today.

I **wrote** spelling words yesterday.

I **have written** spelling words every day this week.

Instructor: In **Exercise 2** of your workbook, I will read each sentence. You will read the sentence after me.

Workbook: 1. That was the sweetest cookie I **have eaten** at this bakery.

2. I already **did** my spelling.

3. I **saw** you at the park yesterday.

4. Last night Mary **sang** a lullaby to the baby.

5. He **has gone** to the store every day.

6. Last Tuesday I **drank** freshly squeezed orange juice with my breakfast.

7. Jin **has come** to play in the pool with us.

8. I **had written** my name on the card before the party.

ORAL USAGE LESSON 3

Irregular Verbs

The student needs to have completed Lesson 30 before this lesson. This oral usage lesson focuses on using the correct forms of the verbs "to ring," "to draw," "to begin," "to bring," "to run," "to give," "to throw," "to think," and "to wear." Here is a chart for your reference.

Present	Past	Past with Helping Verb (like *have*, *has*, or *had*)
ring	rang	rung
draw	drew	drawn
begin	began	begun
bring	brought	brought
run	ran	run
give	gave	given
throw	threw	thrown
think	thought	thought
wear	wore	worn

Instructor: Sometimes people use the wrong verb—so we want to practice saying the correct verb. In **Exercise 1** read each group of sentences to me. The first sentence in each group has a verb that shows present time, or tense. The second sentence has the form of that same verb that shows past tense. The third sentence has a special past form of the verb that needs a helping verb to go along with it.

Workbook: I **ring** a bell today.

I **rang** a bell yesterday.

I **have rung** a bell every day this week.

I **draw** pictures today.

I **drew** pictures yesterday.

I **have drawn** pictures every day this week.

I **begin** my daily chores today.

I **began** my daily chores yesterday.

I **have begun** my daily chores every day this week.

I **bring** pencils today.

I **brought** pencils yesterday.

I **have brought** pencils every day this week.

I **run** around the house today.

I **ran** around the house yesterday.

I **have run** around the house every day this week.

I **give** help today.

I **gave** help yesterday.

I **have given** help every day this week.

I **throw** the ball today.

I **threw** the ball yesterday.

I **have thrown** the ball every day this week.

I **think** about summer today.

I **thought** about summer yesterday.

I **have thought** about summer every day this week.

I **wear** a coat today.

I **wore** a coat yesterday.

I **have worn** a coat every day this week.

Instructor: In **Exercise 2** of your workbook, I will read each sentence, and you will read the sentence after me.

Workbook: 1. Last Fourth of July, the bell in the tower **rang** four times.

2. Tommy **drew** a picture and gave it to his mother.

3. The parade **began** at eight o'clock yesterday morning.

4. I **brought** my mother flowers on her last birthday.

5. My brother **has run** a race.

6. I **have given** a cracker to the baby every day.

7. Joe **threw** the ball over the fence last night.

8. I **thought** I had lost this money.

9. He **has worn** out his best pants.

ORAL USAGE LESSON 4

Irregular Verbs: Lay Versus Lie, Set Versus Sit

The student needs to have completed Lesson 42 before this lesson.

You will need eight index cards for the last exercise in this lesson. You may wish to prepare these ahead of time.

Instructor: There are two verbs that are often confused: *lay* and *lie*. The verb "to lay" means "to put or place something." You lay a book on your desk. *Lay* is always followed by a direct object, the thing you put or place somewhere. You must always lay **something**. You lay a book. In **Exercise 1** read the sentences with different forms of the verb "to lay." The verb is in bold print. After you read each sentence aloud, I will ask you "whom" or "what" after the verb to help you find the direct object.

Prompt the student to find the direct object by asking "[Verb in bold print] **what?**" for every sentence except number 2. For number 2, ask "Is laying **whom?**"

Workbook: 1. I **lay** my head on my pillow.

2. The mother **is laying** the baby in her crib.

3. The chicken **laid** a brown egg in the nest.

4. I **laid** my flashlight on the table last night.

5. Every past Memorial Day people have **laid** flowers on graves of soldiers.

Answer Key:
1. head
2. baby
3. egg
4. flashlight
5. flowers

Instructor: The verb "to lie" means "to rest or recline." You lie on the sofa. *Lie* is **never** followed by a direct object. The reason that so many people confuse *lie* and *lay* is because the past tense of the verb "to lie" is "lay." Yesterday you **lay** on the bed. Today you **lie** on the sofa. Read the sentences in **Exercise 2** that contain different forms of the verb "to lie."

Workbook: 1. I **lie** on my bed.

2. The book **is lying** on the table beside my bed.

3. The mouse **lay** in the straw yesterday.

4. Every clear night I **have lain** on the grass to look at the stars.

Instructor: In **Exercise 3** of your workbook, I am going to read you each sentence with a form of the verb "to lie" or "to lay." You read each sentence again after me.

Workbook: 1. Please pick up the book that **is lying** on the floor.

2. Now I **lay** me down to sleep.

3. Jane **lies** on the sofa.

4. Grandma **is laying** her groceries on the table.

5. The goose **laid** a golden egg.

6. Every spring I **have lain** on the hammock and enjoyed the warm weather.

7. Yesterday I **laid** my notebook here.

8. Every past Hanukkah my parents have **laid** presents near the menorah.

9. The rabbit **lay** in the straw last night.

Instructor: There are two more verbs that are often confused: *set* and *sit*. The verb "to set" most often means "to put or place something." It has the same meaning at the verb "to lay"! You set a book on your desk. *Set* is always followed by a direct object—the thing you put or place somewhere. You must almost always set **something**. In **Exercise 4** read the sentences with different forms of the verb "to set." The verb is in bold print. After you read each sentence aloud, I will ask you "whom" or "what" after the verb to help you find the direct object.

Prompt the student to find the direct object by asking "[Verb in bold print] **what?**" for every sentence.

Workbook: 1. **Set** the dishes on the table.

2. Marcus **is setting** the groceries in the pantry.

3. The volunteers **set** extra chairs in the back of the church last Sunday.

4. Every night for the past week I **have set** a book on my bed.

Answer Key:
1. dishes
2. groceries
3. chairs
4. book

Instructor: The verb "to sit" means "to rest in a seated position." You sit in a chair. Sit is never followed by a direct object. In **Exercise 5** read the sentences below that contain different forms of the verb "to sit."

Workbook: 1. I **sit** at the table for breakfast.

2. My sister **is sitting** with me.

3. We **sat** there yesterday, too.

4. We **have sat** there every morning this week.

Instructor: In **Exercise 6** I am going to read you some sentences with forms of the verb "to set" or "to sit." Follow along and then read each sentence aloud after me.

Workbook: 1. I **sat** in the backseat when we went to town.

2. **Set** the laundry baskets on the floor.

3. My babysitter **is sitting** with me.

4. Joseph **is setting** his models on a table.

5. The movers **set** our boxes in the proper rooms last week.

6. You **sit** at the desk.

7. We **have sat** in the bleachers for every game this season.

8. Every day for the past week I **have set** a different toy on the shelf.

The following oral, visual, and auditory exercise reinforces the correct usage of the verbs *lie*, *lay*, *sit*, and *set*. Cards are printed on page 323 of the student's workbook. You or the student should cut along the lines to make eight cards. Give the student a card. He reads the card aloud (being especially carefully to pronounce *sit* and *set* correctly), and then, if you wish, he can follow the direction on the card. Do the cards in order, and then mix them up.

Workbook: 1. <u>Set</u> a plate on the table.

2. <u>Sit</u> in a big chair.

3. <u>Set</u> a stuffed animal on the floor.

4. Make the stuffed animal <u>sit</u> in a chair.

5. <u>Lay</u> a blanket on the sofa or the bed.

6. <u>Lie</u> on the sofa or the bed.

7. <u>Lay</u> your head on your arms.

8. Make a stuffed animal <u>lie</u> on the bed next to you.

ORAL USAGE LESSON 5

Subject Pronouns and Object Pronouns

The student needs to have completed Lesson 59 before this lesson.

Instructor: You know the definition of a pronoun. A pronoun is a word used in the place of a noun. Say that with me, and then say it alone.

Together, then student alone: A pronoun is a word used in the place of a noun.

Instructor: The pronouns you have learned are:

Pronouns

I, me, my, mine
You, your, yours
He, she, him, her, it
His, hers, its
We, us, our, ours
They, them, their, theirs

Instructor: Let's say that list together, and then you say it alone.

Instructor, then student alone:

Pronouns

I, me, my, mine
You, your, yours
He, she, him, her, it
His, hers, its
We, us, our, ours
They, them, their, theirs

Instructor: In this lesson we are going to focus on a few of these pronouns. Read aloud the two columns of pronouns in **Exercise 1**.

Subject Pronouns	Object Pronouns
I	me
he	him
she	her
we	us
they	them

Instructor: The subject pronouns are *I*, *he*, *she*, *we*, and *they*. You always use **subject** pronouns when they are the **subjects** of sentences. Follow along in **Exercise 2** while I read each sentence. Then you read each sentence after me.

Workbook: **I** made some cookies.

He ate the cookies.

She helped him eat the cookies.

We cleaned up the kitchen.

They had a good time.

Fred and **I** rode bikes.

Daphne and **he** made the cookies.

She and Edward built a sandcastle.

We and the rest of the team celebrated the victory.

They and the other neighbors surprised Mary.

Instructor: Do you remember what a direct object is? A direct object receives the action of an action verb (Lesson 29). To find the direct object in a sentence, you ask *whom* or *what* after the verb. Read the sentence in **Exercise 3**.

Workbook: George tickled him.

Instructor: Tickled **whom**?

Student: *Him*

Instructor: *Him* is the direct object. It receives the action of the verb *tickled*. Read again the list of object pronouns in **Exercise 1**—*me*, *him*, *her*, *us*, and *them*. When a pronoun is used as a direct **object**, you always use an **object** pronoun! Follow along in **Exercise 4** while I will read each sentence. Then you read each sentence after me.

Workbook: Doug helped **me**.

Carol thanks **him**.

The dog followed **her**.

The family welcomes **us**.

Mother forgave **them**.

Charles chased Tom and **me** around the yard.

Aunt Bess took **him** and **me** to the library.

The neighbor paid Lucy and **her** for the lemonade.

Grandpa asked Mom and **us** for a ride.

Max invited **them** and **me** to the party.

Instructor: Do you remember what a predicate nominative is? A predicate nominative is a noun or pronoun in the predicate that renames the subject (Lesson 34). Because the predicate nominative refers back to the **subject**, you always use a **subject** pronoun for a predicate nominative. Read again the list of subject pronouns in **Exercise 1**—*I, he, she, we,* and *they*. Then follow along while I will read each sentence in **Exercise 5**. You read each sentence after me.

Workbook: It is **I**.

It is **he**.

It is **she**.

It is **we**.

It is **they**.

It was **I** who brought the cake.

It was **he** who ate some cake.

It was **she** who asked for an extra slice.

It was **we** who finished the whole cake.

It was **they** who baked another cake.

Did you think that it was **I** who won?

It must have been **he** who won.

Was it you and **she** who entered the next race?

Was it **he** and **they** who judged the competition?

Are those the books? Those are **they**.

Was it **he** who lent the books? It was **he**.

Instructor: Let's practice the correct way to answer the phone if someone you know is calling you. If the person says, "Is this *[student's name]*?", you reply, "This is she," or "This is he." These short sentences contain the predicate nominatives *he* or *she*, pronouns that rename the subject. You always use a subject pronoun like *he* or *she* for a predicate nominative.

This exercise is to help the student avoid the common spoken error of saying, "This is her/him" or "This is me." *Her*, *him*, and *me* are object pronouns—they are not used as predicate nominatives.

Instructor: In **Exercise 6** let's read a little play. We'll pretend we are calling each other on the telephone. We will take turns reading. You read the lines in bold print.

Ring! Ring!

Hello.

May I please speak with Alex?

This is he.

Was it you who sent the gift?

It was I.

Ring! Ring!

Hello.

May I please speak with Lee?

This is she.

Was it Joe who sprained his ankle?

It must have been he.

Ring! Ring!

Hello.

May I please speak with Chip?

This is he.

Was it Sam and she who won the prizes?

It was Sam and she.

For extra practice, you may switch parts and reread the play.

ORAL USAGE LESSON 6

Irregular Verbs: "To Be"

The student needs to have completed Lesson 34 before this lesson. This oral usage lesson focuses on using the correct forms of the verb "to be" (*am, is, are, was, were, be, being,* and *been*).

Instructor: Sometimes people use the wrong verb or helping verb in a sentence—so we want to practice saying the correct verb. Follow along in **Exercise 1** as I read each sentence, and then you will read each one after me.

Workbook: I **am** hungry.

Mary and Jen **were** going to the store.

Are you thirsty?

Jimmy's snowballs **are** melting.

I **am** in the car.

She **is** in the car.

You **were** there yesterday.

Ben and I **are** in the third grade.

Roses and daisies **are** flowers.

The boys **were** tired.

I **was** happy.

We **are** going with you.

Were you at the party?

You **are** smart.

Were Sherri and Blake at the store?

My baby sister **was** born in the hospital.

Instructor: The verbs in bold in the sentences in **Exercise 1** are the same verbs that are in **Exercise 2**. Say them.

Workbook: am

            is

            are

            was

            were

Instructor: Remember, these verbs can act like state of being verbs (showing that something exists), linking verbs (linking the subject to a word in the complete predicate), or helping verbs (helping another verb in the sentence). Read each of the sentences in **Exercise 3**, and see if you can find the verb (*am, is, are, was,* or *were*) in it. Point out that verb to me.

Answer Key:

1. Martha is in the kitchen.	is
2. You were outside.	were
3. The people were arriving.	were
4. I was excited.	was
5. Lois and I are ready.	are
6. I am dressed up.	am
7. Joe and Simon were in the yard.	were
8. Are you going to stay?	are
9. Terry's cookies are crumbling.	are
10. I am cleaning up.	am
11. Were you going to leave?	were
12. You are helpful.	are
13. Were Jake and Patsy at the party?	were
14. A napkin and a cup are on the floor.	are
15. We are sweeping up the crumbs.	are
16. My mother was happy.	was

ORAL USAGE LESSON 7

Avoiding Double Negatives

The student needs to have completed Lesson 67 before this lesson.

We try to avoid unnecessarily exposing students to improper grammar. For your resource only, we are providing you with the following incorrect sentences with double negatives (foils for the correct examples in **Exercise 2** of this lesson). This way, if you hear the student use a double negative in his everyday speech, you can quickly correct him.

I'm **not** doing **nothing**.

He **doesn't** want **no** help.

We **won't never** get there.

I **didn't hardly** get any.

I **can't** get **no** help.

I **didn't** get **none**.

We **won't never** cross the street.

I **can't** find **nobody** at home.

I **didn't** go **nowhere**.

I **don't** want **no** more cereal.

I **don't** want **nobody** in my room.

Don't you get into **no** trouble.

I **didn't** have **nothing** to do.

I'm **not** going **nowhere**.

I **ain't** got **none**. ("I haven't got any" is correct according to British usage, but in standard American usage it is more correct to say "I do not have any.")

There **wasn't hardly** anybody on the bus.

I **wasn't** doing **nothing**.

I **don't** get **no** respect.

I **don't** want **none** of those carrots.

I **can't** see **no one** from my window.

I **didn't** hit **nobody.**

The puppy has **barely** had **nothing** to eat today.

The team **doesn't** got **nobody** to cheer for it.

I **don't** want to go **neither.**

I **never** ate **none** of the cookies.

I **didn't** get **scarcely** enough time to finish.

Instructor: In **Exercise 1** read the list of words to me.

Workbook: no

             not

             none

             nobody

             nowhere

             nothing

             no one

             never

             neither

             hardly

             barely

             scarcely

Instructor: Look again at the words at the beginning of the list in **Exercise 1**. Do you see the word *no* in the words *not, none, nobody, nowhere, nothing,* and *no one*? These words, and the other words in the list, are called the "*no* words." And since *not* is a "*no* word," any contraction with *not* in it counts as a "*no* word," too: *doesn't, won't, can't, didn't,* and *don't.* As a rule, you will see only **one** of these "*no* words" in simple sentences. Follow along in **Exercise 2** while I will read each sentence. Then you will read each sentence after me. The "*no* words" are in bold print.

Workbook: I'm **not** doing anything.

I'm doing **nothing**.

He **doesn't** want any help.

He wants **no** help.

We **won't** ever get there.

We will **never** get there.

I got **hardly** any help.

I **can't** get any help.

I can get **no** help.

I **didn't** get any.

I got **none**.

We **won't** ever cross the street.

We will **never** cross the street.

I **can't** find anybody at home.

I can find **nobody** at home.

I **didn't** go anywhere.

I went **nowhere**.

I **don't** want any more cereal.

I want **no** more cereal.

I **don't** want anybody in my room.

I want **nobody** in my room.

Don't get into any trouble.

Get into **no** trouble.

I **didn't** have anything to do.

I had **nothing** to do.

Instructor: Let's do an activity just for fun. Look at **Exercise 3** in your workbook. I will read the first sentence in each sentence pair. It is a silly, ridiculous sentence. Then you will read the sentence beneath it. The sentence you read will have a "*no* word" in it—and the "*no* word" helps your sentence make more sense than mine. The "*no* word" is printed in bold. So when you get to a "*no* word," say it loudly!

Workbook: 1. I could eat a bowl of slimy worms!

   I could **never** eat a bowl of slimy worms!

2. Everybody loves to get shots.

   Nobody loves to get shots.

3. I could climb to the top of a skyscraper.

   I could **not** climb to the top of a skyscraper.

4. A lost ring can be found everywhere.

   A lost ring can be found **nowhere**.

5. I can easily stand on one foot for five minutes.

   I can **barely** stand on one foot for five minutes.

6. I did something to cause it to rain.

   I did **nothing** to cause it to rain.

7. I want chocolate-covered ants for dessert!

   I want **no** chocolate-covered ants for dessert!

If you like, you may repeat the above activity. This time you can switch roles. Feel free to "ham it up"! The person saying the ridiculous sentence can say it proudly or very seriously. The other person can look at her like she is silly—or just plain crazy for saying such a thing!

Instructor: Read the sentences in **Exercise 4** to me. Remember, you will see **only one** of the "*no* words" in simple sentences. The "*no* words" are in bold print.

Workbook: I'm **not** going anywhere.

I'm going **nowhere**.

I do **not** have any.

I have **none**.

There was **hardly** anybody on the bus.

There **wasn't** anybody on the bus.

I **wasn't** doing anything.

I was doing **nothing**.

I **don't** get any respect.

I get **no** respect.

I want **none** of those carrots.

I **don't** want any of those carrots.

I **can't** see anyone from my window.

I can see **no one** from my window.

I **didn't** hit anybody.

I hit **nobody**.

The puppy has had **nothing** to eat today.

The puppy has **barely** had anything to eat today.

The team **doesn't** have anybody to cheer for it.

The team has **nobody** to cheer for it.

I **never** ate any of the cookies.

I ate **none** of the cookies.

I **didn't** get enough time to finish.

I **scarcely** got enough time to finish.

DEFINITIONS, RULES, AND LISTS

DEFINITIONS TO BE MEMORIZED

A **noun** is the name of a person, place, thing, or idea.

A **pronoun** is a word used in the place of a noun.

A **verb** is a word that does an action, shows a state of being, links two words together, or helps another verb.

An **adjective** is a word that describes a noun or pronoun. Adjectives tell what kind, which one, how many, and whose.

An **adverb** is a word that describes a verb, an adjective, or another adverb. Adverbs tell how, when, where, how often, and to what extent.

A **preposition** is a word that shows the relationship of a noun or pronoun to another word in the sentence.

A **conjunction** is a word that joins words or groups of words together.

An **interjection** is a word that expresses sudden or strong feeling.

A **sentence** is a group of words that expresses a complete thought. All sentences begin with a capital letter and end with a punctuation mark.

GLOSSARY OF ADDITIONAL TERMS TO KNOW

command – a sentence that gives an order or makes a request. A command sentence ends with either a period or an exclamation point.

complete predicate – the verb and other words that tell us what is said about the subject. It is the part of the sentence in which the verb is found.

complete subject – the simple subject and other words that tell us who or what the sentence is about. It is the part of the sentence in which the simple subject is found.

compound subject – a subject with two or more parts that are joined by a conjunction.

compound verb – two or more verbs that are joined by a conjunction and that have the same subject.

contraction – two words drawn together and shortened by dropping some letters. Every contraction has an apostrophe in it. The apostrophe tells us where the letters were dropped to form the contraction.

direct object – the noun or pronoun in the complete predicate that receives the action of the verb.

direct quotation – the exact words that someone says. Direct quotations are always enclosed by quotation marks.

exclamation – a sentence that shows sudden or strong feeling. An exclamation always ends with an exclamation point.

homonym – words that are spelled alike and pronounced alike but have different meanings.

indirect quotation – the content of what a person says without using his or her exact words. There are no quotation marks surrounding an indirect quotation.

predicate adjective – an adjective in the complete predicate that describes the subject.

predicate nominative – a noun or pronoun in the complete predicate that renames the subject.

question – a sentence that asks something. A question always ends with a question mark.

simple predicate – the main verb plus any helping verbs.

simple subject – the main word or term that tells us who or what the sentence is about.

statement – a sentence that gives information. Statements always end with a period.

types of sentences – The four different types of sentences are statements, commands, questions, and exclamations.

SUMMARY OF RULES

Forming Plurals

- Usually, add **s** to a noun to form the plural.
- Add **es** to nouns ending in **s**, **sh**, **ch**, **x**, or **z**.
- If a noun ends in **y** after a consonant, change the **y** to **i** and add **es**.
- If a noun ends in **y** after a vowel, just add **s**.

Commas in a Series

Put a comma after every item except the last one in the series.

Direct Address

Put a comma after the name or names of the people to whom you are speaking.

Direct Quotation That Comes at the End of a Sentence

- The exact words a person says are always enclosed by quotation marks.
- Direct quotations begin with a capital letter.
- The quotation is separated from the rest of the sentence by a comma.
- The end punctuation mark always comes inside the quotation marks.

Direct Quotation That Comes at the Beginning of a Sentence

- The exact words a person says are always enclosed by quotation marks.
- Direct quotations begin with a capital letter.
- If the direct quotation would normally end with a period, then the period is changed to a comma. This comma is always inside the quotation marks.
- If the direct quotation ends with a question mark or exclamation point, that mark is always inside the quotation marks.
- Since the direct quotation is only a part of the sentence, the larger sentence must have its own end mark.

LISTS TO BE MEMORIZED

Pronouns

I, me, my, mine
You, your, yours
He, she, him, her, it
His, hers, its
We, us, our, ours
They, them, their, theirs

Helping Verbs

Am
Is
Are, was, were
Be
Being
Been

Have, has, had
Do, does, did

Shall, will, should, would, may, might, must

Can, could

State of Being Verbs

Am
Is
Are, was, were
Be
Being
Been

Linking Verbs

Am
Is
Are, was, were
Be
Being
Been

Prepositions

Aboard, about, above, across.
After, against, along, among, around, at.

Before, behind, below, beneath.
Beside, between, beyond, by.

Down, during, except, for, from.
In, inside, into, like.

Near, of, off, on, over.
Past, since, through, throughout.

To, toward, under, underneath.
Until, up, upon.
With, within, without.

Articles

a, an, the

Common Conjunctions

and, but, or

SAMPLE SCHEDULES

There are 180 days (36 weeks) in a typical school year. This book contains 89 lessons in the main part of the book. These lessons are mandatory. Additionally, there are three optional end units at the end of the book: 7 lessons on writing letters, 7 lessons on dictionary skills, and 7 lessons on oral usage.

Here are three suggested options:

    A. You can do only the 89 lessons in the main part of the book.

    B. You can do the entire book and finish with the optional end units.

    C. You can do the entire book, interspersing the optional end units among the lessons.

The chart on the next page shows these three options and how they would work over the course of a 36-week school year.

Week	Option A Lessons	Option B Lessons	Option C Lessons
1	1, 2,	1, 2	1, 2, 3
2	3, 4	3, 4, 5	4, 5, 6
3	5, 6, 7	6, 7, 8	7, 8, 9
4	8, 9	9, 10, 11	10, 11, 12
5	10, 11	12, 13, 14	DS 1, DS 2, DS 3
6	12, 13, 14	15, 16, 17	13, 14, 15
7	15, 16	18, 19, 20	16, 17, 18
8	17, 18, 19	21, 22, 23	19, 20, 21
9	20, 21	24, 25, 26	22, 23, 24
10	22, 23, 24	27, 28, 29	25, 26, 27
11	25, 26	30, 31, 32	28, 29, 30
12	27, 28, 29	33, 34, 35	31, OU 1, OU 2, OU 3
13	30, 31	36, 37, 38	32, 33, 34
14	32, 33, 34	39, 40, 41	35, 36, 37
15	35, 36	42, 43, 44	38, 39, 40
16	37, 38, 39	45, 46, 47	41, 42, OU 4
17	40, 41	48, 49, 50	43, 44, 45
18	42, 43, 44	51, 52, 53	46, 47, 48
19	45, 46	54, 55, 56	49, 50, 51
20	47, 48, 49	57, 58, 59	52, 53, 54
21	50, 51	60, 61, 62	DS 4, DS 5, DS 6
22	52, 53, 54	63, 64, 65	55, 56, 57
23	55, 56	66, 67, 68	58, 59, OU 5
24	57, 58, 59	69, 70, 71	60, 61, 62
25	60, 61	72, 73, 74	63, OU 6, 64
26	62, 63, 64	75, 76, 77	65, 66, 67, OU 7
27	65, 66	78, 79, 80	68, 69, 70
28	67, 68, 69	81, 82, 83	WL 1, WL 2, WL 3
29	70, 71	84, 85, 86	71, 72, 73
30	72, 73, 74	87, 88, 89	74, 75, 76
31	75, 76	WL 1, WL 2, WL 3	77, 78, 79
32	77, 78, 79	WL 4, WL 5, WL 6	DS 7, 80, 81
33	80, 81	WL 7, DS 1, DS 2, DS 3	WL 4, WL 5, WL 6
34	82, 83, 84	DS 4, DS 5, DS 6, DS 7	82, 83, 84
35	85, 86	OU 1, OU 2, OU 3, OU 4	85, 86, 87
36	87, 88, 89	OU 5, OU 6, OU 7	88, 89, WL 7

INDEX

A

Abbreviations
    addressing an envelope, 405
    months of year/days of week,
        273–275
    titles of respect, 273–275
Action verbs (*see* Verbs)
Adjectives, 47–50, 455
    comparative, 345–349, 364–367
    diagramming, 61–67, 160–164
    possessive nouns, 51–55
        irregular plural, 56–60
        see also Nouns
    predicate, 160–164, 456
        review, 165–171, 203–208,
            259–265, 337–344
    review, 68–70, 93–99, 104–105,
        127–131, 239–243,
        364–367
    superlative, 345–349, 364–367
Adverbs, 455
    diagramming, 74–92
    extent (how much), 249–256
    frequency (how often), 88–92
    location (where), 84–87
    means (how), 74–78
    "no," 290–294
    review, 93–99, 105–106, 127–131,
        244–248, 350–357
    time (when), 79–83
Alphabetizing
    by first and second letter, 413–416
    by third letter, 417–418
Antonyms, 432–434
Articles, 63–64, 459
    review, 69, 94, 241
    see also Adjectives

B

"Bats," 44
"The Beaver is a Builder," 158
"The Bells," 257
"Bull-Jumpers in Early Crete," 335

C

Capitalization (*see* Abbreviations;
    Sentences)
Commands, 177–179, 184–190, 456
    diagramming, 180–183
    review, 195–200, 295–296,
        299–306, 358–363
    see also Sentences
Commas
    in direct address, 281–282
        review, 314–316, 389–393
    and quotations, 296–298, 304–309
    in a series, 276–280, 457
        review, 314–316, 389–393
Common nouns (*see* Nouns)
Comparative adjectives (*see* Adjectives)
Compound subjects (*see* Subjects)
Compound verbs (*see* Verbs)
Conjunctions, 276–280, 455, 459
    diagramming, 276–280
    review, 318–320, 384–388
Contractions, 283–286, 456
    diagramming, 290–294
    review, 290–294, 314–316, 368–
        372
    see also Double negatives
Copywork, 1–2
    see also Dictation

D

Dates (writing), 401–403
    see also Months of the year
Days of the week, 112, 173
    abbreviations, 273–275
Diagramming
    adjectives, 61–67
    adverbs, 74–92
    conjunctions, 276–280
    contractions, 290–294
    direct objects, 123–126
    interjections, 368–372
    nouns, proper, 110–113

Diagramming (continued)
    predicates
        adjectives, 160–164
        nominatives, 147–154
    questions, 192–194
    review, 394–399
    sentences, 40–43
        commands, 180–183
    subjects, 40–43
        compound, 321–324
    verbs
        compound, 325–327
        helping, 114–118
        linking, 147–154
        state of being, 141–146
Dickinson, Emily, 312
Dictation, 2, 4
    see also Copywork
Dictionary skills
    definitions, multiple, 428–431
    entry, parts of, 421–423
    looking up words, 419–420
Dictionary skills (continued)
    see also Alphabetizing; Antonyms;
        Syllables; Synonyms
Direct address, 281–282, 457
    and commas, 314–316, 389–393
Direct objects, 123–131, 456
    diagramming, 123–126
    pronouns, 444–447
    review, 203–208, 259–265, 337–
        344
    see also Sentences
Direct quotations (*see* Quotations)
Double negatives, 450–454

E

Entries (dictionary), 421–423
    see also Dictionary skills
Envelopes, addressing, 405–406, 410
    see also Letters (writing)
Exclamation points, 178, 198, 305,
    308, 310
    review, 391, 393
    see also Interjections

Exclamations, 177–179, 456
    review, 195–200, 295–296,
        299–306, 358–363
    see also Sentences
Extent (adverbs), 249–256

F

Farjeon, Eleanor, 38
Frequency (adverbs), 88–92
Friendly letter, 407–409
Frost, Robert, 201
Future tense (*see* Verbs)

H

Helping verbs (*see* Verbs)
Homographs, 430–431
Homonyms, 428–430, 456
How to use this book
    "four-strand" approach, 1–2
    lessons, 3–5
    parts of the book, 6–7
    schedules, 461–462

I

"I Wandered Lonely As a Cloud," 132
Index, 7
Indirect quotations (*see* Quotations)
Initials, 273–275
Interjections, 368–372, 455
Irregular plural nouns (*see* Nouns)
Irregular verbs (*see* Verbs)
"Isaac Newton's Laws of Gravity," 237

L

"The Land of Nod," 35
lay/lie, 441–443
    see also Verbs
Letters (writing)
    envelope, addressing, 405–406,
        410
    friendly, 407–409
    Thank you, 401–404
Linking verbs (*see* Verbs)
Location (adverbs), 84–87

M

Means (adverbs), 74–78
Memorization
    poetry (*see* Poetry)
    rules and definitions, 1

"The Mongols," 107
"The Months," 401
Months of the year, 112, 173, 401
    abbreviations, 273–275
Mother Goose, 401

N

Narration, 2
    "Bats," 44–46
    "The Beaver is a Builder," 158–159
    "Bull-Jumpers in Early Crete,"
        335–336
    "Isaac Newton's Laws of Gravity,"
        237–238
    "The Mongols," 107–109
    "Spiders," 288–289
Nominatives (*see* Predicates)
Nouns, 8–10, 455
    diagramming, 110–113
        subjects, 40–43
    irregular
        plurals, 18–21
        possessive, 56–60
    plurals, 11–13, 457
        irregular, 18–21, 56–60
        possessive, 56–60
        review, 30–33, 172–176
        words ending in *s, sh, ch, x, z,*
            14–17, 60
        words ending in *y,* 18–21, 60
    possessive, 51–55
        irregular plural, 56–60
        see also Adjectives
    proper, 22–25, 110–113
        review, 30–33, 119–120,
            172–176
    review, 100–102, 373–376
    see also Pronouns

O

Object pronouns (*see* Direct objects;
    Pronouns)
Objects, direct (*see* Direct objects)
Objects of the preposition (*see*
    Prepositions)

P

Past tense (*see* Verbs)
Periods, 177–178, 195, 296–298,
    304–310
    review, 391–392
    see also Abbreviations

Phonetic spelling (*see* Spelling)
Phrases, prepositional, 214–217
    review, 218–222, 233–236,
        327–330, 378–383
Plurals, 11–13, 457
    irregular, 18–21
    review, 30–33, 101–102, 172–176
    words ending in *s, sh, ch, x, z,*
        14–17, 60
    words ending in *y,* 18–21, 60
    see also Nouns
Poe, Edgar Allan, 257
Poetry
    "The Bells," 257–258
    copying, 411–412
    "I Wandered Lonely As a Cloud,"
        132–133
    "The Land of Nod," 34–35
    memorization, 1, 191, 287, 400
    "A Slash of Blue," 312–313
    "A Time to Talk," 201–202
    "A Tragic Story," 72–73
    "Verbs," 38
    "Who Has Seen the Wind?" 411
Possessive nouns (*see* Adjectives;
    Nouns)
Predicates, 134–140, 456
    adjectives, 160–164, 456
        review, 165–171, 203–208,
            259–265, 337–344
    diagramming, 147–154, 160–164
    nominatives, 147–154, 456
        review, 155–157, 165–171,
            203–208, 259–265,
            337–344
    review, 266–272, 373–376
    simple, 456
    see also Sentences
Prepositions, 209–213, 455, 459
    objects of, 223–227
        review, 228–232, 328–329,
            378–379
    phrases, 214–217
        review, 218–222, 233–236,
            327–330, 378–383
    review, 317–318, 377–383
Present tense (*see* Verbs)
Pronouns, 26–29, 455, 458
    object, 444–447
    review, 30–33, 102–103, 373–376
    subject, 444–447
    see also Nouns
Proper nouns (*see* Nouns)
Punctuation (*see individual punctuation
    marks*)

Q

Question marks, 178, 197, 304, 307, 309
   review, 390, 392
Questions, 177–179, 192–194, 456
   diagramming, 192–194
   review, 195–200, 295–296, 299–306, 358–363
   see also Sentences
Quotation marks, 296–298, 304–310
   review, 390–393
Quotations
   direct, 456
      at beginnings of sentences, 299–306, 457
      at ends of sentences, 295–298, 457
      review, 307–311, 389–393
   indirect, 307–311, 456
      review, 389–393

R

Rossetti, Christina G., 411

S

Schedules (sample), 461
Sentences
   commands, 177–183
   compound subjects and verbs, 331–334
   definition, 40–43, 455
   diagramming, 40–43
      see also Diagramming
   direct address, 281–282
   exclamations, 177–179
   questions, 177–179, 192–194
   quotations, direct
      at beginning, 299–306
      at end, 295–298

Sentences (continued)
   review, 373–376
   statements, 177–179
   types of, 177–179, 456
      review, 195–200, 295–296, 299–306, 358–363
   see also Predicates; Subjects
set/sit, 441–443
   see also Verbs
"A Slash of Blue," 312
Spelling (phonetic), 424–427
"Spiders," 288
State of being verbs (*see* Verbs)
Statements, 177–179, 184–190, 456
   review, 195–200, 295–296, 299–306, 358–363
   see also Sentences
Stevenson, Robert Louis, 35
Subjects, 40–43
   complete, 134–140, 456
      review, 266–272, 373–376
   compound, 321–324, 331–334, 456
      review, 384–388
      see also Conjunctions
   diagramming, 321–324
   pronouns, 444–447
   review, 127–131
   simple, 134–140, 456
      review, 266–272, 373–376
   you (understood), 180–183
   see also Nouns; Sentences
Superlative adjectives (*see* Adjectives)
Syllables, 424–427
Synonyms, 432–434

T

Table of contents, 6–7
Tenses (*see* Verbs)
Thackeray, William Makepeace, 72–73
Thank-you letter, 401–404
Time (adverbs), 79–83

"A Time to Talk," 201
Titles of respect, 273–275
to be verbs (*see* Verbs)
"A Tragic Story," 72–73

V

Verbs, 455
   action, 36–43
      review, 373–376
   compound, 325–327, 331–334, 456
      review, 384–388
      see also Conjunctions
   diagramming, 40–43, 114–118, 141–154, 325–327
   helping, 114–118, 458
      review, 120–122
   irregular, 437–440
      to be, 448–449
      lay/lie, 441–443
      set/sit, 441–443
   linking, 147–154, 458
      review, 155–157, 165–171
   review, 103, 127–131, 203–208
   state of being, 141–146, 458
   tenses, 435–440
   types of, 259–265
      review, 337–344
"Verbs" (poem), 38

W

"Who Has Seen the Wind?" 411
Wordsworth, William, 132
Writing skills (*see* Envelopes, addressing; Letters)

Y

You (understood), 180–183

PERMISSIONS

Excerpt from Poem 204 (A Slash of Blue). Reprinted by permission of the publishers and the Trustees of Amherst College from *The Poems of Emily Dickinson*, Thomas H. Johnson, ed., Cambridge, Mass.: The Belknap Press of Harvard University Press, Copyright © 1951, 1955, 1979, 1983 by the President and Fellows of Harvard College.

Excerpt from "Spiders and Their Kin" from *ChildCraft; Volume 10: Nature Excursions* by Mary Geisler Phillips. Copyright © 1935 by The Quarrie Corporation. Reprinted by permission of World Book.

Excerpt from "Bull-Jumpers in Early Crete" from *The Story of the World, Volume 1: Ancient Times* by Susan Wise Bauer. Copyright © 2001, 2006 by Susan Wise Bauer. Reprinted by permission of Peace Hill Press.

Excerpt from "The Mongols" from *The Story of the World, Volume 2: The Middle Ages* by Susan Wise Bauer. Copyright © 2003, 2007 by Susan Wise Bauer. Reprinted by permission of Peace Hill Press.

Excerpt from "Isaac Newton's Laws of Gravity" from *The Story of the World, Volume 3: Early Modern Times* by Susan Wise Bauer. Copyright © 2004 by Susan Wise Bauer. Reprinted by permission of Peace Hill Press.

Excerpt from *The Ordinary Parent's Guide to Teaching Reading* by Sara Buffington and Jessie Wise. Copyright © 2005 by Jessie Wise and Sara Buffington. Reprinted by permission of Peace Hill Press.